Engaging 21st Century Writers with Social Media

Kendra N. Bryant
Florida A&M University, USA

A volume in the Advances in Higher Education and Professional Development (AHEPD) Book Series

www.igi-global.com

Published in the United States of America by
IGI Global
Information Science Reference (an imprint of IGI Global)
701 E. Chocolate Avenue
Hershey PA, USA 17033
Tel: 717-533-8845
Fax: 717-533-8661
E-mail: cust@igi-global.com
Web site: http://www.igi-global.com

                    Library of Congress Cataloging-in-Publication Data

CIP Data Pending
ISBN: 978-1-5225-0562-4
eISNB: 978-1-5225-0563-1

This book is published in the IGI Global book series Advances in Higher Education and Professional Development (AHEPD) (ISSN: 2327-6983; eISSN: 2327-6991)

British Cataloguing in Publication Data
A Cataloguing in Publication record for this book is available from the British Library.

For electronic access to this publication, please contact: eresources@igi-global.com.

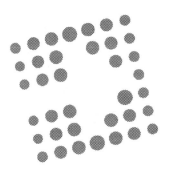

Advances in Higher Education and Professional Development (AHEPD) Book Series

Jared Keengwe
University of North Dakota, USA

ISSN: 2327-6983
EISSN: 2327-6991

MISSION

As world economies continue to shift and change in response to global financial situations, job markets have begun to demand a more highly-skilled workforce. In many industries a college degree is the minimum requirement and further educational development is expected to advance. With these current trends in mind, the **Advances in Higher Education & Professional Development (AHEPD) Book Series** provides an outlet for researchers and academics to publish their research in these areas and to distribute these works to practitioners and other researchers.

AHEPD encompasses all research dealing with higher education pedagogy, development, and curriculum design, as well as all areas of professional development, regardless of focus.

COVERAGE

- Adult Education
- Assessment in Higher Education
- Career Training
- Coaching and Mentoring
- Continuing Professional Development
- Governance in Higher Education
- Higher Education Policy
- Pedagogy of Teaching Higher Education
- Vocational Education

IGI Global is currently accepting manuscripts for publication within this series. To submit a proposal for a volume in this series, please contact our Acquisition Editors at Acquisitions@igi-global.com or visit: http://www.igi-global.com/publish/.

Titles in this Series

For a list of additional titles in this series, please visit: www.igi-global.com

Accelerated Opportunity Education Models and Practices
Rene Cintron (Louisiana Community & Technical College System, USA) Jeanne C. Samuel (Delgado Community College, USA) and Janice M. Hinson (University of North Carolina at Charlotte, USA)
Information Science Reference • copyright 2017 • 316pp • H/C (ISBN: 9781522505280) • US $180.00 (our price)

Preparing Foreign Language Teachers for Next-Generation Education
Chin-Hsi Lin (Michigan State University, USA) Dongbo Zhang (Michigan State University, USA) and Binbin Zheng (Michigan State University, USA)
Information Science Reference • copyright 2017 • 313pp • H/C (ISBN: 9781522504832) • US $185.00 (our price)

Innovative Practices for Higher Education Assessment and Measurement
Elena Cano (University of Barcelona, Spain) and Georgeta Ion (Universitat Autònoma de Barcelona, Spain)
Information Science Reference • copyright 2017 • 471pp • H/C (ISBN: 9781522505310) • US $215.00 (our price)

Handbook of Research on Study Abroad Programs and Outbound Mobility
Donna M. Velliaris (Eynesbury Institute of Business & Technology, Australia) and Deb Coleman-George (University of Adelaide, Australia)
Information Science Reference • copyright 2016 • 754pp • H/C (ISBN: 9781522501695) • US $335.00 (our price)

Setting a New Agenda for Student Engagement and Retention in Historically Black Colleges and Universities
Charles B. W. Prince (Howard University, USA) and Rochelle L. Ford (Syracuse University, USA)
Information Science Reference • copyright 2016 • 343pp • H/C (ISBN: 9781522503088) • US $185.00 (our price)

Handbook of Research on Professional Development for Quality Teaching and Learning
Teresa Petty (University of North Carolina at Charlotte, USA) Amy Good (University of North Carolina at Charlotte, USA) and S. Michael Putman (University of North Carolina at Charlotte, USA)
Information Science Reference • copyright 2016 • 824pp • H/C (ISBN: 9781522502043) • US $310.00 (our price)

Administrative Challenges and Organizational Leadership in Historically Black Colleges and Universities
Charles B. W. Prince (Howard University, USA) and Rochelle L. Ford (Syracuse University, USA)
Information Science Reference • copyright 2016 • 301pp • H/C (ISBN: 9781522503118) • US $170.00 (our price)

Developing Workforce Diversity Programs, Curriculum, and Degrees in Higher Education
Chaunda L. Scott (Oakland University, USA) and Jeanetta D. Sims (University of Central Oklahoma, USA)
Information Science Reference • copyright 2016 • 398pp • H/C (ISBN: 9781522502098) • US $185.00 (our price)

www.igi-global.com

701 E. Chocolate Ave., Hershey, PA 17033
Order online at www.igi-global.com or call 717-533-8845 x100
To place a standing order for titles released in this series, contact: cust@igi-global.com
Mon-Fri 8:00 am - 5:00 pm (est) or fax 24 hours a day 717-533-8661

Editorial Advisory Board

Table of Contents

Section 1
Blogging in the Writing Classroom

Section 2
Exploring Multi-Digital Media in the Writing Classroom

Section 5
Re-Envisioning Wikis in the Writing Classroom

Detailed Table of Contents

Section 1
Blogging in the Writing Classroom

The authors whose chapters are included in this section discuss their classroom experiences with integrating Twitter to assist students both in the scaffolding process and in "exploring networked, digital compositions." Chapters in this section also include discussion on using WordPress to create electronic writing portfolios and to maintain traditional goals of the writing classroom.

Chapter 1

As the landscape for communication changes with new and evolving digital technologies, the format for college composition classrooms must change and adapt as well. If we are moving towards compositions that are created by and mediated through a screen, we must adopt new approaches for talking about and teaching these new forms of language and communication. During the fall 2014 semester, I was given the opportunity to teach a composition class focused on digital rhetoric. As a facet of the classroom experience, my students created and used Twitter accounts for fictional characters. Utilizing Twitter within the composition classroom allowed students to compose as a part of a much larger network of actors that interact with the texts they create. As a form of networked communication, the compositions created by students through this medium demanded interaction and engagement in a way that a classroom composition, shared only between student and instructor, does not.

Despite claims of a decades-long history of multimodal instructional activities, Composition Studies scholars are still slow to embrace many web-based, social media technology tools to help realize traditional goals of the college writing classroom. Microblogging (Twitter) and blogging (WordPress) activities are effective technology companions that support collaborative learning, critical research, and analytical writing models. This chapter suggests online reading comprehension and critical literacy models as guides for microblogging and blogging lesson design. Finally, instructor commentary and student samples from two assignments, (a) blogging communities and (b) using Twitter to critically analyze a text, are offered to illustrate the aforementioned application.

Chapter 3

This chapter explores the idea, and offers three real-life, classroom tested assignments, of using the rules of social media, specifically Twitter, to teach students the rhetorical moves needed to write essays of college length and quality. The assignments provide first-year composition students the tools necessary to read an academic article, understand the rhetoric behind it, and apply rhetorical strategies it to his or her writing. The three assignments: 1) rhetorically analyze Twitter and create a formula for an effective tweet; 2) rhetorically analyzing an academic article 140 characters at a time; and 3) rhetorically analyzing a student's own paper using these same 140-character sound bites, have shown to put students in a position to be successful in the academy. Each assignment has been fully vetted over three years, with a myriad of student examples. This paper shows that the rules of Twitter can be used academically to provide a knowledge base and scaffolding for student writers.

Chapter 4

This chapter illustrates a student-centered pedagogy in process through the example of an electronic portfolio final assignment in two First-Year Writing courses. The philosophy behind the assignment is based in cultural studies, constructivist pedagogy, and multimodal studies. If students learn by doing, they also learn about culture through critique, public writing, and reflection. Students can thus become engaged as writers and citizens through constructing web-based texts focused on social issues and written from personal perspectives.

Section 2
Exploring Multi-Digital Media in the Writing Classroom

In this section, authors discuss how Tumblr, Instagram, Podbean, and Twitter help to promote "Remix Writing," which mirrors the multimodal activities that permeate present rhetoric & composition discourse.

Chapter 5

Remix, as a pedagogical style and teaching method, reframes foundational elements of writing instruction and broadens the traditional practice of writing to include 21st century compositional methods and technological forms. Through Remix Writing, students and instructors learn to compose a networked system of writing that diffuses assumed hierarchies and promotes associative thinking across diverse ecologies of media. We are always already associative thinkers. We build connections to understand, compare, reject, and relate. The digital writing environment offers an assemblage of associations, available in an instant. By disassembling and then reassembling texts, writers can learn to analyze influences and situate works in a web of connections. Students not only write critically about objects of study, but also have the opportunity to produce original work in various styles and media. In mapping the remix process as well as the purpose of each composition, students are able to identify key elements of argument, style, and effective communication – taking ownership of their own writing.

Chapter 6
Katherine Fredlund, University of Memphis, USA

Recognizing that students develop rhetorical skills on social media, this chapter presents a number of writing assignments that ask students to engage with social media and complete a variety of tasks online. These tasks range from taking and posting a photograph, to revising social media posts for honesty, to creating memes. Each assignment then requires students to reflect on these experiences in formal written assignments. This reflective component encourages students to consider writing conventions, processes, and genres in order to develop "high road" and meta-cognitive transfer skills. These assignments have three primary goals: (1) they help students engage with course content, (2) they build student confidence, and (3) they ask students to practice transfer.

Chapter 7
Meghan McGuire, University of Delaware, USA

This chapter explores how multimodal composition and social media conventions can support writing and introduce students to writing to multiple audiences. This chapter will outline an assignment from logistics of Tumblr as a space to help students establish regular writing practices in online spaces. Additionally, this chapter will illustrate some aspects of resistance that students may have with the assignment and provide strategies that respond to these resistances to make the assignment more effective.

Section 3
Theorizing about Social Media Networks in the Writing Classroom

The four chapters that complete this section are grounded in theoretical concepts. While each chapter offers readers ideas about how to implement social media networks into a writing classroom, they more specifically invite readers to interrogate and explore social media networks for their rhetorical characteristics and situations.

Chapter 8
Ken Hayes, Southwestern Oklahoma State University, USA

The goal of this chapter is to act as a primer for scholars looking start working with social networking site (SNS) in the composition classroom. This chapter focuses on research regarding aspects of SNS use in and out of the classroom, such as identity, rhetorical/audience awareness, civic engagement, and SNS pedagogy. This chapter also relies on current discourse, as well as the author's own SNS experiences, to share lists of best practices and SNS activities in the composition classroom. This chapter ends with a call for future research that includes continued efforts to interact more directly with students to learn with them about their use and views of SNS in and out of the composition classroom.

Chapter 9

Erin Trauth, University of South Florida, USA

Despite the Millennial's growing attraction to social media technologies, composition instruction has yet to fully explore the potential of these technologies as resources rather than hindrances to instruction. As instructors of composition, then, it seems logical to apply what we know about these dominant rhetorical and pedagogical theories of the 20th century to the prospective use of social media to better our own pedagogies. Employing the ideas of Mikhail Bakhtin's social construction of knowledge and Louise Rosenblatt's student-centered pedagogy, the author explores the many complementary uses of social media technologies such as Facebook and Twitter in the composition classroom in order to generate a new model of instruction – one which challenges traditional, unilateral exchanges of knowledge and centers on a dialogical, student-centered model of composition instruction.

Chapter 10

Elisabeth H. Buck, University of Massachusetts Dartmouth, USA

Since its original development for use in literary studies by German scholar Hans Robert Jauss in the late 1960s, reception theory has been successfully applied to fields as diverse as media studies, communications, and art history; its efficacy within rhetoric and composition pedagogy, however, has been less fully explored. I argue in this essay that reception theory can provide a meaningful way to understand and discuss social media composing practices, especially as a lens for thinking about why and how we participate in social media as both readers and writers in the 21st century. This essay thus examines the three "aesthetic experiences" of Jauss's reception theory—catharsis, aisthesis, and poiesis— which describe the ways that audiences derive satisfaction from engaging with texts. I apply each aesthetic concept to a corresponding mode of social media composition: practices of social media-based activism, regulation of content on social media, as well as the act of creating "selfies." These applications stand as potential entry points for classroom discussion about how social media draws its users into producing a response. The "aesthetic experiences" represent ways to look at composing practices on social media cohesively, but they also give language to how individual social media users gain enjoyment from participating with these sites. I offer specific strategies for incorporating reception theory in a classroom context, and conclude that this approach helps students think more specifically about the intricacies and limitations of audience(s)—important recognitions for anyone who produces content in social media environments.

Chapter 11

Why are there more than 450 million blogs on the Internet? The answer is simple: blogging is easy, free, and fun. People have opinions they want to share with the world, and blogging is a form of social media that best allows them to do so at length. This chapter examines how blogging can be used as a way to enhance instruction on expository writing. As with any form of social media, using blogs as a teaching tool can be a daunting proposition. Therefore, this chapter provides its readers practical instruction and ideas about how to integrate blogging practices into a composition classroom. Because blogging closely mirrors traditional writing practices, this chapter invites readers to consider blogging as a 21st century model for a 20th century practice.

Section 4
Integrating Social Media as Professional Development in the Writing Classroom

In this section, chapters explore WordPress, LinkedIn, and Twitter as vehicles for helping writing students compose themselves professionally. In this section, audience is carefully discussed as authors suggest students be aware of their professional audience so that they can write more strategically, and therefore, "curate" a professional online identity that makes them more marketable. This section also includes a chapter Q&A between teacher and students regarding students' responses to using social media in their Technical Writing course.

Chapter 12

Using social media to construct a digital, professional presence for the job search is a necessity in today's labor market. Millennials are skilled in using social media for personal purposes but cannot immediately intuit how to use familiar social media outlets in professional contexts. Writing instructors can guide students in enacting an online, professional presence through digitally mediated communication practices that increasingly are seen as valuable in the workplace. Instead of training students away from using "textese," instructors should help students develop an abbreviated writing style that is strategic, consistent, and responsive to the needs of their audience. Twitter is the best social media platform in which to help students achieve these learning goals. This chapter provides readers with a description of a capstone, problem-based learning assignment in which students use Twitter to market their professional selves, network, and improve their digital workplace writing skills.

Chapter 13

Many 21st century student writers have long since mastered the art of crafting a public image through their social media profiles. However, when it is time to make the transition from personal to professional in their public persona, many students have trouble differentiating between the shades of their lives, and subsequently, create less-than-professional public profiles. In this chapter, I explore ways writing teachers can help students transition from a social media experience limited to friends and family to a public persona for job searches, graduate school applications, and the like. More specifically, I discuss how I used LinkedIn to help student writers create authentic, yet professional, public selves.

Chapter 14

Kendra N. Bryant, Florida A&M University, USA

In this chapter, the author argues that although integrating online social media networks into a traditional writing classroom seems timely, cutting edge, and apropos to students' current past-time activities, teachers have the opportunity to create more meaningful classroom activities with social media if they first: consider students' trepidation regarding such non-traditional classroom activities; and second: realize socially-networked students don't necessarily translate into career-ready students. By way of two in-class Q&A sessions, the author discovers that her Technical Writing students need less instruction on how to use social media academically, and more instruction on how to use social media to brand and market themselves professionally. In a chapter grounded in student response, readers receive her student feedback about the effects of integrating social media networks into their writing classroom in an effort to assist teachers more purposely integrate social media into their traditional classroom spaces.

Section 5
Re-Envisioning Wikis in the Writing Classroom

Although rarely referred to as a social media platform, the authors in this section invite readers to explore Wiki's capacity for teaching students how to interact with and write for "real" audiences, while improving student writing skills, including their revising and editing practice.

Chapter 15

Melissa Vosen Callens, North Dakota State University, USA

Unlike first-year writing courses, upper-division writing courses often require students to engage in discipline specific writing. In the author's upper-division course, Writing in the Health Professions, students examine health literacy as it pertains to both oral and written patient-provider communication. Students edit and expand a Wikipedia article for the final course assignment. The advantages of this assignment are threefold. First, students write for an authentic audience, decreasing student apathy. Second, students engage civically, improving health information accessed by millions of people across the world. Finally, students improve content of existing articles and broaden the scope of new articles written, leading to more diverse content and perspectives. In this chapter, the author discusses the above assignment, providing descriptions of scaffolding activities. Potential drawbacks of using Wikipedia to teach students how to write using plain language is discussed, in addition to strategies that might limit these difficulties.

This chapter describes an intervention of a wiki-based course to enhance the practice of academic writing through the process approach. This course was experimented on a freshmen year class of medical students learning English for specific purposes at a university in Saudi Arabia. This chapter draws on the relevant theories and their relationship to the practice of wikis in learning academic writing. Wikis have been introduced into the teaching of writing to afford collaborative assistance and social support. Accordingly, the chapter demonstrates the structure of the course and details the systematic organization between the in-class teaching and on-wiki practice. The intervention of a wiki-based writing course gives emphasis on the background of the tasks assigned. It points out the essential characteristics of the structure of wiki interface that would enable learners to accomplish the process-oriented wiki-mediated collaborative writing (PWMCW) tasks. This new practice reveals the evaluation of this course with its writing tasks, based on the learners' perspectives.

Foreword

When I was in college in the early 1960s, I wrote all my assignments by hand; then I "typed them up" on a tiny manual typewriter, praying I could avoid typos, which were almost impossible to correct. By the time I wrote my dissertation, in 1976-77, I had acquired a miraculous IBM "self-correcting" machine and was as close to technological heaven as I could imagine—which only goes to show how limited my imagination was! Even in 1985, when I got my first computer, I had little inkling of how this technology would change my life as a writer, reader, and speaker.

But I'm getting ahead of myself, because before I could plunge into the digital world, I had to learn to teach print-based writing. As always, my students helped me, but I also had the benefit of amazing intellectual mentors, among them Mina Shaughnessy and Geneva Smitherman. From them I learned to read between the lines of student writing, to listen deeply and rhetorically, and to respect what all of my students bring with them to writing tasks. From "Dr. G," as Smitherman is affectionately known, I especially learned to revel in student experimentation, pushing against and beyond the restrictions and borders of the school essay. Slowly, I began to feel comfortable teaching students to write clear and compelling print-based texts.

The thirty years since then have given me something like Mr. Toad's Wild Ride (from *The Wind in the Willows* and now a Disney ride), as I've learned to create a website, compose digital texts with embedded sound and images, blog, and participate in social media. In my particular journey into the digital age, I've been guided again by my students: working together, we've learned to reach audiences around the world and to build rhetorical prowess through our intense engagements with technology.

In the process, I've also had fine mentors, such as Cynthia Selfe, Keith Gilyard, Henry Jenkins, James Gee, Vershawn Young, and especially, Adam Banks, with whom I had the honor to team teach a course on writing in the digital age. In addition, my ongoing research on college student writing has demonstrated that students today are writing and reading more than ever before, that they are deeply attuned to audiences and how to reach them through use of a wide range of genre and media, and that they are determined not only to *consume* what others have thought and said but to *produce* knowledge themselves. Moreover, in a five-year longitudinal study of student writers at Stanford, I learned that students are deeply enmeshed in communication on the Internet, especially through social media, and that they use these communicative opportunities to make their voices heard.

To achieve such a goal, however, *all* students must have access to today's technological tools. Yet as Adam Banks points out in *Race, Rhetoric, and Technology,* such access is too often limited to students in affluent schools and communities. The technology gap is real, and it is growing. Banks argues for systematically broadening access and bringing all students into the digital world.

Enter Kendra N. Bryant and the authors of *Engaging 21ˢᵗ Century Writers with Social Media*, a volume devoted to achieving broad access to digital literacies in college writing courses. Bryant's Preface makes a compelling case for such a project, and the 16 essays included here provide a wealth of information on how to use everything from Facebook and Twitter to Instagram, Tumblr, Word Press, and Wikipedia to engage student writers in developing personal and academic voices worth listening to. Readers of this volume will, I believe, especially value the very concrete description of assignments and activities, the careful attention to the development of student hearts as well as minds, and the tough-minded assessment of failures or stumbles alongside successes.

If you have integrated social media into your classroom, this volume will provide you with rich comparative data. If you have not integrated social media but are willing to give it a try, you will find here a clear, cogent introduction to how best to do so.

In my view, *Engaging 21ˢᵗ Century Writers with Social Media* goes a long way toward broadening access to the digital literacies students today need to be part of what Henry Jenkins calls a "participatory culture." As I continue on my own journey toward full digital literacy, I am grateful for this thought-provoking volume.

Andrea A. Lunsford
Stanford University, USA

Andrea Abernethy Lunsford *is the Louise Hewlett Nixon Professor of English, Emerita, at Stanford University. The Director of Stanford's Program in Writing and Rhetoric from 2000 through 2011, she has designed and taught courses in writing history and theory, rhetoric, literacy studies, and women's writing, and is the editor, author or co-author of twenty books, including Essays on Classical Rhetoric and Modern Discourse; Singular Texts/Plural Authors; Reclaiming Rhetorica; Everything's an Argument; The Everyday Writer; Writing Matters; The Sage Handbook of Rhetorical Studies; Writing Together; and Everyone's an Author. A long-time member of the Bread Loaf School of English faculty, Lunsford is currently at work on The Norton Anthology of Rhetoric and Writing.*

Preface

Social media is changing the way we communicate and the way we are perceived, both positively and negatively. Every time you post a photo, or update your status, you are contributing to your own digital footprint and personal brand. – Amy Jo Martin, founder & CEO of Digital Royalty

Amy Jo Martin, who began her career in social media while working with the NBA's Phoenix Suns as its Director of Digital Media and Research, broke social media ground when she and former NBA basketball star Shaquille O'Neal partnered to organize the first ever NBA Tweet Up (Gray, 2010). Since partnering with Martin, O'Neal has become the most influential celebrity using social media, (Laird, 2012), therefore encouraging other celebrities like Dwayne "The Rock" Johnson, sports teams like the Chicago White Sox, and businesses like DoubleTree by Hilton to invest in her ideas and practices regarding social media branding. In essence, Martin helps people create the digital universe (read: utopia) they'd like to have.

While our students are not (yet) playing for the NBA, acting in action-packed films, or presiding over major corporations, they definitely are just as engaged in social media networks as the celebrities, sports teams, and corporations that they follow. As a matter of fact, Facebook (est. 2004) and Twitter (est. 2006)—which to date are the top social media platforms used—were created by university students aiming to make long distance connections with their classmates and communicate within small groups. Not surprisingly, then, for the 15 years I've been teaching writing, I have yet to meet a college or high school student unattached to social media. And I totally understand their enthusiasm, for I have been engaged in online social media platforms since I was an undergraduate student at Florida A&M University.

BlackPlanet, an online social networking service that precedes Facebook and Twitter, was designed in 1999 for African American people, and at circa 19 years old, I was a member. However, because BlackPlanet could be accessed through only a desktop computer that most of my peers and I did not own, our participation in online social media sites was quite limited. While we owned cell phones, our mobile devices were not "smart." Therefore, we did not experience the attachments to social media sites and technologies (smart phones, tablets, and laptops) used to access those sites that current 21st century students experience. So, although my peers and I may not have produced writing that our professors believed were indicative of university level students, our writing practice and comprehension were not affected by our current social media use.

The 21st century student writer, however, is having to contend with the demands of academic writing—which are still quite traditional—while absolutely inundated with social media platforms that insist on 140 character tweets, emoticon-filled text messages, and status updates that are often composed of 3-letter words such as "lol," "smh," "wtf," and "idk." While 21st students are absolutely writing and composing more often than I and my peers did—more often than all the previous generations before them did—today's student writer is not necessarily writing as well, or at least to the University's standard.

The traditional 21st century undergraduate student (ages 17-21) often finds himself disconnected from and disinterested in academic writing situations, particularly because they are—more often than not—void of the freedom, flexibility, audience (community), creativity, humor, activism, profanity, and empowerment that social media platforms offer its users. No wonder, then, do teachers find themselves competing with in-class cell phone and social media use. With the World Wide Web in the palm of their hands, along with smart phone applications that allow them to access educational tools and resources—all the while being connected to friends and followers—our students are writing themselves into existence; it's like the biggest explosion of Peter Elbow's "writing without teachers."

However, because students and teachers belonging to an academic institution must hold themselves accountable to the demands of what has been called "academic writing," "good writing," and/or "standard writing," the writing classroom often struggles with being relevant, cutting edge, and affirming. Often times, it may even resemble a counterproductive space; for, many teachers and students find themselves swimming against a current: while writing teachers emphatically prohibit technology use (beyond University endorsed course management systems like Blackboard) in their classrooms, writing students are disengaged from the classroom because they are online, writing in and for their social media networks.

Although traditional writing practices and methodologies feel safe and familiar to many writing teachers who either were born prior to Google's inception or whose pedagogical practices are informed by the pre Google-aged professors who taught them, not inviting students' at-home experiences into the classroom is a disservice. According to Parker Palmer in *To Know as We Are Known* (1993), our classrooms should reflect the real life experiences we want our students to have. Therefore, in an effort to ensure our students are leaving a digital footprint and creating a personal brand that reflects their personhood, as educators, we are responsible for teaching students how to critically analyze, compose with and for, and ethically engage the online social media spaces that occupy more of their mind, body, and soul than television and radio.

Social media allows writing teachers and their students a space to explore multimodal literacies, audience, voice, rhetorical elements and modes, and composition in ways still yet imagined. Our writing classrooms can literally be Wonderland. Be it Facebook or MySpace, Twitter or Tumblr, Instagram or LinkedIn, Pinterest or Snapchat, integrating social media into the writing classroom makes possible a more meaningful learning experience for both students *and teachers*. (More often than not, my students teach me how to use current social media platforms; my job is to figure out how to successfully integrate them into the classroom.)

With all of that said, *Engaging 21st Century Writers with Social Media* is just a point of departure for writing teachers interested in implementing social media in their writing classrooms. While the 16 chapters collected here provide readers some insights regarding contributors' own classroom experiences and theories about social media in the classroom, so much about online communications still needs to be explored, researched, practiced, and shared. Although the World Wide Web is merely 28 years old, it has completely altered the way human beings move in the world, and the system is moving faster than we can keep up with. As a 36-year old writer and English professor, who missed being a member of the Millennial generation (those born between 1982 and 2000) by about five years, I can imagine how daunting, exhausting, and thrilling, this technological phenomenon must be for many. And so, to fulfill the charge to "find a way to bridge the gap between the many years between us" (seasoned and unseasoned folk) that playwright Pearl Cleage made during her 2016 "Essential Conversation" lecture at Florida A&M University, I offer up this text.

In this collection, readers will find chapter essays about blogging with Twitter and WordPress, creating professional personas with LinkedIn, engaging revision practice and the writing process with Wikipedia, and exploring multimodal literacies with Tumblr and Instagram. Additionally, readers will find a compiled list of educational resources and key terms that support their approaches to teaching writing with technology. By no means, however, does this text mean to suggest that teachers do away with traditional approaches to writing instruction. Instead, *Engaging 21ˢᵗ Century Writers with Social Media* aims to offer teachers ideas for *integrating* social media within their current practices as well as provide them with insights regarding the contributions that technological tools make to the learning experience.

Hopefully *Engaging 21ˢᵗ Century Writers with Social Media* will serve as an impetus for future work, for so many other social media platforms like Snapchat, Vine, and Pinterest—which serve as important spaces for (visual) rhetoric and composition discourse and instruction—have yet to be fully realized in a space where blogging so closely mirrors traditional writing practices.

THE PROCESS OF EDITING THIS BOOK

Editor's Note

I became interested in integrating social media in the writing classes I teach while being a graduate student (between 2007 and 2012) at The University of South Florida, Tampa where I was teaching *Professional Writing*. Truthfully, I simply wanted to engage my undergraduate writing students in the online writing communities that my *Rhetoric & Technology* professor required me to engage so that I could learn more about online writing spaces, specifically WordPress. I hoped to garner an appreciation for them. For, as the only Black student in my English graduate program at the time, I was unattached to social media beyond MySpace, and therefore, found the technological demands of my graduate course quite overwhelming. Unlike my White counterparts, I had never heard of WordPress or Twitter, which were recently launched (2005 and 2008), and so, I found myself pushed further against the margins.

When I accepted an assistant professor of English position at the historically Black, Florida A&M University (FAMU)—my alma mater—I committed myself to integrating social media in the *Improving Writing* and *Technical Writing* courses I was assigned to teach, hoping to "uplift the race." I wanted to ensure that the "underprivileged" and "underrepresented" students that FAMU targets are not further marginalized as a result of computer illiteracies. I wanted to ensure that my Black students were strapped with the resources that they needed to compete and perform in all spaces, most of which are Ivory Towers.

However, while I found myself interested in integrating social media in the writing classroom to ensure that my Black students would be able to compete with their White counterparts, I was equally invested in making sure that their social media involvement did not prohibit them from forming meaningful relationships with themselves and real-life relationships with each other. I wanted to create a holistic classroom where heart and brain were invited into the learning experience, but I felt challenged to create a balanced classroom while requiring a potentially distancing online community technology. Therefore, during my first two years at FAMU, I practiced engaging my writing students with online writing communities by way of WordPress, while integrating reading and writing practices that were contemplative in nature, and therefore, encouraged mindful thinking and soul talk (which were eventually expressed in student blogging activities).

In every writing course that I taught, about 98% of my students were like I was: They had not been exposed to WordPress (nor Prezi or LinkedIn), and were not invited into discussions regarding the effects of social media on race, language, composition, identity, and focus. I realized, then, that my Black students, although they were not familiar with WordPress, were absolutely privy to the more "non-academic" social media platforms like Twitter, Instagram, and Tumblr. And surely, most students were not using these popular platforms to compose a professional or academic brand, and they definitely were not interrogating these social media platforms' effects on their personhood. Many of my students were only "shucking and jiving" in their social media spaces, and I—perhaps selfishly—wanted more for them.

My own limitations and curiosities regarding integrating social media into the writing classroom is the impetus for *Engaging 21ˢᵗ Century Writers with Social Media*. In the past year, I have included both Twitter and LinkedIn with my students' WordPress projects, but there's so much more I'd like to explore. And so, I proposed this collection of chapter essays that promises to broaden my own pedagogical practices and hopefully your own.

Call for Proposals

During mid-Spring 2015 semester, I distributed an open call for chapter proposals. I asked for chapter essays that discuss how composition instructors use social media (*Twitter, Facebook, Instagram, Pinterest*) to teach their 21st century learners basic writing skills and encourage their regular writing practice. More specifically, I invited contributors to submit empirically researched, theoretical, or personal narrative chapters on the following topics related to using social media to teach 21ˢᵗ century writing students in Higher Education:

- Using *Twitter* to Teach Succinct Writing,
- Composing with *Pinterest*,
- Blogging as an Approach to Understanding Expository Writing,
- Engaging Audience via *Facebook*,
- Understanding Rhetoric via *Instagram*,
- Traditional Writing Practice with Online Social Media,
- Building a Writing Community by Engaging an Online Community,
- Professional Writing with *LinkedIn*,
- Photojournalism and *Tumblr*,
- Creating an Online Business Portfolio with *WordPress*,
- Using *Twitter* to Write Haikus,
- Understanding Themes by way of #Hashtags,
- Multimodal Composition and *Tumblr*,
- *Snapchat*ting in the Writing Classroom.

I distributed the call for proposals in multiple venues including the Conference on College Composition and Communication, major professional organizations' listservs, and universities like University of South Florida, Florida State University, Purdue University, and Ball State University. I also posted the call for proposals on Facebook, Pinterest, and my website, drknbryant.com. Additionally, the Editorial Advisory Board (EAB) was asked to share the call with other academic institutions, colleagues, and friends.

Chapter Selections

Contributors submitted proposals mid-March of 2015. After receiving a surprising number of proposals, I reviewed each one and accepted those based on their appropriateness for the kind of instructional and informative text I wanted to compile. Authors were notified of their proposal's acceptance and were given until September 15, 2015 to write their full chapters. Chapters underwent a double-blind (sometimes triple) peer review process with my Editorial Advisory Board. The EAB provided invaluable, extensive feedback regarding each chapter. Authors whose chapters were accepted were given until Janaury 30, 2016 to submit their final chapters.

THE ORGANIZATION OF THIS BOOK

Engaging 21ˢᵗ Century Writers with Social Media is divided into five sections:

1. **Blogging in the Writing Classroom:** The authors whose chapters are included in this section discuss their classroom experiences with integrating Twitter to assist students both in the scaffolding process and in "exploring networked, digital compositions." Chapters in this section also include discussion on using WordPress to create electronic writing portfolios and to maintain traditional goals of the writing classroom.
2. **Exploring Multi-Digital Media in the Writing Classroom:** In this section, authors discuss how Tumblr, Instagram, Podbean, and Twitter help to promote "Remix Writing," which mirrors the multimodal activities that permeate present rhetoric & composition discourse.
3. **Theorizing about Social Media Networks in the Writing Classroom:** The four chapters that complete this section are grounded in theoretical concepts. While each chapter offers readers ideas about how to implement social media networks into a writing classroom, they more specifically invite readers to interrogate and explore social media networks for their rhetorical characteristics and situations.
4. **Integrating Social Media as Professional Development in the Writing Classroom:** In this section, chapters explore WordPress, LinkedIn, and Twitter as vehicles for helping writing students compose themselves professionally. In this section, audience is carefully discussed as authors suggest students be aware of their professional audience so that they can write more strategically, and therefore, "curate" a professional online identity that makes them more marketable. This section also includes a chapter Q&A between teacher and students regarding students' responses to using social media in their Technical Writing course.
5. **Re-Envisioning Wikis in the Writing Classroom:** Although rarely referred to as a social media platform, the authors in this section invite readers to explore Wiki's capacity for teaching students how to interact with and write for "real" audiences, while improving student writing skills, including their revising and editing practice.

I organized the book in five sections to make it more accessible. While I hope that readers carefully interact with each chapter included here, I know that many will skim the chapter titles, landing on a few interesting enough to hold their attention—at least through each chapter's introduction. Nonetheless, by sectioning the book into five chapters, all of which intersect with one another, I aim only to enhance the readability of such a thorough text. Therefore, readers may flip through the text, skim sections and their corresponding chapters, and read the works that respond to their pedagogical interests.

CONCLUSION

Florida A&M University's Department of English & Modern Languages has yet to revise their writing courses to include technological writing requirements beyond the university endorsed content management systems that students and teachers use to post grades. As a matter of fact, the department has yet to hold roundtable discussions regarding possibilities for integrating social media and other non-traditional practices into their major course offerings. I imagine then—especially in the historically black college and university setting where tradition often contributes to static methodologies and practices—that many other English departments, professors, and students are far removed from even considering integrating current social media into their neat classroom spaces. Undoubtedly, inviting trends that inform and alter our classroom spaces, pedagogical theories and practices, and rhetorical and composition discourses is scary. But it doesn't have to be. Hopefully, *Engaging 21st Century Writers with Social Media* can serve as your instruction and your guide. I compiled this text especially for you.

This book is also for you, the individual who, like me, promised to be an educator who reminds students of their humanity. As long as we live, there's one thing we know for sure: change is inevitable. Consequently, if we are to impact our students and provide them with meaningful classroom experiences that attend to their mind, body, and soul, we, must adapt to the changes. From Atari to Xbox, the typewriter to the desktop, Woodstock to hip-hop, George Bush to President Barack, change is like a writing process: we invent, we research, we organize, and we write and revise, write and revise, write and revise, all in an effort to know ourselves in relationship to each other.

I hope that *Engaging 21st Century Writers with Social Media* encourages, arouses, and inspirits messy classroom practices, heated pedagogical discussions, and meaningful learning experiences. With a Sankofa spirit, I charge readers to "go back and get it"—to return to heart wherein lies curiosity, creativity, wonderment, and courage—so that we can meet each new semester of students as if we were entering the classroom for the very first time.

Write on!

Kendra N. Bryant
Florida A&M University, USA

REFERENCES

Gray, K. (2010). Laughing, tweeting and eating: the soft power of Shaquille O'Neal. *ZDNet.com*. Retrieved from http://www.zdnet.com/article/laughing-tweeting-and-eating-the-soft-power-of-shaquille-oneal/?tag=main;carousel

Laird, S. (2012). Does every employee need social media training? *Mashable.com*. Retrieved from http://mashable.com/2012/06/13/social-media-digital-royalty/#0G2iqlBBMaqH

Palmer, P. (1993). *To know as we are known: Education as spiritual journey*. New York: HarperOne.

Acknowledgment

Thank you to my mother Choling Bryant Walker who has always told me to keep my eyes on the prize. I am not sure if this is my reward; however, I trust as long as I keep my eyes centered on the gift of love, I will soon enuf exist in all its glory, all ways.

Thank you, too, to my other family members and friends who continue to support my writing endeavors. From poetry to blog posts, Facebook updates and text messages, I appreciate the support, banter, and continued laughter our "pen-palling" generates. One day, I'm sure, one of you will read at least one of my academic essays—in its entirety—and realize I do more than "shuck and jive." (Kiiiiiim, you are definitely the exception.)

Thank you to my University of South Florida classmate-friends, Jessica McKee and Taylor Mitchell, for their continued support. Ya'll are the real deal, for real.

BIG BIG Rattler thanks to my FAMU students who I have worked with, practiced with, and grown with for the past four years. I really do love teaching Black students. I really enjoyed teaching each of you. Thank you, also, to the FAMU Writing Resource Center whose staff has always provided me a communal space in which to work, laugh, debate, and feel the sun on my face. To my colleagues Ceron Bryant, Veronica Yon, Genyne Boston, and Kimberly K. Harding: bOoM! I'm pickin' 'em up & layin' 'em down, yo! Thank you.

And of course, thank you to each member of my Editorial Advisory Board, to each contributing author, to Dr. Ruth Sawh and Lauren Gregory, and to the generous Andrea A. Lunsford.

Finally, thank you to my love, M, whose living room I camped out in while completing the final edits to this text. Thank you for being amazed; thank you for giving me space to work; thank you for opening a door for me.

#ME #xo #ieditedmyfirstbook #its430am #icantbelieveimdone #blackrhetoric #teachpeace #readmychapter #iwroteadecentpreface #andrealunsfordwrotemyforeword #apastyleisaggravating #proofread #edit #thewritingprocess #grantmetenure #blackwomanrhetorontheloose #digitaldividestillexists #blacklivesmatter #famu #eachoneteachone #dropeverythingandread #teachargument #socialmedia #followmyblog #imawesome #blackgenius #engage21stcenturywriterswithsocialmedia

Section 1
Blogging in the Writing Classroom

The authors whose chapters are included in this section discuss their classroom experiences with integrating Twitter to assist students both in the scaffolding process and in "exploring networked, digital compositions." Chapters in this section also include discussion on using WordPress to create electronic writing portfolios and to maintain traditional goals of the writing classroom.

Chapter 1
Networked Digital Spaces:
Twitter in the Composition Classroom

Stephanie N. Phillips
University of South Florida, USA

ABSTRACT

As the landscape for communication changes with new and evolving digital technologies, the format for college composition classrooms must change and adapt as well. If we are moving towards compositions that are created by and mediated through a screen, we must adopt new approaches for talking about and teaching these new forms of language and communication. During the fall 2014 semester, I was given the opportunity to teach a composition class focused on digital rhetoric. As a facet of the classroom experience, my students created and used Twitter accounts for fictional characters. Utilizing Twitter within the composition classroom allowed students to compose as a part of a much larger network of actors that interact with the texts they create. As a form of networked communication, the compositions created by students through this medium demanded interaction and engagement in a way that a classroom composition, shared only between student and instructor, does not.

INTRODUCTION

Before I set foot in my first composition classroom as a graduate teaching assistant at the University of South Florida, I spent the week prior to fall classes assessing the available technology in the classrooms I was assigned. More than anything, I was nervous that I was not skilled enough to even start the projector. I was so fearful of the educational technology provided by the university that I quickly implemented a "no tech" policy within the classroom that asked students to leave their laptops, cell phones, and other electronics in their bags during class. Inexperienced and young, the last thing I wanted was for my students to not respect me, and I thought that technology would only detract from my oh-so-mesmerizing lesson plans about thesis statements.

As I progressed in my own graduate coursework, I began to have positive experiences with projects requiring social media and web writing that were extremely valuable to me as a writer and scholar. Through the creation of personal and professional websites, for example, I began to gain a new respect

DOI: 10.4018/978-1-5225-0562-4.ch001

for modes of writing that diverge from the traditional academic essay. I realized that I was unfairly blaming technology for distracting students from an outdated pedagogical style instead of embracing these varied, interactive, and evolving forms of communication. In Chris Gerben's (2014) "Free and Easy: A Rubric for Evaluating Everyday Technology," he states, "The problem, of course, was not the technology: it was the user" (para. 4). By bringing technologies into my composition classroom, I hoped to share with students many of the same valuable experiences with multimodal writing that I was having as a graduate student.

While I immediately wanted to incorporate as much of this technology as possible into my existing assignments, I needed to consider how these emergent technologies, such as Twitter, change the landscape of the college composition classroom. Chris Anson (1999) notes that, as teachers, "We spend much of our time working within the framework of certain fairly stable educational conditions. These conditions include physical spaces that define the social and interpersonal contexts of teaching," such as classrooms and offices (p. 262). Although written in 1999, Anson's "Distant Voices: Teaching and Writing in a Culture of Technology," aptly makes an assertion that holds true for 2015 writing classrooms: the basic layout, tools, and modes of assessment are largely comparable, and perhaps even identifiable, to a "mid-nineteenth century schoolteacher" (p. 264). New writing technologies drive developments in the way we talk and think about communicable compositions. Thus, we must reevaluate the layout and textual "spaces" that we ask our students to participate in.

If classroom spaces are not changing to meet the needs of students and the digital networks they inhabit on a daily basis, perhaps it is important to recall the warnings of composition theorists who have repeatedly asserted that writing instruction can and will become obsolete if it is unable to meet the needs of students composing as a part of such digitized communities (e.g. Yancey, 2004; Hawk, 2007; Brooke, 2009; Sirc, 2010). Twenty-first-century writing instructors are currently experiencing an inability to engage student writers despite the fact that the vast majority of these students read and write massive quantities of text on a daily basis. These forms of writing that students engage with–text messages, emails, tweets, blog posts, and Facebook updates to name a few–do not resemble the traditional model of academic writing that many composition classrooms still employ as the crux of writing instruction.

In order to engage instruction with the real-world writing that these students create, instructors must consider how composition can include such multimodal formats. As Takayoshi and Sullivan (2007) explain, "Technological practices complicate existing definitions of writers, writing, and publishing, which in turn affect our roles as writers, writing teachers, and writing theorists" (p. 7). Many students in the classroom do not realize that they are all creating and consuming text through social media on a daily basis. By asking students to become more aware of their role as creators within this networked process of writing, composition classrooms can incorporate a fundamental aspect of communication practices in the 21st century.

In this chapter, I seek to:

1. Establish the importance of *digitizing* composition classrooms by integrating assignments that allow students to compose in a multimodal format;
2. Present a sample method for integrating social media, specifically twitter, into the classroom; and
3. Analyze the results of my students' interactions with Twitter in the classroom.

THEORETICAL FRAMEWORK

Expanding the Practice of Teaching Composition

As new writing technologies, especially those that we categorize as "social media," become salient means of interaction and communication, considering how we can expand our use of texts within a classroom to include this new form of composition is important. Building on Kathleen Yancey's 2004 description of how composition studies should expand to meet growing trends in digital literacy, Jody Shipka (2011) reminds us "that a composition is, at once, a thing with parts–with visual-verbal or multimodal aspects–the expression of relationships and, perhaps most importantly, the result of complex, ongoing processes that are shaped by, and provide shape for, living" (p. 17). Shipka challenges the use of academic writing that typically stresses a one-way power dynamic between instructor (the expert) and the student (receiver of expert's information). Marc Santos and Mark Leahy (2014) suggest that

… by presenting our students with a less programmatic writing process, in effect asking them to discover and/or invent new processes to solve a variety of new problems, we are not attempting to remystify writing so much as to acknowledge that the easily-taught, easily-evaluated prescriptivist pedagogy of the last century, with its emphasis on the academic essay and little else, has failed in every imaginable way to account for the unpredictable and ingenious new forms of writing our students encounter and participate in every day. (p. 87)

If composition contains multimodal dimensions and is most effective when placed in relationship with other texts and, importantly, an audience, traditional forms of academic writing and instructor-student relationships are, at their basest, outdated. In order to combat the prescriptivist pedagogy identified by Santos and Leahy, Jody Shipka (2011) expands her composition classroom to include multimodal texts of her students' choosing. While some of Shipka's students may create online writing, others compose more abstract projects, such as research essays literally written directly onto a pair of ballet shoes. Shipka identifies that projects such as the ballet shoes have raised eyebrows and disapproving comments about how composition and college-level writing is *not* writing by hand on an article of clothing. However, Shipka is not interested in such a final product and, instead, seeks to identify and discuss the "final project *in relation to* the complex and highly rigorous decision-making processes the students employed while producing this text" (2011, p. 3).

I agree with Shipka's investment in process and creation and believe that students should analyze the decision-making process that is required while composing, even the small, ephemeral texts produced for social media. In addition, I believe that writing should focus on audience and the affect that any form of text has when received by that audience. Like Shipka, Santos and Leahy (2014) propose a class that focuses on online writing and the work that students do while engaging in specific discourse communities on the Internet. The decision to place students within online networks creates a relationship between the creator (the student), the medium (online blogging forums), and the audience (readers and commenters). As a result of the online writing class, Santos and Leahy claim

… students are generally surprised to see that their writing can reach and even affect people who are not institutionally obligated to read it. We are interested in postpedagogical webwriting, then, as a way

of situating the composition classroom in a world of living writers and writing, not within a simulated experience of imaginary audiences and hypothetical rhetorical scenarios. (p. 86)

The ability to create text in these online spaces allows for a level of engagement, such as the use of comment features, that foster interaction in a way that Shipka's ballet shoes do not.

Given the projects employed by both Shipka and Santos and Leahy, then, I would further the discussion about these new forms of communication by claiming that composition must address a network of creators and audience members that asks all participants to consider the medium of the content that is being created, consumed, and shared. Jeff Rice echoes this sentiment in *Digital Detroit: Rhetoric and Space in the Age of the Network* (2012) when he says that engaging with these digital spaces demands more than spectatorship: we make meaning in these online networks through the interactions we create (2012, p. 9). If, as Rice says, "We live in the age of the network" (2012, p. 5), it is important to build on Shipka's insistence on process and ask students to consider the decisions they make while creating compositions as part of a larger network: compositions do not exist in a vacuum. Compositions, such as the ones created by students through social media on an almost daily basis, interact within networks in a way that more traditional forms of composition, such as an academic essay, do not. In order to best meet students' needs, then, we must help them to develop the skills necessary for becoming digital citizens. This includes the ability to engage appropriately with these networks of communication by understanding the needs and interests of the other networked participants and affecting the dialogue that is taking place within these networks.

The Importance and Impact of Twitter

It is this consideration of networks, then, that prompted me to ask students to engage with Twitter as a tool for composition. Twitter is a social networking tool that allows users to compose 140-character messages called Tweets. Anyone with an account on Twitter can post messages and then tag these messages into sub-categories, or smaller networks, through the use of hashtags. Hashtags are words that begin with the symbol "#" in order to help categorize the content of the message. By clicking on the hashtagged word in a Tweet, the user can view all other messages categorized with the same keyword. If a hashtag becomes popular, it may appear in a sidebar on the Twitter homepage that is marked for trending topics. Hashtags are, by nature, participatory; they ask Twitter users to take part in larger conversations that are found through the use of a hashtag.

Through the use of networks and hashtags, Twitter has grown into a vast public space where information is spread and protests can find a voice. Importantly, marginalized communities can reach enormous participatory audiences. In "The Rules of Twitter" (2014), Dorothy Kim claims that Twitter is a "mediated public space, a hacked public space" (para. 3). Kim elaborates:

Twitter, the medium as a microblogging platform owned by a corporation, was never intended to become such a vast 'public' digital space. Rather, its aims were likely about networking for information and commerce, not for the goals of political and social protest, the vocalization and amplification of minority voices and points of view. Nor was it imagined as the digital space most conducive to the actual mingling of a huge multiracial, multi-bodied, multi-abled population. (para. 5)

Such impressive, mediated, digital spaces, then, furnish the classroom with the ability to participate in discussions that foster engagement and create impact. Hashtags such as #Ferguson and #BlackLives-Matter, for example, are notable demonstrations of Twitter activism and protest.

Twitter is quickly replacing mainstream media outlets as a "primary source of on-the-ground, archived, filtered, and live information" about issues, such as "police brutality, antiblackness, and #JusticeForMike-Brown" (Kim, 2014, "Twitter as a mediated," para. 1). Kim notes that "there were over 1 million tweets before #Ferguson got coverage from mainstream media" (Kim, 2014, "Twitter as a mediated," para. 1). In the past, it was far more difficult to access information or display support on such an immediate level from anywhere in the world.

While many of my composition students chose to write about topics such as immigration reform, gun regulation, LGBT rights, and other issues concerning social justice, Twitter has the potential to advance a student's interaction with these topics by both asking them to engage with a real-life audience and network of participants surrounding such issues, and to learn about the issues from groups previously without the ability to "control conversation" (Kim, 2014). Groups, such as those engaging with #BlackTwitter, #SolidarityIsForWhiteWomen, #Ferguson, and other hashtags used for protesting social injustices, have repurposed Twitter to allow a large percentage of minority and women users to control conversations about these issues (Kim, 2014).

What we see with Twitter when compared to other online spaces, then, is that Twitter is a far more interactive means of communication. This interactivity can help students generate and share knowledge instead of simply consuming it from the "expert" instructor. Giving students this kind of agency, says Alasdair Blair (2013), turns them into "co-producers of knowledge" (p. 142). In other words, with the freedom to post content of their choosing and engage with many of the aforementioned social issues through hashtags, students are given authority through Twitter that, in a more prescriptive form of academic writing and instruction, they do not often have.

Adeline Koh (2015) states,

Introducing social media breaks down the walls of the classroom, because it encourages students to imagine the issues in the classroom beyond the space of the institution, beyond actual class meeting time, and across a wider public who may work on similar things that are being covered in your class. (para. 8)

To return to Anson's (1999) earlier point that we need to reimagine the spaces associated with the writing classroom, Twitter helps to break those all-too-familiar physical spaces by allowing students to engage in a networked and collaborative digital space.

METHODOLOGY AND PEDAGOGY

Bringing Twitter into the Classroom

In agreement with Jesse Stommel (2012) that "the evolution of written language is speeding up at an exponential rate, and this necessitates that we, as writing teachers, reconsider the way we work with language in our classrooms" (para. 3), I accepted an opportunity to implement digital rhetorics in a first-year composition class that I taught during the fall 2014 semester.

As a facet of the classroom experience, my students created and used Twitter accounts for fictional characters in order to explore networked digital compositions. Students developed online personas for these characters and used their accounts to interact with one another and the much larger Twitter network established through hashtags. As a form of networked communication, the compositions created by students through this medium demand interaction and engagement in a way that a typical college composition project, shared only between student and instructor, does not.

My engagement with Twitter in the classroom was inspired by an article by Stommel that proposes a classroom assignment called The Twitter Essay (2012). This assignment asks that "students condense an argument with evidentiary support into 140 characters, which they unleash upon a hashtag (or trending topic) in the Twitter-verse" (para. 9). Stommel acknowledges that, instead of protesting what social media and text messaging do to the structure and grammar that students employ while writing, instructors engage this new evolution in written communication. Before composing, however, students must first know their audience – "the Twitter members engaged in discussion around a particular hashtag" (Stommel, 2012, para. 9). Stommel states that "there is a pleasure in the act of composing with these constraints [140-character limit], an intentional and curious engagement with how sentences, words, and letters make meaning" (2012, para. 7). The results of Stommel's assignment demonstrate the playfulness with which Twitter allows users to engage with language.

Stommel's play with language and structure to create meaning is in direct conversation with Adeline Koh's (2015) concession that we must "reconsider what it means to be *literate* in the twenty-first century" (para. 6). Koh also asks that her students engage with Twitter, though her students use the medium to engage with class content through live-tweeting their classroom meetings. For example, while watching a movie, Koh's students would use Twitter to report what they see in the film and then engage with the content of the film through responding to one another's Tweets or contributing outside content for the class to consider. Koh reports that the tweets composed in class often result in lengthy discussions about the materials outside of the classroom.

While Koh and Stommel offer great suggestions for using Twitter in the classroom, there are noticeable difficulties to discuss before assigning this technology. First, it is important to acknowledge the potential privilege that can inform our interactions on Twitter. Kim (2014) states that "we need to consider how much particular forms of privilege will inform our positionality on this medium" ("Twitter as a space," para. 1). "Respect" and "authority," Kim states, are gained through interactions and not from any given position, such as the position of a college student or even a college instructor. Discussing positions of class, ethnicity, and gender with the class, however, will help to generate awareness for these issues as students begin to navigate Twitter. Second, as the instructor, there is little control over how non-class members interact with students. While the goal of using Twitter is to allow students to engage in real-life conversations, not all Twitter users are positive or friendly. For this reason, I asked my students to create Twitter accounts not linked to any personal, identifiable information.

Building on the assignments created by Stommel and Koh, students were asked to choose a literary character and text that they have prior knowledge of and reimagine that character in the form of a Twitter account. The goal is to present the point of view of this character through a twenty-first century conversation in order to address a modern audience. Thus, the student should engage with the digital format *through* his or her chosen character.

To begin this assignment, my class created a sample Twitter account to use as a group and become familiar with the medium. The class chose the character Dracula from Bram Stoker's *Dracula*. One of the first posts on this fake Twitter account was a flyer asking viewers to participate in a blood drive.

Other students tweeted from Dracula's point of view about the experience of living in London in the twenty-first century. As an "undead" character, we found it humorous to position Dracula in situations that were unique to the twenty-first century audience – learning to use a cell phone, hailing a taxi cab, and visiting a nightclub, to name a few.

Asking students to adopt fictional identities demands that they analyze the points of view of the characters they choose and then understand how these characters would engage with the very technologies we are working to learn in the classroom. While the student's experience with Twitter is mediated through the fictional character, the student must adopt an alternate point of view that allows students to use the technologies they engage with on a daily basis through someone else's perspective. Stoker's Dracula did not engage with any of the modern technologies that are so engrained in our existence, so asking a student to consider how Dracula would have used these technologies requires that student to consider how we use the modern technical conveniences that we often take for granted.

To further introduce this project, my students each chose a different trending topic or hashtag on Twitter and analyzed the members of that community. One student, for example, chose to look at the community surrounding #YesAllWomen. The #YesAllWomen hashtag is used to talk about how all women experience sexual, mental, and physical abuse. The community created through the hashtag is used to share experiences, expose sexism, and promote gender equality through awareness of the sexism that all women face. Like #BlackLivesMatter, #Ferguson, and #BlackTwitter, the community of #YesAllWomen is indicative of a specific audience, and through analysis of the community and the kinds of posts categorized to these hashtags, students discussed how they would make contributions to these kinds of networks. For their audience analysis, I asked my students to consider the following questions:

1. What issues are the members of this community engaged with? What is the overall message that they are trying to convey?
2. What methods are these Twitter users using to convey their message? (Consider tone, content, such as memes or other forms of visuals, and information.)
3. How are the users interacting with one another in this community?
4. What kinds of people would you say represent this community and their interests?

These kinds of questions helped the class to address issues of voice and power in relation to issues of social justice.

Finally, before beginning with their fictional Twitter accounts, my students submitted proposals for the characters that they would be working with. In the proposals, I asked the students to explain what kinds of issues this character would engage with on social media, how their tone and point of view are portrayed in the original work that they appear in, and how this point of view could be remixed to work with a new, digital forum.

For example, earlier in the semester the class worked with graphic novels such as Alan Moore's *Watchmen*. A student might choose to tweet from the perspective of the Comedian, a fictional character from *Watchmen,* and would need to consider what social and political issues this character could be engaged with in 2015. The Comedian is particularly indicative of Goldwater-era politics, so this assignment would ask a student working with the Comedian to adapt this character's point of view to the kinds of current political conversations that Twitter encourages. As Adam J. Banks states, "all technologies come packaged with a set of politics: if those technologies are not inherently political, the conditions in which they are created and which they circulate into a society are political" (2006, p.23). The immediacy of

Twitter creates opportunities for discussing events as they happen and for examining political discourse in terms of these unfolding events.

RESULTS AND DISCUSSION

To demonstrate an instance of how a student could successfully complete this project, I will give examples from a student-created account based on Rorschach, a fictional character from Alan Moore's 1985 graphic novel, *Watchmen*. Rorschach, formerly known as Walter Kovacs before adopting his vigilante name, is a masked anti-hero with a very black and white sense of justice that often ends in violence. The majority of the scenes in *Watchmen* are given from Rorschach's point of view, oftentimes in the form of his diary entries.

The student working with this character used the username @rinkblot85. Rorschach is known for wearing a mask of inkblots, which is where the student derived the account name. This student begins his Twitter page with an origin of Rorschach the vigilante:

@rinkblot85: *broke fingers. cut neck. dirty shirt.*
@rinkblot85: *They constantly taunt me. don't they know that I don't feel. They can do nothing to me*
@rinkblot85: *after that there was no walter. it is rorschach. only rorschach*

Given that Rorschach is a vigilante, it makes sense to begin with an origin story. Using pieces of narrative taken from Rorschach's diary, this student aptly employs Rorschach's dry and blunt style of writing to recreate his origin.

This student also engaged with the hashtag #tbt, which stands for "throwback Thursday." Twitter users will often use #tbt when posting pictures from their childhood. In this project, the student used #tbt to create moments in Rorschach's narrative where the reader is taken to an event in Walter Kovac's past. For example:

@rinkblot85: *#tbt to when i partially blinded that kid and bit the other one cuz i was angry. don't cross me*

Although #tbt does not represent a specific community working towards social justice, it is one of the most common hashtags used on Twitter. This hashtag is also particularly useful to the character Rorschach because much of his narrative in the graphic novel is expressed through flashbacks to past events. The student behind @rinkblot85 worked closely with the original narrative to tell Rorschach's story through more modern narrative techniques than the diary that Rorschach keeps in the novel. When Rorschach believes that he will be killed in the novel, for example, he seeks to present his diary to a newspaper that will print his story. In response to the change of medium, @rinkblot85 posted: "If I die I want my Twitter to be seen so people know my story."

@rinkblot also posted articles about current political events and used the character to discuss these events. One particular downfall of this account, however, is that the student demonstrated little interaction with other Twitter users. Two other students, also choosing to work with *Watchmen*, chose to portray Laurie Jupiter and Dr. Manhattan. In the novel, these characters are in a romantic relationship with one another. The Twitter accounts created by these students often interacted with one another and demonstrated a more conversational element to their Twitter use. Again, however, these two students were mostly engaging with each other through Twitter and not with larger communities. This assignment does not necessarily require that students interact with many varied Twitter communities, but it does introduce them to the potential of this technology and ask them to compose in a space that is designed to engage them in networked communication.

Assessment

Given that this assignment, and most other forms of webwriting, looks very different than the traditional academic essay, I needed to consider how I would assess the students' engagement with the medium. In Jody Shipka's *Toward a Composition Made Whole* (2011), she discusses how she asks students to reflect on the non-traditional compositions, such as writing an academic essay directly onto ballet shoes, that they created for class. Specifically, she asks students to respond to the following two questions:

1. What, specifically, is this piece trying to accomplish – above and beyond satisfying the basic requirements outlined in the task description? In other words, what work does, or might, this piece do? For whom? In what contexts?
2. What specific rhetorical, material, methodological, and technological choices did you make in service of accomplishing the goal(s) articulated above? Catalog, as well, choices you might not have consciously made, those that were made for you when you opted to work with certain genres, materials, and technologies. (p. 114)

Shipka's questions emphasize the process of creating compositions and the choices the students had to make before and during creation. For Shipka, then, the process is more important than the final product – the student could have poorly executed the composition, but the ideas make the project worth discussing.

I adapted Shipka's reflection assignment and asked my students to respond to the following questions:

1. What is the process you used for selecting your fictional character? How did Twitter effect your character selection?
2. Before creating your character's account, what topical goals did you establish? Were the goals different for unilateral communication, communication with other specific Twitter users, or for communication with the larger Twitter network?
3. Did your choice of fictional character assist or limit the communication goals you established? Did the account achieve the level of interaction with other characters and users you envisioned? What aspects of the character you chose limited your ability to successfully communicate with the Twitter network as a whole?
4. How did Twitter assist or limit your communication goals?

The goal of the reflection assignment is to ask students to consider the decision-making process that went into the composition of their Tweets. If the assignment is effective, the students are thinking about the character they would like to work with and their ability to engage with the networks inherent in this medium before we begin the project.

I gave the students the above questions as a guide for writing their reflections, though many students also included points that I had not considered to ask them about. For example, some students discussed the decisions they made when choosing a username, an avatar (identifying picture), and a border picture for their Twitter homepage. The aforementioned account for Laurie Jupiter, for example, used an avatar picture of Laurie hugging Dr. Manhattan, her love-interest. The student noted that her choice of avatar represented the content that she was creating on Twitter, such as discussions with Dr. Manhattan and reflections on her relationship with Dr. Manhattan. The student also noted that her choice to use images of Laurie with Dr. Manhattan reflected the concept that Laurie's identity is very tied to her relationship with Dr. Manhattan and that, as many young adults on social media do, Laurie would surely post a picture of herself and her partner if she was using social media. By imagining Laurie Jupiter participating in the writing practices common among young people, the student demonstrated an awareness not only of appropriate subject matter, but also the appropriate genres and methods of online performance.

All of these decisions helped students to create the identity of their fictional character and engage with the tools provided by this medium. While I did not initially consider adding questions about design to the reflection assignment, I would add these kinds of questions in the future and, perhaps, spend more time talking about how such design elements, like an avatar, can help establish identity. In Kristin Arola's "The Design of Web 2.0: The Rise of the Template, the Fall of Design" (2010), she emphasizes that design, particularly the design of social media and its content, impacts identity formation. While Arola focuses primarily on MySpace and Facebook, the notion that choosing an avatar and other content to place on a social media page impacts perception by an audience and ultimately helps shape an online persona and identity, is applicable to Twitter as well. Like my reflection assignment, Arola notes that we should spend time asking students to consider the implications of design elements on their social media pages:

One avenue is to analyze the interfaces of Web 2.0. Teachers can ask students how Facebook would be different if there were no user profile pictures, or if the rectangular listing of the News Feed was replaced by pink thought bubbles, or if one's status appeared vertically instead of horizontally and could only be displayed through the use of animated emotive stick figures. Such interrogations help students see how the design of every element impacts the overall effect. (p. 12)

Reflections on the design further help students to make connections between the designs that they choose and content that they are creating through posts.

CONCLUSION

Asking my students to engage with Twitter in the classroom provided them with the opportunity to learn to work with the medium in an encouraging and monitored setting. While I think that many of the students were initially hesitant to work with Twitter in a classroom context, some of these students have reported that they have since created their own personal accounts on Twitter and continue to engage with the many networked discussions that take place through this tool. Those that learned the most from this project were able to successfully engage with other members of the class by sharing information or adding the opinions of their fictional characters to an ongoing discussion. In the future, I would ask that the students attempt to connect with users outside of their classmates to interact with. Interacting with users other than peers would better connect them to trending political and social issues and better observe how these concerns are discussed and spread through Twitter networks. I would also ask that they discuss in the reflection assignment how their characters may respond to these trending issues on Twitter. While the students completed an analysis of the types of networks that exist within Twitter, asking them to actually take part in some of these discussions would better demonstrate how a Tweet could effectively convey meaning as a part of a larger conversation.

It is important that we consider and include these emergent forms of communication technologies, such as Twitter, in the classroom because, with a deeply symbiotic relationship emerging between technology and communication, writing teachers must reexamine what it means to be literate in the twenty-first-century and how we can equip our students with the skills they need to write successfully using this technology. These skills need to include audience awareness, the ability to enter into an already existent discussion with meaningful contributions, establishing ethos for social networking, and both the ability to work within the constraints of a particular medium while simultaneously demonstrating mastery of that medium to work in the writer's interests.

As I have discussed, Twitter is the perfect tool to develop these skills because, in order to be used productively, it mandates an awareness of its many networks and the users inhabiting those networks. Twitter also allows for instantaneous action towards issues of activism and social justice. Further, given the 140-character limit, the medium asks users to consider each word that they choose in order to ensure that meaning is created through language and imagery. Stommel (2012) would agree with the benefits of using Twitter in the classroom and states,

There is both the end result of concision and the fun to be had in attaining it. There is both the undoing of language for the purpose of making meaning and the undoing of language for its own sake, calling attention to the fundamental oddity of its rules and structure. ("Instructions," para. 3)

I do acknowledge, however, that incorporating digital technologies into the composition classroom arouses concerns over accessibility and computer literacy. One of the benefits of a digital, multimodal approach in the classroom is that while it asks students to engage with new communication technologies (i.e., social media), the composition classroom itself remains largely a place of discussion and reflection on student writing. As such, the technological requirements within the classroom are modest. As Takayoshi and Sullivan noted in 2007, "some level of technological access is now available at most colleges and universities, as technology has been and continues to be of high priority for schools and institutions of higher learning across the country" (p. 8). At universities where connected classrooms are scarce, this approach can be implemented with little difficulty, provided students have access to and are conversant with social media outside the classroom.

While many instructors in the humanities are still, as I once was, wary about the inclusion of too much technology in the classroom and this technology's ability to destroy "writing as we know it," in order to remain useful as a discipline, we need to consider how our teaching practices can adapt to modern modes of writing and communication. It is a common fear, as demonstrated in Clary Shirky's (2014) manifesto, "Why I Just Asked My Students to Put Their Laptops Away," that students are distracted by technology and that these distractions will inhibit their ability to learn. If our students and, admittedly we as teachers, are so engrossed and invested in these kinds of technological communication tools, however, we must consider how they may be changing the landscape of education, particularly for writing instructors. Instead of instituting a technology ban, as I thought was the correct policy when I first started teaching, we should rearrange our perception of college composition in order to help students better use the technologies that "distract" them.

If our goal as instructors is to create students with effective and compelling communication skills, then we must meet students' needs in terms of how they are communicating and with whom they are communicating. Continuing to reject the technology that our students engage with based on the assumption that it is not academic writing ignores the fact that many of the most valuable sites of discourse, interaction, and activism are online, digital spaces.

REFERENCES

Anson, C. M. (1999). Distant voices: Teaching and writing in a culture of technology. *College English*, *61*(3), 261–280. doi:10.2307/379069

Arola, K. L. (2010). The design of web 2.0: The rise of the template, the fall of design. *Computers and Composition*, *27*(1), 4–14. doi:10.1016/j.compcom.2009.11.004

Banks, A. J. (2006). *Race, rhetoric, and technology: Searching for higher ground*. New Jersey: Lawrence Erlbaum Associates, Inc.

Blair, A. (2013). Democratising the learning process: The use of Twitter in the teaching of politics and international relations. *Political Studies Association*, *33*, 135–145.

Brooke, C. G. (2009). *Lingua fracta*. Creskill, NJ: Hampton Press.

Gerben, C. (2014). Free and easy: a Rubric for evaluating everyday technology. *The Writing Instructor*. Retrieved from http://parlormultimedia.com/twitest/gerben-2014-03

Hawk, B. (2007). *A Counter-history of composition: Toward methodologies of complexity*. Pittsburgh, PA: University of Pittsburgh Press.

Kim, D. (2014). The rules of Twitter. *Hybrid Pedagogy*. Retrieved fromhttp://www.hybridpedagogy. com/journal/rules-twitter/

Koh, A. (2015). Teaching with the Internet; or How I learned to stop worrying and love the Google in my classroom. *Hybrid Pedagogy*. Retrieved from http://www.hybridpedagogy.com/journal/teaching-with-the-internet-or-how-i-learned-to stop-worrying-and-love-the-google-in-my-classroom/

Rice, J. (2012). *Digital Detroit: Rhetoric and space in the age of the network*. Carbondale: Southern Illinois University Press.

Santos, M. C., & Leahy, M. H. (2014). Postpedagogy and web writing. *Computers and Composition*, *32*, 84–95. doi:10.1016/j.compcom.2014.04.006

Shipka, J. (2011). *Toward a composition made whole*. Pittsburgh, PA: University of Pittsburgh Press.

Shirky, C. (2014). Why I asked my students to put away their laptops. *Medium*. Retrieved from https://medium.com/@cshirky/why-i-just-asked-my-students-to-put-their-laptops-away7f5f7c50f368

Sirc, G. Serial composition. In S. A. Selber (Ed.), *Rhetoric and Technologies* (pp. 56–73). Columbia, SC: University of South Carolina Press.

Stommel, J. (2012). The Twitter essay. *Hybrid Pedagogy*. Retrieved fromhttp://www.hybridpedagogy. com/journal/the-twitter-essay/

Takayoshi, P., & Sullivan, P. (2007). *Labor, writing technologies, and the shaping of composition in the academy*. New Jersey: Hamilton Press, Inc.

Yancey, K. B. (2004). Made not only in words: Composition in a new key. *College Composition and Communication, 56*(2), 297–328. doi:10.2307/4140651

Chapter 2
Blog Love:
Blogging (And Microblogging) Communities as Writing Classroom Companions

Clarissa J. Walker
University of Rhode Island, USA

ABSTRACT

Despite claims of a decades-long history of multimodal instructional activities, Composition Studies scholars are still slow to embrace many web-based, social media technology tools to help realize traditional goals of the college writing classroom. Microblogging (Twitter) and blogging (WordPress) activities are effective technology companions that support collaborative learning, critical research, and analytical writing models. This chapter suggests online reading comprehension and critical literacy models as guides for microblogging and blogging lesson design. Finally, instructor commentary and student samples from two assignments, (a) blogging communities and (b) using Twitter to critically analyze a text, are offered to illustrate the aforementioned application.

Technology allows us to live out theoretical perspectives; but sometimes technology appropriates those theoretical positions, amplifies and transforms them. It is not always theory to embodiment. It is sometimes embodiment to theory. – Cynthia Selfe

INTRODUCTION

Although there is a more companionable embrace of technology in the composition classroom, blogs and microblogs, such as Twitter, are too infrequently employed as viable tools for helping writing students reach long-discussed course goals. The merits of collaborative learning, writing that contributes to the proverbial "Burkean parlor," and discovering the usefulness of outside knowledge in writing classroom creations are often delineated as important instructional components (Lunsford, Ede, Moss, Papper,

DOI: 10.4018/978-1-5225-0562-4.ch002

Walters & Brody, 2012; Bruffee, 1984). Still, there are few in Composition Studies who turn to technology companions such as blogging and microblogging as a means to that end.

In this chapter, I submit that student blogging (Wordpress.com) and microblogging (Twitter) facilitate several of the historical aims and still emerging traditions of the composition classroom. Emphasized is the application of a pedagogical lineage respectful of a sociocultural lens, collaborative learning and rhetorical situation instruction. Most importantly, I demonstrate how online and offline reading comprehension models of literacy scholars offer guidelines for engaging blogging technologies in ways that strengthen student research writing, evaluation and strategic reading abilities. In this chapter, I will discuss Composition Studies and reading comprehension scholarship that inform sought after critical evaluation practices in the writing classroom; profile two in-class activities using Twitter and community blogs; and, offer teacherly observations and student examples that illustrate how they use social media for textual analysis and collaboration. By sharing student creations, descriptions of writing activities and commentary, I hope to encourage others who may be tentative about experimenting with technology tools; this chapter joins a body of work that widens the scope of composition instructional practices and makes the incorporation of multimodality, albeit deictic, more normative.

THEORETICAL FRAMEWORK

Growing Pains: Student Writing Traditions, Multimodality, and "New Media"

Pedagogical approaches that incorporate technology often illustrate how participatory culture[1] manifests in the classroom; these approaches are anchored in a liberatory education lineage that is also taken up by composition scholars. Adopting critical pedagogy precepts (Freire, 1972; Shor, 1996), writing teachers seek to nurture student agency and independent thought. This advocacy for student agency, clarity about their own positionality and voice is often articulated with metaphors such as the "Burkean parlor,[2]" named after Kenneth Burke. This trope situates student writing in an existing conversation (Lunsford et al., 2012). Connecting the dialectic traditions of the field to collaborative meaning making, Kenneth Bruffee (1984) claims that one of the main goals of collaborative learning is to provide students with a social context and a community of knowledgeable peers. Discourse communities as invaluable outside knowledge (Gee, 1989), which is knowledge that is also a meaningful guide to textual analysis (Huckin, 1992), reflect the sociocultural underpinnings of composition educators work.

According to Jason Palmeri (2012), new media in the composition classroom has pedagogical roots that date back to the 1960s with the use of analog technologies. Because computers in the writing classroom grew more prevalent in the late 1980s, some composition studies scholars both encouraged and admonished teachers who were eager to incorporate new media into writing course activities; they warned that, without strategic use, this "new" classroom companion could inadvertently reinforce old problematic practices. Cynthia L. Selfe and Gail E. Hawisher (1991) cautioned that computers are cultural artifacts destined to mirror dominant values of the educational system (Hawisher & Selfe, 1991, p. 55). They observed that classroom culture with computers maintained what Paulo Freire (1972) described as "the banking" model of education or continued to form "Siberianized" students (Shor, 1996) who subscribed to teacher-pleasing, rendered expected responses to problems and wanted to ingest, rather than create new knowledge. "We argue that computer technology offers us the chance to transform our writing classes into different kinds of centers of learning if we take a critical perspective and remain sensitive to the social and political dangers that the use of computers may pose" (Hawisher et al., 1991, p. 56). To some, the useful incorporation of classroom computers was slow moving and the field's resistance to purposeful digital literacy instructional models was noted. In an April 2010 *Composition Forum* interview, Selfe discusses writing classrooms and English departments that are resistant to the "the vernacular of multimodal literacy practices in digital environments":

I still know plenty of teachers who avoid teaching students how to compose or produce such texts because they personally don't feel it's their responsibility to compose, or to teach composition, in any modality except the alphabetic. (Selfe, 2010)

Selfe (2010) continues:

On the humanist side: We are more sophisticated about technology than we were twenty years ago, but we're nonetheless resistant to seeing technological or digital texts as 'serious' texts or even resistant to seeing multimodal composition as even 'real' composition. On the other side, (there are) computer enthusiasts who... are always hopping from one technology to the next technology without sufficient critical attention. I think the reactions of both camps result in the same problem, that is, the lack of critical examinations and uses of technology. (Selfe, 2010)

Kenneth Bruffee (1984) also attributes some composition classroom constraints to humanistic traditions. "Humanistic study, we have been led to believe, is a solitary life, and the vitality of the humanities lies in the talents and endeavors of each of us as individuals" (Bruffee, 1984, p. 645). It follows that university merit systems, which celebrate singular rather than group achievement, account for student resistance to engage in collaborative classroom work. Also, as we further embrace pedagogy as a shared responsibility, the loss of power and control inherent to such structures since the Enlightenment Era must be factored into any new teacherly effort; concomitant divisions of high culture and low culture nurture the broader resistance to seeing social media content as serious texts.

Rethinking the Twitterverse and the Blogosphere

How we continue to theorize these teaching practices will continue to be a cobbling of frameworks that are multidisciplinary in nature and deictic. Media literacy scholars assert that blogs (and microblogs) provide students with the opportunity to practice summarizing, textual analysis, collaborative learning and to infuse knowledge from their various interconnected discourse communities as a viable academic context (Jenkins, 2006; Middlebrook, 2010; Hobbs, 2015). In addition to identifying intersections in composition studies curriculum goals, media literacy scholars often provide "embodiment to theory" instructional models for successful social media use in the college classroom. Media literacy scholar Renee Hobbs offers what is arguably one embodiment in her description of the classroom as an open network learning environment, which steers student work toward collaboration and classroom activities that are not content-centered and paradigm-laden. "Open-source digital tools, such as Twitter, YouTube and WordPress, can be used as a means to escape the walled garden of the learning management system (LMS)" (Hobbs, 2015, p. 8). Hobbs describes instructor observations of student Twitter use over three months in a graduate-level library science class and reports that students learned concision writing for

140-character limit. Library science content was analyzed in the posts. Learners engaged in peer-to-peer relationships, responding to ideas of their classmates. And, students shared resources related to the course discussions and goals (Hobbs, 2015, p. 14). This type theorizing is anchored in observation of the student's social media activity.

In the work, "Blogging as Social Action: A Genre Analysis of the Weblog" authors offer one conceptualization for understanding student-as-blogger positionality (Miller & Shepherd, 2003). This work explores the merit of a weblog genre, including the evident community building and self-disclosure that serves as a catalyst for establishing authority and voice, something that routinely occurs in the blogosphere. The work indicates that bloggers operate from a "particular rhetorical subject-position" that could allow for self-expression that constructs an "experimental" or "constitutive" identity (Miller et al., 2003, p. 9). Here, this is an ongoing creative event, drawing from multiple experiences over a continuum and with the potential to counter some of the formulaic, restrictive paradigms that historically have been problematic in the writing classroom. Doreen Massey's (2010) suggestions about space as a product of human interrelations is arguably applicable in the blogosphere discussion; this discourse content space is created by students together making a social product. And, each contributor has their own connections with other spaces (Massey, 2010, p. 9): "From my perspective, this also includes cyberspaces and other public and private media spaces, which are important parts of the youth identity." Massey reiterates that the student reality is that their school literacies merge with literacies from other domains, suggesting that classroom activities should reflect the complex and heterogenous nature of the students' reality.

Acknowledging an ever increasing presence of technology tools in the everyday lives of most students and that this forever changing terrain calls for new or extended abilities, literacy scholars offer a dual-level theoretical system that classifies these literacies: Lowercase (new literacies) and Uppercase (New Literacies) (Leu, Kinzer, Coiro & Castek, 2013, p. 1152). Lowercase "new literacies" is the theory used to understand specific areas of literacies and technology, capable of facilitating different disciplines and the pace of innovation because "they are closer to the specific types of changes that are taking place and interest to those who study them within a particular heuristic" (1157). Uppercase "New Literacies" is theory that isolates patterns developing over multiple lowercase theories, more broadly considers research and "maintains a close focus on many different aspects of the shifting landscape of literacy" (1157). As we adjust instructional practices, reconsider the changed role of teacher, student and required literacies for both and as we communicate on a landscape that is not writing inscribed flat on the page, but that functions as networked, living, scrolling, co-content, narratives and archives, the way that we theorize this engagement must be transformative and integrative.

Social Identity Kits: Student-Generated Texts and Prior Knowledge

Many claim that the most transformative classroom activities are student-led. Ira Shor (1996) recommended in-class speech communities to avoid grounding the classroom culture in teacher-centered rhetoric; in these speech communities, teachers and students engage in meaning making work that consistently promotes equity (Shor, 1996, p. 29). Identifying several of the same constraints previously referenced in Freire's *Pedagogy of the Oppressed* (1972), Shor introduces the notion of the "Siberian Syndrome" as the antithesis of power sharing. In his description, the classroom culture is defined by the teacher's dominating discourse and the pre-emptive didactic presentations. This disempowerment produces and reinforces "'Siberianized' students, who expect (the instructor) to address them in one-way teacher-talk"

(Shor, 1996, p. 30). Further, this style of classroom management blocks opportunities for the inclusion of outside knowledge in in-class meaning making. "Students should talk a lot and produce a variety of texts which educate the teacher about their interests, levels of development, idiomatic diversity, cultural backgrounds and thematic preferences vis-a-vis the syllabus" (Shor, 1990, p. 30). Multimodality, an assortment of student creations and a "variety of texts" in the writing classroom are indicated as vehicles for student contribution, ownership and leadership.

Deborah Brandt (1990) also explores antisocial characterizations of reading and writing in the field of Composition Studies, saying that this idea of "a strong-text account of literacy" underscores a self-referential quality of written language. While Brandt offers one concept of literacy as "private contemplation and reflection" (p. 3) of the single participant, Bruffee presents this engagement as the imprint of a system: Students resist collaborative work because they are situated in a system that rewards and promotes individualistically. He continues with the example of expository writing activities, saying they "involve demonstrating to students that they know something only when they can explain it in writing to the satisfaction of the community of their knowledgeable peers" (Bruffee, 1984, p. 652). In this case, familiar writing classroom instruments are restrictive paradigms, preserving fixed ideas about knowing and how knowledge should be demonstrated. Also, a stale criterion for which products qualify as legitimate academic texts may inhibit a fluid acceptance of new patterns of student production, including their creations in social media fora. The social nature of technology tools, such as blogs, could potentially support more productive student-led meaning making and create needed space for modes of student expression not yet considered, or even, not yet invented.

There is a sustained interest in understanding writing as a social action that is located in a social context and to discover more pronounced ways to capture and honor the prior knowledge students bring with them to the classroom. This includes composition scholarship that celebrates the practical, functional and everyday uses of writing (Barton & Hamilton, 1998; Cushman, 1998) and those who assert that writing is never untethered from sociocultural underpinnings and the influence of discourse community membership of its creator (Huckin, 1992; Gee, 1989). With the infusion of multiple sources of knowledge and with the introduction of varied epistemological considerations, there is a need to rethink even the language used to describe the writing and reading process. For example, Huckin (1992) offers a simplified and functional definition of *a text:* "the product of an attempt by a writer to communicate meaning to one or more readers," adding that a text is successful when the intended audience receives the writer's intended meaning (87).

In Huckin's explanation, metalinguistic and interpersonal content of the writing informs the intended audience's interpretation. "Writers belong to multiple discourse communities and the texts they write often reflect their divided loyalties," reflecting lush nonstandard usage, voice, errors associated with membership in family, academic institution, special interest groups, inner circle of peers, etc. (Huckin, 1992, p. 89). Since the 1980s, James Paul Gee has claimed that language and grammar are not most important in literacy; a composition reality is that neither the writing nor its creator can be divorced from a social function. "Discourses are ways of being in the world; they are forms of life which integrate words, acts, values, beliefs, attitudes and social identities as well as gestures, glances, body positions, and clothes" (Gee, 1989, p. 7). Gee describes discourses as identity kits. It follows that a text should be conceptualized as an artifact that reflects the respective identities of the student creator. As such, a blog or microblog may easily facilitate identity building content.

The Collective: Instructional Reading Models that Inform Writing Instruction

The subsequent WordPress and Twitter-based inquiry activities are structured by, not only the elements of the rhetorical situation[3], but also by online reading comprehension and critical literacy instructional models. Scholarship about student approaches to conducting research online and their critical handling of texts in electronic environments is still emergent, experimental. For example, there is no universal cataloging mechanism comparable to a conventional Dewey Decimal System for students who now by and large conduct research online. However, among several assertions, online reading comprehension scholars affirm that group activities provide a productive forum in which students "skillfully facilitate collaborative interactions" and negotiate complex online texts (Castek, Coiro, Guzniczak & Bradshaw, 2012). The collection of instructional models is used here to begin to establish personal teaching protocols that aim for meaningful student engagement with online texts and technology tools.

These instructional approaches to comprehending and evaluating online texts are born from a lineage that includes the RAND Reading Study Group[4] (2002) and scholarship on Reciprocal Teaching (RT). The RAND Group report, a study that responded to a 30-year lack of improvement in reading comprehension across multiple demographics, emphasizes the importance of prior knowledge, external and internal motivations and how conflicting motivations lead to incomplete comprehension (RAND, 2002, p. 15). Reciprocal Teaching is an instructional framework in which instructors gradually release to students' full responsibility for using reading strategies and for leading group discussions (Johnson, 2014, p. 24). RT involves group processing of a text by employing four strategies: summarizing, questioning, clarifying and predicting (24). Extending RT practices to include technological support, literacy scholars developed Internet Reciprocal Teaching (IRT) so that students may "develop their own lines of inquiry and collaboratively work with others using the Internet to solve the important problems they have defined" (Coiro, 2012, p. 414). Julie Coiro delineates the actions for this engagement as (a) identify the problem, (b) locate information, (c) evaluate (accuracy and currency), (d) synthesize, and (e) communicate the information online. Blogs are identified as one such forum (Coiro, 2009, p. 60).

Arguably, this progression embodies the elements of the rhetorical situation, especially considerations of a text's purpose, the credibility and stance of the creator/rhetor and publication. Added are phases, such as locating and communicating online, which are specifically mindful of additional skills needed to manage search engine, databases, networked fora, etc. There is an emphasis on collaboration also. The IRT model involves teachers supporting student groups or pairs as they use technology tools to do interactive work, have strategy discussions and "engage with authentic curriculum-based challenges" (414). Finally, E. Honan (2003) characterizes Luke and Freebody's "Four Resource Model" (1999) as a critical literacy instruction tool that provides guidelines to help instructors be more cognizant of their own teaching practices. Under four categories of engagement, code breaker, text participant, text user and text analyst, the model suggests a map of possible textual practices (Honan, 2003, p. 1). I submit that guides like the Luke and Freebody's Four Resource areas may help writing instructors more deliberately provide activities that isolate specific online and offline reading comprehension abilities. In the inquiry exercises that follow, the types of questions posed were taken from some of the following categories:

- **Code Breaker:** Prompts students to decode and encode, isolate terms, etc.;
- **Text Participant:** Prompts students to make meaning, identify or even personalize the content by applying prior knowledge, prior experiences;

- **Text User:** Prompts students to examine the functionality of the text, to understand how various types of media function;
- **Text Analyst:** Prompts students to understand how texts are constructed and operate within a greater, even socio-political, context.

There are evident intersections between critical literacy, online reading comprehension and rhetorical situation frameworks. When anchored in activities for student groups and/or student pairs, these models offer ways to help students develop habits that cause them to handle online texts more deliberately, to learn to monitor themselves as they move through texts or links, and to help facilitate purposeful use of technology tools in the writing classroom.

METHODOLOGY AND PEDAGOGY

Two Tech-Tool Activities from My Own Teacher Portfolio

In their writing practices, composition students are often guided by learned behaviors that reflect what Paulo Freire calls the "banking model of education" (Freire, 1972). It has been long-discussed that too often the single purpose of their writing product is to garner a validating score from an audience of one, the instructor. Not only does this teacher-pleasing preconditioning undermine pedagogical efforts to amplify the concepts of collaborative learning, but this submissive ("un-radicalized") posture serves as a constraint in an important way. It is rare for composition students to consciously engage texts seeing themselves as valued voices nor do they see themselves as contributors to a preexisting discussion. The emblematic "Burkean parlor" is described in *The Philosophy of Literary Form*:

Imagine that you enter a parlor. You come late. When you arrive, others have long preceded you, and they are engaged in a heated discussion, a discussion too heated for them to pause and tell you exactly what it is about. You listen for a while, until you decide that you have caught the tenor of the argument; then, put your oar in. (Burke, 1941)

I submit that although the content of microblog technology tools, such as Twitter, may be deemed by some as a news wire for inane banter, the user governance of these forums mirrors the operations of the Burkean parlor in that hashtags represent gatherings and collections of posts by contributors who are often "creating new knowledge," collaboratively, and often about a single topic. Also, online reading comprehension scholarship coupled with frameworks like the Four Resource Model offer useful guidance for composition classroom activity design. This use allows for productive text analysis and the application of student outside knowledge.

Activity #1: Tweeting the Hits - Using Twitter for Critical Analysis of an Online Text

Background and Rationale

This activity has been repeated with literature, first year writing and African American history courses. In this chapter's example, the nonfiction text, an essay by author Amy Tan called "Mother Tongue," was included in a first year writing course lesson. A stated purpose of this course is "to introduce students to the ways in which the academic community uses writing to discover, to think, to inform, and to act"; and, the academic community is robustly represented in many social media properties that the students already use. In fact, the design of the activity mirrors that of several discussion feeds connected to academic conference hashtags and scholarly meetups that I have attended on Twitter. Hoping to make the activity more interesting and focused, I asked students to do all of their contributing on Twitter only, no verbalized analysis.

I observed a classroom full of students engaged in this cycle: their eyes moved from the Twitter feed to monitor their classmates' critical analysis and to catch the next question; then, their gaze shifted to the essay searching out passages and evidence; finally, they went back to their devices in order compose a 140-character contribution to the discussion. The Tan essay and others selected for this activity carried familial and personal-level tensions (her mother being stereotyped), institutional-level discrimination (at department stores and local schools) and national-level debates (the merits and effectiveness of achievement testing).

The texts I curated for this activity were intended to have diversity of content, making it possible for learners at all levels to possibly lead in an area of the discussion. Thus far, I have completed this exercise with more than 60 students and the incorporation of technology uniquely addresses level variance that is the norm in general education courses.

Activity Purpose and Connection to the Course Objectives

The purposes of this activity are (a) to practice creating one succinct and well-summarized annotation in preparation for an upcoming annotated bibliography assignment, (b) to practice composing defendable, one-sentence claims, and (a) to continue learning to "interrogate the text" by asking questions of the author. Having read, Tan's "Mother Tongue," students composed an abstract (summary paragraph) of the text, isolating the author's reasoning, evidence, big claims, and persuasive detail. Next, for the Twitter phase of the activity, students responded to questions tweeted by the instructor about the text, posting under the Twitter hashtag "#FYWbbforumTan", which was created for this exercise. Here, the Four Resource Model was one guide for critical evaluation of the text, as the students were responding to questions inspired by the four quadrants of this inquiry model (code-breaker, text participant, text user and text analyst). As they evaluated, questioned and completed close reads of text sections on Twitter, their feed created a new text. Ultimately, the students and instructor create new questions, by including student responses and inviting identified students to pose their own questions to the class.

Instructions for Students

The purposes of this activity is to (1.) practice creating one succinct and well-summarized annotation in preparation for next week's annotated bibliography assignment (2.) to practice composing our own defendable, one-sentence claims, and (3.) to learn to "interrogate the text" by asking our own questions of the author.

PART I: 1. Read the essay called "Mother Tongue" at least once. 2. Compose a one-paragraph annotation of the text isolating Tan's key claims, supporting evidence, notable examples/details and the author's reasoning. We have about an hour for Part I.

PART II: When directed, we will Tweet responses to questions as they appear in the class's feed under #FYWbbforumTan. This online discussion will take place for the last hour of class.

Instructor Procedure

As preparation, I set up and shared the Twitter hashtag with the students. Then, I populated our new forum with images and relevant quotes by Tan. I added microbursts of her biography and other published works as the first anchor Tweets of the feed. In time, I asked a student leader to post background on Tan to acclimate classmates. Once the activity began, I gave students several moments to respond between each of the questions, because they referenced the text during the activity:

Q1: Who might be Tan's intended audience in "Mother Tongue"?
Q2: What do you think the author means by "language of intimacy"? Do you have such a language?
Q3: What might Tan be persuading her audience to believe or understand?
Q4: How might an advocate of achievement tests respond to the essay?
Q5: If all U.S. students were required to learn Hindi and Mandarin, how might this essay be different?

Also during lesson preparation, I composed the first 10 questions. However, while the feed is live, I took advantage of opportunities to feature student Tweets and introduced unplanned questions into the feed. I invited students to ask their own new questions in response to patterns and meaning making flowing up the Twitter feed, new text creations by their classmates.

Figures 1-6 are images of Tweets generated by writing students during Activity #1. Prompted by questions posted on the Twitter feed, the composition students critically analyzed the Amy Tan essay, "Mother Tongue."

Figure 1. Tweet 1

@PecolasAdvocate Our language/limitations do not define who we are or what we are capable of doing. #FYWbbforumAmy

Figure 2. Tweet 2

@PecolasAdvocate Broken Eng is the way shes able to communicate with everyone it doesn't reflect her intelligence in any way #FYWBBFORUMAMY

Figure 3. Tweet 3

@PecolasAdvocate Amy tought us that her mothers "broken" english is an extension of their ethnic background in a sense #FYWbbforumTan

Figure 4. Tweet 4

The most significant idea in "Mother Tongue" is tolerance because the use of language and intelligence can be unrelated. #FYWBBForumTan

Figure 5. Tweet 5

@PecolasAdvocate Tan is looking to show the reader that language can not be the only judgement for integrity. #fywbbforumamy

Figure 6. Tweet 6

@PecolasAdvocate A4: The public perception is more impressed with the expression rather than meaning itself. #FYWbbforumAmy

Teacherly Observations of the FYW Activity Using Twitter

- **#Hashtag as the "Burkean Parlor":** One main idea of this essay is Tan's commentary on how we measure intelligence in the United States. The author discusses how often her mother's intelligence is assessed by her heavy Chinese accent. Another key and timely commentary is the author's critique of the nation's various achievement tests, which she indicates is a failed system of measurement. During the Twitter activity, #FYWbbforumTan served as the "Burkean Parlor" where the students assembled to weigh in about such widely discussed topics. Prompted by the questions, they isolated several central themes. However, as the discussion continued, they introduced new themes of their own, such as their own immigrant experience, judgement and the absence of empathy. By using Twitter in the composition classroom, we capitalized on the existing hashtags as connected parlors, which created endless possibilities in this networked space. The scrolling live commentary potentially will allow students to better understand their own subjectivity, the proverbial "tardiness" of the scholar of this famed metaphor. As contributors to, in some cases, several hashtags, students gained a greater knowledge of writing for an audience beyond the instructor and their composition is more purposeful than mere writing to get a grade. By adding ideas to these digital parlors, students operationalize the precepts of participatory culture as well.
- **Gaining Rhetorical Knowledge:** With the Twitter discussion of the text, the students have the opportunity to gain more rhetorical knowledge immediately. For example, when we considered intended audience of our Tweets, students named themselves as the intended viewers and creators of the feed. However, the discussion about audience was complicated when we noted that, with the simple addition of "@AmyTan" in a post, we now included the author, a new intended audience.

- **Writing Claims, Composing Succinctly:** While the majority of the students who shared that they used Twitter in their everyday lives, several stated that formulating a claim about the text in 140 characters was the greatest challenge. Early in the first year writing course, I observed students composing several sentences, calling the assemblage of ideas their "thesis statement". The microblog character limit provides guard rails and exercises the writer's ability to say it succinctly in a low stakes activity. In this classroom situation, students develop their ability to produce Tweets, or short claims, that are relevant and direct.

- **Critical and Creative Thinking:** Thinking about writing that persuades and compels audiences to listen or act is a foundational goal for writing courses. In these microbursts of ideas, I observed students discussing the author's tone and possible motive. As they did a close read of the text sections, they used Tweets to suggest the author's multiple implicit and explicit messages.

- **Student Agency and Accountability:** This activity places an emphasis on the value of a collective student voice, their analysis, or "their take" on things. A summary of what *Tan said* is a key purpose of the activity's second step, writing the abstract paragraph. The Twitter feed is dedicated to ideas about the text, what it means, what is implied, for speculating about Tan's motivation, and for examining the effectiveness of her persuasion. With the Twitter "Reply" function, the student Tweets eventually become the centerpiece of the next question. Agency is tethered to the next big idea, rather than the published author's text, the instructor or questions pre-printed in a composition reader.

- **The Online Reading Comprehension and Critical Literacy Models in the Composition Classroom:** In the notes above, Q1/Q3 are text participant questions; Q2 is a code-breaker questions, and Q4/Q5 are text analyst questions. One useful Twitter feature is that the students pace the feed, giving them time to return to the text, think critically about the content and perform close reading during the discussion. Students began to understand Twitter used in the composition classroom may have a slower pace so that questions may be answered thoughtfully. Working this critical literacy muscle also helped to prepare students for the upcoming argumentative essay and provide engagement in inquiry that prompts them to evaluate, question and communicate, following effective online reading comprehension models.

The activity provided a heuristic for understanding how scholars use their critical analysis and their ideas to join an existing conversation. Twitter immediately complicates this process because the hashtag may be instantly connected to related hashtags, or other fora, further revealing the networked nature of this environment and collaborative learning. Eyes widened when we remembered that adding @AmyTan meant that the author may become a part of our classroom. The capability to quickly shift audience provides yet another rhetorical exercise for the student writer. The limitation of the 140 characters caused the students to compose succinct claims, which is excellent practice for writing thesis statements and for thinking through the process of creating in, what some argue is, a new genre. Finally, online reading comprehension and critical literacy models offer an effective way to layer the difficulty-level and to guide the type of inquiry.

Activity #2: The Oyster Knife - Using Blogging Communities for Critical Writing and Collaboration

Background and Rationale

Community blogging is a bi-weekly activity intended to provide students with a low stakes forum to engage the weekly reading for a course titled *Short Stories by Women of Color*. Students collaborate on the visual design of their blog space, its mission statement, and they respond to each others posts throughout the semester. The course readings are written by authors from India, Colombia, Haiti, Dominican Republic, Ghana, the U.S., specifically the southern states. Supplementary texts are primarily video footage of author interviews, images and some literary criticism. In part, the blogging community serves as a writing workshop, a forum where several important actions comprise the community culture: (a) struggling students learn how stronger students question, evaluate and communicate meaning from the texts, (b) students consciously write for audiences other than the instructor; now their classmates and, potentially, the World Wide Web may be influenced by their ideas, and (c) by regularly reading and responding to classmates, the bloggers learn each other's vocabulary, writing styles and have the opportunity to see other students modeling language use. "The Oyster Knife" was the name chosen by one of the blogging communities. In their mission statement, the group explained how they were inspired by a Zora Neale Hurston's quote from the first week's reading: "I do not weep at the world. I am too busy sharpening my oyster knife." The following activity and observations draw from the activities of 110 students who participated in blogging communities for the writing and literature classes. This set represents student bloggers who managed their community blogs between 2013 and 2015.

Activity Purpose and Connection to the Course Objectives

The purposes of this activity are:

1. To provide an alternative way for all students to be contributors, as they differ in their learning styles and comfort levels with public speaking,
2. To offer a reoccurring opportunity for bloggers to construct their own student-led discussion space,
3. For students to help each other make meaning and ask questions of texts that are often set in cultures and environments that are unfamiliar to them.

In terms of assessments and student products, this activity accompanied a weekly, multiple choice, online (open book) reading comprehension quiz. Also, there are four required essays that satisfy more traditional literary criticism and close reading requirements of the English department for this general education course. However, in the blogging communities, students created and shared iMovie video documentaries of their favorite authors, documentaries that they created. Student bloggers added images and content that they curated and responded to the ideas captured in their classmates' blog posts. I observed that this was a more creative space, and in some ways, an experimental space. My role was to offer prompts and set the guard rails, which, honestly I am not always sure is necessary. The question remains: For lower-level Gen.Ed. courses, how do I remove the instructor (the prompts, the rubric, etc.) and still have certainty that the activity will not peter out by the end of the course?

Instructions for Students

The blogging communities responded to two types of prompts: "formal" and "informal". Informal prompts inspire journal writing in first-person, during which students experiment with language around new issues, tensions, ideas that are raised during the class discussion and from the readings. Typically, we decide on the "informal" topics together. Sometimes there is a vote on the next informal blog post in the middle of a class discussion. The following is an example of a "formal" blogging prompt.

Instructions: *Each community member must submit one 500-word blog post and three responses to other community member posts.*

Your Post: *For your 500-word post, compose a critical essay comparing the depictions of womanhood in "No Sweetness Here" (Aidoo) and "Everyday Use" (Walker). You may use any of the tools of analysis that we have used/discussed in class to express your observations. Please include any questions that you still have about the pieces that you read this week. (The "tools of analysis" in this course employs several of the principles underscored in the online reading comprehension model: question, locate, evaluate, summarize, and communicate.)*

Your Responses: *Write three responses to your community members' posts. In your responses consider the following: (a) Did this blogger clearly state an arguable thesis statement or claim? (b) Did the blogger adequately support this thesis statement with evidence from the text? (c) Discuss the elements of the post that really worked for you as a reader. (d) Discuss the elements that you wished were more developed, that made you want to hear more.*

Grading rubric for the blog community posts:

The blog posts and responses comprise a total of 30% of your grade. The blogs will be graded using the following criteria:

*[1] **30 PTS** = Does your work reflect an understanding of what the assignment asked of you?*
*[2] **30 PTS** = Did you engage in useful and thoughtful dialogue with your community members (your responses)?*
*[3] **30 PTS** = Was your blog well-organized? (Informative heading, your claim stated first and paragraphs that offer support, evidence, and reasoning). Did you use MLA style in-text citations where appropriate?*
*[4] **10 PTS** = Did you include design, charts, images or video that you located online or elsewhere to help illustrate your point to your followers?*

Instructor Procedure

Over the years, I have explored different blog sites for this activity and I have no preference; however, it is important that the teacher and students use the same interface for access reasons. For the blogging communities activity, I prepare a mini-lecture and demonstration of the selected blog site and help students create accounts. I have observed that students are proficient and quick with the social media properties that they use daily. However, if the technology tool is new, guidance is needed (sometimes repeatedly). I arrange student writers in blogging communities and there are usually 5-6 members in each community with varying levels, varying competencies. The activity begins when students hold their first community meeting. In groups, I suggest introductions, an exchange of available contact information, and I inform them that the meeting should yield:

1. The blog community's name
2. The mission statement, and
3. The related design or theme.

These decisions, their community's presentation and appearance, will be shared with the class. I find it easier if all students and instructor hold "administrator" status. That access makes it easier to help groups and to grade. Moving forward, students access the bi-weekly blog community prompts/assignments on the course website, which corresponds with the deadlines indicated on the syllabus.

Teacherly Observations of a Literary Analysis Activity Using Blogging

-   **Students Staking Their Claim:** The blogging communities support several of the key writing department goals for literature and writing courses. The student-led forum, which houses a visible archive of their work, allows for their close reads and assessments of their *own* creations. For example, students did a close read of their claims, comparing the thesis statement from an earlier assignment to the last one of the semester. In this low-stakes forum, their self-assessments were sincere and enlightening:
    -   **Blogger #1:** *While looking at these two thesis statements, I realize that my first statement is a little too wordy and isn't proving anything. I didn't write what kind of hardships I was talking about. In my thesis from my third blog post, I improved and was more direct. I did a better job of finding the important things in the story and picked out the symbolism of innocence and strength.*
    -   **Blogger #2:** *I feel that I have progressed greatly from my first (post). My thesis statement is more informative but still does not really provide an argument. Honestly, while looking at this it is definitely better than my first but still nowhere close to a truly good thesis statement. I'm still just summarizing the plot rather than giving an argument, which I feel is necessary.*

The community members offered each other new criteria for revision; quite often, struggling bloggers took cues from stronger writers in their group.

-   **Bloggers' Synthesis of Multiple Texts:** For several of the "formal prompts," students were asked to explore intersections between two or more texts: "If authors Ama Ata Aidoo and Alice Walker were in your Burkean Parlor, what would these two say to each other about the topic of 'Motherhood'?" Because the post is limited to 500 words, students consolidated and curated more economically. The shorter, more focused analytical writing and synthesis of the blogging communities provide meaningful practice for polishing future, lengthier writing.
-   **Creation of Multimedia Texts:** Students selected images that they asserted carried narratives connected to or that supported the blog post claim. To teach their classmates about authors they chose to feature, some bloggers created documentaries using iMovie and other technology tools to profile these women from countries worldwide. In this literature course, the author profile docu-

mentary was presented as an extra credit option. Over the semester, the content (student-created or student-curated video and images, artwork, writing, responses to writing and headings) formed a lush archive that embodied the student-led multimodality model. With permission, I was able to use their multimedia blog content, their own creations, as teaching tools and routinely incorporated their blogging into my class demonstrations.

- **A Celebration of Collective Identity and Individual Competencies:** Students established the collective identity of the blogging community by writing the mission statement together and by maintaining and designing the site as a group. During the first community meeting, the bloggers co-authored a mission statement for their blog. Together, they decide on a name and choose colors, themes, etc. This discussion about identity and what they want the World Wide Web to know about their content is one of the most fruitful collaborative exercises. Equipped with varying skills, prior knowledge and multiple literacies, the bloggers owned tasks within the community that underscored their personal strengths. For example, in one class, the art major stepped up and took the lead on design decisions. The group decided that he should feature his original work as the main art for the site. The orators and public speakers weighed in more on how to shape ideas into what they all decided was mission-statement speak; and, the students who possessed more digital literacies were trusted by the group to assemble all of the content elements.

As an activity in a 200-level general education literature course, the blogging communities exercised muscles - producing critical commentary, close reading and synthesizing fiction works - that are characteristically tethered to such a course. The "formal" blogs were, by design, more dedicated to the conventions of the English department. However, content from the "informal" assignments, the blog design, mission statement and the author video profiles extended this function to include prior knowledge of the students and evidenced an intermingling of their many discourse communities.

In *Short Stories by Women of Color* course, the authors' works presented these students with international, unknown, distant communities and cultures. The stories challenged patriarchal paradigms and exposed gender discrimination. Many of the groups, from the authors' own countries, were sociopolitically marginalized. This made the video documentary profiles very important teaching tools for separating the storytellers' realities from their stories.

At the end of the semester, this blog content functions as an unconventional location for an archive of student creations and a lush repository of teaching materials. I continue to rethink the rubric and blog assignments, more specifically, the rigidity of these two elements. Because this is relatively new as a learning tool, this structure provides comfort, familiar boundaries, and ways to measure, as we are still operating in a university's grade-driven meritocracy. Students come to class with their own understanding of what makes a great, high-scoring student essay, but there is not a comparable standard in their minds for "a great student blog post." This is an area that I continue to negotiate and that is still emergent.

CONCLUSION

If successful collaboration in the writing classroom is a sincere priority, it is important to acknowledge that students are more willing to work together using fitting technology tools than they are without them. Seemingly, among several of the classroom-level constraints are the long-discussed misperceptions of instructors (Jenkins et al., 2006). We make assumptions about student proficiency with social media (participation gap); we assume that students are mindfully moving through Internet properties and electronic environments simply because they do these things several hours each day (transparency problem); and, we leave it up to students to teach themselves standards and ethics of use (the ethics challenge). However, by anchoring student research writing in models that amplify questioning, evaluating, locating, communicating skills, we are empowered as writing instructors to teach students uses of technology for academic purposes and to incorporate fruitful writing activities into these familiar social media environments.

REFERENCES

Barton, D., & Hamilton, M. (1998). *Local literacies: Reading and writing in one community*. New York: Routledge. doi:10.4324/9780203448885

Brandt, D. (1990). *Literacy as involvement: The acts of writers, readers, and texts*. Carbondale: Southern Illinois Univ. Press.

Bruffee, K. (1984). Collaborative learning and the "conversation of mankind". *College English*, *46*(7), 635–652. doi:10.2307/376924

Burke, K. (1941). *The philosophy of literary form: Studies in symbolic action*. Baton Rouge: Louisiana State University Press.

Castek, J., Coiro, J., Guzniczak, L., & Bradshaw, C. (2012). Examining peer collaboration in online inquiry. *The Educational Forum*, *76*(4), 479–496. doi:10.1080/00131725.2012.707756

Coiro, J. (2009). Rethinking online reading assessment: How is reading comprehension different and where do we turn now. *Educational Leadership*, *66*, 59–63.

Coiro, J. (2012). The new literacies of online reading comprehension: Future directions. *The Educational Forum*, *76*(4), 412–417. doi:10.1080/00131725.2012.708620

Cushman, E. (1998). *The struggle and the tools: Oral and literate strategies in an inner city community*. Albany: State University of New York Press.

Ebner, M., Lienhardt, C., Rohs, M., & Meyer, I. (2010). Microblogs in higher education: A chance to facilitate informal and process-oriented learning? *Computers & Education*, *55*(1), 92–100. doi:10.1016/j.compedu.2009.12.006

Freire, P. (1972). *Pedagogy of the oppressed*. New York: Herder and Herder.

Gee, J. (1989). Literacy, discourse and linguistics: Introduction. *Journal of Education*, *171*, 5–17.

Hawisher, G., & Selfe, C. (Eds.). (1991). *Evolving perspectives on computers and composition studies: questions for the 1990s*. Urbana, IL: National Council of Teachers of English.

Hobbs, R. (2015). Twitter as a pedagogical tool in higher education. In R. Lind (Ed.), *Producing theory in a digital world 2.0*. New York: Peter Lang.

Honan, E. (2003). *Teachers as researchers: Using the four resources model as a map of practices. Teachers as leaders: Teacher education for a global profession. International yearbook on teacher education. 48th world assembly.* Melbourne, Australia: ICET.

Huckin, T. (1992). Context-sensitive text analysis. In Methods and methodology in composition research (pp. 84-104).

Jenkins, H., Purushotma, R., Clinton, K., Weigel, M., & Robinson, A. (2006). *Confronting the challenges of participatory culture: Media education for the 21st century.* Chicago: The MacArthur Foundation.

Johnson, D. (2014). Reading, writing, and literacy 2.0: Teaching with online texts, tools, and resources, K-8. Teachers College Press: Columbia University.

Leu, D. J. Jr, Kinzer, C. K., Coiro, J., & Castek, J. (2013b). New literacies: A dual-level theory of the changing nature of literacy, instruction, and assessment. In R. B. Ruddell & D. Alvermann (Eds.), *Theoretical models and processes of reading* (pp. 1150–1181). Newark, DE: International Reading Association. doi:10.1598/0710.42

Luke, A., & Freebody, P. (1999). Further notes on the four resources model, reading online. Retrieved from http:www.readingonline.org/research/lukefrebody.html

Lunsford, A., Ede, L., Moss, B., Papper, C., Walters, K., & Brody, M. (2012). *Everyone's an author with readings.* New York: W.W. Norton & Company.

Miller, C., & Shepherd, D. (2009). Blogging as social action: A genre analysis of the weblog. In S. Miller's (Ed.), The Norton book of composition studies. (pp. 1450-1473). New York: W.W. Norton & Company, Inc.

Palmeri, J. (2012). *Remixing composition: A history of multimodal writing pedagogy.* Carbondale: Southern Illinois University Press.

RAND Reading Study Group. (2002). *Reading for understanding: Toward an R&D program in reading comprehension.* Santa Monica, CA: RAND.

Selfe, C. (2010, April). If you don't believe that you're doing some good with the work that you do, then you shouldn't be doing it: An interview with Cindy Selfe. *Composition Forum*, 21. Retrieved fromhttp://compositionforum.com/issue/21/cindy-selfe-interview.php

Shor, I. (1996). *When students have power: Negotiating authority in a critical pedagogy.* Chicago: University of Chicago Press.

ENDNOTES

[1]   Henry Jenkins et al. (2006) define participatory culture "as culture with relatively low barriers to artistic expression and civic engagement, strong support for creating and sharing creations, and some type of informal mentorship whereby experienced participants pass along knowledge to novices. In a participatory culture, members also believe their contributions matter and feel some

degree of social connection with one another (at the least, members care about others' opinions of what they have created)."

[2]   In *The Philosophy of Literary Form* (1941), Kenneth Burke offers the well-known metaphor: "Imagine that you enter a parlor. You come late. When you arrive, others have long preceded you, and they are engaged in a heated discussion, a discussion too heated for them to pause and tell you exactly what it is about. You listen for a while, until you decide that you have caught the tenor of the argument; then, put your oar in".

[3]   Textual analysis that considers the creator (rhetor), purpose, audience, media and stance.

[4]   The RAND Group responded to a 30-year lack of improvement in reading comprehension across multiple demographics and offered a definition of reading comprehension that categorically considered the reader, the text, and the activity (RAND, 2002, p.11). The RAND Group reports on the understood purposes for reading or that the associated activity informs educators about the development of needed "operations to process the text at hand" (11).

Chapter 3
Using Twitter to Scaffold English Composition

Brian C. Harrell
The University of Akron, USA

ABSTRACT

This chapter explores the idea, and offers three real-life, classroom tested assignments, of using the rules of social media, specifically Twitter, to teach students the rhetorical moves needed to write essays of college length and quality. The assignments provide first-year composition students the tools necessary to read an academic article, understand the rhetoric behind it, and apply rhetorical strategies it to his or her writing. The three assignments: 1) rhetorically analyze Twitter and create a formula for an effective tweet; 2) rhetorically analyzing an academic article 140 characters at a time; and 3) rhetorically analyzing a student's own paper using these same 140-character sound bites, have shown to put students in a position to be successful in the academy. Each assignment has been fully vetted over three years, with a myriad of student examples. This paper shows that the rules of Twitter can be used academically to provide a knowledge base and scaffolding for student writers.

INTRODUCTION

In 2011, as a University of Akron graduate assistant pursuing a master's degree in English Composition, I was charged with teaching a class of 25 first-year college students to become writers and learn how to succeed in academic settings. In order to do this, students would need to understand the writing process, be able to rhetorically analyze, and respond appropriately to, any academic situation and text, be able to engage in critical reading and writing, and be able to write for different genres in the academy.

As the semester began, I quickly realized that many of the students were not capable of entering into academic discourse as easily as I had hoped. I was going to have to find a way to build a bridge, or, as David Wood, Jerome S. Bruner, and Gail Ross (1976) suggest, scaffold the student's learning. According to Wood, Bruner, and Ross, scaffolding consists "of the adult 'controlling' those elements of the task that are initially beyond the learner's capacity, thus permitting him to concentrate upon and complete only those elements that are within his range of competence" (p. 90). To properly scaffold the class I was

DOI: 10.4018/978-1-5225-0562-4.ch003

teaching, I had to determine the student's range of competence and begin to build. By gaining an understanding of the writings of Wood, Bruner, and Ross, Lev Vygotsky, Peter Elbow, Bruce McComiskey, and other respected scholars in the field, I began to guide my writing students through the requirements of English Composition, by creating a social network *inside* the class.

Each day that I entered the classroom, students were on their cell phones, composing on various social networks. It was then that I realized, instead of asking the students to put away their phones in order to learn composition, I could use social media and their phones to create a genesis. I chose to focus on Twitter. My students came into the classroom proficient at being able to compose, not in the ways of academia, but on social media. It was my job to take this developed social function and begin to build.

The essay that follows explains how I have created ways to use Twitter in my first-year English Composition classroom, results as well as implications these assignments can have on other composition classrooms are also explicated here.

THEORETICAL FRAMEWORK

Learning through Scaffolding

The *Oxford English Dictionary* defines scaffolding as, "The temporary framework of platforms and poles constructed to provide accommodation for workmen and their materials during the erection, repairing, or decoration of a building." Without strong scaffolding, buildings are not able to be built; however, the scaffold is temporary. It does not remain with the structure forever. There is a larger goal than just forming the framework. Often, the scaffold takes time to create. Constructing a scaffold in the classroom assures students can be supported as they work to develop their education.

While Wood, Bruner, and Ross's (1976) definition is suitable to be used, many other scholars during the 1970s discussed the process of development of their writings. John Nordlof (2014) wrote, "Lev Vygotsky can therefore offer us a model for understanding student learning; it is a developmental process in which concepts are internalized through social interaction." Vygotsky's (1978) theory of the student's zone of proximal development is defined as, "The distance between the actual developmental level as determined by independent problem solving and the level of potential development as determined through problem solving under adult guidance or in collaboration with more capable peers" (p. 86). For teachers, Vygotsky provides a place of reference for the student. If a teacher is able to identify the zone of proximal development in a student, the teacher can begin to develop the scaffolding. Most importantly, as Nordlof suggests, this is through social interaction.

Prior to Vygotsky and Wood, Bruner, and Ross, Peter Elbow's text, originally published in 1973, *Writing without Teachers*, uses the term scaffolding when considering his own writing process. Elbow (1973) wrote, "X. It seems great. But then I find next day that it seems mediocre. But further writing produces an extension of it. That's better. The original was scaffolding that I had to use to get to the second one" (p. 37). Elbow's writing process included building on writing, creating this scaffold. Later in the book, he begins to apply this same concept to the development in students. Elbow wrote, "It is the characteristic of living organisms, cell creatures, to unfold according to a set of stages that must come in order. The paradigm is the fetus going through the stages" (p. 43). Elbow also mentions that great thinkers like Freud, Erik Erikson, and Piaget, all have different models explaining this development. Elbow (1973) wrote:

The developmental model explains a lot about human affairs and makes many paradoxes come clear. The main thing is that these stages must all be gone through in order. None may be skipped. A person is held back from attaining a certain stage if he hasn't completed or done justice to some previous stage… Have you ben pretending or trying from the neck up to live at a later stage than you are really at? (p. 44)

Teachers can be guilty of this when trying to educate students. *Has the instructor not created a scaffold which allows the stages to be built? Has the teacher not considered the zone of proximal development as he or she attempts to deliver the information?* As teachers work to create good writers and thinkers, scaffolding is a necessary step in this effort.

Learning through Collaboration, Social Interaction, and the Internet

The concept of learning through social interaction, mentioned in Vygotsky's research, provides an additional building block to support learning. Vygotsky wrote (1981), "Any higher mental function necessarily goes through an external stage in its development because it is initially a social function" (p. 162). That external stage is crucial to the development of the writer. By harnessing the social interaction of writing, teachers can guide students through learning. Many scholars (Prensky, 2001; Boyd & Ellison, 2008; Ferriter, 2010; Moody, 2010; Lin, Hoffman & Borengasser, 2013; Yakin &Tinmaz, 2013; Bryant, 2014; Jacquemin, Smelser & Bernot, 2014) believe that students have a better chance of success if they harness the power of the Internet to lead in this social function.

Parker Palmer (1983) provided a compelling argument to keep the social and collaboration aspect in the classroom in his text *To Know As We Are Known: Education As A Spiritual Journey*. Palmer, in looking at how the conventional educational education is administered, addresses the need for collaboration in the class. He wrote:

We become manipulators when education denies and destroys community, placing us in an endless competition for supremacy over each other. Throughout our education we learn to manipulate in order to survive, and we carry that habit into our post graduate lives. If we gained knowledge through a collaborative, communal process, we would process a knowledge that can be used in cooperative, not manipulative, ways. (p. 38, 1983)

Collaboration and cooperation in the classroom can provide students with the opportunity to be more fully educated. It is in the composition classroom where academic community can best be fostered. If social media can bring strangers from around the world into a single conversation, then using it in the classroom can be equally successful.

Deanna C. C. Peluso (2012) wrote in the article, "The Fast-Paced iPad Revolution: Can Educators Stay up to Date and Relevant About These Ubiquitous Devices?" "In this technological era of iPads and Twitter learners and educators alike have access to some of the most intuitive and engaging forms of communication and expression ever available" (p. E125). Scholars from many different fields have researched, and published on, these new forms and using social networking services to understand the practices, implications, culture, and meaning of the sites, as well as users' engagement with them (boyd & Ellison, 2008). It produces an increase in the scholarship for teaching professionals who are finding ways to use social media to share resources and lend quick support to peers with similar interests (Ferriter, 2010) and provides instructors new ways to connect with the 21st century writers while still remaining scholarly. It has been suggested that even while Twitter has worked in some classes, to use Twitter to its greatest potential, educators must provide scaffolding, address privacy, establish purpose, and model use with structure (Lin, Hoffman & Borengasser, 2013).

While it has been shown that incorporating Twitter into a course provided a "rapid method for disseminating current topical information but failed to readily facilitate discussion" (Jacquemin, Smelser & Bernot, 2014 p. 26), it is still possible to assert that the more students engage themselves with Twitter in a learning context, the more they will apply it for both personal and instructional purposes (Yakin & Tinmaz, 2013), thus giving the student a real world application. Many believe that the ultimate goal of using Twitter is to foster a classroom with a high level of energy, sharing, and, above all, greater understanding of the world around us (Moody, 2010). This can be accomplished by using Twitter to teach students how to create the academic essay.

Learning through Twitter

Twitter went online in 2006, and as Evan Williams (2009) explains in his TEDTalk, "The Voices of Twitter Users," it, "is based around a very simple, seemingly trivial concept. You say what you're doing in 140 characters or less, and people who are interested in you get those updates." Twitter uses brief sound-bites to create conversations and interactions via the Internet. Students can have access to Twitter through a computer, tablet, or phone, and, according to *Statistics Brain Research Institute,* there are over 645,750,000 registered users, 289,000,000 active users, and an average of 9,100 tweets per second (StatisticsBrain.com, 2015). The world of Twitter is full of usernames, hashtags, tweets, characters, likes, mentions, retweets, quotes, trends, and follows. Students like the brevity and the immediacy of Twitter, giving them the chance to say what they want, when they want, to whomever they want, all in 140 characters or less. Users follow people they know, famous people, interesting people, funny people, news organizations, companies, or just about anyone they want.

Once an account is followed, every tweet written will be seen by the user on their timeline. In order for others to read the tweet of a user, they must be followed. Add a hashtag to tweets and users who are interested in the subject of the tweet instantly sees the user's thought and can reply in kind. By adding a mention (the username of a Twitter user) to an individual tweet, a user may direct a comment to a specific person and that person will be notified of the tweet. If a particularly interesting or thoughtful tweet is read by a user, they can retweet the tweet so everyone who follows them can have access to it. The most important rule is that of brevity. No tweet can be over 140 characters long; therefore, tweets have an average of 14-16 words to clearly get the point across.

Using Twitter in the classroom harnesses the power of the social and the power of succinctness in writing, giving students a scaffold to develop critical thinking, to understand rhetorical concepts, and to create clear ideas using words, all in a real-life setting which, as Parker Palmer and Arthur Zajonc (2010), wrote, "If higher education cannot deal with the messiness of real life, educated people will not be prepared to use their knowledge amid the complexities and cruelties that constantly threaten to undue civilization" (p. 38). It is clear to me that by using Twitter to scaffold composition education, students will not be as intimidated while learning the rhetorical moves necessary in academic writing.

Creating Spaces for Twitter in Academics and Critical Thinking

While many educators have been able to successfully bring social media into the classroom, some scholars (Wolf, 2007; Carr, 2008; Richtel, 2009; Richtel & Wollan, 2011; Turkle 2012) have legitimate concerns that if we are perpetually connected to the Internet, we run the risk of losing the ability to think critically outside of 140 characters at a time. Sherry Turkle (2011) in the article, "The Tethered Self: Technology Reinvents Intimacy and Solitude," wrotethe power of the Internet actually changes one's ideas and ideologies and that, "technology is the architect of our intimacies, but this means that as we text, Twitter, e-mail, and spend time on Facebook, technology is not just doing things for us, but to us, changing the way we view ourselves and our relationships" (p. 28).In the 2012 *TED Talk*, "Connected, but Alone?"Turkle related, "I believe it's because technology appeals to us most where we are most vulnerable. And we are vulnerable. We're lonely, but we're afraid of intimacy…we're designing technologies that will give us the illusion of companionship without the demands of friendship" (*Ted. com*). Her research began to show that by implementing social media in the classroom to encourage collaboration and community, it may have the opposite effect.

Maryanne Wolf (2007) warned in an opinion article in the *Boston Globe*, "Children need to have both time to think and the motivation to think for themselves, to develop an expert reading brain, before the digital mode dominates their reading" (*Boston.com*). Perhaps, by bringing these technologies into the classroom, I am creating immature creative thinkers? This would defeat the learning goals of the composition classroom. Wolf (2007) made a strong statement that I had to consider, "The immediacy and volume of the information should not be confused with true knowledge" (*Boston.com*). This, coupled with Nicholas Carr (2008), in the seminal article, "Is Google Making Us Stupid?" who pointed out when thinking about his reading skills, "Now my concentration often starts to drift after two or three pages. I get fidgety…begin looking for something else to do…The deep reading that used to come naturally has become a struggle" (*theatlantic.com*), gives cause to reflect on how this can be avoided in the composition classroom.

While these authors correctly point out the inherent dangers of using technology, they also acknowledge that they are consistently enjoying the benefits of its use. Carr (2008) admitted, "For more than a decade now, I've been spending a lot of time online, searching and surfing and sometimes adding to the great databases of the Internet. The Web has been a godsend to me as a writer" (*theatlantic.com*) and Turkle (2012) acknowledged, "And so there you have it. I embody the central paradox. I'm a woman who loves getting texts who's going to tell you that too many of them can be a problem" (*Ted.com*). Each of these concerns should be acknowledged by instructors as they integrate social media and technology into the classroom. However, I believe that the benefits of using these technologies outweigh the potential negatives. And whether or not instructors want to admit it, students are encased in this world, and the likelihood of it changing is slim. I believe students can learn better if I implement these concepts in my classroom.

Understanding the Link between Integrative Education, Writing Instruction, and Twitter

Palmer and Zajonc (2010), in their book, *The Heart of Higher Education*, created a scaffold of integrative education by discussing how one must eliminate the divide between inside the academy and the outer world, or real life. They wrote, "A truly integrative education engages students in the systematic exploration of the relationship between their studies of the 'objective' world and the purpose, meaning, limits, and aspirations of their lives" (p. 10). When students enroll in the university, most of them have specific goals in mind. These goals often include getting a good job so he or she can make a lot of money and support future spouses and children, finally saving enough to make it to retirement, and live in a warm climate waiting for the grandchildren to come visit. While perhaps not expressed in those terms, a student rarely enters into the academy for the purpose of remaining in this objective world, free of the goings on of real life. Educators must be willing to work toward an integrated pedagogy, which will, according to Parker, "lead to moral engagement because it engages more of the learner's self and teaches by means of engagement: the curriculum and the 'hidden curriculum'…that involves much if not all of the whole self in learning about the world" (p. 32).

To include the whole self, real life, and writing instruction in the composition classroom, one should consider the theory of social process and how writing instruction can be scaffolded by using Twitter. Bruce McCominskey believes writing teachers should not ignore the rhetorical levels of composing, which I believe is necessary for first-year students, but rather students must use the social contexts and ideologies of both the processes and products of writing. Bruce McCominskey (2000) wrote in *Teaching Composition as a Social Process*:

In terms of writing instruction: 1) teachers ought to articulate the kinds of activities they want their students to perform outside of the classroom, and they should design pedagogical techniques that develop skills in their students consistent with these future activities; 2) teachers ought to theorize the nature of the social context within which these activities will be performed, and they should design curricula based on the structure and processes that comprise this context; and 3) teachers ought to predict the positive and negative effects on these activities in these future contexts might have on both students and society alike. (p. 113)

By designing pedagogical techniques around conventions that students are currently using outside of the classroom, the author has been able to build that bridge between the classroom and the "messiness of real life." Twitter is real life writing. First-year composition classes give the students unique opportunities to practice being good citizens. Students are able to make mistakes and receive support from classmates and the instructor.

Using Twitter to teach writing skills can begin to introduce students to the world of academic writing, while nesting itself in activities and skills learned outside of the classroom. To be a successful teacher, the theory is fairly simple; get the students to buy into the knowledge you are trying to sell and make sure they retain it. In practice, it can prove to be challenging. In 2001, Marc Prensky, in the article, Digital Natives, Digital Immigrants," where he explained, "The single biggest problem facing education today is that our digital immigrant instructors, who speak an outdated language (that of the pre-digital age), are struggling to teach a population that speaks an entirely new language" (p. 3). Students are learning every day. Usually, it is not about comma usage, or how to write a great transition; instead, many are learning about the technology devices in their hands. Our modern day students want to spend hours on their phone, texting their friends, creating social commentary for all who want to hear. Not becoming experts at writing academic essays, most modern students are experts at social media. Students speak this language. In order to get them to do composition, instructors can teach writing by co-opting the knowledge and skills students have using social media, and begin to design pedagogy using the mastered talents students already possess.

While not an exhaustive list, most composition instructors' goals are to get students to think critically, analyze a text, understand the value of audience awareness, develop a writing process, enter into different conversations, use appropriate voice, tone, and level of formality, develop ethos, logos, and pathos in their writing, and recognize different rhetorical situations in the academic setting. While these goals may not become fully developed until years later, it is crucial that instructors begin to plant the seeds. What they must realize, and take advantage of, is students are already able to perform these rhetorical moves in their daily lives on social media. Creating that bridge between the real world and the world of academics becomes the ultimate challenge.

In any given composition classroom, teachers often ask students to read and discuss texts with the goal of rhetorical analysis. Mike Bunn (2011), in his article, "How to Read Like a Writer,"while speaking directly to students, illustrated, by rhetorically analyzing texts, "You work to identify some of the choices the author made so that you can better understand how such choices might arise in your own writing. The idea is to carefully examine the things you read, looking at the writerly techniques in the text in order to decide if you might want to adopt similar (or the same) techniques in your writing" (p. 72). Instructors should be able to hand a student a well-crafted essay, give him or her time to read, examine, analyze, and then move to a place where students can produce their own high-quality texts. Bunn's theory is admirable, but as any instructor who has taught more than a day in the classroom can tell you, this is not the starting line for labor. This would be like asking a student to fix a car after showing them a wrench. Instead, reading like a writer comes near the end of the process, after the students have internalized the rhetoric. I believe the best method to scaffold writing for a student is to start where he or she is already reading, analyzing, and mimicking the writers they admire on social media and look at what they do to compose strong posts.

METHODOLOGY AND PEDAGOGY

Purpose

The purpose of this essay is to show how I have used Twitter in my English Composition classes at the University of Akron beginning as a grad student in 2011 through the fall of 2015. During that time, the University of Akron had nine goals that English Composition classes were supposed to meet during the two semesters of English Composition 111 and 112:

1. Rhetorically analyze and think critically;
2. Effectively structure and organize an essay;
3. Understand the writing process;
4. Integrate one's own ideas and incorporate the ideas of others into academic papers;
5. Develop a thesis;
6. Understand tone, voice, and levels of formality in their writing;
7. Learn argumentative strategies and various persuasive appeals;
8. Anticipate and respond to audience concerns and counter-arguments; and
9. Critically analyze and evaluate different sources for validity and relevancy.

In Comp 111, the English Department required students to write a minimum of four formal essays totaling a minimum of 20 pages of polished writing. In Comp 112, the students had the same basic requirements, four formal essays and a minimum of 20 pages of polished writing, but they were also required to write a capstone essay, which was a minimum of six pages of researched argument, and an annotated bibliography based on the capstone essay. Instructors were given carte blanche as to how these goals and requirements were met.

Since I was given free reign when it came to course delivery, I tried to keep courses taught since 2011 immersed in the many aspects of technologies in the classroom. The University of Akron used the Desire2Learn platform, specifically Springboard. Every student had access to the class Springboard account, which provided a drop box to turn in all assignments, a discussion page to discuss readings and conduct online peer-review, reading content to supplement the textbook, access to TED talks and YouTube videos, online quizzes, the grade book, and the ability to email his or her classmates as well as the instructor. The only part of the course that was not online was the textbook, *Creative Composition* by Eileen Pollack, Jeremiah Chamberlin, and Natalie Bakopoulos.

By using Twitter to teach and apply rhetorical analysis to the composition class, it was my pedagogical goal to ensure students had the best chance of successfully navigating Comp 111 and 112. I hoped I would be able to guide the students through some of the rhetorical moves of composition, and create scaffolding that would develop the skills students needed for future contexts.

Participants and Setting

The University of Akron is located in Akron, Ohio. According to the United States Census Bureau, in 2014, the city of Akron had an estimated population of 197,859, 62% identify as white alone (quickfacts.census.gov, 2015). In the fall of 2015, the enrollment at the university was 25,177 total, 21,158 being registered undergraduate students. The university offers five types of degrees: baccalaureate, associates, master's, doctoral, and law. The university reports in the fall of 2015, 73.2% of students identify as white alone (uakron.edu, 2015). Of the 27 courses I have taught since 2011 and used Twitter to scaffold learning, 85% of the students self-identified as white only.

A unique demographic of The University of Akron as a whole, and of the classes I have taught over the last four years, is the number of high school students who have taken Comp 111 and 112 as post-secondary students. During these years, the university had a strong synchronous distance learning (DL) program. Comp 111 and 112 were taught to students in high schools, allowing them to earn college credit while still enrolled in high school. Because I taught multiple DL classes, the number of post-secondary students was inflated compared to other composition classes. Of the 27 classes taught using Twitter to scaffold learning, there were 576 students enrolled. Thirty-seven of these students were enrolled in a 100% online asynchronous comp 111 class. Two hundred forty-four of the 576 (42%) of the students enrolled were also enrolled in an area high school. One hundred sixty-four of the 244 high school students were enrolled in a distance learning section, taking the class through DL technology at their local high school. Many of these students were enrolled in Comp 111 in the fall and Comp 112 in the spring. The enrollment figures do not represent unique students, just the number of students enrolled in each course. In other words, if Student A was enrolled in Comp 111 in the fall and again in Comp 112 in the spring, Student A would be counted as two different students.

There is an assumption that every student enrolled at the university had computer and Internet access, whether it was in the student's home or on campus. In order to turn in all assignments and have access to

Springboard, one of the requirements of the 164 high school students enrolled in the DL sections of the courses was to have access to a computer and the Internet. This is required of all DL classes throughout the university. These students were required to sign a contract. The 37 students who were enrolled in the 100% online course were also required to have access to a computer and the Internet. It is also a reasonable expectation for students enrolled in face-to-face courses taught on campus to have access. The university provides seven computer labs to students, free access to laptops to check out and use, and wireless Internet throughout campus. Each dormitory provides Internet access to students living in the individual dorm.

While not every student had access to the Internet via a smartphone, all 576 students self-identified proficiency using social media. Since 2011, 445 (77%) students had a Twitter account prior to enrolling in my Comp. 111 and 112 courses. According to Maeve Duggan, Nicole B. Ellison, Cliff Lampe, Amanda Lenhart, and Mary Madden's (2015) report, "Demographics of key Social Networking Platforms," 23% of adult Internet users currently use Twitter. Those in the 18-29-year-old category, in which all but two of the 567 students belong, 37% use Twitter (*pewinternet.org*).

By the end of the first week, all students were required to create a Twitter account, follow me, and compose a tweet about the class, tagging me in the process and use the class hashtag. Of the 132 students who began using Twitter in one of these courses, I was asked by 23 to help them create an account and to assist in the first assignment. After the first week, zero students asked for help using Twitter, suggesting it is accessible to most students after minimal assistance.

Opening a Space for Twitter and Language in the Composition Classroom

After students have been given some time to understand how to follow an account, tweet, use a hashtag, and feel comfortable doing so, the first assignment is to discuss the linguistics of using Twitter (text-speak) versus using Standard English in the classroom. Michelle Drouin and Brent Driver's (2014) in their article, "Texting, Textese and Literacy Abilities: A Naturalistic Study," indicate there have been many studies done on the relationship between textspeak and literacy. In this report, Drouin and Driver (2014) concluded:

The average proportion of textese used within actual text messages (textism density) was significantly and negatively related to single word reading and spelling. Although the magnitude of these correlations was weak overall, the negative relationships were consistent, which provides some evidence that use of textese is associated with lower levels of literacy. (p. 264)

This gives concern that the use of textspeak in the classroom may be counter-productive. In addition, Amanda Lenhart, Sousan Arafeh, Aaron Smith, and Alexandra R. Macgill's (2008) published the *Pew Internet and American Life Project.* They wrote that many people, "are concerned that the quality of writing by young Americans is being degraded by their electronic communication, with its carefree spelling, lax punctuation and grammar, and its acronym shortcuts" (p. i). Begging the question, how can composition instructors prevent the sabotage on their own teaching if using the language of social media downgrades the literacy of students?

In another study, this one by Graham G. Scott, Jason Sinclair, Emma Short, and Gillian Bruce (2014), it is suggested that, "The language individuals choose to convey information online could have unforeseen consequences" (p. 562). The researchers found:

While the type of language used to convey information on SNS profiles did not affect perceived social, physical, or task attractiveness, targets who used correct language were judged as being more intelligent, competent, and employable than those who used incorrect language, and more intelligent and employable than those using text speak. (p. 564).

If using the language of social media reflects the intelligence of students, especially in the view of future employers and colleagues, it would be wrong for the instructors to allow the use of textese to continue. However, it is my belief that textspeak is not a reflection on the inability to write using Standard English; instead, it is a different language. It is rule governed and can constantly changing.

This theory has been shown by linguist scholars. Kristen Hawley Turner (2009) believes students can easily code-switch and the goal of instructors should be to get the students to be aware of language as they use it. She writes:

Perhaps we can see its [text speak] use in school as a difference, rather than a deficit, and teach students how to code-switch from this language that has become part of their primary discourse into the more formal language of school and the larger society. (p. 64)

Finally, John McWhorter (2013), in his TED Talk titled, Texting is killing language, believes that textspeak, is not, in fact, written language. McWhorter believes it is actually, written speech. Students are encouraged to learn languages. In fact, by language acquisition is a sign of intelligence. Because of this, my class watched McWhorter's TED Talk and it fosters a tremendous amount of discussion.

Students are given a place to start thinking about the use of words in composition, as well as how they use words in their everyday writingby watching McWhorter (2013), reading Turner (2009), and the summary of the Pew Internet and American Life Project (2008). This discussion begins the scaffolding by making students aware of their use of language. Students are then invited to write a formal response to McWhorter and the uses of text speak, opening the door to the first major assignment using Twitter: the rhetorical analysis.

First Writing Assignment: A Rhetorical Analysis of Twitter

When we analyze an academic article for the rhetorical moves made, such as the thesis statement, the audience awareness, the counter-argument, the history of the topic, and the future of the topic, students often lose focus and begin to summarize the article in a step-by-step fashion, missing the rhetorical moves made by the author. When done well, the rhetorical analysis can be an excellent tool in helping students to write a strong academic paper. They are able to see how other established writers in the field are able to put together a strong paper, and students can emulate these steps. While not a formula, per se, academic writing has definite steps students must consider. Instructors ask students to read a myriad of articles, both as classroom assignments and as research, with the assumption that rhetorical analysis is being done. But when we ask students to discuss and write down the rhetorical concepts the author uses, we often get a summary of the argument. We need rhetorical analysis so that students can begin to understand the necessity of these articles, for not only what they say, but how they say it. In actuality, most students want examples of papers prior to writing them. Students are already able to rhetorically analyze text; it is only when we ask them to identifythese moves on paper that confusion sets in. This first assignment attempts to take away the confusion by asking them to rhetorically analyze a nonacademic source that many students are already familiar with, Twitter. The intention of this assignment is to lead the students through a well-thought out, academic rhetorical analysis without the added pressure of academic writing, using what the students already know and understand.

For the *Rhetorical Analysis of Twitter* project, students are assigned the following prompt:

1. Create a document with the rules (spoken and unspoken) of Twitter. There should be at least 10 rules that you have discovered on using Twitter.
2. Discover what makes a great tweet. Find great tweets and quote them. What was the most retweeted tweet in history? You may even screen shot them and copy them onto this document. If they have a picture, make sure the picture is included in this document. Create a formula that would provide a user the best likelihood to be retweeted, favorited, or followed. It is your job to analyze Twitter and provide a how-to document.
3. You are also being asked to provide a separate document which will explain the original document. What is the purpose of the how-to document? Who is your intended audience? What choice did you make in terms of creativity and the visual? What evidence did you use to show the audience that your formula and rules are correct and will work? What is the true language of Twitter?
4. The how-to document should be colorful and creative. The ultimate goal of this document is to provide a real life education and analysis of Twitter to be given to someone who wants to "do" Twitter the best way possible.

I have assigned this project as group work (four to five students) as well as an individual assignment. Students have completed the assignment both ways.

Second Writing Assignment: A Rhetorical Analysis of an Academic Article

It was my experience when first-year college students are asked to write a rhetorical analysis of a peer-reviewed, academic article, they experience difficulty. On a good day, with no written analysis required, students struggle with basic understanding of texts. Just getting the student to summarize the main points of the article can prove to be daunting. Then asking the students to find meaning in what they have read can cause some students to hide in the corner in the fetal position. However, if we take the tools learned in the *Rhetorical Analysis of Twitter* project and use those on an academic article, students are likely to feel more in control of the assignment.

For this assignment, students were asked to read an academic article, Nicholas Carr's (2008), "Is Google Making Us Stupid?" This article was accessible to the first-year students and modeled solid academic writing.

The following prompt is provided to the students:

1. Read the article provided and write a one-page summary. This summary should only summarize the basic concepts of the article. What are the main points the author is trying to get across? What does the author want you to do once you have read the article?

2. Consider how the author wrote the text. Consider these ideas, answering each section 140 characters at a time. This is not an essay. Instead, it is a series of Tweets considering each question being asked:

   a. The main and supporting claims presented within the essay: What is the main claim/thesis of this essay? What reasons are offered in support of this thesis? And how does this claim fit into the larger conversation on this topic? (Your analysis should include a general overview of the topic as well as a brief summary of the essay itself.)

   b. The types of appeals used by the author: To whom is the essay directed (audience)? How does the author attempt to connect to the reader? Where do you see evidence of this?

   c. The use of evidence within the essay: What types of evidence does the author bring in to support his/her claims and appeals? Personal experience? Factual information? Expert testimony? Statistics? Analogies? Hypothetical examples? Is this evidence credible? Does it adequately support the author's argument? Why or why not? Does it cover all the necessary perspectives on the issue? If not, what perspectives does it seem to overlook?

   d. Overall development of the essay: does the essay move logically from one point to the next? Are there evident gaps or fallacies embedded within the reasoning process or overall presentation of the argument? How does the movement/organization of the essay attempt to engage the reader in the subject? What techniques does the author use to draw the audience into the larger conversation and debate?

   e. The use of language, tone, and style within the essay: Is the language of the essay inviting? Colorful? Vivid? Descriptive? Or is it dull? Flat? Highly technical or jargon-rich? Is the author's use of language suited to the audience and purpose at hand? How would you describe the overall tone of the essay? Is this tone appropriate, given the target audience and the subject matter being addressed? What stylistic devices does the author use to present and support the argument?

This assignment, very often, will generate 25-30 tweets per student. Students submitted the tweets as a Word document.

Third Writing Assignment: A Rhetorical Analysis of a Student's Own Paper

The third assignment is assigned at the end of the semester. Prior to this third Twitter assignment, students draft a six to eight-page argument paper. The argument paper, or the Capstone, included writing a personal narrative, literature review, thesis statement, evidence, responding to naysayers, the future of the topic, and a call to action. Students are asked to rhetorically analyze this draft using the skills they acquired using Twitter. This analysis assignment specifically accomplished two pedagogical goals:

1. It made sure students had completed the different goals of the learning assignment; and
2. It ensured the argument paper had made all of the rhetorical moves that created a strong essay.

To understand how the third assignment accomplished these goals, it is important to understand the Capstone paper assignment that they analyzed. Students were given this prompt:

For the Capstone paper, you will compose a six to eight-page evidence-based argument on the issue, topic, and question of your choice based on the theme of the classroom. For this paper, you will be required to develop and support a thesis using a strategic array of evidence, good reasons, and rhetorical appeals. You are encouraged to draw your evidence from a combination of primary and secondary source material, and to find your sources in places relevant to your chosen interests and experiences (personal narratives and observations; interviews; anecdotal evidence; relevant web sites; news magazines; radio, TV, and newspaper analyses) as well as in academic databases, such as Academic Search Complete and Opposing Viewpoints. This paper should showcase your ability to analyze your rhetorical situation and construct a purposeful, well-designed, audience-oriented, and engaging argument. As a Capstone paper, in other words, this essay should represent the culmination of your work as a student who has completed the composition sequence.

Students were given at least four weeks to research, draft, and complete a draft of the assignment. Prior to the final, graded draft being turned in, but after the papers were peer-reviewed, the Twitter analysis prompt was assigned:

Students are asked to consider, in 140 characters or less, seven different learning objectives of the composition sequence. How did the paper:

1. Develop, support, and defend a thesis,
2. Identify and avoid faulty reasoning,
3. Analyze/employ argumentative strategies and persuasion,
4. Anticipate and respond to counterarguments,
5. Support thesis with researched evidence,
6. Integrate the student's ideas with others.

Students are asked to look at the draft of the Capstone paper they have composed and provide evidence that, in 140 characters, they have completed all seven objectives.

RESULTS AND DISCUSSION

First Writing Assignment: A Rhetorical Analysis of Twitter

Students who completed a Rhetorical Analysis of Twitter were able to understand how Twitter works, what makes for a good composition in Twitter, and begin to grasp how rhetorical analysis works.

Examples of some of the rules students created when thinking about doing Twitter were:

Twitter Do's

1. Be interactive. Hashtag super #trendy subjects, follow people, and interact with friends and celebrities.
2. Be funny. Tell jokes, be witty, and make your Twitter profile a fun a place to be!
3. Be intelligent. Use adequate spelling and grammar; don't be a dummy!

4. Follow ratio rules. Don't be over eager. Nobody likes a super-stalker or a super-stalkee. So please, keep your followers and following ratio in control.
5. Trust no one. The government is out to get you. Let the world know.

Twitter Don'ts

1. Be in a relationship, not about it. It's fine to tell people about who you're dating and that you love them, but it only needs to be said once.
2. Passive Aggressiveness is a no-go. Sub-tweeting is an acceptable form of communication within your friend group only. No one else knows what you're talking about.
3. Your muscles say something about you; never say something about your muscles. Enough said.
4. We all know you think you're hilarious. But let others decide whether your tweets are Twitter gold. Don't favorite your own tweets.
5. Fishing should not be done online. Fishing is not supposed to be done through a screen, so fishing for compliments should not be happening.
6. Personal issues are personal for a reason. That's none of my business.

While some of the rules are personal preference and not rules that must be adhered to, students feel strongly that in order to be successful on Twitter, a user must follow these guidelines. For example, "Be in a relationship, not about it. It's fine to tell people about who you're dating and that you love them, but it only needs to be said once," is probably not a rule, but students see it as a guideline. Students tend to come up with strong rules that, when followed, provide for a better Twitter experience. One thing is certain; by thinking about what rules should be followed to be successful on Twitter, they have begun to rhetorically analyze writing.

Other rules students have developed from their analysis are:

1. "Don't post too many selfies; selfies are for Instagram not Twitter;"
2. "No nudes. Have respect for yourself. You should not be posting inappropriate pictures on Twitter at all. If you wouldn't want your grandparents to see the picture you are posting, than you probably shouldn't be posting it;"
3. "Don't have an inappropriate Avi; make sure your avatar is a picture with you in it. If it's a picture of a car and your Twitter handle is something ridiculous how do you expect people to know who you are?"

Each rule created indicates that a student rhetorically analyzed Twitter and thought about what makes a good tweet, which in turn, can be applied to academic compositions and essays.

Second Writing Assignment: A Rhetorical Analysis of an Academic Article

Students who rhetorically analyze an academic essay using 140-character sound bites were able to identify the rhetorical moves made and coherently discuss them in the writing.

When analyzing Nicholas Carr's (2008), "Is Google Making Us Stupid?" based on these different rhetorical moves, 140 characters or less at a time, students were able to provide accurate descriptions of the rhetorical concepts. The bold typed questions are questions I posed, and italicized statements are student answers.

1. What is the main claim/thesis of this essay?
   a. The Internet is changing the way people read and write. "Once I was a scuba diver in the sea of words. Now I zip along the surface like a guy on a Jet Ski" (Carr 2).
   b. *That the internet is chipping away at our capacity for concentration and contemplation.*
   c. *Google/technology machines have been making us dumber in the fact that it messes with neurology and our actual brains.*
   d. *That too much reliance on the internet will only lead to a decrease in your knowledge.*
2. Who is the audience of this paper?
   a. *Fellow internet and technology users*
   b. *Everyone. All can be targeted and find useful apps or web pages that suit their needs.*
   c. *The audience the author is targeting is today [sic] society and more importantly people whose lives are based around technology and machines.*
   d. *The audience is directed towards writers and readers like Carr who is on the Internet.*
3. How does Carr use evidence in his paper?
   a. *Personal experience, experience from other literary friends, and statistics were all used as evidence.*
   b. *He brings in sources from all over time. He uses many people like Frederick Winslow Taylor to describe the formation of efficiency.*
   c. *To support his claims, Carr uses personal experience, factual information, expert testimony, and statistics.*
   d. *There is research on personal experience, factual information, expert testimony, statistics, analogies, and hypothetical examples.*
4. How does the essay develop?
   a. *It starts off with explaining the topic and then moves into chronological order.*
   b. *It takes the facts from one setup to lead into the events of the next.*
   c. *The movement of the essay attempts to grab the reader's attention by connecting to the reader with each piece of evidence.*
   d. *Carr showed a small glimpse (I would have liked more detail) of the opposite argument.*
5. What did you see in the use of language, tone, and style within the essay?
   a. *The language used throughout this essay is diverse and educated. I enjoy the word choice.*
   b. *Changes tones a few times when the topic shifts which makes a nice read. It is also very vivid and paints a picture straight in my head.*
   c. *There are a few big words that might need looked up to understand the point of the sentence.*
   d. *The language is very descriptive, inviting readers in with the vivid imagery.*

By understanding how these different concepts work in Carr's article, students began to understand how they might work in their own writing. Having the students take small sound bites, made the rhetorical analysis much more manageable. This gave students a stronger grasp of what is needed in order to write effective, quality, academic essays.

Third Writing Assignment: A Rhetorical Analysis of a Student's Own Paper

Students who rhetorically analyzed their own writing 140 characters at a time created strong academic essays and were given a way of entry into academic writing.

Examples of this assignment can vary, but they all have one common theme surrounding them; they understand what each rhetorical move is and the purpose of these moves, giving credence to the work being done. As before, the bold typed questions are questions I posed, and italicized statements are student answers.

1. What is your thesis statement in this paper?
   a. *Ultimately, the removal of the DDR would benefit the organ transplant community because it would open up many new opportunities to harvest needed organs.*
   b. *Expressive art therapy lets patients tell their therapist what they are feeling without physically saying it.*
   c. *Nutrition therapy should be the first line of defense for patients, illness permitting.*
2. How have you been able to identify and avoid faulty reasoning?
   a. *My first quote can be classified as pity because I am making the audience feel compassionate and sad that a parent realizes they can't cure their child. Any parent who read this would find it devastating.*
   b. *I have an appeal to authority in the paper currently. I quote Einstein to begin my paper. I will remove it.*
   c. *I point out the fallacy that Harry J.Anslinger brought marijuana use to the attention of the nation by making connections between marijuana to racism and violence.*
3. What argument strategies have you employed and how did you do it?
   a. *I believe the intensive research I performed (Ethos) has allowed me to grasp a greater understanding of how the medical practice works.*
   b. *I made sure to use mostly female authors, as Heidi Thoenen showed me because it helps me employ my argument that Title IX should be changed.*
   c. *I used a story in my introduction to capture my audiences' attention. I used a story that would relate to most people who have relatives or friends in other states or countries.*
4. How did you employ naysayers in your paper?
   a. *Kathleen Patrice Gulley does not view technology as beneficial for students and teachers. I quoted her extensively and responded to her arguments in order to enter into my argument.*
   b. *Teachers don't like the idea of having to plan for technology because they don't have the material or knowledge about the subject. This was the stepping stone for my call to action.*
   c. *Some people claim it is impossible to teach everyone due to different learning habits, but with effort, it can be achieved.*
5. How did you support your thesis using researched evidence?
   a. *In "Learning Matters: The Role of Learning in Concept Acquisition," Eric Margolis agrees that concepts need to be learned for everyday life.*
   b. *Huss' previous study on the effects of school uniforms "revealed a greater sense of student respect, a decrease in discipline problems, and a sense of belonging" (32).*

c.   "I think that if you have more hands on activities, I would learn more" (Birchall 24). This is evidence for my thesis because it shows one technique of teaching Spanish in a beneficial manner.

6.   How did you integrate your ideas with the ideas of others?

a.   Griel writes, "Learning about MI theory changed the thinking of teachers and students" (20). The way in which we learn is outdated, as is the way of thinking about education.

b.   "Doesn't permit to maintain easily accessibility at the level of programming can usually find in simpler types of robots" (58) a major road block is the aspect of understanding how to run robots to do what we need them to.

c.   I used multiple real world examples and applications, scholarly journals, personal narratives, and TED Talks to back up my capstone.

These examples show that, during English Composition, students can achieve class objectives and be aware they are doing so. Ensuring students understand the rhetorical move of composition is an important aspect of teaching composition. Once students can rhetorically analyze a text, they are able to be successful in a myriad of academic environments.

CONCLUSION

In 2014, after the semester had finished and students were getting their overall grades for the semester, a student asked to make an appointment with me to discuss the semester. His first words have resonated with me since:

Mr. Harrell, I entered your class knowing that I could not write school essays; at least that is what my high school teachers told me. All I could do was sit on my phone and write status updates and texts. I was really good at that. But when you showed me that if I figured out how to tweet, I can figure out how to write papers for school, I really took that to heart. This class was hard for me. But I slowly realized that it was no different than learning what my readers wanted in my tweets. I have 400 followers on Twitter because I am good at it. In the last four months I did what I was never able to do, become good at writing in class. Thank you!

Social media can be used as an academic tool to guide students in composition classes. Many students are experts at using social media. By using the tools students already have in their tool belt, we are setting them up for greater success. Teaching rhetorical analysis in the language of the student provides an entry way into academic thought that many students struggle finding. While not all students initially understand the language of Twitter, especially older, non-traditional ones, many students do, and by breaking down these rhetorical concepts 140 characters at a time, they can access the moves of academic writing and the language of composition.

Students love their Smartphones and devices. The first thing they do in the morning is check their phones. At the end of the day, after all of the lights are out, the subtle blue glow can be seen from the space under their bedroom door, as they finish the conversations, started hours prior. Just one more tweet, one more direct message, one more broadcast. And yet, when I ask students what they struggle the most with in the classroom, it is writing. Most modern day students do not like to read and write. In fact, some will claim they do not read or write on a daily basis, until the instructor points out that every time the student logs into Twitter, Facebook, Periscope, or whatever social media site is trending today, they read for hours on end, and often write more than Hemingway did in a single day. Harnessing this enthusiasm is a way to get students to become successful writers, and then, I can say I have done my job.

REFERENCES

Boyd, D. M., & Ellison, N. B. (2008). Social network sites: Definition, history, and scholarship. *Journal of Computer-Mediated Communication, 13*(1), 210–230. doi:10.1111/j.1083-6101.2007.00393.x

Bunn, M. (2011). How to read like a writer. *Writing Spaces: Readings on Writing, 2*, 71-86. Retrieved from http://writingspaces.org/sites/default/files/bunn--how-to-read.pdf

Carr, N. (2008). Is Google making us stupid? What the Internet is doing to our brains. *The Atlantic.* Retrieved from http://theatlantic.com

Drouin, M., & Driver, B. (2014). Texting, textese and literacy abilities: A naturalistic study. *Journal of Research in Reading, 37*(3), 250–267. doi:10.1111/j.1467-9817.2012.01532.x

Duggan, M., Ellison, N. B., Lampe, C., Lenhart, A., & Madden, M. (2015). Demographics of key social networking platforms pew research center. Retrieved from www.pewinternet.org

Elbow, P. (1973). *Writing without teachers.* New York, NY: Oxford University Press.

Ferriter, W. M. (2010). Why teachers should try Twitter. *Educational Leadership, 67*(5), 73–74.

Jacquemin, S. J., Smelser, L. K., & Bernot, M. J. (2014). Twitter in the higher education classroom: A student and faculty assessment of use and perception. *Journal of College Science Teaching, 43*(6), 22–27.

Lenhart, A., Sousan, A., Amith, A., & Macgill, A. R. (2008). Writing, technology, and teens. *Pew Internet and American Life Project.* Retrieved from http://www.pewinternet.org

Lin, M.-F., Hoffman, E., & Borengasser, C. (2013). Is social media too social for class? A case study of Twitter use. *TechTrends, 57*(2), 39–45. doi:10.1007/s11528-013-0644-2

McCominsky, B. (2000). *Teaching composition as a social process.* Logan, UT: Utah State University Press.

McWhorter, J. (2013, February). John McWhorter: Texting is killing language [Video File]. Retrieved from http://www.ted.com/talks/john_mcwhorter_txtng_is_killing_language_jk

Moody, M. (2010). Teaching Twitter and beyond: Tips for incorporating social media in traditional courses. *Journal of Magazine & New Media Research, 11*(2), 1–9.

Nordloff, J. (2014). Vygotsky, scaffolding, and the role of theory in writing center work. *Writing Center Journal, 34*(1), 45–64.

Palmer, P. (1983). *To know as we are known: Education as a spiritual journey.* New York, NY: Harper One.

Palmer, P., & Zajonc, A. (2010). *The heart of higher education: A call to renewal.* San Francisco, CA: Jossey-Bass.

Peluso, D. C. C. (2012). The fast-paced iPad revolution: Can educators stay up to date and relevant about these ubiquitous devices? *British Journal of Educational Technology, 43*(4), E125–E127. doi:10.1111/j.1467-8535.2012.01310.x

Prensky, M. (2001). Digital natives, digital immigrants. *On the Horizon, 9*(5), 1–6. doi:10.1108/10748120110424816

Scott, G. G., Sinclair, J., Short, E., & Bruce, G. (2014). It's not what you say, it's how you say it: Language use on Facebook impacts employability but not attractiveness. *Cyberpsychology, Behavior, and Social Networking, 17*(8), 562–566. doi:10.1089/cyber.2013.0584 PMID:24949532

Turkle, S. (2011). The tethered self: Technology reinvents intimacy and solitude. In *Continuing Higher Education Review* (pp. 7528-7531).

Turkle, S. (2012, February). Sherry Turkle: Connected, but alone? [Video File]. Retrieved from http://www.ted.com/talks/sherry_turkle_alone_together

Turner, K. H. (2009). Flipping the switch: Code-switching from text speak to formal language. *English Journal, 98*(5), 60–65.

Vygotsky, L. S. (1978). Interaction between learning and development. In M. Cole, V. John-Steiner, S. Scribner, & E. Souberman (Eds.), *Mind in society: The development of higher psychological processes* (pp. 79–91). Cambridge, MA: Harvard University Press.

Vygotsky, L. S. (1981). The genesis of higher mental functions. In J. V. Wertsch (Ed.), *The concept of activity in soviet psychology* (pp. 144–188). Armonk, NY: Sharpe.

Williams, E. (2009, February). Evan Williams: The voices of Twitter users [Video File]. Retrieved from http://www.ted.com/talks/evan_williams_on_listening_to_twitter_users

Wolf, M. (2007). Learning to think in a digital world. In M. Bauerlein (Ed.), The digital divide: Arguments for and against Facebook, Google, texting, and the age of social networking (pp. 34-37). New York, NY: Penguin.

Wood, D., Bruner, J. S., & Ross, G. (1976). The role of tutoring in problem solving. *Journal of Child Psychology and Psychiatry, and Allied Disciplines, 17*(2), 89–100. doi:10.1111/j.1469-7610.1976.tb00381.x PMID:932126

Yakin, I., & Tinmaz, H. (2013). Using Twitter as an instructional tool: A case study in higher education. *TOJET: The Turkish Online Journal of Educational Technology, 12*(4), 209–218.

Chapter 4
From Expository Blog to Engaged E-Portfolio:
A Student-Centered Pedagogy in Process

Jill Darling
University of Michigan, USA

ABSTRACT

This chapter illustrates a student-centered pedagogy in process through the example of an electronic portfolio final assignment in two First-Year Writing courses. The philosophy behind the assignment is based in cultural studies, constructivist pedagogy, and multimodal studies. If students learn by doing, they also learn about culture through critique, public writing, and reflection. Students can thus become engaged as writers and citizens through constructing web-based texts focused on social issues and written from personal perspectives.

INTRODUCTION

Years ago I taught two versions of an upper level writing class in which students learned html and designed their own web pages as their semester-long writing projects. Students had the whole semester to read and discuss topics related to internet and society, work on related writing assignments, do research for their final projects, and design and build websites. When I no longer had the opportunity to teach that class, I stopped using web technology other than the basic course management systems for each class; integrating web design into First-Year Writing or creative writing courses seemed more distracting than productive. In the academic writing courses, I wanted students to focus on traditional reading and writing skills and not add extra work with the introduction of technology requirements. Eventually, though, I began to assign weekly blog writing to replace hard-copy response writing in creative writing classes, and I started more fully utilizing the course management systems for writing and discussion in composition courses. I've also come to believe that web technology can no longer be compartmentalized or kept separate from the rest of the course content in any of my courses. Since web 2.0, internet use has become more interactive, and our uses of internet and social media cannot always be neatly separated

DOI: 10.4018/978-1-5225-0562-4.ch004

from other daily practices. It is now also easier to make writing available online without having to learn html, transfer files, or figure out web hosting. In all of my courses, students now write responses and reflections on blogs, and create electronic portfolios as their final semester projects.

This chapter describes and reflects on my experience giving a final e-portfolio assignment and the related pedagogy and assignment scaffolding. The samples of student work included here come from two recent First-Year Writing courses focused on community, citizenship, and culture. The course content and assignments during the semester were designed within a context of critical, constructivist, and multimodal pedagogy. The final portfolio assignment was both specific in terms of requirements and open to students' creative interpretations, though not all students were comfortable with the creative freedom. Although I have learned a great deal about integrating web-based technologies, social media culture, and student writing into the pedagogical goals for this course, I still feel new to the design and implementation of the final portfolio assignment. With each iteration I encourage students to participate and construct on their own terms, offering them both structured guidance and space for their own creativity and innovation. This student-centered pedagogy integrates theory and practice with the goal of deeper engagement in both teaching and learning, and within the context of community, collaboration, and public writing.

THEORETICAL FRAMEWORK

Community, Citizenship, Culture

Aristotle asserted that no matter what one calls it, whether democracy or oligarchy, a government only works when its members have equal access, as citizens, to education and participation in the system of governing (Jacobis, 2013). Benazir Bhutto knowingly risked her life, after her own father and two brothers had been killed, to fight for democracy in Pakistan (Baughman & Siegel, 2010). Frederick Douglass emphasized the importance of critical literacy for emancipation from mental and legal slavery (Douglass, 1892). Martin Luther King, Jr. called on white and black mainstream America to come together to change the laws that kept segregation legal, as a step toward justice for all Americans (King, 1963). Jonathan Kozol and Marian Wright Edelman show readers how as a society we are failing the poorest and most vulnerable in our society: the children in under-resourced communities, and that we are responsible to do better (Loeb, 2004). And in *Soul of a Citizen* (2010) Paul Loeb encourages individuals to overcome feeling overwhelmed or helpless in the face of social ills and to take even small actions toward change. Grace Lee Boggs exemplified this in her life's work advocating for justice for people in Detroit and in motivating others to join the cause, reiterating the idea that we can be the change that we want to see (Boggs, 2012). These examples tell us a lot about how social change has happened throughout history: extraordinary individuals take on issues and work to create that change. What we don't always realize is that these same individuals began as ordinary citizens.

Contemporary students are overwhelmed with responsibilities including working part or full-time jobs while going to school, or having caretaking responsibilities in their families. But they are also especially vulnerable under changing economic conditions and decreased social safety programs. They are leaving college burdened by debt and at risk of not finding professional work for which their degrees have prepared them. Social Security and healthcare loom as big question marks in the future for those for whom retirement is a long way off. What some students don't realize is that they are also citizens who can participate in creating a future that will benefit more people in society. As Loeb writes, although being involved in community activism may not lead to instant improvements, many people claim "social activism gives them a sense of purpose, pride, and service; teaches them new skills; shows them how to confront daunting obstacles; and lets them experience new worlds. It offers camaraderie and helps them build powerful friendships" (2010, p. 11). We have numerous historical examples of individuals working on behalf of others, but we don't always think of ourselves as having real voices for progress and change. Social change can be said to begin with individual awareness. This can lead to small actions that potentially spread (Loeb, 2010).

In the First-Year Writing classes that I discuss here, I introduced students to the concepts of community and citizenship, and invited them to engage through active reading and writing on related topics over the course of the semester. We discussed the above and other texts to more fully explore these concepts. Students were encouraged to synthesize the general concepts with their own values, interests, and experiences. In theory, this course could lead to a second semester service-learning course that would further engage in public writing in the kinds of ways described in *Community Literacy and the Rhetoric of Public Engagement* (Flower, 2008). Flower advocates not simply writing for or about public issues, but writing in cooperation and collaboration with the publics most directly affected by those issues. A goal of this kind of writing is to engage in a public sphere and participate in transformative practices (p. 4).

Academic and Personal Writing

One challenge in the writing classroom involves offering students opportunities to deeply engage in both academic and personal writing. I believe that students can benefit from reading and writing widely, and so I require that they practice writing in a variety of genres. Students move through academic summary, analysis and response, reflection, personal essay writing, and blog posting. They also do in-class free-writing, short homework writing, group collaborative writing, and other activities. About two-thirds of the way through the semester, students begin to think about final writing projects that integrate a personal interest or experience with the topic of the course. This assignment can be related to, or come out of, previous reading and writing assignments, or go in a related but different direction. They are also required to include a few different kinds of sources in order to push their ideas beyond the personal. In my experience assigning personal essays that require outside textual sources, students tend to be more interested, engaged, and produce better writing than with earlier versions of research paper assignments. An important aspect of teaching writing includes focusing more on writing process and less on product. In particular, this means helping students to grow as writers and not simply to produce perfect papers. I also believe that *both* process and product improve when students are personally engaged with the material, and when they are invested they make the process work for them. In any class that I teach, my job is to scaffold context and structure so that they can work through low-stakes writing and other activities that lead toward larger, interactive and engaged, final projects. If the process is strengthened, the products will also benefit in more holistic ways.

Social Media, Public Writing, Audience

A recent Pew Research Center study (Perrin, 2015) looked at social media use from 2005-2015 and found that 90% of people age 18-29 use social media, and usage among groups older than 29 has been increasing. The study reported that 35% of people 65 and over now use social media, which is up from only 2% in 2005. The study highlighted the disparities in terms of education level, household income, and race. Having only some college education can increase likelihood for use compared to those with only a high school education or less. Households with higher incomes are consistently greater users of social media. And only 56% of African-Americans use social media compared to 65% of whites and 65% of Hispanics (Perrin, 2015). The Pew Research Center Fact Sheet (2014) breaks down the data more specifically and also includes discussion of "Social Impact" from a 2010 survey. It was found, among other things, that "social networking sites" can be instrumental to helping people maintain social ties, feel less isolated, and be more politically engaged than those less involved in social media.

The importance of social media, especially in the lives of young adults, should give us a great deal to reflect on in terms of teaching practice. The use of internet in general, and social media in particular, is now intimately integrated into so much of our students' lives. It seems to only make sense to bring this knowledge and practice into the classroom.

Pedagogy

After Paolo Freire (2000) a critical pedagogy is invested in student participation and engagement. My own pedagogy comes, in part, out of Freire and through James Berlin, especially in terms of encouraging students to read and develop their own critical literacy practices. As Berlin (2003) writes, "for Freire ... to learn to read and write is to learn to rename the world, and in this naming is a program for understanding the conditions of our experience and, most important, for acting in and on them" (p. 105-6). This kind of critical exercise includes engaging students in democratic and dialogic activities in the classroom; inviting them to participate across age, race, culture, and experiential differences; helping them to understand the rhetorical power of language; and encouraging their abilities to rewrite narratives in order to create and inspire community (Berlin, 2003). Contextualized by this philosophy, instead of acting as an authoritarian figure telling students what to learn, an instructor can instead facilitate critical and independent thinking while helping to create community in the classroom (Darling, 2015). In terms of rhetorical context, audience is also important; students act as audience for each other, and speak and write as engaged citizens in the world.

Theories of multimodality bring together pedagogy and practice in ways that help contextualize the integration of electronic media into the writing classroom. Jonathan Alexander and Jacqueline Rhodes (2014) claim that thinking new media from a pedagogical perspective "challenges us to reconceive ... how we communicate with and through media, how media interact with one another, and how we re-flexively understand ourselves, individually and collectively, in our interactions across different media platforms" (p. 60). We can use this kind of perspective to investigate relationships between writing, rhetorical practices, and the public sphere (p. 67). Our personal and public lives have, in fact, become integrated by and through these new media, and it is through these that we are also able to learn more about ourselves in the world.

Anne Frances Wysocki (2004) argues that "new media needs to be opened to writing" (p. 5) by which she means bringing more reflection and engagement into the new media classroom. She explains that "new technologies do not automatically erase or overthrow or change old practices" and that writing teachers are in a good position to examine and critique the role of media in classrooms and culture "precisely because of how [writing teachers] see texts as complexly situated practice embedded in the past but opening up possible futures" (p. 8). Because our students are already communicating through a variety of media, we have an opportunity here to examine, discuss, and exercise both traditional and new practices with our students, preparing them for further work inside and outside of the classroom.

Further, Jason Palmeri (2012) argues that composing and teaching multimodal texts reinforce process pedagogy and a "collaborative investigation of composing processes" (p. 24) (for more on process pedagogy see Elbow 1973; Emig, 1983; Moffet, 1991; Tobin, 2001). Blending image, sound, and language in their composing processes, for students meaning-making thus becomes more personalized and encourages invention. Palmeri also points out the importance of reflection writing in order to "develop a more nuanced understanding of the unique affordances of visual, aural, and alphabetic forms of communication" (p. 47). Critical and active engagement and reflection, across modes and contexts, can be seen to potentially enhance students' personal development, skills, and confidence in the writing classroom.

Additional arguments in support of inclusion of multimodal pedagogies and student projects appear every day. Claire Lutkewitte (2014) has assembled a powerful collection of scholarship in *Multimodal Composition: A Critical Sourcebook* which includes previously published articles that present a diverse array of perspectives. Included in the collection, Kathleen Blake Yancey (2004) cites "the proliferation of writings outside the academy" and the speed at which "technologies of writing" are contributing to new genres of communication in various modes. The New London Group (1996) advocates the concept of "design" in regard to learning processes and multiliteracies. In this framework, acknowledgment of difference is key and "classroom teaching and curriculum have to engage with students' own experiences and discourses, which are increasingly defined by cultural and subcultural diversity and the different language backgrounds and practices that come with this diversity" (p. 207). The New London Group calls this kind of difference "productive diversity" and it extends out of the classroom and into the world. They argue that as "designers of our social futures" we can harness pluralism in the meaning-making practices of community building. Multimodal pedagogy further asks what is privileged and excluded from classrooms and "if writing rhetorically means being responsive to the changing technological, economic, social, cultural, and political conditions in a society then we cannot demand that students only compose in one mode using only one technology" (Lutkewitte, 2014 p. 279-80; Jewitt, 2005). Multimodal composition can open space for this greater diversity of voices not only in the classroom but also in public realms. And it affords students access to greater toolkits for skill-building and occasions for meaning-making (Lutkewitte, 2014; Hull & Nelson, 2005).

METHODOLOGY

When I began to think beyond reading response blog posts as discrete assignments to consider the integration of more comprehensive e-portfolios in my courses, I had to also contemplate purpose and framing in different ways. Further understanding of traditional and more contemporary pedagogies, in both theory and practice, became especially useful to me. Not only was I changing the assignment on paper, but through reading about others' experiences teaching new media and incorporating multimodal activities and assignments, I came to better understand the value for students from a variety of perspectives.

In his article, "The Maker Movement and the Rebirth of Constructionism," Jonan Donaldson (2014) shares his experiences of a transformed "understanding of pedagogy, teaching, and learning" through his foray into constructivist educational theory. Connecting his intuitive and practical teaching experiences, he explains how he came to realize that "at its heart constructionism argues for what I had been trying to articulate: learning happens best when learners construct their understanding through a process of constructing things to share with others" (para. 6). My own experiences echo, in different ways, this kind of personal, pedagogical epiphany. Students learn best when they make, create, and engage in materials on their own terms. This is not to say that a college writing class, for example, should be unstructured so that students can do what they want. But rather, a class might be structured in such a way as to get students to pursue their own interests and personal connections to course materials; they should be encouraged to develop their own skill sets through the lenses of their own experiences. When Donaldson modified his writing assignments, in the context of contemporary "remix" and media culture, he realized that having real-world audiences in mind helped students to become more invested and engaged in their own writing. Giving them access to tools and media that they could use to construct their own projects, he saw students feel empowered and surprised at their own abilities to do kinds of work they hadn't thought themselves capable. He opened writing to include forms beyond the traditionally textual, such as podcasts or animations.

Further, he began to emphasize reflection. As he explains, "when the students explained to the reader what they had created and why, their own learning was consolidated and deepened" (para. 5). The opportunities for reflection combined with collaborative practices helped students to think, create, interact and progress by way of their own interests and abilities and through learning from each other. My own experience mirrors these conclusions. Students tended to engage more personally with blog writing and in creating e-portfolios, and their reflection writing often articulated that leaning even more clearly.

In their Preface to *Writer/Designer*, the authors (Arola, Sheppard, & Ball, 2014) lay out their goals for multimodal pedagogy, which include helping students to be "more prepared for the complex rhetorical challenges they face as students and future professionals." They discuss the enriched learning experience students receive by "doing," similar to Donaldson's ideas about "making," and coming out of the New London Group's idea of "situated practice." They assert that these kinds of engagements, by way of experiment and reflection, will help students "develop the confidence and competence they need to leverage both old and new technologies and media for successful communication" (p.vii). Through the examination of a variety of real-world, multimodal texts, students learn about genre, which can help them to create their own writing across contexts and situations. The e-portfolio assignment, introduced early and integrated into the content of the whole semester, gives students practice navigating through traditional, hybrid, and media texts which may benefit them in their academic and professional lives.

Recent studies advocate integrating the use of technology with constructivist pedagogy. This kind of pedagogy engages the teacher as facilitator and promotes a learner-centered classroom in which students learn by doing. (Keengwe & Onchwari, 2011; Keengwe, Jared, Onchwari, Grace, Agamba & Joachim, 2014). The use of technology is closely tied to a focus on pedagogical praxis, in which the tools are used to deepen thinking and engagement of students immersed in their own critical learning practices. "Interactive multimedia generally present multiple ways that a problem could be solved thus allowing for greater thinking and exploration from students rather than just a one way. At the core of an effective constructivist pedagogy is an approach that integrates various technologies with active learning while allowing for the teacher to act as a guiding partner" (Gallant, 2000 as cited in Keengwe, Jared, Onchwari, Grace, Agamba & Joachim, 2014, p. 890). Interaction, collaboration, and reflection are shown to encourage engagement and student success in the classroom (Keengwe, Jared, Onchwari, Grace, Agamba & Joachim, 2014). Because we can no longer ignore the role of internet and social media in our daily lives, helping students to critically and creatively use these technologies can offer them more than the basic skills of the past.

Arming students with tools and knowledge will also help them to recognize the downsides of internet technologies. If our thought processes and relationships in the world are changing as a result of increased internet and social media use (see Carr, 2011; Turkle, 2012) we may have to learn how to better manage our technological endeavors. Douglass Rushkoff (2010) argues that our awareness of the potential dangers can, in fact, help us to be more in control of our choices in regard to internet use. And other arguments about the negative consequences seem simultaneously hopeful that we can alter our practices for healthier outcomes (Turkle, 2012). As instructors in this Web 2.0, 21st Century, we can raise the level of awareness with our students and give them access to tools and strategies so they are not overtaken and lost in a virtual space of no return. How can we help students to use the internet creatively, productively, and in ways that will benefit them as active and engaged citizens of a larger world? I believe part of the answer lies in the learner-centered, critically pedagogical practices of integrating these technologies into our classes. Keeping the tools out of the classroom will not help students learn to negotiate these mediated spaces in critically literate ways.

The potential perils may be more acute when we consider the digital divides in relation to race, class, and access issues (see Bryant, 2014). Those with less access, education, and fewer resources are the most vulnerable to being swept away by surface-level practices. These are the students who need the most support to give them a technological, critical edge. In the two classes discussed here, when we began the semester, only a few of students had used blogs previously and only one or two had done some kind of web site design or construction. Over the course of the semester, through homework assignments and in-class work time, students learned how to set-up and design WordPress or Blogger sites and then turn these into complete e-portfolios. By the end, most everyone felt a tangible sense of having created a comprehensive web site portfolio basically from scratch.

Audience, Blogs, and E-Portfolios

In First-Year Writing courses we talk about purpose, focus, and audience, yet academic hard-copy papers are rarely seen outside of the student-teacher context. Students miss the opportunity to think deeply about audience in terms of purpose and focus, but also in terms of engaging themselves in the presentation of their work. Why is audience important? In this world of digital media, students are on Facebook and Twitter, Instagram, Snapchat and other sites writing, developing, and negotiating their ideas and identities in the world. Academic writing that remains cordoned off from the ways that students participate in the world does them a disservice; they may learn basic skills and how to write strong papers, and some students will be engaged and do that successfully, but this additional kind of "making" for a larger audience can also encourage students to become more confident, and maybe even come to enjoy writing. By shifting the audience beyond the teacher to the peer-space of the class and the public audience of the internet, the writing may be, potentially, exponentially diffused. This is not to say that one should water down the idea of audience so that a piece of writing can reach any person, but that while focusing purpose toward a particular kind of audience, students will also be aware of their rhetorical choices for an online audience. This can include critical examination of what and how audience functions, and how we might all think about ourselves as writers online and via social media in our personal and professional lives.

As a space of "rhetorical opportunity" (Miller and Shepherd, 2004), a blog can function as the private "cultivation and validation of the self" and simultaneously occur at the intersection of private and public, or a space of identity formation and questioning (Miller and Shepherd, 2004, para. 1). In 2009, a second study asserted that alongside the development of social media and enhanced interactive possibilities online, the blog as a site of connection became more profound. Whether they are blogs from celebrities for their readers, or personal blogs written for self or others, the need to feel a part of a larger physical or virtual world is at the center of blogs' exigence (Miller and Shepherd, 2009). Inherent to the basic design of a "web-log" is an understanding of audience and rhetorical context, even while the blog, for the personal user, can function like a journal, offering a space for low stakes writing, reflection, agency, and creative expression with few rules for formality (Bryant, 2014).

I began to have a different view of using blogs in the classroom when I was invited to teach a class that had a required final e-portfolio. The class was relatively open in terms of overall design though there were basic goals and outcomes, including the students' development and online publishing of their portfolios. Using examples from previous sections of the class, and rubrics and advice from other instructors, I implemented the assignment in that section and further opted to include it as a similar assignment in another class I was teaching. Although I had already been assigning weekly reading response blog writing in my creative writing classes, I had not introduced blog writing in my First-Year Writing courses. As I moved further into teaching the e-portfolio, I came to realize that I had been underutilizing students' blog response writing in the creative writing classes. I saw the e-portfolio as a way to further the discussion of purpose and audience in more complex ways. Instead of turning in a final paper, on paper, to the instructor, the e-portfolio would allow students to publish their work online for a specific peer audience as well as a larger potential general audience. I began to encourage students to do reflective blog writing and make connections among texts and ideas, instead of writing generic summaries in response to reading assignments. I hoped this might encourage students to invest in personal writing that would more thoughtfully lead to the larger portfolio project.

The e-portfolio is appealing in the ways it offers the potential to bring together personal writing, reflection, creative expression and an understanding of rhetorical context with greater stakes. It can serve as a space for writing accumulated over the course of a semester like a traditional hard-copy portfolio, but it also becomes hybrid, hypertextual, and multimodal because of its web form. Considerations of layout, design, organization, structure and other elements take on greater meaning and require more attention. Instead of simply collecting materials, an e-portfolio can also serve as a single or cohesive project, like a fully formed website for a comprehensive paper bound together with a common focus, purpose, and sense of audience. Designing a single project into an interactive portfolio can potentially allow for more time and thought—within the confines of the semester time frame—for creative and organizational choices. Further, integration of other media including graphics, video, audio and other forms can turn the portfolio into a dynamic, multi-dimensional experience.

These are skills that go beyond the classroom. As Helen L. Chen (2009) argues, considering the increase in life span there will be a need to "help individuals think less in terms of terminal degrees and academic credentials and more in terms of transitions facilitated through the development of key work skills and personal competencies" (p. 31). She emphasizes the philosophy of lifelong learning which "places the *needs* of the individual at the forefront" (emphasis Chen's) and "the importance of exploration and preparation for change and adaptability in both formal and informal learning environments" (p. 31). The "efolio" combined with "reflective thinking," she explains, can be considered an example of "a learner-centered pedagogy focused on providing structured opportunities for students to create learning portfolios for the purpose of fostering coherence and making meaning" (p. 31). Students can learn by doing, but that learning is deepened and made more profound when they are required to reflect and make connections on their own terms.

Participants and Setting

The two classes observed here, although at different campuses, had a number of relative similarities in terms of demographics and classroom setting. The nearly identical syllabi had small differences in reading and writing assignments. Both sections were composed of students from a diversity of ethnic, cultural, racial, gendered, and economic backgrounds. One section was taught in a computer classroom in which each student had access to a computer, and when students were not working on computers we sat around a large table for class discussion. Many of the students in this section also brought personal laptops to class, had access to computers at home, and all students had access to a number of computer labs and resources on campus. The other section was not in a computer classroom but almost all students had personal laptops that they brought to class regularly. That campus also provided resources for students to borrow laptops to use for free for the semester. That classroom also had moveable desk-tables so we could arrange a circle as a whole group, or small groups could easily spread around the room. Physical space is an important consideration because of the collaborative nature of student-centered, constructivist practice; in less-amenable classroom spaces, an instructor may need to be more creative in terms of helping to engage conversation and collaboration.

In both sections we spent a number of class periods working on blogs and e-portfolios so that students could help each other, and I was available to work with whole groups of students or individuals. Although it is true that most students now use internet and social media regularly, in general they tend to have less experience setting up, designing, and manipulating sites for blog posting and turning these into whole portfolios. Early in the semester, I gave students the assignment to set up a WordPress or Blogger site, create a home page and a blog posts page, and publish an initial reflection post. Although a couple of students in each section were able to accomplish the task with little trouble, most students needed extra instruction and support. Over the course of the semester, all of the students developed the skills to make pages, create links, work on design elements to some degree, and post and revise their own writing. Some included additional media and spent more time on layout, font, color, readability and other considerations. Because this was a first-semester course, the requirements for media and design were minimal. The basic goals included introduction to the idea of the e-portfolio, extended consideration of purpose and audience, and general practice in philosophically and practically transferring traditional text writing to web form. Some students struggled with these basic ideas—especially thinking of their traditionally written papers in web form—while others were able to harness a deeper creative process of media integration.

Scaffolding

For these classes I utilized both the Instructure Canvas class management sites, and WordPress sites that I designed specifically, one for each class. The Canvas sites included course readings and prompts for short, weekly homework writing assignments. The class WordPress sites included detailed and regularly updated schedules of assignments, pages for links to articles and topics of interest in relation to assigned course readings and class discussions, pages with the lists of student blog sites, and miscellaneous other information. During the semester, students wrote short, weekly homework responses to readings and class conversations and posted those on the Canvas sites. Periodically, I also assigned longer blog reflection writing which extended and reflected on ideas from the weekly short homework assignments, readings, and conversation. I encouraged students to include quotes and references, but also to personalize and be creative in the presentation of their responses. They posted these on their blog sites, and I made a list of the class blog sites on each class WordPress site that everyone could access.

The formal writing assignments ranged from academic summary to analysis to personal essay, and the final paper integrated personal essay and research. For the final paper, students chose topics from their own experiences or interests and in relation to community, citizenship, culture, and/or social activism. Papers topics ranged from education to animal abuse. Because the final paper went through a process of mind-mapping, freewriting, drafting, peer review on paper, and then peer review on-screen, it was easy for me to keep track of who was writing about what. That meant I could also intervene and assist at any point if a student went off track or got stuck somehow.

Small group peer-review helped students learn by doing and from each other. Not only did they receive feedback for strengthening their papers over the course of the semester, and building their sites, they were able to see what others were working on, to share information and skills, to practice effective communication, and to build confidence through collaboration. By the time groups started to peer-review their projects online, the process became messy and seemingly less effective. Working on-screen is distracting; students often have a hard time sticking with a linear process for reading through others' sites, and the feedback is given in parts and pieces. Often students ended up working on their own sites-in-progress instead of focusing on others' work. Because the sites are continually in process, they are never really completely finished before the end of the semester. Although I have tried to refine the guidelines for on-screen peer review from one semester to the next, I also believe some of the messiness is an important part of the process. The collaborative part of construction is counterintuitive to working in a linear fashion, but working in this non-linear way to read, comment, and help others create quality work can be especially beneficial.

The challenges in these courses included having enough time to effectively integrate discussion of the portfolios and class time to work on them. In these classes, with so many parts and pieces, it sometimes seemed as if the portfolio was not holistically integrated throughout the semester. At the same time, the course content, including theoretical grounding for assignments and the e-portfolio, did seem to overlap in serendipitous ways. Reading about and creating their own social media platforms helped students to think about audience and presentation in more real-world ways. In relation to the content of their final projects, it seems likely that they were able to form more critical perspectives in regard to audience and presentation than they may have if not for the public online forum.

DATA COLLECTION

Below I include samples selected from students' final portfolios, and reflection writing on the final projects and writing process. The samples come from the two classes described above. The figures below show the variety of approaches to audience, presentation, layout, and design. The reflection writings point to different concerns and feelings about processes and products. Students volunteered the inclusion of selections from their portfolios here. Two of the students, each with a keen awareness of audience, purpose, and online presentation, wanted their names included with their work, and their sites remain active online.

RESULTS AND DISCUSSION

Audience

The portfolios take into account a sense of audience in different ways. Figure 1 shows a welcome page created by a student who had done volunteer work in the community. It calls attention to the value of community work by asking "How willing are you to help out in your community?" and incorporating an active poll for readers to respond to. In a different way, Figure 2 shows the home page from a portfolio that asks readers to rethink perceptions of Muslim-Americans. Showing a woman wearing an American Flag hijab, or head scarf, and repeating the image on the borders of the page, the author creates a strong visual argument. The project is divided into pages with titles including, "Ignorance," "Racial Profiling," and "My Experience." From a personal perspective, the author appeals to readers' sense of fairness to consider how Muslims and other minority groups are discriminated against in contemporary American society. Instead of attacking or telling a reader how to feel, the author brings the reader into her personal experience to show how misinformation leads to mistreatment for many groups in America.

Personal Investment, Layout, and Design

Many students began with a personal experience, or interest in a topic, related to community and social good. One student asserted that world peace might be possible if we start by thinking about personal happiness (Figure 3). Telling a story about her relationship with her grandmother, this student made a strong argument for the relationship between the individual and society that was at the center of our reading and discussion all semester. Although she didn't use those terms explicitly, the connection and sense of reciprocity in that relationship was clear.

Figure 1. Welcome page of a student portfolio; this page encourages its audience to get involved with their communities.

Figure 2. We Are All Equal; this is the home page of a student portfolio. It engages its audience by showing that Muslim-Americans are patriotic and argues against discrimination in contemporary society.

Figure 3. World Peace; this student project begins with a personal engagement with the idea of world peace and the relation to personal happiness.

Road To Peace & Love

Anything is possible....it just takes a little while

CAN IT HAPPEN? · POSTS PAGE · SOLUTIONS · WHAT IS THE PROBLEM? ·

WORLD PEACE CANNOT BE OBTAINED?

World peace cannot be obtained?

World Peace Cannot be Obtained?

Why is world peace such a huge aspiration? Many of the people that ask this question have not achieved true happiness. In today's world, conformity has drained every bit of what makes humans happy. We think we are happy, but in reality, we are blinded by the surroundings of temptation, greed, and the excessive need for power. Because of this, equality amongst all people ceases to exist. This new way of living has conquered because many people in the world forgot how to love and overpass judgment, diversity, and social class. But the sad truth is that many people are so weak and afraid to face adversity, that they are willing to lose their sense of pride and civil liberties. Being strong minded has turned into something wrong. Individualism as far as having your own mind is now something foreign. It will take a long while, but we will again learn to love. We as humans will once more find love. Selfishness will be replaced with selflessness, and the spirit of conformity will forever be broken. But this will not happen if we as people choose luxuries and power over self-worth and freedom.

search

Search ...

Recent Posts

Amazing grace

Karl Marx "Communist Manifesto" Main Idea Summary

Benizar Bhutto

Recent Comments

Archives

November 2015

October 2015

Another project (Figure 4) foregrounds a strong personal investment in advocating for feminism in contemporary society, and attentively takes into account the web format in the presentation of text. Although the writer simply copied her final paper into a single page on the WordPress site, instead of dividing it among multiple pages, the text is engaging and visually pleasing. It reads like a long blog post, includes reader-friendly fonts and white space, and the text is often interrupted with images, links to other articles and sites, and additional elements. The page becomes a hypertextual reading experience, with which readers can interact. Images include "We All Can Do It #Feminism is worthless without intersectionality and inclusion," a graphic play on Rosie the Riveter with three women representing intersectionality (made by Chelsea Valentin Brown at soirart.tumblr); the You Tube link to Emma Watson's speech to the UN about gender equality; and a number of other comics and graphics. The page is colorful, and the writing is appealing, like many short articles posted on journalistic kinds of web sites that get shared among social media. This student has a clear sense of web audience, reader engagement, visual rhetoric, and her own writing style.

This site is also a great example of the final portfolio as a comprehensive project that incorporates other writing from the semester. The blog reflection posts—accessible from the Blog tab at the top—compliment the long paper with discussion of equality, and political and economic rights, through various course readings. Here Lemees writes an especially thoughtful reflection on the Black Lives Matter movement:

The issue of individual and systemic racism and discrimination has always been a highly critical topic, but it seems that ... with the high profile case of the death of Trayvon Martin ... this controversy is now being debated more than ever. With the rise of highly influential activists and leaders such as Alicia Garza ... who coined the notorious hashtag #BlackLivesMatter, it's almost inevitable that change is upon

Figure 4. Confessions of a Teenage Activist; this student supports her personal statement on feminism with outside sources.

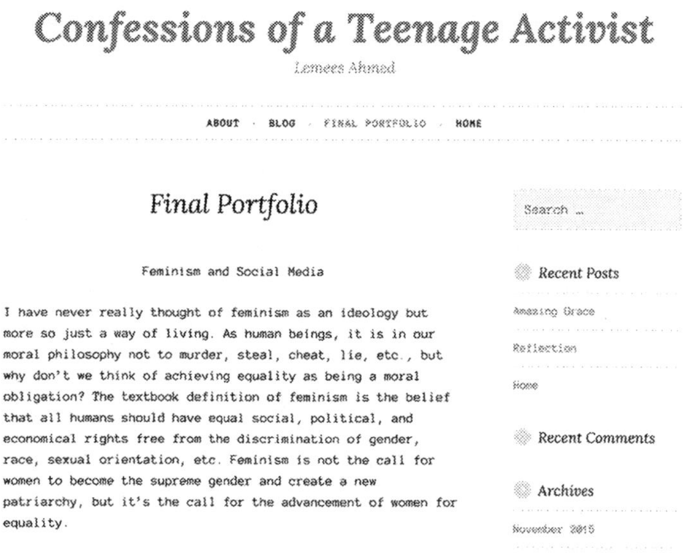

Confessions of a Teenage Activist

Lemees Ahmed

ABOUT · BLOG · FINAL PORTFOLIO · HOME

Final Portfolio

Search …

Feminism and Social Media

I have never really thought of feminism as an ideology but more so just a way of living. As human beings, it is in our moral philosophy not to murder, steal, cheat, lie, etc., but why don't we think of achieving equality as being a moral obligation? The textbook definition of feminism is the belief that all humans should have equal social, political, and economical rights free from the discrimination of gender, race, sexual orientation, etc. Feminism is not the call for women to become the supreme gender and create a new patriarchy, but it's the call for the advancement of women for equality.

Recent Posts

Amazing Grace

Reflection

Home

Recent Comments

Archives

November 2015

us. "I've been praying for a moment like this one my entire life," says Garza when speaking about how the social media trend has brought so many young activists of all color together.

The beauty of the movement is not only that it gives a voice to African American men who are highly subjected to racial profiling, but it also plays a big role in other types of discrimination such as gender, sexuality, gender identification, etc. The leader and co-founder of the movement herself is an African-American, queer woman which in itself is essentially the most discriminated classification there is. It is already typically known that a white woman makes 76 cents to every dollar her male counterpart makes, but what most are not aware of is that African-American males make 75 cents to every dollar a white male is making. And shockingly, black women make roughly 65 cents to every dollar, that's a 35 cent margin!

Consequently, if as a society we remove the social and political stigma against black, queer women and unlearn and baptize our minds of racial prejudice, it is possible that equality will be granted to all races, religions, genders, sexual orientations, etc. I, a Muslim, Arab-American woman, experience discrimination on a regular basis and am an advocate of the #BlackLivesMatter movement. Though I'm aware that the mission is directed towards black people, the message of equality and ending racism affects me as well. The fact of the matter is, everyone on earth will experience some type of prejudice and by ending it for the group most affected by it, we can end it for all.

This portfolio ultimately does a really nice job connecting readings, themes, and outside sources to explore a personal relationship to an issue of importance for this student in the world. By relying on both traditional textual examples and visual and other media from the Web, she is able to personalize and make this site her own in a thoughtful, academic, and critically literate way.

From a different design perspective, Figure 5 offers an example of a comprehensive consideration of layout and organization in a project about cyberbullying. A drop-down menu from the main menu at the top divides the project into multiple pages for easier reading and accessibility, and titles include, "Effects of Cyberbullying," "Personal Experience," and "How cyberbullying Can Be Avoided." Some of the pages include images, graphs, and links to other sites for facts and information. This site and the student's reflection, described below, illustrate a clear sense of rhetorical situation, purpose, audience, and personal investment through the choices she has made in terms of content and organization.

Some students further personalize their sites by including their mind maps (see Figures 6 and 7) or other elements. The mind map is an assignment that helps students to begin thinking about the final project with a low-stakes, visual, free-writing practice. For Kristina (Figure 7), the mind map served as a starting point and also an important visual rhetorical marker within the project itself. As an interactive web document, her portfolio incorporates short, easy to read sections of text organized over multiple pages as well as visuals and graphics to make readers' experiences more stimulating. The handmade mind map draws our attention to the ideas in the paper in a way that reiterates the arguments, because we are seeing them in a visually creative format. This writer/designer has a keen sense of digital rhetoric and presentation.

Reflection Writing

Connections between the personal and the social are further made in many of the reflections students wrote after completing their final projects. During the semester, they also composed short reflections

Figure 5. Cyberbullying; this student portfolio incorporates a comprehensive consideration of organization and layout.

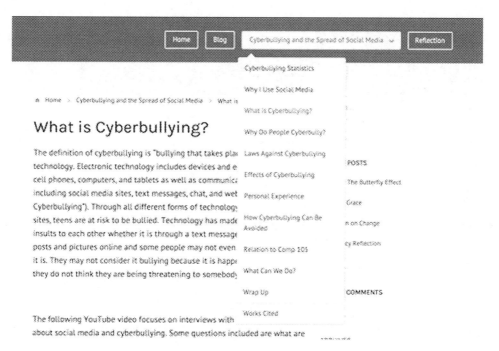

Figure 6. Hunger in America; some students included their handmade mind maps in their portfolio.

Figure 7. Civic Engagement; this student portfolio incorporates a clear sense of organization and creative presentation.

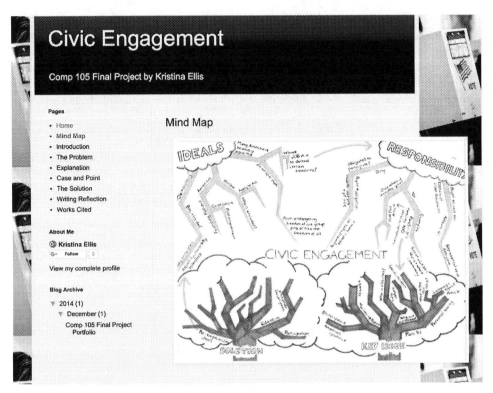

after each major writing assignment, and the periodic blog posts also functioned, in part, as reflection writing. Some of the students' final reflections focused more on the basic writing process, while others delved further into making connections between course content, the final paper topic, and the writing process. It is through the combination of the final projects and the reflections on those that the levels of student engagement become most apparent. The relationships between traditional process pedagogy, multimodality, and construction, or making, are also especially noticeable here.

Student Sample #1

This reflection brings together the project on cyberbullying referenced above (Figure 5) and the writer's personal interest in the topic.

While doing research for this paper, I learned a lot more about cyberbullying than I expected. I always knew the basics of what it was and how it happened, but when I was researching, I learned about the statistics of who is cyberbullied and why it happens. Cyberbullying happens way more than I ever thought. This was evident when I connected cyberbullying to the article we read about when President Barack Obama joined twitter and the racist comments followed immediately. This shows that cyberbullying hap-

pens to everybody, not just teenagers. While writing the paper, I started with only a few sources, but as it expanded, I started to find more and more. One of the hardest parts about this paper for me was the length. I was able to write everything that I needed to say in about six pages and I struggled to get to eight. This is when I began to include more of my personal thoughts and soon, I had eight pages. I felt like adding personal thoughts and experiences about the subject made the paper easier to write. Although I haven't personally been cyberbullied, I do know people who have and I have seen the effect it has had on them. I also liked writing about how what I am planning on studying … can hopefully help me be a part of stopping cyberbullying in the future. One of the sources I used included a lot of information and tips about how to avoid being cyberbullied. I knew about some of these things, such as using privacy settings or blocking whoever is bullying, but this article discussed other ideas that I hadn't heard about before. I think sites like this are very beneficial for teenagers to stay aware and avoid being cyberbullied.

Student Sample #2

One challenge in this kind of class is that not all students will be interested in the material related to community, citizenship, and social activism. I believe, however, that giving them the context of course readings and assignments, and then also offering the freedom to reflect, write from a personal perspective, and ultimately choose a topic that is of interest to them, helps them to find something to write about from a personal perspective.

The first time I read through the assignment I had no idea what I would write about. It seemed to me that this paper was supposed to be about a social issue. I didn't consider myself a social activist so I had no idea what to write about. I decided to call my mom … We began to talk about the topic of education. This is something that she feels very strongly about and has transferred this passion to me. I started writing down some of the problems with education. Then I wrote down ways that I could support these ideas. These consisted of facts and life experiences. This part of the writing process was very unorganized because I was writing down points as my mom and I talked about them. After getting off the phone with her I reorganized my thoughts into a bubble map. This helped me isolate the ideas and find places where I would need to come up with more support.

Now that my ideas were organized it was fairly easy to write my paper. The first draft I wrote I did so without stopping. The support I used to back up my ideas was based entirely on my own experiences. When I finished writing the first draft I went back through the paper and found places where it would be helpful to include factual evidence. After the places for additions were identified I gathered the facts I needed and added them to the paper. Once this was done, my paper met the length requirement and I had run out of things to say. When editing I focused on refining my phrases and removing grammatical errors.

I think that this paper taught me how important the pre-writing process is. I found that the more organized I was before I began writing my paper, the easier it was to write. I was able to transition more effectively because I prearranged the order that I would present my points. Overall, the writing process went much smoother for this paper because of the additional planning I did.

Student Sample #3

This student wrote about the importance of social activism in general, through his experience working for the Smile Foundation in India. His reflection is personal, and makes strong connections between course readings, his experience, and reflecting on why all of that is important to share with his readers.

During the writing process I would often think back to the days when I used to serve as a volunteer in the Smile Foundation, a non-profit that helped provide education to the poor and needy in the streets of India. This was mainly due to the nature of the topic that I was discussing in this essay. I viewed the assignment of 'Social Engagement/Activism' from the stance of charities and I leveraged my prior experience in this field. I planned to use many statistical data files as well as imagery to further bolster my point, initially. However, I was unable to do so as I deviated from my initial focus which was on economics and the dwindling employment rates. Instead, I decided to divert my attention towards historical evidence and events that mirrored the contemporary financial and economic times.

To shed more light on what activism meant and its modern day interpretation, I quoted and referenced works of great political leaders who acted bravely for the benefit of society. These leaders include Martin Luther King Jr. and his fight for Civil Rights for all African-American people. I also used examples from Frederick Douglass's memoirs to complement King's instances of struggle for both his own identity and for the welfare of his community. Finally, I used samples from Jonathan Kozol's Amazing Grace to bring the economics side of things into my essay. I tried to invoke the same sympathy with the readers as he did with his book.

Finally, I felt my essay was a nice amalgamation of what I have learnt during the last few weeks of my writing course. I have tried to include an adequate number of pictures and graphs to depict my point and to keep the reader entertained with some visual stimulation. By writing this essay I can see how far I have come by taking this course. I was able to write this assignment more fluidly without having to keep thinking of new ideas and topics. My vocabulary has also greatly improved by continuously writing essays throughout the semester. I hope that this learning process continues throughout my life and I can keep writing critically and analytically to improve myself and my audience.

IMPLICATIONS

The use of new media, combined with readings about community and culture, and navigated through blog reflection writing and the construction of the final e-portfolio, encouraged my students to have the confidence and to build the resources to be active, community oriented, and engaged citizens in the world. Scaffolding ideas, topics, and assignments helped students develop thinking and practical skills while also constructing active portfolios of their own work that they could save or use further after the semester ended. It seems clear that introducing students to new ways of using media can have enormously beneficial consequences. Students are already involved with media, and the final e-portfolio assignment helped them to navigate that relationship in more critical ways.

After leading students through the process of setting up blogs and turning those into whole portfolios, I more firmly believe there is no turning back to earlier ways of teaching. The class framed around issues of community and citizenship—and including discussion of social media and other contemporary technology topics—seemed to logically include public internet writing in the end. During the semester we read from articles posted on the class WordPress site which included links to other articles and information. Students did most of their own writing in Word documents and then uploaded those to the class Canvas site. Additionally, adding their writing to the public blog space extended their audience beyond the instructor and encouraged students to think of themselves as writers and thinkers in a larger public context. After discussing contemporary social issues during the semester, students then situated themselves in relation to topics of their choosing to construct their final projects, making them more engaged in personalizing those projects.

This approach thus offered a complex rhetorical context, giving the students a more mature sense of purpose, audience, and personal ethos as the writers and designers of their own texts in the world. This also positioned them as active citizens in the world, thinking and acting through writing, and offering persuasive thought-pieces for public consumption. The course content, student involvement, and integration of the various teaching strategies showed the importance of pedagogy in relation to practice. A critical pedagogy helped to engage students in their own learning and making processes. The integration of media as subject of study (e.g. class discussion of social media) as well as a tool for the construction of the final portfolio projects reiterated in practice what the theories outlined above described. Students benefited from active participation as well as became, to some degree, more practiced users of internet technologies across various modes of reading and writing. Development of media savvy and practical skills generally benefited rather than resulted in negative consequences for students.

CONCLUSION

In *The Rise of Writing*, Deborah Brandt (2014) explains how people are spending more of their work-day time communicating through writing, and that workers are increasingly expected to write in a variety of forms and media on a daily basis. As she explains:

While writing has always been used for work, more and more people are now involved in it and spend more time at it. Writing as a dominant form of labor means that for the first time in the history of mass literacy, writing has become a major form of mass literate experience. So rapacious are the production pressures on writing, in fact, that they are redefining reading, as people increasingly read from the posture of the writing, from inside acts of writing, as they respond to others, research, edit, or review other people's writing or search for styles or approaches to borrow and use in their own writing. (p. 17)

Giving students the tools to develop the kinds of skills outlined by Brandt will assist them in moving through their work as students, and eventually as professionals, in a highly mediated world. Reading and writing strategies are continually in process, and as writing teachers we are in a good position to help students build awareness and technical capabilities. These skills and technologies, however, should also be considered within a larger cultural context in which critical thinking and analysis play crucial roles.

Stuart Hall describes "culture" not as a set of things but as "a set of practices." This means that "culture is concerned with the production and the exchange of meanings … between the members of a society or group" (p. 2). People contextualized within the same or similar cultural contexts may then "interpret the world in roughly the same ways and can express themselves, their thoughts and feelings about the world, in ways which will be understood by each other." This is how meaning is produced and circulated, and in turn, these similarities in ways of meaning-making propagate and maintain culture. As Hall further explains, "meaning is constantly being produced and exchanged in every personal and social interaction in which we take part. In a sense, this is the most privileged, though often most neglected, site of culture and meaning." It is also important to consider how culture is "produced in a variety of different *media*; especially … in the modern mass media, the means of global communication, by complex technologies, which circulate meanings between different cultures on a scale and with a speed hitherto unknown in history" (p. 3). Invention of new media, and the quickly changing uses of and relationships with media, affect our responsibilities as teachers, students, citizens, and participants in this larger cultural context. Reading, writing, and critical thinking have taken on new forms and morphed into processes that are similar to, and yet different from, those of the past.

But these are not things I can simply *tell* my students. I have learned that students learn best when they make and construct meaning on their own terms. I can set up the structure and context, and then I can facilitate their practices of engagement. This is what Donaldson (2014) refers to as "authorship learning":

The core elements of authorship learning include multiple senses of authorship, including students authoring their creations, students authoring their own meanings and understandings, students engaging in self-authorship, and broader public authorship … Other key aspects of authorship learning include student ownership of learning, authentic audiences, and metacognitive practices. These aspects emerge from research and the experience of educators: students learn best when they construct their own meaning. This is facilitated most powerfully through a process of having them construct meaningful physical or digital things in the real world which are intended for a real audience, and these artifacts are constructed in collaboration with others. (para. 11)

The move from writing on paper with an individual instructor as audience, to writing for a larger audience of peers and a public audience online, models the potential for a democratic, community oriented, critical literacy in practice. As Berlin (2003) asserts, "literacy enables the individual to understand that the conditions of experience are made by human agents and thus can be remade by human agents. Furthermore, this making and remaking take place in communities, in social collections" (p. 110). The democratic classroom can model this social space, provide students the opportunity to develop writing skills, and encourage them to become critically literate in regard to how individuals are shaped by, and can shape, culture. The writing classroom in the 21st Century can thus give students access to the practices that will enable them to be collaborative and community-oriented citizens in a technologically complex world.

REFERENCES

Ahmed, L. (2014). Confessions of a teenage activist. Retrieved from https://lemeesahmed.wordpress.com/

Alexander, J., & Rhodes, J. (2014). *On multimodality: New media in composition studies*. Urbana: National Council of Teachers of English.

Arola, K., Sheppard, J., & Ball, C. E. (2014). *Writer/designer: A guide to making multimodal projects*. MacMillan Education.

Bauerlein, M. (2011). *The digital divide: arguments for and Against Facebook, Google, texting, and the Age of Social Networking*. USA: Archer Perigee, Penguin Books.

Baughman, D., & Siegel, M. (Producers), & Baughman, D. & O'Hara, J. (Directors). (2010). *Bhutto* [Motion Picture]. USA: First Run Features.

Berlin, J. (2003). *Rhetorics, poetics, and cultures*. West Lafayette, IN: Parlor Press.

Boggs, G. L., & Kurashige, S. (2012). *The next American revolution*. Berkeley: University of California Press.

Brandt, D. (2014). *The Rise of Writing: Redefining Mass Literacy*. Cambridge: Cambridge UP.

Chen, H. L. (2009). *Electronic portfolios 2.0*. Sterling, VA: Stylus Publishing.

Darling, J. (2015). Community and citizenship in the computer classroom. *Hybrid Pedagogy*. Retrieved from http://www.digitalpedagogylab.com/hybridped/community-and-citizenship-in-the-computer-classroom/

Donaldson, J. (2014). The maker movement and the rebirth of constructionism. *Hybrid Pedagogy*. Retrieved from http://www.hybridpedagogy.com/journal/constructionism-reborn/

Douglass, F. (1898). From narrative of the life of Frederick Douglass, an American slave. In L. Jacobis Editor (Ed.), A world of ideas (pp. 327-340). Boston: Bedford/St. Martin's.

Elbow, P. (1981). *Writing with power, writing without teachers*. Oxford: Oxford UP.

Ellis, K. (2014). Civic engagement. Retrieved from http://kristinaellisfinalproject.blogspot.com/

Emig, J. (1971). *The composing process of twelfth graders*. NCTE Press.

Emig, J. (1983). *The web of meaning*. UK: Heinemann Educational Books.

Flower, L. (2008). *Community literacy and the rhetoric of public engagement*. Carbondale: Southern Illinois UP.

Freire, P. (2000). *Pedagogy of the oppressed*. UK: Bloomsbury Academic.

Hall, S. (1997). *Representation: cultural representations and signifying practices*. Los Angeles: SAGE Publications.

Jacobis, L. (Ed.). (2013). *A world of ideas. Boston*. Bedford: St. Martin's.

Keengwe, J., & Onchwari, G. (2011). Fostering meaningful student learning through constructivist pedagogy and technology integration. *International Journal of Information and Communication Technology Education*, 7(4).

Keengwe, J., Onchwari, G., & Agamba, J. (2014, December). Promoting effective e-learning practices through the constructivist pedagogy. *Education and Information Technologies*, 19(4), 887–898. doi:10.1007/s10639-013-9260-1

King, M., Jr. (1963). Letter from Birmingham jail. In L. Jacobis (Ed.), A world of ideas (pp. 375-392). Boston: Bedford/St. Martin's.

Loeb, P. (Ed.). (2004). *The impossible will take a little while*. New York: Basic Books.

Loeb, P. (2010). Soul of a citizen (new and revised edition). New York: St. Martin's Press.

Lutkewitte, C. (Ed.). (2014). *Multimodal composition: a critical sourcebook. Boston*. Bedford: St. Martin's.

Miller, C., & Shepherd, D. (2004). Blogging as social action: A genre analysis of the weblog. University of Minnesota. Retrieved from http://www.webcitation.org/5j9YtAGiO

Miller, C., & Shepherd, D. (2009). Questions for genre theory from the blogosphere. In J. Giltrow & D. Stein (Eds.), *Genres in the Internet: Issues in the theory of genre*. Amsterdam: John Benjamin's Publishing. doi:10.1075/pbns.188.11mil

Moffett, J., & Wager, B. (1991). *Student-centered language arts, K-12*. Portsmouth: Heinemann.

New London Group. (2014). From a pedagogy of multiliteracies: designing social futures. In C. Lutkewitte, (Ed.), Multimodal composition: a critical sourcebook (pp. 193-210). Boston: Bedford St. Martin's.

Palmeri, J. (2012). *Remixing composition: A history of multimodal writing pedagogy*. Carbondale: Southern Illinois UP.

Perrin, A. (2015). Social media usage: 2005-2015. *Pew Research Center*. Retrieved from http://www.pewinternet.org/2015/10/08/social-networking-usage-2005-2015/

Rushkoff. (2010). *Program or be programmed: Ten commands for a digital age*. Berkeley: Soft Scull Press.

Social Networking Fact Sheet. (2014). *Pew Research Center*. Retrieved from http://www.pewinternet.org/fact-sheets/social-networking-fact-sheet/

Turkle, S. (2012). *Alone together*. New York: Basic Books.

Wysocki, A. F. (2004). *Writing new media*. Utah State UP.

Yancey, K., Robertson, L., & Taczak, K. (2014). *Writing across contexts: Transfer, composition, and sites of writing*. Boulder, CO: Utah State University Press.

Section 2
Exploring Multi–Digital Media in the Writing Classroom

In this section, authors discuss how Tumblr, Instagram, Podbean, and Twitter help to promote "Remix Writing," which mirrors the multimodal activities that permeate present rhetoric & composition discourse.

Chapter 5
This Is the Remix:
Remediating Pedagogy Practices

Shannon Butts
University of Florida, USA

ABSTRACT

Remix, as a pedagogical style and teaching method, reframes foundational elements of writing instruction and broadens the traditional practice of writing to include 21st century compositional methods and technological forms. Through Remix Writing, students and instructors learn to compose a networked system of writing that diffuses assumed hierarchies and promotes associative thinking across diverse ecologies of media. We are always already associative thinkers. We build connections to understand, compare, reject, and relate. The digital writing environment offers an assemblage of associations, available in an instant. By disassembling and then reassembling texts, writers can learn to analyze influences and situate works in a web of connections. Students not only write critically about objects of study, but also have the opportunity to produce original work in various styles and media. In mapping the remix process as well as the purpose of each composition, students are able to identify key elements of argument, style, and effective communication – taking ownership of their own writing.

INTRODUCTION

Remix is not a new idea. Art, music, and writing have a long history of "cut-up" techniques, remix, and sampling from William Buroughs and Marcel Duchamp to Led Zepplin and Grandmaster Flash. Copying, recycling, adapting, and appropriating have all helped create art, culture, technology, and texts. In music, recording equipment and sound machines alter tempo, tone, instrumentation, intensity, and style to create something new – all while using common notes and chords. In writing, new media formats and technologies alter common composition methods for authoring texts and communicating ideas. As Mickey Hess (2006) notes, "Like academic writing, hip-hop sampling requires more than cutting and pasting existing material. Sampling, at its best, uses sources to create new meaning" (p. 281).

The free market economy of Internet information makes untold amounts of data available to users, not just as read-only texts, but data available for consumption, production, remix, and circulation. While

DOI: 10.4018/978-1-5225-0562-4.ch005

the term 'remix' may originate with musical composition and hip-hop sampling, the act and ideas of remix inhabit all forms of writing and design, from fashion appropriating emerging trends and language evolving signs and signifiers, to technology tweeks of code that blur the lines between remix, invention, and innovation.[1] Even people can be considered genetic remixes of family traits and cultural experiences. Remix as a combinatorial generative device is encoded in evolutionary biology and culture, a code that has only grown in size and variation with the proliferation of digital media.

Remix already describes the writing process. Authors rewrite and revise all the time. Multimedia writing uses the skills of remix to both transform existing texts and also create new ones. The particular arrangement of notes, images, or words matters, but so does the rearrangement, adaptation, and remix of key ingredients or common ideas. As many writing classrooms move to incorporate emerging technology and modalities, remix offers a framework for composition that reworks pedagogical aims through everyday digital practices.

Writing Departments commonly ask students to demonstrate mastery in various styles, situations, or contexts without acknowledging the routine use of social media as a form of writing. Instead, word counts and page numbers often define "successful" writing and establish requirements for composition curricula. Educators want students to 'write more,' but many first-year writing classes pick and choose what counts as writing while lamenting the sorry state of literacy today. Students are writing, prolifically, but the writing process has evolved beyond traditional page-based formats. According to the 2014 Writing Program Administrators Outcomes Statement "[s]ucessful writers understand, analyze, and negotiate conventions for purpose, audience, and genre, understanding that genres evolve in response to change in material conditions and composing technologies" ("WPA Outcomes," 2014, p. 3). Students successfully participate in a vast web of composition across multimodal platforms: Twitter posts, Facebook status updates, Instagram photos, Youtube mashups, Vine videos, and messaging programs, which each engage rhetorical skills conventionally taught and typically valued in academia. Acknowledging social media in the classroom empowers students to take ownership of their writing, all forms of writing, and encourages learners to *remix* conventional perspectives on authorship, criticism, and what defines writing.

Using Remix Writing as a framework, this chapter confronts the traditional limits of page-based pedagogy by offering multimedia strategies to remix composition and supplement teaching.[2] Working with a tautology of second-hand ideas alongside an overview of classroom assignments, I explain the benefits of remixing and remediating conventional rhetorical methods through web applications and alternative technologies such as *Podbean, Instagram,* and *Twitter.* Through Remix Writing, words, images, platforms, and technologies all become data available for update, shuffle, repurpose, and replay.

THEORETICAL FRAMEWORK

Writing as Remix

Remix centers on hybridity, a state of culture always already in play. Literacy and media scholars Michele Knobel and Colin Lankshear (2008) define remix as "taking cultural artifacts and combining and manipulating them into new kinds of creative blends" (p. 22). Kirby Ferguson (2012), documentarian and author of the influential video series 'Everything is a Remix,' offers an even more simple equation:

Remix = Copy + Transform + Combine.

Figure 1. Remix equation
Adapted from Kirby Ferguson's Everything is a Remix Video Series.

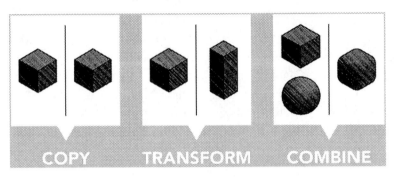

Remix centers on the creation of a new text, not merely copying, but dividing elements into identifiable parts and then transforming compositional elements to craft a new meaning (see Figure 1). In order to transform and recombine, remixers must first understand the parts to create a new whole.

People exist in a web of associations assembled by the way we experience and interpret the world.[3] In a global "network society," we sift through influences and artifacts that have become a part of our culture, memories, and experiences, encoded in the world around us and often mediated through digital technologies (Castells, 2009). As we write new meanings for ourselves, we pull from a list of recognizable signs and symbols. The Oxford English Dictionary adds new words every year built from the foundations of existing language, using pieces combined or transformed to fit a different purpose or describe a new situation. 'Unfriend' emerged from a Facebook application, 'selfie stick' from a social media adaptation, 'hangry' from a physical combination of feelings, and 'slow food' from a cultural movement. Evening existing words like 'tweet' now have a new meaning because of technologies authoring new communication forms. And each year, companies release 'new' technology that builds on previous versions of the same product – remixed versions of the iPhone 5, 5s, 6, Apple Watch, etc.

However, remix occurs beyond the corporate level and outside of institutional authority. Individual media users create millions of mashup videos and mixed media projects for a variety of rhetorical purposes - entertainment, political parody, and advertisement, to name a few. Technology is changing the way audiences understand and access various forms of information, in turn facilitating new forms of authorship, authority, and commentary. Multiple media theorists and writing scholars advocate for the importance of remix as a frame for writing and many consider remix one of the most significant practices for composition (Burwell, 2013; Lessig, 2008; Manovich, 2005; Navas, 2012). In 2008, Creative Commons advocate Laurence Lessig even argued that remix is a form of writing necessary for art and commerce to thrive in the networked digital age. Remixes pick apart the texts we consume daily and help facilitate new kinds of representations while also helping users recognize how 140 characters and concepts of 'un-friending' transforms the way we communicate and compose.

The point—remix happens all the time, all around us. We are always already remix writing. The cultural production of new remix texts occurs across communities as individuals use the tools around them and the encoded knowledge of existing media to create new combinations. Remix offers a way of thinking about the breakdown of texts, the sampling and transformation of pieces to create a new whole, a new text with a specific purpose and audience. Media theorist Eduardo Navas (2012) extends the definition of remix writing and argues that "remix is a binder—a cultural glue. . . Remix is more like a virus that has mutated into different forms according to the needs of particular cultures" (p. 15). The participatory aspect of media circulation often transforms, repurposes, or distorts information as it passes through diverse communities. Remix not only writes texts through simple combination, but also acts as a connective tissue, filling in gaps between existing texts to author new meaning. By disassembling and then reassembling media texts, remixers are able to make largely invisible messages visible—learning how to map associations and situate texts in a web of connections. So perhaps scholar Paul Miller (2008)—aka DJ Spooky—says it best when he claims that remix helps turn analog writing into that which is decidedly digital.

Remixing in the Classroom

Pedagogically, remix subverts an endgame style of learning that ticks a checklist of skills. Instead, Remix Writing interrogates mastery by inviting students to re-envision writing as an ongoing skill and continuous practice. As DeVoss and Ridolfo (2009) note, teachers have always encouraged students to remix their own work through revision – copying, pasting, merging, and reorganizing words and sentences to refine their own texts and create a better, more cohesive pieces of writing. Instead of passing notes in class, our students are live tweeting, posting status updates, and taking selfies. And while some may see social media as a disruption to conventional writing, I offer a way to reframe the disruption, to remix and reuse it for instructional purposes.

Remixing composition in writing classrooms allows us to re-frame the value system of texts and push back against the traditional hierarchy of originality and institutional authority. Writing Departments often list aims such as 'to understand and demonstrate various styles, situations, or contexts of writing' and to 'demonstrate mastery' in several styles or forms. However, Johndan Johnson-Eilola and Stuart A. Selber (2007) suggest that prioritizing textual authority through citations and plagiarism can create a separation between work studied and work created. Such separation can imply a hierarchy in terms of the writing process and what might be considered 'derivative' works. Mickey Hess echoes this concern and argues, "to equate sampling with plagiarism ignores the ways that sampling transforms, critiques, and responds to sources" (p. 282). If writing classrooms should "use composition processes and tools as a means to discover and reconsider ideas," then the remix writing process repositions students as already skillful writers who can interrogate texts and create new meaning ("WPA Outcomes, 2014, p. 2).

Additionally, critical pedagogy scholar James Berlin (1996) calls for a writing classroom that resists indoctrinating a particular worldview by teaching students to "negotiate and resist semiotically enforced cultural codes" (p.121). While students need to understand how to read and write within academic discourses, remixing in a critical classroom helps students become active agents of social change—producers as well as consumers, writers who can breakdown arguments and understand the multiple meanings of texts in a variety of environments. As social media writers, students are already blurring the distinction between consumer and producer. By authoring as well as circulating texts, writers become a node in the network of associative meanings and compose texts with an active awareness of influences. Remix becomes a hub for writing and a filter through which to analyze ideas and create new texts, resist traditional hierarchies, and focus on the writing process as an ever growing web of connections, in and outside the classroom.

METHODOLOGY AND APPLICATION

The Art of Form and Style: Remix Writing Assignments

I first taught a Remix Writing course as a University of Florida ENC 1131: *Writing Thru Media* class. Based on theories of Roland Barthes, the introductory writing course works to meld the divide between traditional literacy and post-literacy, or electracy (digital literacy), by positioning the students as both consumers and makers of new media. Writing becomes an umbrella term that explores the production of meaning by tracing the style, form, content, persuasive appeal, and technology involved in the composition process.

The course started with a podcast assignment focusing on sound and style, then moved to a film analysis that introduced components of visual rhetoric, and concluded with a remediation project emphasizing media form and adaptation. Additionally, students were periodically required to post to a discussion blog reflecting on assignments and commenting on various elements of remix writing. Each remix writing assignment coupled different forms of media with a specific agenda, progressively building skills as in any writing course, but used video, sound, digital media, images, and traditional text based writing as objects of study and methods of response.

In the following section, I offer suggestions for how to integrate social media in the classroom through two multimodal remix writing assignments. Alongside a discussion of each assignment are the assignment title, prompt, as well as guides for the main components and how to model them in class. Each assignment relies on different forms of media to teach basic writing and rhetorical analysis skills with an emphasis on student agency and participation.

Assignment #1: Podcasts - Understanding Style and Structure

Prompt: You will work with a partner or group to create a podcast in the style of another podcast. The assignment is an exercise in imitation and adaptation. Choose a podcast available to the public and diagnose the content, structure, and key elements through a style analysis. Then create your own podcast by imitating the style of the analyzed podcast.

The key to the assignment is to close read and make sense of the original text. Diagram the structure, analyze the elements, and work to adapt your imitation to best represent the character of the original. You should see your podcast as an episode of the original series—able to fit in the archive and match the other episodes. You will be responsible for conceiving, researching, scripting, recording, and editing your own podcast. In addition, you will compose a rhetorical analysis arguing for the accuracy of your imitation. Remember to document specific elements and use evidence to support your claims. (4-5 weeks to complete)

You will turn in:

1. **Style Analysis:** A breakdown of podcast elements (Due week 2).
2. **Discussion Post:** 500-word analysis of podcast (Due week 3).
3. **A 10-12 Minute Podcast:** An imitation of an original (Due week 4).
4. **Rhetorical Analysis:** An argument validating your imitation (Due week 4/5).

Beginning with sound and style, the Podcast assignment allows the students to strip away the visual and evaluate communication through orality and imitation. Social media often melds the lines between orality and writing, we type what we would say into a phone text or 'chat' with friends through messaging. Eliminating a visual text forces the students to articulate observations as we listened to example podcasts in class and compose original close reading/listening notes. Immediately students must create their own written texts and consider diverse methods of assessment. The character or 'ethos' of the Podcast as well as any format specifications for creating adaptive podcasts come from evaluating the original to understand style.

Imitation revolves around understanding the specific elements of style individual to each text. For example, when a comedian does a celebrity impression, the walk, speech, posture, or even general demeanor may change to reflect the individual style of the celebrity and prompt recognition. As students deconstruct and analyze Podcasts for specific elements, they begin to understand the context as well as the constraints of the form. The Podcast assignment hinges on skills rhetorical analysis, understanding purpose and style. The character of a piece is not just the content, but who it was made for and how – understanding the parts and the whole to recognize what a text does and how. In the next few sections, I break down the graded Podcast components as parts and offer strategies for teaching podcast remixes as a whole (feel free to copy, transform, and combine for your classroom).

1. Choose a Podcast and Model a Style Analysis

I introduce the Podcast assignment by listening and close reading popular podcast episodes in class. NPR, Podbean, Stitcher, ITunes, and other hosting sites have free Podcasts categorized by genre and available for download. *Wait, Wait, Don't Tell Me*, a humorous news quiz show and weekly NPR podcast, serves as a great classroom example.

Before listening, I ask the students to pay attention to the production and content of the broadcast:

- What are the first sounds you hear?
- Is the production live or in a closed studio?
- Is there an introduction – how long is it?
- How many different voices do you hear?
- What else fills the broadcast – any music, sound effects, silence?
- Is the format divided into sections?
- If so, do any sections repeat and how many sections for how long?
- Is the podcast serious, funny? How can you tell?

I usually start the discussion with a few questions and then encourage students to think about the many elements involved in production. We write questions on the board and try to create a large list, asking each student to contribute a close reading question. While the list might seem long, the broad coverage shows students how many elements authors and producers of texts must consider – a valuable lesson in close reading any type of text. In addition, the questions provide a great starting point for groups as they begin to evaluate podcasts on their own for imitation.

As the class listens to the podcast, I ask students to write down key elements of the production and content like they would in a log—specific details of what happens when. If the opening has an instrumental piano theme song that last four seconds and then fades out to an announcer, then students would document the time and detail the action. Once we finish listening to the podcast as a class, we collectively compile a working document of podcast features and create a sample style analysis through class observations. You can formulate a more specific set of guidelines for the assignment depending on the needs of your students, but I generally ask for 30 style observations to be turned in evaluating the original podcast – basic notes describing the imitated text. The style analysis then becomes a blueprint for creating an imitation and part of the graded criteria for evaluating how well students close read and adapt style elements.

For example, a *Wait, Wait Don't Tell Me* episode begins with theme music and an announcer introducing the host, Peter Segal, as well as the featured quiz panelists for the episode. Peter then asks each player a current event question. Since the podcast focuses on real-life stories based in humor, many of the questions are satiric and highlight funny quotes or awkward incidents from the last week's news. By the conclusion of the episode, *Wait, Wait* has aired diverse segments involving call-in players from the broadcast audience, conducted an interview with a celebrity who plays a game called "Not My Job," and closes with a lightning round of panelist questions to determine who wins for the week. Student observations would detail this format, but also describe the length of each segment, the character of panelists, the type of music included, any voice or tone modulations, and anything else that might help the class understand individual style components of the media. In essence, students gather sound evidence from the episode, diagraming the structure and analyzing elements to build a list of criteria for imitation.

Remix writing emphasizes parts, combinations, and purpose, often, in that order. Breaking down a podcast and constructing a style analysis helps students focus on the evidence actually present in the object of study instead of starting with grand theories or vague generalizations. Too often writing teachers receive argument analysis papers that begin something like: 'Throughout time, argument has persuaded people.' Several more sentences follow that generalize the importance of argument or how persuasion can change the world and, hopefully, at some point, the writer narrows to make a thesis claim about a specific text. By starting with listening, note taking, annotation, and observation, students come to understand writing as a process that can build from evidence to analysis in order to craft a specific, well-reasoned theory about the text.

2. Discussion Post

The discussion post is an opportunity for students to start creating an argument out of the style analysis. Students compose a 500-word reflection detailing what style points they are remixing to persuade the listener that the imitation version is a good copy or adaptation. For each point, writers focus on how the style element described represents the character of their chosen podcast—emphasizing specific word choice and phrasing to carefully dissect key elements. The discussion post should have a thesis that students use in the larger rhetorical paper and at least one detailed point of analysis.

Working from evidence to analysis to build theories also refines synthesis skills. Once students have evidence, they can move from taking notes to grouping style points into categories and craft nuanced arguments about the character of the podcast, synthesizing information to support claims. For example, in the Podcast Assignment students work like crime scene detectives to break down the text into pieces of evidence, documenting each element in detail with the style analysis. Then, students can synthesize information and propose a profile for the podcast, using specific evidence to back up a claim (see Figure 2).

The discussion post pushes students to connect and explain observations, formulating claims about process and adaptation that can later build towards the final component of rhetorical analysis. In build-

Figure 2. Discussion excerpt (screenshot)

Sofia Luna
May 23, 2015

Not Too Deep, hosted by Grace Helbig, is a comedy podcast that focuses on not having thoughtful and informational conversations with her weekly guests. Instead, she guides the podcast with witty and random questions about a variety of topics and her guests respond accordingly. The podcast is divided into two segments; the first segment is composed of questions created by Helbig and the second segment involves the listeners asking a question on Twitter. To reproduce the podcast, I decided to emphasize on the type of questions asked and her comedy style by imitating particular phrases and her ways of speaking. The nonsensical nature of the questions and a hesitant style of speech are the most important characteristics of the podcast and the elements that are crucial for emulation.

ing a discussion post from the style analysis, the 'parts,' students learn to construct arguments about the purpose, argument, or character of a text from the ground up, adding parts to interpret and argue a whole.

3. Create Content and Adaptation

Podcasts in the public sphere vary in length and many last the span of an hour. Requiring students to compose a 10-12-minute imitation podcast also invites students to analyze and pick parts that best represent the original text—even if that means adapting formats by remixing elements. Often, students have to make choices about content and create more of a 'mini-episode' instead of a full-blown imitation. For example, a student working with *Wait, Wait Don't Tell Me* would have to imitate a 44-minute podcast in 10-12 minutes. The writer must decide which elements of style to imitate, abridge, or remix in order to accurately adapt the original podcast, understanding how to evaluate, synthesize, and adapt a text for a specific purpose. Composing a convincing imitation means identifying the key qualities of the original podcast and adapting elements for an abbreviated version.

In addition, students must create content appropriate to the character of the podcast series. One student, Stephani Harrison, inspired by the popular 2014 *Serial* podcast, decided to compose an imitation mini-episode based on the HBO series *Game of Thrones* (see Figure 3).

The original podcast *Serial* features Sarah Koenig, a journalist investigating the story of Adnan Syed, a teen convicted of killing his girlfriend in 1999. Each episode runs over an hour and features distinctive theme music, phone calls from a prison, interviews with witnesses, and Sarah Koenig's questioning tone of voice. The *Serial* student adaptation, titled *Game of Serial*, investigates the murder of King Joffrey Baratheon from *Game of Thrones* by Tyrion Lannister and includes copycat theme music, phone calls from King's Landing prison, interviews with witnesses, and a deliberately questioning tone of voice – all in 10 minutes. Figure 4 is an excerpt of Stefani's discussion post detailing her analysis of the original Serial podcast as well as how she creates the *Game of Serial* podcast adaptation.

Although the content differed, the adaptation was convincing because the student copied the key features that best told the story of an accused criminal and used skills of rhetorical analysis - evaluation, synthesis, and adaptation - to remix Serial source material with her own creative content (see Figure 4).

Figure 3. Game of Serial remix (screenshot used under fair use)

Figure 4. Discussion post analysis 5

Stefani Harrison

May 23, 2015

My podcast is a remix from Serial, a podcast that challenges the audience to analyze and formulate their own perspective on a real-life criminal case based on the information Sarah Koenig presents in a 12-episode season. My remixed version attempts to imitate the theme and style of Serial in a 10-minute podcast. Serial convinces the audience of its authenticity through the use of interview recordings, evidence of Koenig's research, and the relaxed but dynamic tone of Koenig's voice.

Pursuing a real-life criminal case requires a lot of research, dedication, and time. As a college student, I could not hope to dedicate myself to a story as Koenig had. Instead, I represented Serial with a case from fiction. As a "Game of Thrones" fan, I decided to cover the case against Tyrian Lannister after his trial for the murder of King Joffrey Baratheon. Since "Game of Thrones" is a work of fiction, I had my friend voice multiple characters to function as interviewed recordings in my podcast. His knowledge of the show greatly helped to produce recordings in the tones of the characters. I included numerous interview recording similar in style to Koenig's interviews to imitate Serial to the best of my ability. Most of the time in Serial, you cannot hear Koenig in the recording, but instead she refers to the recordings or talks over them from what sounds like her studio. I did the same for my interview recordings. For example, when Koenig talked to Adnan Syed he sounded choppy because it was recorded off a telephone, so when I interviewed Tyrian Lannister I tried to achieve the same effect.

4. Rhetorical Analysis

The Rhetorical Analysis component works more like a traditional argumentative paper except students argue for the quality of their own work. With a clear thesis and supported claims, students compose a persuasive argument for the accuracy of their podcast remix and detail key elements of style observed and imitated as evidence. The analysis should be 1000 words and organized into essay form with intro, body, and conclusion paragraphs. Student can choose which elements to write about, but the rhetorical analysis is graded on clarity, organization, tone, language, use of evidence, and persuasive appeal. The rhetorical analysis pushes students to see the connections throughout the Podcast assignment – how the process of writing works across different media forms and which rhetorical practices remain the same despite medium differences. Examining media making through the remix lens, students not only analyze, but also make and reflect on the entire project. The rhetorical analysis combines the writing skills employed throughout the multimodal podcast assignment - evaluation, analysis, synthesis, creative composition, comparison, discussion, and adaptation – to culminate in a persuasive argument grounded in the rhetorical process.

Assignment #2: Remix as Remediation

Prompt: You will document a story or event through three different forms of media, Instagram, Twitter and a media of your choice, using both images and written accounts to remediate the same source content. The first text will be a photo essay, composed through Instagram. Once you finish your Instagram narrative, you will remediate the same event through Twitter posts. You will then choose a third form to remediate your content. In addition, you will also write a short rhetorical analysis essay in which you reflect critically upon the differences between media forms and the changes remediation and remix brought to each composition's meaning and method of communication. The assignment is an exercise in adaptation, understanding each format and how to best remix content and purpose through multimodal writing (5-6 weeks to complete).

You will turn in:

1. Instagram Narrative (40 posts – Due week 4).
2. Twitter Narrative (25 posts – Due week 4).
3. Third Remediation of Content (Due week 5).
4. Rhetorical Analysis (1200 words—Due week 6).

Building on many of the principles taught in the Podcast assignment that opens the semester, the Remix and Remediation final project challenges students to analyze, interpret, and compose across diverse forms of media. Again playing on imitation and adaptation, each remediation requires students to consider purpose, tone, format, and persuasive appeal in order to create content for a specific medium.

As mentioned, remix transforms existing parts to create a new text. Yet, sometimes the primary element of remix involves altering and adapting the media form. Jay Bolter and Richard Grusin (1999) define remediation as "the formal logic by which new media refashion prior media forms" (p. 273). But Bolter and Grusin (1999) are careful to note that while digital media has increased the production of remediated texts, media forms have been "commenting on, reproducing, and replacing each other" since at least the Renaissance (p. 55). Remediation exists as another type of remix that transforms through form and context. Remediating one story in three media helps students understand a different approach to remix while using the same 'copy+transform+combine' process. For example, narrating the same story of a family vacation could occur in 40 photos, 25 Twitter posts, and a blog—but 'copying' the story onto different platforms would transform the narrative or emphasize a different perspective due to changes in medium. Composing in a variety of social media formats encourages students to consider how the remix writing process transforms the 'parts and whole' depending on media and message.

1. Instagram Narrative

The Remix and Remediation project hinges on understanding different media and how to adapt a narrative across different platforms. Beginning with 40 Instagram posts, students compose a photo narrative by ordering a sequence of images to tell a clear story. Picking an appropriate Instagram narrative is key since the remediation story should remain somewhat consistent across several types of media. I recommend that students take photos with a camera or phone first, even take extra photos to see what works best, then work to select and organize the photos into a cohesive and clear story before officially posting to Instagram. Once posted, the Instagram component is complete. Each photo should be original and taken by the student at the time of the assigned project. The subject matter of the photo narrative, and the remediation project as a whole, depends on student interest. Often, students photo journal music festivals, chronicle a trip, document a football game, tell a brief love story, or report on a local news event (see Figure 5).

The Instagram interface allows hashtags and comments, but centers on the visual, providing users multiple filters and photo augmentation options in every post. Using the same filter, creating collages, or choosing specific photo angles can help convey messages in each picture and create cohesion throughout the photo narrative. Remix Writing student Victoria LaGreca chose to narrate a walk in the woods where she gets separated from her boyfriend and finds him by following a trail of marshmallows (See Figure 6).

Using perspective, framing, and one specific filter, Victoria codes the images with specific meaning, composing associations for the audience and building a narrative structure. Images that feature individu-

Figure 5. Collage of student Instagram narratives

Figure 6. Select images from Lost and Found-student Instagram narrative collage

als are taken from further away to signal a loneliness or isolation. In contrast, images where the couple is together use a light yellow filter and show hands held to signify unity and love (LaGreca, 2014).

The Instagram narrative does not have to depict a public place, dramatic story, or feature a distinctive style to work well for remediation. One student, Sarah Bullock, after finding an old recipe from her grandmother, decided to document making dinner for her parents using only family recipes. The Instagram feed started with faded photos of relatives past and recipe cards handed down, then moved to shopping for the meal, preparing dishes, setting a formal table, and enjoying food with family (see Figure 7).

The messages in Sarah's photos came through in her framing, order, and image composition. Allowing students to choose the Instagram narrative for remediation promotes many of the decision-making skills of prewriting and analysis. Composingthe remediation remixes requires understanding platforms, audience, organization, drafting, revision, and adaptation. Students must work with mixed media forms and evaluate key features of each to figure out how to best craft a narrative that copies, transforms, and recombines well.

Examining various image forms and narrative situations in class helps students understand the components of visual rhetoric that persuasively construct a clear narrative. In class, I reference *Time Magazine* photo essays, comic books, and graphic novels to discuss visual storytelling, creating a narrative through line, and how media can affect visual messages. Scott McCloud's *Understanding Comics (1993)*[4] offers great visual examples for defining how sequential images can form a cohesive narrative through a concept called closure (see Figure 8).

McCloud argues that missing elements in images or even the space between images in comics, much like the space between pictures in a photo narrative, break up images in time and space, but closure allows us to "connect these moments and mentally construct a continuous, unified reality" (p. 74). Although McCloud is writing about comics, applying his concepts to electronic media such as film, television, or Instagram shows students how we naturally 'close' moments of action between images and brings

Figure 7. "A Family Dinner" collage from Sarah Bullock Instagram narrative

Figure 8. Scott McCloud Understanding Comics p. 63
Image used under fair use provisions.

up the associations embedded in the way we compose texts as a whole (see Figure 9). Seeing how the parts create the whole reminds students that remixes can act as 'closure' as well, connective tissue that pulls together individual samples to create master narratives suited to a particular purpose or medium.

In conjunction, Allie Brosh's *Hyperbole and a Half* (2013) is a great example of remixing memories and media forms to depict an event. Her book compiles existing blog posts and previously unpublished

Figure 9. Scott McCloud Understanding Comics p.68
Image used under fair use provisions.

material to tell childhood stories in a graphic novel form. In each story, Brosh narrates a particular memory or moment and uses the program Paintbrush to create accompanying drawings with what she calls "a very precise crudeness" (Brosh, 2011).

The result is a simplistic style and tone that unites all her narratives and builds a comedic sensibility that translates across media (see Figure 10). Examining how Brosh remediates a consistent narrative from blog to traditional book helps students evaluate what kind of stories could work for their remediations. Using comparison and contrast methods, the class can make a list of narrative elements that remain consistent despite shifts in medium.

For example, *Hyperbole and a Half* illustrations remain in the same style and text acts as captions or explanations for each image, regardless of digital or print publication. However, in the shift from blog to book form, the audience experiences the narratives in a different order. Instead of clicking on a sidebar and ordering stories as the user wants, the book presents the individual narratives in a particular set order. Like the style analysis for the Podcast assignment, the comparison and contrast list helps students hone close reading skills by breaking down specific elements in each text. However, in comparing more than one text and across media forms, the evaluation adds considerations of authorial intention, representative images, audience reception, and adapting associations.

Figure 10. Home page of Brosh's hyperboleandahalf.com
Image used under fair use provisions.

Writing through visuals plays on an assemblage of signs and encoded associations engaged by the author, but often subject to the interpretation of the reader or the limits of a media form. The Instagram narrative has to understand and employ these associations to convey a message and initiate closure among images as well as across media platforms. Identifying the specific elements or associations necessary to convey a visual narrative helps writers see what can remain consistent and what can transform to remix a narrative through remediation.

2. Twitter Remediation

Once the Instagram Narrative is complete, students retell the same story in a series of 30 tweets. Reducing the number of posts from 40 Instagram photos to 30 tweets pushes remixers to again evaluate the key elements of the narrative and construct brief statements, 140 characters long, to describe a particular situation or feeling. Students must consider language, the posting format, networked hashtags, and the continuity of form in order to facilitate expression and argument.

Twitter is often referred to as a microblog – a short text media form similar to word of mouth communication. When Twitter came online in 2006, the platform connected users in a sort of status update forum. Many people expressed their sentiments or situation in a tweet and followed a set group of users to create a unique online community. However, Twitter now serves as business tool, a social media hub, and a spreadable media form (Jenkins, 2013).

Through the Twitter medium, participants have created new essay forms, new methods of circulation, and new aggregates of data beyond traditional paragraph text-based forms. Abbreviations, hyperlinks, hashtags, retweeting, and following create a networked archive of users and associations. The Twitter form may be brief, but the posting format invites a new connected continuity that augments traditional composition and publication.

To discuss the Twitter format and remediation, our class reviews and discusses Teju Cole's short story, 'Hafiz.' In 2014, Teju Cole, fiction author and prolific Twitter user, contacted his Twitter network and invited users to participate in a 'storytelling experiment.' Each contact received one sentence to post and Cole retweeted the entire community, 31 tweets, to publish his story (see Figure 11).

Cole's unique use of the Twitter medium and 'retweet' feature avoided traditional publication authorities to engage readers online in an everyday form of digital literacy. Retweeting plays on the 'viral' capability of sharing and linking, but also participates in what Henry Jenkins (2013) calls spreadable media. The networked reality of everyday communication is like a childhood game of *Telephone*, ideas change through sharing. Henry Jenkins' work with 'spreadable media' engages the viral and a sense of replication - but also acknowledges the participatory aspect of media circulation – a process that often transforms, repurposes, or distorts information as it passes through diverse communities. The Twitter community facilitated Cole's remix of a short story composition by playing on the combinatorial code of viral connectivity while transforming the publication and reception processes of creative works.

Just as remix can transform works by putting samples into a different context or comment on a work by remaking and reinterpreting a message, the Twitter remediation offers remix writers an opportunity to shift perspective or create new networks. Sarah Bullock, the student who documented a family dinner, chose to shift the message in her Twitter narrative by tweeting stories about each recipe alongside memories of making Southern food with her grandmother. Sarah's tweets remediate not only the communication of the initial narrative, but also remix associated memories through a new medium of net-

Figure 11. Screenshot of Teju Cole's Hafiz Twitter feed

worked associations. Now categorized with hashtags, her Twitter narration offers a new aggregate and context for her experience, a digital archive of memory.

3. ReReMediating: Choose Your Own Adventure

Students pick the third remediation and alter the argument to best fit the chosen form. In the past, students have composed songs, created blogs, written poetry, constructed Pinterest boards, and put together playlists with liner notes. The final remediation for "A Family Dinner" used a Pinterest board to organize and pin 60 traditional Southern recipes and compose an archive similar to the family cookbook (see Figure 12). Meanwhile UF student Stefani Harrison chose to remediate the narration of an *Urban Safari* by coding a blog, writing with numbers, images, and words to describe a wildlife walk through a nearby city (see Figure 13).

Regardless of the third media form, the students engage remix writing through remediation and continue to evaluate methods, means, and messages in arguments. The form doesn't really matter and that is the point – composition occurs all the time and, just like remix is a cultural glue that always already builds the world around us, writing and argument do the same. Writing is ubiquitous, regardless of media. Teaching students to write through and in spite of form cultivates critical thinkers, persuasive writers, and successful communicators.

4. Rhetorical Analysis

The Remix and Remediation rhetorical analysis works as it does in the Podcast assignment. Using their work as evidence, writers organize an essay with a specific thesis and supported claims about how remix as remediation affected the analysis, production, and reception of each text. The analysis should be 1200

Figure 12. Screenshot of Pinterest archive by Sarah Bullock

Figure 13. Urban safari

words with a clear thesis and intro, body, and conclusion paragraphs and should detail key elements of narration and demonstrate how each new media form copied, transformed, and recombined to remix the narrative. Students can choose which elements to write about, but are evaluated on the effectiveness of their clarity, organization, tone, language, use of evidence, and persuasive argument. Examining media re-making through the remix lens helps students not only analyze, but also make and reflect on the entire project. While the instructor might determine the final grade for the project, the rhetorical analysis offers the remix author some authority in the evaluation process. The student becomes part of the evaluation and acts as consumer, producer, and reviewer for the text as a whole. The rhetorical analysis combines the writing skills employed throughout the entire course and across different formats, challenging students to evaluate their role as makers of media and hubs for an already networked system of associative writing.

RESULTS AND CONCLUSION OF REMIX WRITING

Before the *Remix Writing Thru Media* course, many of my previous introductory writing courses primarily focused on analyzing and writing traditional essays. Courses such as ENG 1001, ENC 1101, ENC 1102, and even Business Writing or Writing About (insert discipline here) classes emphasized 'academic writing and research' and 'writing in the professional domain,' which most often translates to paper and page-based formats. Technology and social media were used in lessons or to provide examples, but students delivered work written in Microsoft Word with specific word counts and page numbers.

To be fair, the pedagogical aims of each course did not exclude social media or multimedia composition; however, in presenting a particular methodology for understanding academic or professional writing the university, college, or course *implies* a hierarchy of writing for learning specific skills. Students absolutely need to learn how to write to different audiences and understand what is and is not appropriate for academic genres. Using remix writing can help students meet writing program guidelines and "understand why genre conventions for structure, paragraphing, tone and mechanics vary" or how to "learn common formats and/or design features for different kinds of texts" ("WPA Outcomes," 2014, p. 3). Remix writing by nature is associative and adaptive. My goal is not to undermine page-based writing, but instead to make room for incorporating alternative compositional methods as part of the writing process.

In contrast to my more traditional (page-based) first year writing classes, my *Remix Writing Thru Media* students were more engaged, excited about their work, and willing to revise. Also, they made better grades. In using media forms native to everyday digital literacy, students felt that their writing was relevant and purposeful regardless of the platform or public forum (Patel, 2014). Students were not just writing for the classroom, but learning and using a set of skills applicable to diverse writing environments. Participants became agents in negotiating rhetorical methods and identifying argumentative approaches to best fit each project and purpose. Instead of merely consuming or responding to writing prompts, instead of modeling a method or attempting to demonstrate mastery, individuals became both creative composers and skillful writers – aware of the growth and change necessary to continue becoming good writers in any situation. Remix writing made the everyday academic and the academic everyday by positioning writing across disciplines, across media, and beyond the page.

Writing occurs in the ordering of pieces, using words, sounds, images – all fragmentary and distinct - to build a cohesive idea and purpose. Remix writing not only deconstructs texts, it updates the instruction of rhetorical methods by embracing a media user's ability to code switch. Originally a linguistic term, code-switching describes "the use of two or more linguistic varieties in the same conversation or interaction" (Carol Myers-Scotton and William Ury, 1997, p. 5). Instead of switching languages, multimedia writers code switch between digital formats to compose texts in diverse platforms, exercising knowledge of rhetorical practices through everyday digital literacy.

In the classroom, instructors often tell students to consider audience and purpose. A cover letter to a potential employer should not sound like a text to a friend. Composing in social media updates this lesson to employ a digital literacy that recognizes multiple forms of fluency alongside considerations of audience, medium, and message. When writers tweet 140 characters, they might use abbreviations, links, hashtags or even retweet to connect to a larger conversation or draw on shared knowledge within the writing community. A similar message in Instagram would primarily feature a picture, and perhaps hashtags, but less text. For example, a status update that reads "Feeling gr8 today. New haircut. #feelingfine" might work on Twitter, but an Instagram post could express a similar idea with a selfie and hashtags reading #newhaircut #feelingfine. The Twitter update assumes audience understanding of text language abbreviations while the Instagram post plays on the shared cultural implications of selfies. The hashtags unite the writing through the repetition or 'sampling' of the same text, but also digitally connect the two posts. Users can click on hashtags to group similar posts across mediums or search specific terms. Across both media platforms the act of writing and the message remain constant, a continuous conversation or interaction, but users must understand audience, medium, and purpose to fluently communicate.

The classroom should provide a space for students to understand that in using social media they *are* writing; they are participating in a writing community much larger than academic institutions. A classroom is only one site of learning. To connect institutional learning and what Andrea Lunsford (2007) calls life writing, (composition outside of the classroom) Terry Dean (1989) suggests that teachers "structure learning experiences that both help students write their way into the university and help teachers learn their way into student cultures (p. 23).

With today's ubiquitous use of writing technologies, writing programs that want to prepare students for professional writing environments must work to cultivate productive writing practices in and out of the classroom. Remixing social media composition into curricula fosters writing skills that will continue to grow beyond the boundaries of academic institutions. Adapting social media for the classroom helps nourish writers across all fronts, recognizing purpose and form, but also helping students better understand the fluidity and adaptability of writing.

Through remix, students and instructors learn to compose a networked system of writing that diffuses assumed hierarchies and promotes associative thinking across diverse ecologies of media. We are always already associative thinkers. We build connections to understand, compare, reject, and relate. As Jonathan Lethem (2007) notes,

By necessity, by proclivity, and by delight, we all quote. Neurological studies have shown that memory, imagination, and consciousness itself is stitched, quilted, pastiched. If we cut-and-paste ourselves, why can't we foster it in our work? (p.10)

The digital writing environment offers an assemblage of associations, available in an instant. Share, pin, post, retweet, and forward tools organize a network of viral connectivity and often-ambiguous origin. By disassembling and then reassembling texts, writers can learn to analyze influences and situate works in a web of connections. Students not only write critically about objects of study, but also have the opportunity to produce original work in various styles and media.

In mapping the remix process as well as the purpose of each composition, students are able to identify key elements of argument, style, and effective communication – taking ownership of their own writing. Remix, as a pedagogical style and teaching method, reframes foundational elements of writing instruction and broadens the traditional practice of writing to include 21ˢᵗ century compositional methods and technological forms.

NOTE

Student projects sampled, collaged, and remixed with permission from:

- Sarah Bullock (2015),
- Steven Einbinder (2014),
- Stephani Harrison (2015),
- Victoria LaGreca (2014),
- Sofia Luna (2015),
- Erik Nyman (2014),
- Viral Patel (2014).

REFERENCES

Berlin, J. (1996). *Rhetorics, poetics, and cultures: Refiguring college English studies*. Urbana, IL: NCTE.

Bolter, D., & Grusin, R. (1999). *Remediation: Understanding new media*. Boston, MA: MIT Press.

Brosh, A. (2011, May 6). FAQ (Blog). Retrieved from http://hyperboleandahalf.blogspot.com/p/faq_10.html

Brosh, A. (2013). *Hyperbole and a half: Unfortunate situations, flawed coping mechanisms, mayhem, and other things that happened*. New York, NY: Simon & Schuster.

Burwell, C. (2013). The Pedagogical Potential of Video Remix. *Journal of Adolescent & Adult Literacy, 57*(3), 205–213.

Castells, M. (2009). *The Rise of The Network Society: The Information Age: Economy, Society and Culture*. Oxford, UK: Wiley-Blackwell.

Council of Writing Program Administrators (CWPA). (2014, July 17). *WPA Outcomes Statement*. Retrieved from http://wpacouncil.org/positions/outcomes.html

Dean, T. (1989). Multicultural classrooms, monocultural teachers. *College Composition and Writing, 40*(1), 23–37.

DeVoss, D. &Ridolfo, Jim. (2009). Composing for Recomposition: Rhetorical Velocity and Delivery. *Kairos: A Journal of Rhetoric. Technology, and Pedagogy, 13*(2), n2.

Ferguson, K. (2012, August). Embrace the remix [Video file]. Retrieved from www.ted.com/talks/kirby_ferguson_embrace_ the_remix.html

Ferguson, K. (2012). Everything is a remix. Retrieved from vimeo.com/kirbyferguson

Ford, S., Green, J., & Jenkins, H. (2013). *Spreadable media: Creating value and meaning in a networked culture (postmillennial pop)*. New York, NY: New York University Press.

Hess, M. (2006). Was Foucault a plagiarist? Hip-hop sampling and academic citation. *Computers and Composition, 23*, 280–295.

Johnson-Eilola, J., & Selber, S. (2007). Plagiarism, Originality, Assemblage. *Computers and Composition, 24*, 375–403.

Knobel, M., & Lankshear, C. (2008). Remix: The art and craft of endless hybridization. *Journal of Adolescent & Adult Literacy, 52*(1), 22–34.

Kress, G. (2010). *Multimodality: A social semiotic approach to contemporary communication*. London, England: Routledge.

Lessig, L. (2008). *Remix: Making art and commerce thrive in the hybrid economy*. New York, NY: Penguin.

Lethem, J. (2007). The ecstasy of Influence. *Harpers Magazine*. Retrieved from http://harpers.org/archive/2007/02/the-ecstasy-of-influence/

Lunsford, A. (2007). *Writing Matters: Rhetoric in public and private lives*. Athens, GA: University of Georgia Press.

Manovich, L. (2005, November 15). Remix and remixability. Rhizome. Retrieved from rhizome.org/discuss/view/19303/

McCloud, S. (1993). *Understanding comics: the invisible art*. New York, NY: HarperCollins.

Miller, P. (2008). *Sound Unbound*. Boston, MA: MIT Press.

Myers-Scotton, C., & Ury, W. (1977). Bilingual Strategies: The Social Functions of Codeswitching. *Journal of the Sociology of Language, 13*, 5–20.

Navas, E. (2012). *Remix theory: The aesthetics of sampling*. New York, NY: Springer.

ENDNOTES

[1]   Musical composition has a long history of appropriation, from folk songs to blues and rock and roll. Hip-hop is one of the first genres to openly use existing material/samples to create a new song. See Mickey Hess, John Tehranian, Clay Shirkey, Kirby Ferguson, and Lawrence Lessig for additional information.

[2]   I capitalize 'Remix Writing' together to emphasize the method of writing, the name of the style. Remix as a composition process remains lowercase.

[3]   Although humanist in approach here, network theory can be applied to writers of all forms. The 'we' as people is used since the focus of the chapter is student writing. One could argue that Facebook the technology authored 'unfriend.' See N. Katherine Hayles, Sidney I. Dobrin, and Donna Haraway.

[4]   McCloud's text can also be used to help define basic theories of semiotics and icons. In addition, see David Chandler's *Semiotics for Beginners* and Elaine Scarry's *Dreaming by the Book* for help with visual rhetoric and narrative language.

Chapter 6
Social Media and the Rhetorical Situation:
Finding Common Ground Between Students' Lives and Writing Courses

Katherine Fredlund
University of Memphis, USA

ABSTRACT

Recognizing that students develop rhetorical skills on social media, this chapter presents a number of writing assignments that ask students to engage with social media and complete a variety of tasks online. These tasks range from taking and posting a photograph, to revising social media posts for honesty, to creating memes. Each assignment then requires students to reflect on these experiences in formal written assignments. This reflective component encourages students to consider writing conventions, processes, and genres in order to develop "high road" and meta-cognitive transfer skills. These assignments have three primary goals: (1) they help students engage with course content, (2) they build student confidence, and (3) they ask students to practice transfer.

INTRODUCTION

Twenty-first century students use complex rhetorical practices daily; they consider their audience, compose arguments, and revise posts on Facebook, Instagram, Twitter, SnapChat, and elsewhere. Yet many are unaware of their resulting rhetorical prowess. As educators, we can empower students to recognize how their social media use has made them practiced and successful writers by bringing social media into the classroom and helping students make connections between the rhetorical practices of their daily lives and the rhetorical demands of the academy. In fact, as educators, we must find new ways to reach our students because they don't think or learn in the same way as past generations. As Prensky (2001) has pointed out, "It is now clear that as a result of this ubiquitous environment and the sheer volume of their interaction with it, today's students think and process information fundamentally differently from their predecessors" (p. 1). If our students really do think and learn differently, then as educators we must find ways to teach differently.

DOI: 10.4018/978-1-5225-0562-4.ch006

Teaching differently is no easy task. In Shaughnessy's 1976 "Diving In: An Introduction to Basic Writing," she recognized,

... that this system of exchange between teacher and student has so far yielded much more information about what is wrong with students than about what is wrong with teachers, reinforcing the notion that students, not teachers, are the people in education who must do the changing. (p. 311)

This continues to be the case, especially now that we teach what Prensky calls "Digital Natives" or "'native speakers' of the digital language of computers, video games and the Internet" (p. 1). Thus if we want to reach our students, we must stop focusing on the ills of social media and its impact on writing. Instead, we must teach differently. While Carr's *New York Times* column (2015), "The Media Equation," often discussed the negative impact of social media, he also often recognized the positive impact of such media:

The enhanced ability to communicate and share in the current age has many tangible benefits . . . Many younger consumers have become mini-media companies themselves, madly distributing their own content on Vine, Instagram, YouTube and Snapchat. It's tough to get their attention on media created for the masses when they are so busy producing their own. (para. 9)

Social media is not a fad or at least not one that is going to disappear anytime soon. Thus as writing teachers in the twenty-first century, we cannot simply decry student use of social media; we must find a way to use this social media use to our own (and our students') advantage.

One way to do this is to incorporate students' social media use into classroom discussions and writing assignments. By asking students to engage with, post to, and reflect on social media through formal and informal assignments, my writing courses aim to help them recognize their ability to successfully adapt to a variety of rhetorical situations. Helping students understand their social media posts as acts of rhetorically-situated writing allows them to gain confidence in their general writing skills. In their award-winning book, *On Multimodality: New Media in Composition Studies* (2014), Alexander and Rhodes explain, "In our push to assert our own disciplinarity, we have perhaps privileged text-based forms of writing to the extent that we rarely address the specific invention, delivery, and rhetorical possibilities of other types of composition in our classes" (p. 3). When we only teach text-based writing, we are narrowing students' understanding of writing to writing that can be done in a Word document, but by addressing the "specific invention, delivery, and rhetorical possibilities" (p. 3) of social media, we can encourage students to recognize that they already do a lot of what we are asking of them in their daily lives. Thus while the negative effects of social media on writing are hard to ignore, a different approach to social media recognizes and focuses on the strengths students have gained through their incessant posting. If we encourage our students to think of social media use as writing, then we can help them transfer their rhetorical knowledge from their social (and online) lives to their academic lives. Perhaps, this can also work in reverse, and such assignments can help them transfer their new academic understanding of rhetorical situations to help them become savvier social media users as well.

THEORETICAL FRAMEWORK

Students often struggle when attempting to transfer their rhetorical knowledge from one situation to another. Yet administrators, teachers in other fields, and even parents often expect writing courses to prepare students to write in a variety of situations. As a result, part of our job as writing teachers is to help students compose not only in our own classes but also in future classes in a variety of disciplines. In order to do this, we must teach them how to transfer the knowledge they gain in our courses, but this is, of course, easier said than done. Wardle's (2007) "Understanding 'Transfer' From FYC: Preliminary Results of a Longitudinal Study" concludes:

We cannot prepare students for every genre, nor can we know every assignment they will be given or the genre conventions appropriate to those assignments across the disciplines…What FYC can do, however, is help students think about writing in the university, the varied conventions of different disciplines, and their own writing strategies in light of various assignment and expectations. (p. 82)

One way to encourage transfer, then, is to ask students to compose reflective assignments that ask them to think about writing, conventions, and processes.

Thinking about writing in the University alone, however, might not be enough. Perkins and Salomon (1988) define "high road" transfer as the "deliberate mindful abstraction of skill or knowledge from one context for application in another" (p. 25). This high road transfer necessitates "reflective thought in abstracting from one context and seeking connections with others" (p. 26). The skills students use in high road transfer are often referred to as meta-cognitive skills in transfer research, and finding ways to teach such skills presents writing teachers with a challenge because we cannot foresee or plan for every writing situation our students will encounter. Rounsaville, Goldberg, and Bawarshi's (2008) article in *Writing Program Administration* found that "despite possessing a wide genre base, and despite having experience writing in multiple domains, students utilized only a fraction of these discursive resources when encountering new academic writing situations" (p. 108).

With this research on transfer in mind, I designed a variety of short assignments that ask students to reflect on the rhetorical skills they develop and use when posting to social media. While new social media platforms are constantly being introduced, my assignments are not developed for a specific platform. Instead, I design them to work for any social media platform that asks students to post for an audience. This allows me to incorporate new social media platforms as they become popular without having to completely redesign my assignments. This incorporation of social media encourages students to begin the meta-cognition necessary for transfer during our writing courses instead of assuming they will know how to do this once they complete the course. Thus we don't need to prepare students for every rhetorical situation that they will encounter; instead, we can ask students to practice identifying rhetorical situations, adapting their writing to fit genre expectations, and considering a variety of audiences by incorporating social media use into our writing assignments. In doing this, I recognize and use students' "wide genre base" in order to teach both writing and transfer in FYC.

METHODOLOGY AND PEDAGOGY

Practicing Transfer and Building Confidence with Social Media

By incorporating social media into short reflective writing assignments, my students are asked not just to consider transfer but to also practice this "high road" transfer. Such writing assignments do not simply tell students that they will have to use the skills we teach them in different ways later. Instead, they encourage meta-cognition by asking students to practice transferring their knowledge from rhetorical situations on social media to the rhetorical situations in our classroom. Thus, rather than hoping students will transfer the writing skills I teach, I try to teach them transfer skills as well as writing skills when incorporating social media into writing prompts.

In order to foster this transfer, I assign a variety of short assignments throughout the semester and ask students to respond to those assignments in a blog they create at the beginning of the semester. Blogging in classrooms is certainly nothing new. Many teacher-researchers have written about how blogs can be used for freewriting and to encourage students to interact with their own and others' writing (Ferdig & Trammell, 2004; Goodwin-Jones, 2003; Bryant, 2013). Yet the reason I incorporate blogs in my classroom is not to encourage interaction among students, though such a benefit is indeed valuable. Instead, I incorporate blogs because they allow students to compose short written assignments that can include screen captures and images of their own social media use, and these shorter assignments encourage them to practice the transfer that will be necessary for them to succeed as college students and professionals.

Most of my students are between the ages of 18 and 25 attending a mid-size State University with a population around 14,000. The classes are generally fairly diverse, with most students coming from either small, rural towns in Indiana or Illinois or the cities of Indianapolis, Chicago, or St. Louis. On the second day of class, students are asked to create their own blog using WordPress where they will turn in all of their work throughout the semester. They turn in their short blogging assignments as blogs on the homepage, and they turn in their lengthier written assignments as pages that appear as menu items on the top of the website. The blogs are required to be a minimum of 400 words and also must include images or other media elements. The larger assignments range in length from 800 to 2,000 words. While many millennial students are tech-savvy, many of them do not blog and struggle to create their website when asked to do so out of class and without instruction. WordPress is new to them, and getting the blog set up takes up a good portion of the second day of class. I am careful to slowly lead my students through the blog creation process, pausing to keep everyone on the same step. Below I outline three short writing assignments that incorporate social media use in order to promote student confidence while requiring them to practice transferring their rhetorical knowledge from one situation to another.

Recognizing Rhetoric Online: Making Social Media Honest

In order to help students form connections between the composing they do on social media and the composing they will be asked to do for my course, the first blog prompt (seen in Figure 1) challenges students to analyze and then revise two status updates (one of their own and one of a friend). Students are asked to revise these status updates in order to make them "honest." In other words, they are asked to revise social media posts to say what they actually mean. This assignment encourages students to see the writing they do online as rhetorical. We first discuss how each time they post to social media they are attempting to convince their audience of something. Students often quickly recognize that what they say on social media isn't always what they actually mean. For example, we discuss selfies and what the message of a selfie might be. Since they can't just write "I am SO beautiful" on Instagram without sounding self-involved, they instead post a selfie and hope their audience will receive their intended message. We also discuss a variety of posts that almost everyone sees on social media. These common posts (like people posting photos of or statuses about working out) allow us to dissect the true meaning of the post as a class before students are challenged to go do this on their own.

This prompt serves as an introductory assignment and asks students to analyze what they have already done on a variety of social media platforms. Students can choose to revise posts from facebook, Instagram, SnapChat, or Twitter. With this blog, students are being prepared to think rhetorically about social media while also practicing revision. In revising their own posts, they can easily recognize that when they posted a status or photo, they were attempting to persuade their friends or followers, and that in order to do so, they made rhetorical choices intended to appeal to an audience. While it has been many years since Ken Macrorie asked his students to write the "truth," the practice, when combined with social media, doesn't just help produce better writing, it helps students see themselves as writers (Schroeder & Boe 5). With a new rhetorical situation (honesty), my students recognize the importance of revision and audience awareness. Building on this rhetorical awareness of social media, the next two prompts ask students to actively post on social media sites.

Figure 1. Making social media honest blog prompt

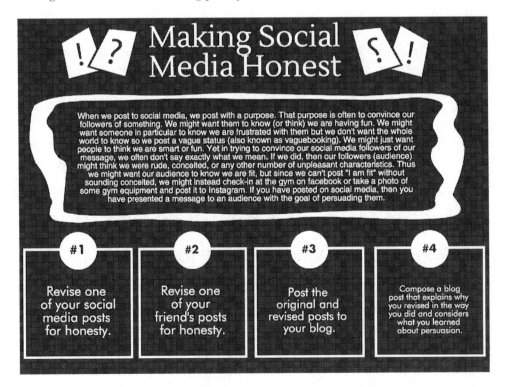

Considering Audience: Photography as a Rhetorical Process

After introducing my students to what our textbook, Morey (2014), calls the rhetorical tetrahedron (an extension of the rhetorical triangle for new media writing that adds medium, genre, and design to writer, message, and audience), I challenge my students to take a photograph with their camera phone, post it to a social media platform of their choice, and then compose a blog that reflects on the rhetorical choices they made from the moment they decided to take a photo until the moment the photo was posted to social media (pp. 22-23). The full prompt, seen in Figure 2, asks my students to consider and then write about why they included or left things out of the frame, what message they were trying to convey to an audience, and how the social media platform they chose altered how they took and presented the photograph.

This blog prompt is assigned during the second week of the semester, and it is intended to begin building student confidence. Students in my classes often admit that they are intimidated by their writing courses, and with this assignment, students learn that they are already composing messages, considering audiences, and meeting genre expectations. Since it is early in the semester, students are asked to share their social media posts with the class during discussion before they begin composing their response to the prompt. During class, students are asked to post a photo (not necessarily the one they will end up writing about) to their blog, and using a projector, we visit each student's blog and discuss the photo, its message, and the way they used filters, the zoom feature, or other editing tools to convey that message to their audience. As a class we analyze each student's photo and guess the message before the photographer (or writer) then explains what the student was actually trying to convey. After projecting each

Figure 2. Photography as a rhetorical process blog prompt

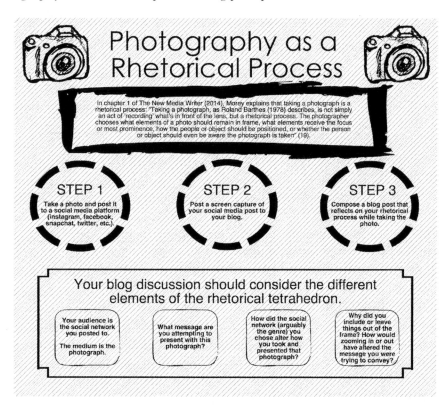

photo for the whole class to see, the class asks the photographer why he or she made certain decisions and provides suggestions for how their message might have been improved with design elements such as cropping, filtering, or editing. This in class exercise prepares students for the written portion of the assignment by providing them with the terminology (genre, message, audience, design, zoom, filter, etc.) they are expected to use and also giving them a chance to revise their photograph (or start fresh) before posting it to social media and composing their blog.

The written portion of the assignment makes the rhetorical process of photography explicit, and this helps my students understand that they already do what the larger writing assignments in the course will ask of them. They just do them in different (non-academic) rhetorical situations. For example, a written assignment might ask students to consider what their audience needs to know and provide all of that necessary information through research. Similarly, when taking a photograph, students must consider what needs to remain in frame in order for the photograph to make sense to the viewer or to portray the intended message. Thus when students take images for Instagram or Snapchat, they are considering their audience and revising or editing their photos in order to make sure their audience receives their message.

While photographs and alphabetic texts are quite different, students are rhetorically engaged during the composition of both, and I have found this helps them understand the importance of audience. Further, the written portion of the assignment encourages students to consciously consider the process they go through when posting to social media, and this not only prepares them to transfer those skills into the classroom but also helps them become more cognizant of the messages they are sending when they post to social media platforms.

Practicing Revision: Adapting Rhetoric for Social Media Genres

Because my students often struggle to transfer their writing skills from one rhetorical situation to another, the next writing prompt I assign asks them to practice (and recognize) their ability to transfer this knowledge when posting to social media platforms. While students might think of genre as an artistic composition, Miller's (1984) concept of genre as social action makes genre a useful concept for writing instruction. She explains,

What we learn when we learn a genre is not just a pattern of forms or even a method of achieving our own ends. We learn, more importantly, what ends we may have . . . We learn to understand better the situations in which we find ourselves and the potentials for failure and success in acting together. (p. 165)

With this in mind, using genre to teach students about what they do on social media platforms helps them understand the complex rhetorical process they enact each time they post to one of these sites. Thinking of different social media platforms as genres of social media that require compositions with similarities and differences in form, style, and even content (think Twitter vs. Facebook), allows students to understand that they have developed complex rhetorical practices through their use of social media. Thus this prompt, seen in more detail in Figure 3, asks students to post the same message to three different social media platforms. Students are expected to revise each post to fit the genre expectations of the platform.

This assignment allows students to practice a number of skills they will need in order to succeed as student writers. They are asked to identify the genre expectations of three different situations and revise their writing (or message) according to those genre expectations. After they have practiced this revision,

Figure 3. The genre expectations of social media platforms blog prompt

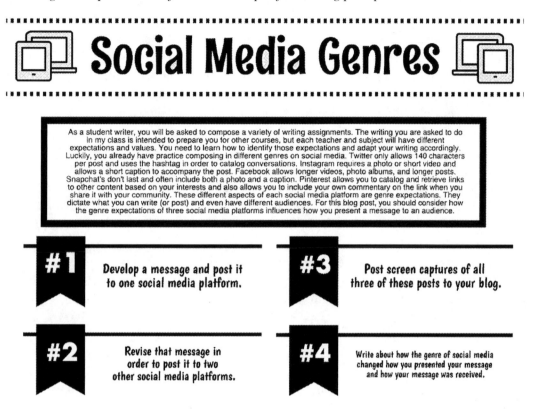

they are asked to reflect on the process they went through when revising each post, thus practicing the meta-cognitive skills necessary for successful transfer. The prompt asks students to explain and even justify the choices they made. In these blog posts, students often discuss how the genre impacted who composed their audience. For example, if students start with a Snapchat but then need to revise the post for Facebook, my students often note that now their families are part of their Facebook audience, and this impacts how they present their message. My students also recognize how the genre expectations of Twitter (140 characters or less) make some posts from Facebook impossible to replicate in a single post. This exercise helps students understand what it means to transfer their writing skills from one situation to another and builds on the previous blog prompt by asking them to actually practice revision and consider three different audiences for the same message. The "Social Media Genres" assignment continues to build their confidence while also asking them to practice transferring their rhetorical knowledge from one situation to another.

Each of these short assignments builds upon the others in order to prepare students to transfer their rhetorical knowledge from their social lives to their academic lives. By asking students to reflect on the writing choices they make on social media in short written assignments, they begin to understand that their daily social media practices have helped them develop rhetorical abilities. In my classes, I notice that this recognition leads to confidence in their writing skills while also preparing them to attempt to transfer their rhetorical skills from one situation to another.

Practicing Argumentation and Considering Kairos with Memes

In addition to these smaller social media assignments, I also assign one major assignment that asks students to compose and consider a genre of new media argument that they often encounter on social media: memes. Originally defined by Richard Dawkins as "small units of culture that spread from person to person by copying or imitation" (Shifman 2), memes have become a popular form of argument on social media. They most often include a single image accompanied by a pithy saying that appears in white text at the top and/or bottom of the image. (To see an example of a meme, see the image in Figure 5.) In *Memes in Digital Culture*, Shifman (2013) defines memes as "(a) a group of digital items sharing common characteristics of content, form, and/or stance; (b) that were created with awareness of each other; and (c) were circulated, imitated, and/or transformed via the internet by many users" (pp. 7-8). Memes, then, are socially constructed public discourses. "Another fundamental attribute of Internet memes is intertextuality: memes often relate to each other in complex, creative, and surprising ways" (Shifman p. 2).

While our students encounter memes often, many of them aren't familiar with the term and the variety of free meme-creator websites available to them (Imgflip, MEME DAD, Make a Meme, etc.). When I ask my students how many have seen a meme before, all 25 of them (no matter their age, class, gender, or race) raise their hands. When I ask how many have created a meme before, only a few younger students raise their hands, illustrating that our students consume new media compositions far more than they produce them. Thus this assignment also asks students to compose in a format that they are not familiar with (a meme), and, as they often write in their reflections, meme creation is not as easy as it looks.

This assignment challenges students to practice a number of rhetorical skills while continuing to connect academic writing to the writing they encounter on social media. I ask students to compose three different memes for the assignment so that they can experiment with different rhetorical appeals. The creation of a meme requires them to consider Kairos (the best or opportune moment to present an argument and, in this case, post their meme). In class, we discuss a variety of memes and their reasons for success. We pay careful attention to the time that the meme was originally posted. For example, if a meme concerns a football game, then the meme needs to be posted within 24 hours of that game (with the most effective memes being posted during the game or within an hour or two of the game's completion). If a great meme is created 4 days after the game, then the meme creator has lost their Kairotic moment, and the meme will not have the same popularity it might have had days before. Meme creation also forces students to compose a challengingly concise argument without relying on logical fallacies, and it requires students to consider how image and text can work together, a skill that is becoming more and more important as writing occurs less on paper and more online.

The reflection portion of the assignment asks students to justify and explain their rhetorical choices. As a class, we read about and then discuss a variety of rhetorical appeals that might be useful in meme creation. While we discuss logical, emotional, and ethical appeals, students are asked to use concepts such as analogy, juxtaposition, enthymeme, adaptation, visual narrative, celebrity, and others in their meme creation. Thus in order to prepare them for this aspect of the assignment, I assign a blog post that asks students to find memes that use these concepts and explain how the meme uses the concept. I direct students to look for memes that have been posted to their own social media platforms or to do Google image searches such as "best memes" or "college memes." The full blog prompt can be seen in Figure 4.

This blog prompt asks students to think about how memes use rhetorical tactics in order to persuade. Our students likely do not think about a meme's rhetorical tactics when they scroll by a meme on Ins-

Figure 4. Understanding how memes persuade blog prompt

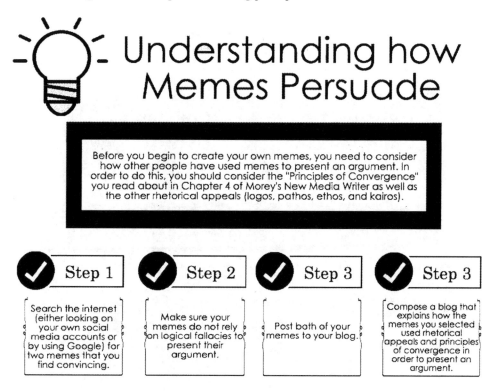

tagram or Facebook and consume its content. Similarly, the rhetorical aspect of meme creation is likely not a conscious one for many meme creators, but my students find that the most effective memes rely on the same rhetorical tactics such as celebrity, adaptation, juxtaposition, or enthymeme. The goal of this blog assignment is to prepare them to begin the composition of their own memes while helping them better understand the rhetorical tactics they have read about in their readings. They learn that juxtaposition (two images placed next to one another in order to create a comparison) and visual narrative (many images placed next to one another to create a story) are frequently used in memes. Celebrity (using famous people to create ethos) and adaptation (taking a movie or character your audience likely knows and changing its meaning with a purpose) are also frequently used tactics within meme composition. After considering how other people have used these rhetorical tactics, students are finally ready to begin creating their own argumentative memes.

At their very core, memes are imitations, and for student writers, imitation is a useful skill. As Bartholomae (1985) explains in "Inventing the University," "It may very well be that some students will need to learn to crudely mimic the 'distinctive register' of academic discourse before they are prepared to actually and legitimately do the work of the discourse, and before they are sophisticated enough with the refinements of tone and gesture to do it with grace and elegance" (p. 650). This assignment asks students to practice imitation within a genre that they are far more familiar with than academic writing. Thus before students even begin the formal written part of the assignment, they are considering their audience, composing remarkably concise arguments, waiting for a Kairotic moment, and practicing the imitation that will help them as they move on to imitate more complex forms of discourse.

Figure 5. Meme project assignment sheet (Part 1)

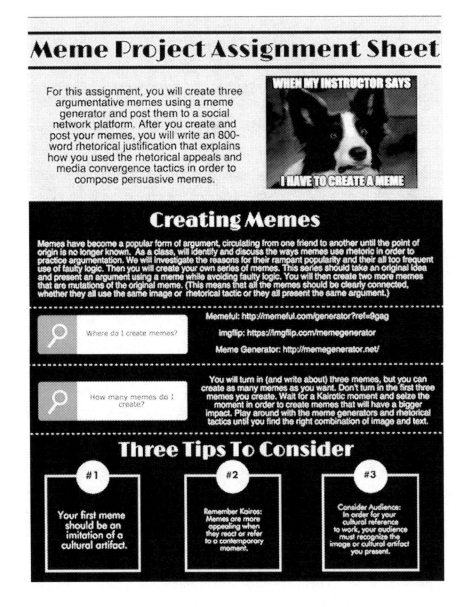

The written portion of the assignment asks students to justify and explain their decisions by using the rhetorical terms (juxtaposition, adaptation, celebrity, pathos, ethos, logos, kairos, etc.) we discuss in class. This portion of the assignment asks students to practice academic writing while analyzing and justifying their own meme creation. In previous assignments and blog posts, students used narrative or conversational tones, but for the written part of the meme assignment students are asked to use rhetorical terms and write in formal, academic prose. While they are still writing about memes they composed for a social media audience, they are now challenged to write about social media in academic prose. Yet because students are still talking about something they are familiar with (social media), they do not experience the same level of uncertainty or self-doubt they might encounter if their first academic writing assignment engaged with a more traditional topic. The full assignment sheet can be seen in Figures 5 and 6.

Figure 6. Meme project assignment sheet (Part 2)

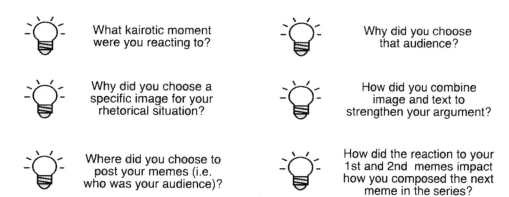

Writing About Memes

As constant users of technology, we don't often pause to consider our rhetorical situation. Yet each time you post to social media, you are a composer targeting an audience. Thus this assignment does not only ask you to create a series of memes; it also asks you to think about how you can (or did) make that meme as effective as possible. In an essay of at least 800 words, you should explain why you made the rhetorical choices you did. You should use the applicable rhetorical terms from the "Media Convergence" chapter of The New Media Writer, consider how you used rhetorical appeals, and respond to the questions below.

What kairotic moment were you reacting to?

Why did you choose that audience?

Why did you choose a specific image for your rhetorical situation?

How did you combine image and text to strengthen your argument?

Where did you choose to post your memes (i.e. who was your audience)?

How did the reaction to your 1st and 2nd memes impact how you composed the next meme in the series?

At first, my students struggle to present the concise arguments that memes require, but that struggle leads to an important lesson about language. Memes use very few words to get their point across. Yet without these words, the images behind them can be interpreted in a variety of ways. The written portion of the meme, then, helps students understand the importance of clarity in their writing. Without a clear, concise message, the words will cover the image, and they won't meet the genre expectations. Further, the words have to work with the image, so students are also learning about visual rhetoric and the importance of explaining an image with words, an aspect of writing that will become important if they move into technical writing or digital writing courses later in their college careers. Such courses teach genres of writing that value and include images, charts, and graphs and expect student writers to make clear connections between the written and visual aspects of a text.

Another benefit of the meme assignment is that it requires students to make conscious rhetorical choices and justify those choices in writing. While the earlier blog posts asked for formal writing, this assignment helps students transition from formal writing to academic writing while not stepping too far out of their comfort zone. It slowly moves them from a discourse community they are completely comfortable with to an academic discourse community. The transition to academic writing is made smoother because the topic of the assignment concerns their own rhetorical choices and social media. Further, this assignment continues to ask students to reflect on the writing situation and their writing process during meme creation. Students, then, continue to build the meta-cognitive skills necessary for transfer with this assignment.

The meme assignment also helps students continue to work on transferring the rhetorical skills they use on social media while challenging them to compose in a genre they are not comfortable with. This challenge helps them think about language use, the impact of concise language, and the ways text and image work together. The rhetorical justification helps them make their rhetorical process explicit while slowly introducing students to academic writing assignments. The meme project completes our time working with social media, and students are now asked to move on to research-oriented assignments with new confidence and transferable writing skills.

RESULTS AND DISCUSSION

"Making Social Media Honest" Example

As my students progress through the social media assignments, they slowly build their rhetorical confidence and skillset. We begin with the "Making Social Media Honest" assignment because it helps students recognize rhetoric in their (digital) lives, asks them to practice revision, and encourages them to see themselves as capable of producing rhetoric. For example, Student # 1 revised his Disney World Instagram post (seen in Figure 7) from "A great day at the happiest place on earth in the books. #DisneyWorld" to "Everyone look where I am! I like to travel!" He then discusses his revision, claiming,

I revised it the way I did because that was the underlying motive for the post. Posting in the revised way would create the perception of showing off and add a negative connotation to the post. The way in which I wrote in the actual post creates a more lighthearted and fun undertone. In both versions of the post, the underlying point is to still show that I am at a well-known and liked travel destination, but the way in which the wording is used sets the entire tone of the message . . . Persuasion is a tactic we all use in day to day conversation, many times without even realizing it. The way we state things in our posts create a certain context that would not be utilized elsewhere. Many examples of this can be found by simply scrolling down a social media wall, where we can see persuasion being used to save face through what are mostly self-centered statements.

Figure 7. Student # 1's original Instagram post

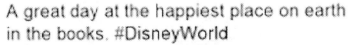

As the excerpt from Student #1's blog indicates, the reflection aspect of this assignment made the often-unconscious rhetorical decisions that go into the composition of a social media post conscious for this student while also allowing him to consider the importance of tone. Further, this student was able to make connections not only between persuasion and social media but persuasion and everyday life.

"Photography as a Rhetorical Process" Example

The next blog assignment, "Photography as a Rhetorical Process," asks students to move from revising old posts to creating new ones. This assignment aims to help students see that they go through a rhetorical process when they do something as simple as take a photograph and post it to social media. In Student # 2's blog post, it becomes clear that the blog allows for a playful tone, but the response, while conversational, indicates that the student has a complex understanding of audience:

Like every other hardworking college student, I find myself juggling both class and work. (Two cheers for being a broke college student!) That being said, I have been lucky to not only find a job, but to find a job that I love. And, more than anything, what kind of Millennial would I be if I didn't post about it on social media?

Recently, I was promoted at [my] campus radio station, from Assistant Promotions Director to Program Director of the station. For anyone who has been around to hear my saga, they know that this is a huge step for my professional career. A few days before this photo was posted to Instagram, I had just received my keys to the station.

The message behind the picture is that after much toil and struggle, I have finally gotten a promotion that I want everyone to know about. Utilizing Instagram as the medium for the message, I snapped a pic of those long sought after keys, labeled Program Dir and typed a brief caption. Because Instagram is unarguably a social media that revolves around the artistry of the picture, I focused more of my attention on the snap rather than the cap. This is because the caption, while still important (especially to all the girls out there who spend hours on their inspirational and ultimately unoriginal quotes), it is not the primary focus of the medium. Another important aspect of Instagram is audience. For me, it is a much tighter circle of friends than either Facebook or Twitter, making the message more intimate. The people that I want to know about my success, my handful of Instagram followers, are the ones that will receive that message rather than a broad audience of distant relatives and elementary school crushes who would scroll right past the news on some other site, like Facebook.

Also, they way that the picture is taken is just as important. What elements do you choose to focus on and what ones do you choose to crop out? That is all encompassed in the split second it takes for one to snap a picture. In my case, I chose to zoom in on my brand new set of keys with the Program Dir tag in the forefront of the picture while opting to crop out the rest of my jumbled set of keys because they weren't pertinent to the message that I was trying to convey. In essence, zooming in on the particular set of keys helped to create a more concise message for my audience to read.

More than anything, however, social media platforms allow us to express our thoughts, feelings, and ideas in a way that lets us to connect to the world around us. Understanding how to properly communicate those messages is something that is hardwired into our brains. We realize how to read these different messages, like someone like me who is fishing for compliments on a new promotion, and know to double tap to show them some love.

Student # 2's blog illustrates how the "Photography as a Rhetorical Process" assignment helps students think about how they make rhetorical decisions in order to persuade an audience in their everyday lives (see Figure 8). This student thought about the rhetorical process of taking and posting a photograph and then was able to make conclusions about persuasion on social media in general, even recognizing how a specific genre of social media (in this case Instagram) meant having a different and more ideal audience for her post about a promotion. This student further considers how zooming in allowed her audience to better focus on her message, illustrating how this simple blog assignment can help students make connections between posting to social media and writing for other less-familiar audiences.

"Social Media Genres" Example

The "Social Media Genres" blog post asks students to practice transfer by posting the same message to three different social media platforms. Students will need to transfer what they learn in their writing courses when writing assignments later in their college careers, and this blog asks them to practice this transfer. Student # 3 chose to post to Facebook, Twitter, and Instagram. Her reflection on this process explains what she learned from the exercise:

Figure 8. Student # 2's rhetorical photograph

There are so many different types of social media that a message can be adjusted and changed depending on the location of the posting. Not only do people tend to adjust their word usage, but it can also be perceived differently on different sites. With this in mind, I posted on three different Social Media sites. I chose to start with a post on Facebook, altered it for Twitter, and further adjusted it for Instagram. My Facebook Post reads "We're finally getting to that point in the semester where things are getting crazy busy. I have so much to get done within the next few weeks! Prayers are appreciated!" My friends on Facebook are largely family members, members of my church, and members of my campus ministry. I also have high school classmates as friends as well. Not only did I explain my situation, I asked for prayers. I chose Facebook to ask for prayers because it is my social media account with my largest group of prayer warriors. This also lets my parents know that things are getting intense and that I may not be in communication with them for a while due to the stress that is being piled on.

When I moved my message from Facebook to twitter it got shorter, and was written in a different form (Figure 2). When I posted on Facebook it was an explanation, on twitter it becomes more of a challenge, and an attempt at getting retweets by making it relatable and funny. I honestly do not post too much on twitter, I have very few followers and I struggle with being concise and making an impact. I am on Twitter all of the time reading others tweets; I just lack the skills to create successful tweets myself.

After my post worked its way to Instagram, it remained shortened like twitter, but now with an added visual aspect: a picture of my computer and textbooks showing different things that I have going on right now. This is my favorite Social Media site, probably because I am a design student and between the photographs and filters I get really excited! I also like the simplicity of Instagram, It lacks the insanity and complication of the other Social Media sites. This post will not only be seen by my measly amount of followers but may show up in someone's "Explore Posts" section. It can also be found by searching the hashtags. For this reason I tagged different terms than I had previously on twitter. Not only were typical college terms tagged, but since I displayed some of my design work on my computer, I tagged Design and Graphic Design to reach other students in similar situations as I.

The roles different types of Social Media play are very interesting. Seeing how the same post is manipulated and changed for different interfaces and platforms is a great example of how the medium is the message. My post on Facebook, Twitter, and Instagram changed not only based on the platform but also on the audience. For this reason, I can understand more clearly how genres, mediums, and messages go hand in hand.

Student # 3's blog reflects on how genre influenced her message. Recognizing how the different sites forced Student # 3 to change the post, this student's blog illustrates an impressive understanding of how the rhetorical situation should dictate the writer's message. Further, Student # 3 also discusses how the audience changed depending on the genre. Such knowledge is useful for students as they move from this assignment to other assignments in the course and later to unfamiliar genres in courses in other disciplines.

Meme Assignment Examples

The final social media blog asks students to find memes using a Google image search or their own social media accounts. It also asks them to think about how the memes they find rely on rhetorical tactics such as juxtaposition, celebrity, adaptation, and enthymeme. This final blog prepares students for the larger meme assignment that asks them to compose their own memes and justify their rhetorical choices. After finding a meme with a picture of comedian Kevin Hart with his hand raised as if to say "stop" covered with the words "How you act when Bill Cosby offers your friend a drink," Student # 4 explained,

The maker of this meme uses many forms of principles of convergence to make the argument. One principle of convergence that is used is celebrity. The producer of the meme uses the facial expression of Kevin Hart to fit the argument it is making. Kevin Hart is a well-known comedian, so the creator of the meme can usually catch the audience's attention by using a picture of him. Another principle of convergence that is used is adaptation. The meme producer uses a screen shot from one of Kevin Hart's comedic presentations to make the meme. They used an image that was produced for another reason in order to make the argument. Along with the principles of convergence, the meme creator also uses rhetorical appeals to appeal to the audience. One rhetorical appeal that is used in this argument is kairos, which is the best, most strategic time to make an argument (Morey 40). The Bill Cosby incident is fairly recent, so it is fresh in many people's minds. The meme writer appeals to the audience by making an argument about an event that happened within the past few years.

This assignment, then, slowly moves students from writing about only social media and simple concepts such as audience or genre to discussing argumentation in a more sophisticated manner while using the rhetorical concepts we have read about in our textbook in their writing. This blog also allows students to analyze memes before they are asked to create their own memes for the larger meme assignment, helping to prepare them for their most challenging assignment yet.

The social media unit of the course ends with a larger assignment that asks students to create three memes and compose a written justification of the rhetorical choices they made during their meme composition. This assignment asks students to purposefully combine an image with concise text while avoiding logical fallacies. The major goal of this assignment is to ease students into academic writing while allowing them to write about social media and memes, a topic they are familiar and comfortable with. A selection from Student # 5's essay illustrates how the student is able to talk confidently about their meme creation while using an appropriate tone for academic audiences:

This meme [seen in Figure 9] utilizes adaptation and enthymeme as two methods of argumentation. Adaptation is used because I have taken an image from SpongeBob SquarePants and repurposed it to create an argument that is otherwise unrelated to the show. Also, this could be considered to be using the rhetorical force of celebrity. While it is quite true that cartoon characters aren't actual celebrities, their likenesses are held to that type of stature. Especially with a show that has had such a long track record of cultural permeation, the characters have a well-established celebrity status, at least among millennials who are my target audience. More than anything, however, this meme's argumentation is clearly enthymematic. An enthymeme is very similar to a syllogism but is missing either a major premise, minor premise, or a conclusion. Here, the conclusion is missing which states that I don't like to go out if I don't have to. Because of the use of enthymeme, I don't have to explicitly state this; rather, I can let the reader fill in the blanks with the other context clues that have been established...

Student # 5's essay evidences that while students are still talking about social media, this final assignment allows them to do so while using academic prose, discussing meme creation with more complex

Figure 9. Student #5's meme

language than was required in the previous blog posts. Yet because the student is still talking about creating memes for social media, she is not intimidated by the normally unfamiliar genre. Student # 5's essay concludes,

After diligently working on this assignment, it has become abundantly clear that creating the perfect meme is a nuanced art that takes some skill and practice to fully master. One of the most important things that I've discovered is the relevance of audience when it comes to meme creation. You must know who you are targeting in order to make the argument more effective. Also, and perhaps just as importantly, finding the right kairotic moment to post your meme is key to making it successful. Like the old adage says, sometimes magic happens when you're in the right place at the right time. Finally, above all else, memes are meant to be fun! Let your creativity and your humor shine through!

This conclusion illustrates that this student has also thought about meme creation with regards to the rhetorical situation, recognizing the relevance of audience and the importance of timing. My goal as a writing instructor is to help students recognize their own rhetorical abilities while making the course and assignments engaging and fun. Using social media helps students engage with the course initially, but it also helps them think about themselves as writers capable of convincing a variety of audiences. By the time we move from the meme assignment to more traditional writing assignments, students believe in their own abilities to adapt to new genres of writing, know how to consider their audience, and are capable of finding the best available means of persuasion because they have already done all of these things on social media. Social media assignments help my students build their confidence, preparing them to face the daunting tasks that lie ahead in my course and beyond.

IMPLICATIONS: THE BENEFITS OF SOCIAL MEDIA ASSIGNMENTS

As a teacher-scholar whose research focuses primarily on the history of rhetoric, I was, admittedly, wary of incorporating social media into my previously traditional writing classrooms. However, since

I have started to do so, I am convinced that social media assignments enable students to recognize and transfer their rhetorical knowledge from social networks to our classrooms and their academic writing while also engaging them with the course. When I began incorporating social media into my assignments, the most noticeable benefit was increased student engagement. Suddenly, my students were more confident in both class discussion and their short writing assignments. More importantly, they felt they had something to say—and they were excited to have something to contribute to class discussions. This changed the complexion of my writing courses. Both teacher and student benefit when students are engaged with the course material.

The second benefit of incorporating social media into the classroom is that students' experimentation with the rhetorical situations of social media allows them to see themselves as capable and practiced writers and rhetors. Students see themselves as novices when it comes to academic writing. Yet they are experts at writing for social media, and recognizing themselves as experts in one sense, makes the idea of them becoming experts at academic writing more conceivable. At the very least, the fact that they are experts in one setting makes them more willing to build their expertise in another.

While there is still a lot of work involved in transferring their newly recognized skills into an academic environment, this confidence makes them far more willing to attempt to achieve this transfer. Student confidence is often lacking in writing courses because they struggle to write within an unfamiliar discourse community, but once students know they already have rhetorical skills, the inevitable failures and roadblocks become far more manageable.

Perhaps the most important benefit of incorporating social media in the classroom is that students get to practice the transfer of writing skills that is often the ultimate goal of college writing courses. They begin by transferring those skills from one social media website to another before they are asked to take the skills they use on social media and apply them to their experimentation with memes. Since most, if not all, of my students are inexperienced meme creators, this assignment asks them to transfer their rhetorical skills to a new genre without pushing them to move straight from social media to academic writing. This assignment provides a middle step that allows them to practice this transfer before asking them to approach the intimidating task of transferring their social media writing skills to academic writing tasks.

Thus the social media unit of my course ends with a rhetorical analysis of their own meme creation, asking students to write in academic prose without asking them to write about a necessarily academic subject. Ultimately, incorporating writing prompts and assignments that ask students to reflect upon and experiment with social media encourages students to see themselves as capable writers while practicing the transfer they will inevitably find challenging. Practicing this transfer with digital forms of writing, however, builds student confidence enough to prepare them for the often daunting and always challenging task of learning academic writing.

REFERENCES

Alexander, J., & Rhodes, J. (2014). *On multimodality: New media in composition studies.* Urbana, IL: National Council of Teachers of Teachers of English.

Bartholomae, D. (1985). Inventing the university. In V. Villanueva (Ed.), *Cross talk in comp theory: A reader* (2nd ed., pp. 623–653). Urbana, IL: National Council of Teachers of English.

Bryant, K. (2013). Composing online: Integrating blogging into a comtemplative classroom. In K. Pytash & R. Ferdig (Ed.), Exploring technology for writing and writing instruction. (pp. 77-99). Hershey, PA, USA: IGI Global.

Carr, D. (2015, January 4). Selfies on a stick, and the social-content challenge for the media. *The New York Times*. Retrieved from http://www.nytimes.com/2015/01/05/business/media/selfies-on-a-stick-and-the-social-content-challenge-for-the-media.html?_r=0

Ferdig, R. E., & Trammell, K. D. (2004). Content delivery in the "blogosphere." *T.H.E. Journal Online*. Retrieved from http://thejournal.com/articles/2004/02/01

Goodwin-Jones, B. (2003). Blogs and wikis: Environments for on-line collaboration. *Language Learning & Technology*, *7*(2), 12–16.

Miller, C. (1884). Genre as social action. *The Quarterly Journal of Speech*, *70*(2), 151–167. doi:10.1080/00335638409383686

Morey, S. (2014). *The new media writer*. Southlake, TX: Fountainhead Press.

Perkins, D., & Salomon, G. (1992). *Transfer of learning. International Encyclopedia of Education* (2nd ed.). Boston, MA: Pergamon Press.

Prensky, M. (2001). Digital natives, digital immigrants. Retrieved from http://www.marcprensky.com/writing/Prensky%20-%20Digital%20Natives,%20Digital%20Immigrants%20-%20Part1.pdf

Rounasville, A., Goldberg, R., & Bawarshi, A. (2008). From incomes to outcomes: FYC students' prior genre knowledge, meta-cognition, and the question of transfer. *WPA*, *32*(1), 97–112.

Schroeder, J., & Boe, J. (2004). An Interview with Ken Macrorie: 'Arrangements for Truthtelling'. *Writing on the Edge*, *15*(1), 4–17.

Shaughnessy, M. P. (1976). Diving in: An introduction to basic writing. In V. Villanueva (Ed.), *Cross talk in comp theory: A reader* (2nd ed., pp. 311–317). Urbana, IL: National Council of Teachers of English. doi:10.2307/357036

Shifman, L. (2013). *Memes in digital culture*. Cambridge, MA: MIT Press.

Wardle, E. (2007). Understanding 'transfer' from FYC: Preliminary results of a longitudinal study. *WPA*, *31*(1/2), 65–85.

Chapter 7
Reblogging as Writing:
The Role of Tumblr in the Writing Classroom

Meghan McGuire
University of Delaware, USA

ABSTRACT

This chapter explores how multimodal composition and social media conventions can support writing and introduce students to writing to multiple audiences. This chapter will outline an assignment from logistics of Tumblr as a space to help students establish regular writing practices in online spaces. Additionally, this chapter will illustrate some aspects of resistance that students may have with the assignment and provide strategies that respond to these resistances to make the assignment more effective.

INTRODUCTION

Students are writing more now than ever before. This is due to what Andrea Lundsford (2013) referred to in her study on the writing habits of Stanford University freshmen as "life writing": text messages, tweets, status updates; most of their communication is facilitated by smart phones, tablets and social media applications. Yet, even with this increase in writing they do on their own time, when students enter the writing classroom, some students may still struggle with the composing process; sometimes the very act of writing seems daunting, and often they wonder how the writing we ask them to do will be applicable to them outside the classroom and in their future careers.

Writing teachers struggle as well to find ways to help students see that writing is not just a classroom activity, but will benefit them in their professional and civic communities for the rest of their lives. If writing teachers can find ways to capitalize on these "life writing" skills, there may be more opportunities to provide richer moments for context-specific writing, where scenarios replicate the kinds of writing students will encounter in professional capacities, at the same time giving them reasons to think more critically about who their audience is. While incorporating social media seems like a useful way to help students transition from life writing to academic writing to professional writing, the challenge for writing instructors is to find ways to use these applications in purposeful ways that complement the learning objectives of writing courses.

DOI: 10.4018/978-1-5225-0562-4.ch007

This chapter outlines a meaningful approach to incorporating social media into the writing classroom that gives students the opportunity to think about writing in larger situations than writing essays for their teachers. Using Tumblr in particular, students can explore the writing process in their future professions and develop regular writing habits by composing messages with text and images according to social media conventions.

THEORETICAL FRAMEWORK

Tracing Technology in Writing

The availability of technology has had a large impact on writing. As The New London Group (1996) wrote, "New communications media are reshaping the way we use language…that effective citizenship and productive work now require that we interact effectively using multiple languages, multiple Englishes, and communication patterns that more frequently cross cultural, community, and national boundaries" (p. 64). While new media scholars were noticing the impact of new media in all communication areas, educators have been slow to acknowledge these changes in practice. While people in professional and personal settings were more often using tools that allowed them to communicate in words, images, and sounds, Takayoshi and Selfe (2007) argued that, "*inside* many of these classrooms, students are producing essays that look much the same as those produced by their parents and grandparents" (p. 2). While technology was increasingly giving users the opportunity to write in new ways to reach larger audiences, students were still being prepared to write essays that catered to a very specific, scholarly audience, and not to the audiences they would encounter in their future careers or personal lives.

In her 2009 report to the National Council of the Teachers of English, Kathleen Blake Yancey argued that writing in the 21st century was "a call to help our students compose often, well and through these composings, become citizen writers of the country, citizen writers of the world, and citizen writers of the future" (p. 1). She, too, stressed the need to prepare our students for writing outside the classroom. To do that, educators must evolve how they teach writing along with how people write in situations outside the classroom. One way to respond to this call is to take writing off the printed page. Takayoshi and Selfe contend that students should be "composing in multiple modalities, if they hope to communicate successfully within the digital communication networks that characterize workplaces, schools, civic life, and span traditional cultural, national, geopolitical borders" (p. 3). Faigley (2003) further argues, "I can think of no scenario for the revival of public discourse that does not involve digital media" (p. 179). If students are to understand that writing and communication in their lives goes beyond the printed essays they are asked to write in the classroom, they need to practice with the ubiquitous tools and spaces they use in other facets of their lives.

To have students understand that writing, especially the writing they already do, is a social action where they can interact with larger audiences than their teacher and peers, then they must write for audiences beyond the four walls of the classroom. Finding opportunities for students to do this is imperative. While educators are quick to acknowledge technology is changing the shape of communication, integrating digital writing in the public sphere into the classroom remains a slow process. And with social media facilitating so much global digital communication, this integration is crucial.

To respond to these changes in technology, educators must rethink writing in the classroom. Clark (2010) writes:

The future of writing–based on a global, collaborative text, where all writing has the potential to become public–informs our classrooms and forms a new 'digital' imperative, one that asks how we can reshape our pedagogy with new uses of the technologies that are changing our personal and professional lives. (p. 28)

Teachers must not only think about technology's potential as a tool for writing, but about how it can promote writing and become part of the writing process in meaningful ways. Santos and Leahy (2014) believe that "[e]ducation in the digital era means acting as architects who design learning spaces, not as suppliers delivering a product" (p. 86). Educators can address this digital imperative by helping students explore the writing process with social media, rather than have them view social media as an end product.

As students will be writing in these spaces for more than just personal communication, they must be prepared to think about how audiences communicate not only through social media, but also in other digital spaces and situations beyond the research essay. Because of these considerations, the complexities of writing on social media are also worth exploring as a class as well. As Wolff (2014) argues, social media are "spaces for writing that, like more traditional print-based writing, have their own grammars, styles and linguistics" (p. 212). Tumblr in particular can allow students to delve into writing in a public space where they can practice using these different styles for social media and examine how they can relate to the writing they will do in various situations and with various audiences.

Tumblr as a Tool for Writing

Tumblr is a microblogging[1] site where users compose short posts. While it includes tools similar to those found in other social media applications such as, liking a post and/or replying to a post–which is equivalent to leaving a comment–there are also some differences that make it more flexible for writing in the classroom. It can be used for more conventional writing activities, such as daily responses or free-writing that can get students in the habit of practicing writing. Tumblr can also be used to explore writing and composing in different forms, such as images and source sharing.

Tumblr supports multimedia content such as video and images, and allows for more than 140 characters, unlike Twitter, which is also a microblogging site. The Tumblr site encourages users to "put anything they want" on their blogs ("Tumblr," n. d.). This self-described openness to different types of content can encourage students to explore all the possibilities of what writing can be. Because Tumblr makes it easy to integrate multiple modes of composition, it is a more functional social media site for slightly longer writing exercises. While Twitter can be helpful for conciseness, Tumblr provides a little more room for expository writing.

Visuals

Although Tumblr offers more room for text-based writing, its microblogging status comes from its emphasis on small-scale bits of information, most often through visuals. Because it facilitates visuals, students can also experiment with and explore how to use images to convey messages and respond to audiences' different information needs, which is important for the kinds of large-scale communication that students will be a part of in their professional discourses.

Among the most common posts on Tumblr are memes or gifs. Memes are images, videos or GIFs (animated images) that are passed among users online, making them viral and becoming recognizable and commonplace to large audiences. Dawkins (1976) defined memes as ways cultural information spread (p. 192). They become a part of cultural moments that appeal to large audiences and they are often altered and parodied to respond to other cultural moments. Because Tumblr so easily supports multimedia, as well as longer, text-based blog posts, it is a space that gives students the opportunity to think about using all the available means of composition for responses – text, still images, film, and audio. This is important, especially as multimodal texts become more commonplace in professional communication.

Information across many professional discourses often includes images or hyperlinks, especially as many of documents are created to read online. In fact, Mike Isaac (2015) recently reported in *The New York Times* that GIFs are even making their way into professional discourse with people including them in email conversations. Again, practicing the meaningful use of memes and GIFS in various situations prepare students to compose for audiences that are becoming increasingly used to reading short content and expect to find their information in a variety of modes.

Reblogging

Reblogging is another capability of Tumblr that can help students think about collaborative writing and sharing sources. Reblogging is when a user reposts another user's content in a way that gives credit to the original poster. The original post is accompanied by notes, which are an account of who has reblogged the post and where it has been reblogged. This allows students to think about writing as social action in terms of collaboration and sharing.

In reblogging, whether by simply reposting as the post originally was or adding to it by including additional information by replying with a comment, users are entering into and extending a conversation, giving others the opportunity to become part of the conversation and keep it going. Reblogging and commenting show how social media can be a beneficial tool to teach students about the collaborative nature of writing. They can understand the importance of being a part of and sharing information with community. They can also think about their own credibility as a source of information contributing to an existing conversation. And as a part of this, they can reflect on the rhetorical choice of what they reblog and the decisions they make regarding best information or mode of writing to contribute to their community.

Lunsford, Fishman, and Liew (2013) found that interacting through writing with their professional communities built "a sense of purposeful connection between students and their writing, allowing them to see that writing as something of worth" (p. 479). If students are reblogging posts from their professional communities, they can see the relevant topics of information for their field while becoming an active part of these discussions. The use of Tumblr can help students begin to make connections between their professional communities and their writing and to see that writing does have consequences outside the classroom.

Diverse Voices

Another facet of Tumblr that makes it a rich environment for writing in the classroom is that Tumblr users focus more on topics and issues, rather than focusing on crafting identities and connecting with people a user knows or wants to know. People often remain anonymous and still make meaningful contributions to discussions. It is not necessarily considered unethical to go by a pseudonym on Tumblr. While this Tumblr convention of anonymity does not always make the conversations richer, it does provide the potential for voices or stories that are often overlooked to be heard. In fact many users join Tumblr under a pseudonym so they can post more freely as the person they identify as and about issues they are passionate about without the backlash of possibly insensitive opposition.

Communities involved with issues of race and LGBT use Tumblr as a space for discussion because it can be more empowering to discuss these issues safely without the fear of repercussion. As feminist scholar Moya Bailey stated, "I see many more diverse images on Tumblr than I see anywhere else. It's one of the few places where I see fat people, trans women and trans women of color who are celebrated" (as qtd. in Safronova, 2014). Having access to a space where students can observe a diverse group of voices talking about diverse issues in ways they may have not seen before can be critical to helping students understand audience, the power of writing, and how the rhetorical situation of communication on social media can be much larger than their immediate surroundings and can contribute to much larger cultural conversations.

METHODOLOGY AND PEDAGOGY

In the classes I teach at the University of Delaware (UD), I prepare students to become professional writers such as medical writers, technical writer, public relation specialists, editors, etc. To prepare them, I ask them to write in genres and scenarios they will likely encounter in the workforce such as memos and proposals. Increasingly this has also included social media and how to consider its use in professional situations. Although students communicate on social media daily, I found that many of my students struggled to make the connection between the writing they did on social media in their personal lives with writing they may do in other contexts, such as school or work.

Because so much communication occurs on social media, students must be prepared to think about how audiences interact with information in these spaces. Writing has changed in large part because of how people read online. Audiences need to consume and share information quickly, so timeliness and length of writing is important to consider. A 2012 study by the Smart Data Collective found that a personal Facebook status of 70 characters or less will get 66% more engagement than a status that is more than 231 characters. That is a significant writing situation for students to consider, and the earlier students start to think about writing to those situations, the better. Creating short posts and images will be a beneficial and useful writing experience for them, and using social media in the classroom can promote this.

To address this, I asked my students to regularly write on Tumblr throughout the semester to practice writing in a space other than traditional notebooks, Microsoft Word documents or discussion boards. The major goals of the assignment were for students:

- Develop a rhetorical understanding of writing in different modes according to different social media conventions;
- Develop an understanding of writing as a process through regular writing practice; and
- Explore professional discourse on Tumblr.

By writing in a public space, students could see writing with an audience other than me as their teacher and practice responding to the diverse rhetorical situations of writing in social media at the same time as simply practicing writing. Students started with smaller writing exercise, responding to specific prompts or discussion. I also asked them to respond with various modes popular on Tumblr, including text-based posts, images (including memes and gifs), videos, links, and reblogs. Additionally, I required that each post include a hashtag in order to categorize it into both classroom conversation and larger, public conversations. As the assignment progressed, I began to ask students to write some posts on their own without any constraints. The Tumblr site also became a space to post in-class activities, as well as a repository of sources available for larger research projects comprised of the articles the students posted.

PARTICIPANTS

I used this assignment in a class I taught in the English Department at UD, "Topics in Professional Writing." This particular class was focused on professional uses of social media. For example, the class examined topics such as how NASA used Twitter or how social media was used for emergency response during Hurricane Sandy. The students were primarily sophomore, junior, and senior English majors with a concentration in Professional Writing, but additionally there was a Business major, Engineering Major and Food Science major taking the class to complete their second writing requirement.

These students were considered what Prensky (2001) coined a "digital native"; they had spent their entire lives surrounded by technology and do not remember a time without it. Every single one of them had their own laptop, tablet, or at the very least, a smart phone, that they brought to class. In fact, because the class was about social media, I encouraged them to bring whatever technology they felt comfortable using in class to work on. While many of them were familiar with social media applications like Facebook, Twitter, Instagram and Snap Chat, after doing an informal, oral survey of the class, I found that only a couple of students had used Tumblr.

EXPLORATION

To give students an understanding of the various kinds of writing on Tumblr, I began the semester-long assignment by asking students to analyze different Tumblr accounts, exploring the writing that was done on Tumblr in discourses they were interested investigating the social media conventions that are specific to Tumblr and the kinds of rhetorical choices, both effective and ineffective, that were made in those accounts. Banks (2006) writes that it is important for students to learn not only how to use the tools, but, "individually and collectively to be able to use critique, resist, design and change technologies in ways that are relevant to their lives and needs, rather than those of the corporations that hope to sell them" (p. 41). Students should be able to decide how these spaces are going to work for them and their own communicative purposes, rather than use them blindly.

They should also understand how the space works for the rhetorical situation at hand and what choices will be best for audiences to interact with information. I encouraged students to look at Tumblr accounts that were related to their interests or future professions. For example, students interested in doing social media marketing followed digital media website, *Mashable's* Tumblr, and students interested in publishing followed the publishing house, Harper Collin's Tumblr. The class took note of the tone of the posts, the mode of the posts, what hashtags were being used, whom they followed and how they interacted with other accounts. This gave students the chance to see the difference between personal, informal content and how Tumblr can be used professionally.

The kinds of images that were integrated into the professional posts and how the professional posts used memes effectively were likewise analyzed. We also spent time analyzing the layouts of various accounts and how some templates aided in facilitating information delivery better than others. For example, if the hashtags for each post were on the side of the post, it was easier to see how they are categorized or what the post might be about than if the hashtags were at the very bottom of the post.

COMPOSING ON TUMBLR

Creating Accounts

When students were ready to put their Tumblr to practice, I invited them to a group Tumblr for the class. Each student needed a Tumblr account to participate in the group blog; many students already had a personal account, but they decided to create a new account to keep their personal and professional thoughts separate. This was helpful as many students worried about their classmates and me as the teacher having access to parts of their personal lives. This also opened up a space to discuss professional identities. As I discussed earlier, the anonymous aspect of Tumblr is important, but for the purpose of the class, there did need to be some visibility to see who was writing what, especially as students moved into investigating their professional discourses. How they crafted their Tumblr profile was aided by the research they did into their professional discourses. They were able to see how others in their field presented themselves or their organizations. By creating a more professional online persona, students were learning how to build their own ethos as they began to interact in these professional conversations and build their professional literacy in terms of how to represent themselves.

In addition to navigating personal and professional writing on Tumblr, many students were also concerned with navigating a new space. To help remove this fear or anxiety about writing in a new space, the first half of a 75-minute class period was set-aside for students to set up their accounts. While we were not in a computer lab, all students in the class had a laptop, tablet or smart phone with them to set up their accounts. This in-class time could also be used for instructors to present a tutorial on how to post different content to the Tumblr, as well as how to reblog posts and how to comment on posts. The class, as a group, also decided on the template for the account and considered how the interface of the Tumblr template could better help readers access their information.

Posting Content

To encourage the habit of writing, I asked students to contribute to the class Tumblr a total of five times a week for the rest of the semester. They responded to specific prompts I gave them or responded to a reading, either in-class or as homework, two to three times a week. For example, I asked them to discuss a protest movement that social media figured predominately in, like Occupy Wall Street. Another example asked them to analyze a business or organization's social media presence based on the strategies from "A Social Media Primer for Technical Communicators" by Meredith Singleton and Lisa Meloncon (2011). They were also asked to post on their own outside the structured writing prompts two to three times a week. Often these posts responded to current news stories that involved social media.

In keeping with social media writing as shorter units of information and text, students were asked to keep their posts to a certain length. They began with 250 words, and by the end of the semester, they were responding with less than 150 words. This encouraged them to be concise, while still providing substantial responses that illustrated engagement with the reading or topic of discussion. The brevity of texts also supported their posts as they began using images in responses.

In addition to their text-driven responses, they were asked to respond with a meme or an image (see Figure 1), or a link to another article that related to a class reading or discussion, or that responded to an issue or added to professional discourse. I also occasionally asked them to reblog from another account or respond to a Tumblr post from an account of someone outside the class, such as a writer from their specific industry (see Figure 2). By asking students to specifically post in modes that reflect Tumblr, teachers can, as Santos and Leahy further argue, "engineer such discovery and help students explore forms of writing they may not have considered by periodically asking that some portions of the students' online writing to adhere to certain constraints that we have set" (p. 90). I felt that by directing students to the kinds of communication available to them, they could see how including images or links can be beneficial to their communication. They were then challenged to make thoughtful choices about how to convey information to their audiences in meaningful ways.

A further component to the assignment was that every post, no matter what the mode, was hashtagged. Hashtags were used in two ways:

1.   To connect the course conversations through their readings and prompt responses.
2.   To enter their professional discourses.

After some discussion of hashtags as a rhetorical strategy, students worked together to choose the course hashtag. For our specific class, they chose #UDENG413. This showed the university they were part of, the department the course was in, and the course number. Then they individually discovered what hashtags were typically used in other Tumblr accounts in their future professional communities or accounts dealing with topics that they were interested in. This gave them the opportunity to see what

Figure 1. A response with a meme

For all of the Seinfeld fans IN CLASS, I saw this and thought of the conversation we had a couple weeks ago.

Figure 2. A reblogged post

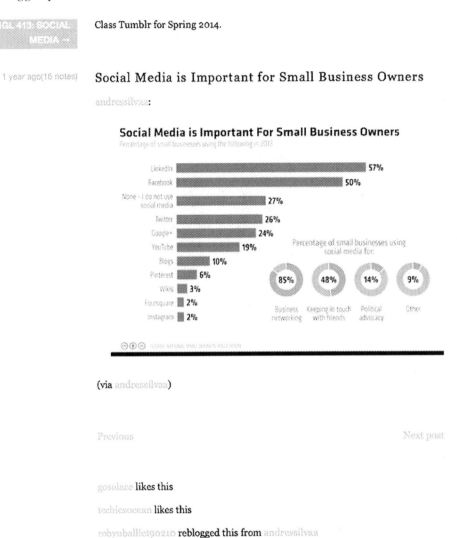

language or practices are privileged by certain discourses. It also assisted in their work getting categorized and interconnected with other Tumblr posts on similar topics and becoming a part of a larger network of conversations. This helps students, as Santos and Leahy write, "explore the many kinds of writing available on the web and determining what kinds of writing practices privileged by their online communities are best for expressing their own interests" (p. 88). If a student was interested in the fashion industry or video game design, he or she saw what hashtags are used most often and began to incorporate them into their own posts to connect the professional discourse (see Figure 3).

Figure 3. Professional discourse

ENGL 413: SOCIAL MEDIA →   Class Tumblr for Spring 2014.

11 months ago   Cosmopolitan Magazine Mission Statement →

Cosmopolitan: Like #ElleWoods says, we are the "Bible."

Cosmopolitan: We are #FunFearlessFemales.

Cosmopolitan: Fashion, relationships, and health, oh my!

Cosmopolitan: Driving conversations that matter since the 1960s.

RESULTS AND DISCUSSION

Ultimately, there were some students who struggled with aspects of the assignment. Many were challenged by the word limit of their responses. Some students were not as successful in finding a professional discourse to take part in. Additionally, some began to rely heavily on posting visuals and had to be reminded to occasionally compose text. And for some, Tumblr was an assignment to complete for a grade, and there was little engagement in the learning. However, for a great deal of students, this was a successful activity that prompted interaction with writing in various ways.

While this assignment began in a more structured format where I assigned the writing prompts, modes of responses, and due dates, students eventually began to write on their own, even when not directed. As the semester progressed and students became more acquainted with Tumblr and developed a writing routine, the posts took on different shapes as students began exploring different modes of writing. They included images, such as memes, with their reading responses (see Figure 4). They also began to respond to each other's posts, as well as posts by users outside the course. The more time they spent writing on Tumblr, the more comfortable they began to feel writing on their own. These unguided posts students composed showcased that they were less intimidated and they felt acknowledged by a larger audience than me alone.

The longer students spent on Tumblr exploring other blogs and crafting their own content, the more their posts began to seem less like traditional writing responses and more like typical Tumblr posts (see Figure 5). Students became encouraged when their class writing began to take the shape of a typical Tumblr blog and would begin to check in with it throughout the day. Occasionally a student would come to class with a story of how someone they did not know liked or reblogged something they had posted. For many students, this was an opportunity to take notice of how they were interacting with a world outside the classroom.

Resistances and Challenges

Because many students are adept at "life writing" and are familiar with social media applications like, Facebook, Twitter, and Instagram for personal communication, instructors often assume students can complete these assignments without any guidance or preparation. But writing in these spaces for purposes unlike what they are used to can be difficult for students, especially if writing in general feels

Figure 4. An undirected post

Class Tumblr for Spring 2014.

Although this is not an article, I thought this was really relevant to our class
discussion. As a person who does not have a smart phone, I have found that this
sort of judgement has been passed on me. Ten years ago, this phenomenon was
not observed. The evolution of the smart phone is just one of the many ways that
technology has impacted our culture.

Figure 5. Typical looking Tumblr response

Class Tumblr for Spring 2014.

Taco Bell advertisement circa 1979. Their target audience today clearly has not
changed since then: guys in the 18-25 y/o range. Social media has only
perpetuated this target, using "young" and "hip" lingo on Twitter and staying
very relevant on other social medias (Vine, Snapchat). The blonde guy in this ad
could easily fit into one of Taco Bell's Vine or Instagram videos today, nearly 35
years later.

(The also looks like me. Weird.)

uncomfortable to them prior to class. This is why there are some challenges for instructors to keep in mind when using social media, specifically Tumblr, in the writing classroom

Many educators make the assumption that students come to the classroom already well equipped to do projects with social media. As Purdy (2010) notes, educators assume that because students use these applications for personal communication outside of class, they should easily be able to jump right into an assignment using social media without much discussion or tutorial (p. 56). Carrying these assumptions into this assignment can alter or limit its effectiveness. Instructors must consider that some students may not easily transition to these new writing situations. Moving the academic writing process from traditional paper to alternative spaces already feels risky, but asking them to write in a space they associate with more personal communication can be paralyzing to some students.

Often, when many of the students were faced with a new writing situation, their anxiety about the new tool often impeded the content of the composition. In the classroom, students expect to write for certain purposes (research essays) and in certain modes (the printed page). When students are asked to write in new ways for academic purposes, they let their fear of failure get in the way. They most likely have composed a message with an image or included a hyperlink in a post to a friend, but that was a different situation, without a grade attached. The complexities of a new space and a larger audience outside the teacher seem risky to them. Even if they are very comfortable using social media for personal reasons, it is often hard for them to transition to using it for academic reasons. Although they may understand that the idea of an audience is much more public in these spaces, students still worry about anyone who is not their teacher seeing their work.

Additionally, some may not be familiar with Tumblr in the same ways they are Facebook or Twitter. Approaching the assignment with the expectation that students can easily move from one social media space to another can also impact the assignment. In fact, according to the Pew Internet Research Center (2015), only 14% of teenagers ages 13-17 use Tumblr, as opposed to Facebook (71%) and Twitter (33%). Further, many students are not as digitally savvy as they are expected to be, and not every student has had access to social media or the technology it is used with. There are still areas of the United States where access to these tools is limited. To many students, Tumblr is a brand new application that some may have difficulties navigating.

When they are asked to write in an unfamiliar space, students often get caught up in the logistics of that space, rather than focusing on the content or how the space can aid in writing. For example, Tumblr, like many social media spaces, occasionally updates its interface, and when students could not find the option needed to post a blog entry or an image in the same place they found it before, they would often panic that they would not be able to complete their assignment. Educators should, as scholars such as Vaidhyanathan (2008) and Thomas (2011) argue, acknowledge the varying levels of technological expertise students bring to the classroom and recognize that there may be some limitations in the learning curve. For these reasons, finding the right means to integrate writing on Tumblr successfully is important to help students feel less anxious about a new writing situation.

DEVELOPING SUCCESSFUL STRATEGIES

In-Class Writing Time

One suggestion to encourage students in this transition is to provide some class time to get acclimated to Tumblr and how it works. In addition to setting up the class Tumblr together, giving students brief in-class time to write their posts in the first few weeks of the semester can be helpful. This way, if they have questions about how to insert a link or image, or reblog from another site, they have an opportunity to ask the people around them. One option is to have students do a reading for a class and then have the instructor pose a question to respond to on Tumblr as the class period begins. This helps students get used to how the space works for certain modes and to get in the habit of writing regularly, which will improve their overall writing skills. The in-class writing can also be used as a springboard for class discussion. As David Gooblar (2014) states on *The Chronicle Vitae* blog, the in-class writing activity

... lays the groundwork for a good class discussion. Not every student is equally talented at thinking on her feet. By giving your students a chance to think and write about the day's topic, you'll improve your chances of having an interesting and constructive discussion.

In-class writing helps students reflect on the reading and focus for the rest of the class. Additionally, this gives shyer students a chance to participate. If classrooms have a computer and projector in the room, instructors can display the class Tumblr so that it becomes a community activity and students can talk through their responses.

Community Learning

One of the best ways to support student learning as community is to ask students in the class who have used Tumblr to be peer tutors for the space. Inevitably, one or two students have some experience with Tumblr and are willing to help their peers. At the beginning of the assignment, instructors could split the class into small groups, making sure that a Tumblr "expert" is in each one to help with the initial process of joining the site and crafting the first posts. This helps build community in the classroom and enables students to be more resourceful in helping each other. This can help students feel more comfortable with a new writing situation that may seem daunting to them. DeVoss, Johansen, Selfe, and Williams (2003) suggest that by being able to observe their peers and ask questions of them, students will feel more comfortable when they do work on their own (p. 166).

Interacting with peers doing the same projects can help alleviate some of their anxiety. In the first week weeks of this class, students often found new ways Tumblr worked and would come in and share these tips in the first few weeks. For example, one student discovered that to separate multiple hashtags, users must hit return or enter rather than just inserting a space in between each one. The New London Group (1996) call this "Overt Instruction." These types of activities "focus the learner on the important feature of their experience and activities within the community of learners; and that allow the learner to gain explicit information at times when it can most usefully organize and guide practice..." (p. 33). Exploring in a community of learners can help students feel more comfortable writing in an unknown space.

Reflection

A final recommendation would be to have check-in days or points in the semester where students can give feedback on the experiences of writing on Tumblr. Students can write reflective memos to the instructor detailing their experiences writing on Tumblr for class. This was helpful because I was able to gauge the assignment and see where some adjustments can be made. For example, some students noted that they found it hard to remember to post on their own outside of class, so I began including a reminder with other homework announcements. These reflective assignments also give students some agency in their learning process. When they are given an outlet to share their experiences, they may engage with the assignment more.

Students can also take time to reflect on the experience of writing in their future discourses. They start to understand language choices and issues relevant to their fields. As they step back and look at the choices they made, they will feel more confident knowing that they are capable of writing to these larger audiences. This is a good opportunity to ask them to consider the experience of using a social media space for classroom writing as compared to their personal social media use and to see if there has been any impact or intersection between the two writing situations or if they are more conscious about their rhetorical choices in their personal social media communication.

For example, one of my students mentioned that they started thinking more about proofing their posts in other social media applications because they had gotten in the habit of reading over their posts before the published them on Tumblr. Another student mentioned they were surprised at how many organizations post memes on their Tumblrs and that made her see how social media conventions are for more than personal use. The ability to be critical of the how these spaces promote writing in larger contexts is a valuable tool for students to make decisions about writing on social media for many different purposes.

Taking this knowledge to future writing projects, no matter what mode they are written in, can help them work more efficiently. This helps them feel more comfortable with the composition process. Selber (2004) writes that reflection is "valuable in that the connections between language and practical experience are not always made clear in technological contexts" (p. 205). Yancey (1998) contends that reflecting and asking themselves about the modes they choose to use over other modes help students "to develop as members of a writing public" (p. 311). It gives them a sense of responsibility and helps them see where their choices impact a larger picture.

CONCLUSION

Teaching writing can be challenging. Instructors must not only prepare students for writing in their academic careers, but in their professional and civic lives. In fact, a study done by The National Association of College and Employers (2015), found that 73.4% of employers want candidates with strong written communication skills, so it is more critical than ever that students are prepared to write, research, and think critically in any situation. In addition, instructors must acknowledge the continuously changing landscape of digital communication technology that is prevalent in all areas of lives. Using social media in the writing classroom is no longer just about engaging students as writers, but has become a necessity to equip them to communicate effectively in these social media spaces - especially when, according to the Pew Internet Research Center, as of January 2014, 74% of adult Americans are online and gathering information.

By incorporating social media applications such as Tumblr into the writing classroom, teachers can help students prepare to communicate for academic and professional purposes, as well as to become articulate community members online, where they are living a large part of their lives. As Clark writes, "The public domain is just one facet of the new critical democracy in which our students will be asked to live and work" (p.34). Integrating social media shows students that it is not just a tool for writing, but is also meaningful space to communicate in important ways.

Outlining Tumblr as a writing space demonstrates its value in the writing classroom and that it can be used within the context of other writing courses. With strategic Tumblr use, students are first able to acclimate to the process of writing, rather than focus on the finished product. Second, they are able to understand the larger context of writing and how it benefits them beyond their role as students, and in this particular assignment, how they are preparing themselves for their careers and begin to situate themselves within that context. Tumblr can also be used to explore the many different ways of exploring how people write about a large number of issues and topics in a global context, including both text-based and multimodal writing. Finally, by allowing students to empower themselves by learning the various components and tools of Tumblr and assisting their classmates as well, teachers can give them some agency in their own learning and enable them to find pride and ownership in what they have done.

REFERENCES

Adsanatham, C. (2012). Integrating assessment and instruction: Using student-generated grading criteria to evaluate multimodal digital projects. *Computers and Composition*, 29(21), 152–174. doi:10.1016/j.compcom.2012.04.002

Banks, A. (2006). *Race, rhetoric, and technology: Searching for higher ground*. Mahwah, NJ: Lawrence Erlbaum.

Clark, J. (2009). The digital imperative: Making the case for a 21st-century pedagogy. *Computers and Composition*, (27): 27–35.

DeVoss, D. N., Johanson, J., et al. (2003). Under the radar of composition programs: Glimpsing the future through case studies of literacy in electronic texts. In Bloom, Daiker and White (Eds.), Composition studies in the new millennium: Rereading the past, rewriting the future (pp. 157-173). Carbondale: Southern Illinois University Press.

Faigley, L. (2003). The challenge of the multimedia essay. In Bloom, Daiker and White (Eds.), Composition studies in the new millennium: Rereading the past, rewriting the future (pp. 174-187). Carbondale: Southern Illinois University Press.

Gooblar, D. (2014, July 2). The obvious benefits of in-class writing assignments. *The Chronicle Vitae*. Retrieved https://chroniclevitae.com/news/588-the-obvious-benefits-of-in-class-writing-assignments

Isaac, M. (2015, August 3). For mobile messaging, GIFs prove to be worth at least a thousand words. *The New York Times*. Retrieved from http://www.nytimes.com/2015/08/04/technology/gifs-go-beyond-emoji-to-express-thoughts-without-words.html

Optimizing Facebook engagement – the effect of post length. (2012, June 27). *Smart Data Collective*. Retrieved http://www.smartdatacollective.com/morgan-j-arnold/52456/optimizing-facebook-engagement-effect-post-length

Prensky, M. (2001). Digital natives, digital immigrants. *On the horizon.*, (9): 1–6.

Purdy, J. (2010). The changing space of research: Web 2.0 and the integration of research and writing environments. *Computers and Composition*, 27(1), 48–58. doi:10.1016/j.compcom.2009.12.001

Safronova, V. (2014, December 20). Millennials and the age of Tumblr activism. *The New York Times.* Retrieved from http://www.nytimes.com/2014/12/21/style/millennials-and-the-age-of-tumblr-activism.html

Santos, M., & Leahy, M. (2014). Postpedagogy and web writing. *Computers and Composition, 32,* 84–95. doi:10.1016/j.compcom.2014.04.006

Selber, S. (2004). *Multiliteracies for a digital age.* Carbondale: Southern Illinois University Press.

Social networking fact sheet. (n. d.). *Pew Internet.* Retrieved from http://www.pewinternet.org/fact-sheets/social-networking-fact-sheet/

Takayoshi, P., & Selfe, C. (2007). Thinking about modality. In C. Selfe (Ed.), *Multimodal composition: Resources for teachers* (pp. 1–12). Cresskill, NJ: Hampton Press.

Teens, social media & technology overview 2015. (2015, April 9). *Pew Internet.* Retrieved from http://www.pewinternet.org/2015/04/09/teens-social-media-technology 2015/

The New London Group. (1996). A pedagogy of multiliteracies: Designing social futures. *Harvard Educational Review*, (66): 60–93.

The skills/qualities employers want in new college graduate hires. (2014, November 18). *National Association of College and Employers.* Retrieved http://www.naceweb.org/about-us/press/class-2015-skills-qualities-employers-want.aspx

Thomas, M. (2011). *Deconstructing digital natives: Young people, technology, and the new literacies.* New York, NY: Routledge.

Tumblr. (n. d.). Retrieved from tumblr.com

Wolff, W. (2013). Interactivity and the invisible: What counts as writing in the age of web 2.0. *Computers and Composition, 30*(3), 211–225. doi:10.1016/j.compcom.2013.06.001

Yancey, K. (1998). *Reflection in the writing classroom.* Logan, Utah: Utah State University Press.

ENDNOTE

[1]   Microblogging is posting short online updates.

Section 3
Theorizing about Social Media Networks in the Writing Classroom

The four chapters that complete this section are grounded in theoretical concepts. While each chapter offers readers ideas about how to implement social media networks into a writing classroom, they more specifically invite readers to interrogate and explore social media networks for their rhetorical characteristics and situations.

Chapter 8
Socializing Composition:
Entering the Conversation of SNS in Composition

Ken Hayes
Southwestern Oklahoma State University, USA

ABSTRACT

The goal of this chapter is to act as a primer for scholars looking start working with social networking site (SNS) in the composition classroom. This chapter focuses on research regarding aspects of SNS use in and out of the classroom, such as identity, rhetorical/audience awareness, civic engagement, and SNS pedagogy. This chapter also relies on current discourse, as well as the author's own SNS experiences, to share lists of best practices and SNS activities in the composition classroom. This chapter ends with a call for future research that includes continued efforts to interact more directly with students to learn with them about their use and views of SNS in and out of the composition classroom.

INTRODUCTION

As I find myself transitioning from life as a college student to that of a professor of composition, I realize how Social Networking Sites (SNS) have been a continuous presence for me in and out of the classroom. My academic life has been punctuated by moments of engaging with SNS. I remember spending plenty of time as a freshman in campus computer labs trying to find all of my high school friends who had just signed on to Facebook, and building my MySpace wall. In my last year as an undergraduate, classrooms were making more frequent use of computers and it was becoming more and more common to see students scrolling through their Facebook walls during class or spending time in the computer labs between classes updating profiles and posting.

Then, as I began to transition into the world of graduate school, I found myself walking the line between student and teacher, and I remember teaching classes and seeing my own students trying to hide the fact that they were signed into their SNS instead of working on an activity or participating in a discussion. In many ways my experience with SNS as an undergraduate echoes the experiences of the undergraduates I was teaching, whether or not I initially realized it.

DOI: 10.4018/978-1-5225-0562-4.ch008

I also remember the dissatisfied feeling I got when I sat in on the first workshop for the department that discussed the use of Facebook in the classroom. As a Graduate TA in my second year of teaching, I was intrigued by the idea of incorporating something new into the composition classroom. However, as a student who was still grappling with the fact that Facebook had just recently been opened for access to the general public and as someone who was unsure what that meant about his personal interaction with family and acquaintances, I was skeptical when the primary pedagogical suggestion from the individual running the workshop was to simply use Facebook as a space to meet with students and connect. I did not like the idea of so blatantly mixing school with personal life, and I was sure many of the undergrads who had just begun to sign up to the SNS, and just starting to carve out a place for themselves in those spaces, would probably not respond positively to such implementation either. The pedagogue in me decided to keep SNS and classroom activities separate from one another.

However, as I finished my Masters in Literature and began life in the Rhetoric and Writing Doctoral program, I began to use a greater variety of SNS, and I started to view my own, and others', use of SNS with a more critical lens. I began to see that the rhetorical moves and considerations we were discussing in the seminars were being played out in these online spaces. Fellow grad students, as well as the FYC students I taught in my own classes, were having debates on SNS. They were creating new kinds of content that entertained, informed, and connected them to people with various perspectives on the world. I perceived the term multimodal composition for the first time, and after seeing classroom activities being built around analyzing websites and witnessing the incorporation of digital tools to discuss audience, and rhetorical composition, I began to consider SNS as spaces with legitimate potential for expanding the discussion of rhetorical composition in the composition classroom.

As I considered the idea of using SNS in the composition classroom, I began to further reflect on the ways in which I had seen instructors attempt to incorporate online technology, and SNS in particular, into the classroom: often without success. I also thought of the workshop I had attended as a masters student and it occurred to me that in so many instances the instructors using SNS in the classroom, or the workshop leaders discussing how to incorporate SNS in the composition classroom, often did so independently, without input from the students who would be working with these technologies in the classroom. This is problematic for at least two reasons. First, there are often discrepancies between how students use technology outside the classroom, and how instructors attempt to use the same technology inside the classroom, which can cause a disruption in the students' ability and willingness to engage with such technologies as learning tools. Second, the use of SNS can be a deeply personal experience, and if certain instructors incorporate SNS too heavily or inappropriately in the classroom, students may not fully participate for fear of having some of the personal element of SNS stripped from their experiences.

SNS is an important part of life for composition students and SNS use is becoming ever more prevalent in the day-to-day interactions of society. Selfe (1999) argues that awareness of what she calls a "new literacy agenda" is:

An integral part of educator's larger responsibility to understand the way in which our culture thinks about and values literacy. Perhaps even more important, this awareness is part of our ethical responsibility to understand how literacy and literacy instruction directly and continually affects the lived experiences of the individuals and families with whom we come into contact as teachers. (p. xix)

Over the last decade, SNS have become some of the primary avenues through which to shape literacy in the lived experiences of so many students. Thus, it is important as ever to pay attention to the ways in which students and SNS impact one another in order to develop ways of understanding SNS, while critically thinking about, talking about, and rhetorically using SNS to make a positive impact on the personal, professional, social, and civic lives of all who may be impacted by the use of SNS.

As a frequent user of SNS for social, personal, and professional reasons, I strive to use SNS in the most effective and responsible ways possible for my given purposes, which include my use of SNS in the composition classroom as pedagogical and rhetorical tools. Thus, this project comes about out of a continuous personal desire to better understand SNS and their use, in order to responsibly, ethically and effectively work with such sites in the composition classroom.

Therefore, it is with this attempt at paying attention or, remaining aware, that I proceed with the remainder of this chapter. My goal is to use this chapter as a kind of starting point for an emerging scholar in the field like myself to begin to understand the ways in which SNS are already being viewed and used in and for the composition classroom. Then, by calling on these valuable resources and concepts while using my own experiences with SNS (as a student, teacher, and citizen), I use this chapter to list ideas for potential best practices and classroom activities utilizing SNS, while discussing what I see as important trajectories for myself and others to follow for future research on the subject of SNS in the composition classroom.

ESTABLISHING THE CONVERSATION

Today, our college-age youth are engaging in composition on Social Networking Sites (SNS) more than ever before. According to the Pew Research Center (2014), 89% of Internet users between the ages of eighteen and twenty-nine use social networking sites, and 35% of all Twitter users are in that age range. Moreover, because of SNS popularity, teachers are continually trying to incorporate them into the classroom. Yet, while such integration has the potential to engage teachers and students alike in critical activities regarding the use of such sites and their potential as rhetorical tools, there is also a potential danger in promoting the use of these sites without teaching students to think critically about the positive and negative consequences of SNS use.

In order to determine ways of viewing SNS practices and their (potential) roles in the composition classroom, my primary goal is to establish what is already being done in the field regarding SNS. As teachers continue to consider the role SNS can and do play in and out of the composition classroom, considering issues of identity, rhetorical/audience awareness, civic engagement, and privacy are of paramount importance. Indeed, as computer technology and SNS are integrated more into the lives of users, and more time is spent engaging with these technologies, it becomes more important to consider the impact these interactions have on users' establishing and maintaining their online identities.

Moreover, as incorporation of SNS becomes more prevalent in our day-to-day personal, social, and professional lives, it becomes increasingly necessary to build skills identifying when and where to use SNS effectively and responsibly, all while being able to understand who will be engaging with what is posted. To this end, it is also important to help students consider the large-scale social ramifications of their interactions on SNS, whether intentional or not, and to consider ways in which they can use SNS for active and positive civic engagement—should students choose to do so.

Of course, in order to ethically and effectively engage with students in the classroom with SNS, student privacy is of utmost importance. Thus with any discussion of SNS in and out of the FYW class, issues of privacy must always be on the minds of educators. From the potential for hacked student accounts, to the students willingly engaging on SNS and all of the data tracking processes that go on online, there are a number of privacy concerns that students may not be fully aware of, and providing them with such information throughout the incorporation of SNS in the composition classroom should be a priority.

What follows is a brief introduction to some of the key conversations that inform my early understanding of SNS use and understanding, which include issues of identity, rhetorical/audience awareness, civic engagement, and privacy, as well as the ways instructors can consider these ideas to incorporate SNS in the classroom in a pedagogically sound manner.

Identity

Perhaps at the core of all these considerations of SNS use and their impact is the potential role SNS plays in identity creation. With society's increased interaction on SNS spaces, individuals are inevitably going to be further influenced by such spaces, not only when thinking about those that they interact with, but when thinking about who they are as individuals. Arola (2010) points to the design of interactive sites on the web as limiting user experiences and impacting how they create their online identity. Arola (2010) posits, for instance, that:

The visual dominance of the News Feed suggests its importance, and because it is so much larger than any other section of the page, it encourages us to understand others through their actions in Facebook. It also encourages us to understand ourselves in relation to the actions of others. (p. 8)

Thus, not only does Facebook use privilege following the lives of others in their day-to-day lives, but it similarly forces users to consider their own lives relative to the lives of those they are following.

Wandel and Beavers (2010) discuss ways users connect to one another on Facebook, suggesting:

When my friends list is populated by people from different parts of my life, any pretending I engage in to find a self-concept happens in front of all of them. I am thus no longer radically free to engage in creating a completely fictive self. I must become [someone] I am allowed to be and what I am able to negotiate in the careful dynamic between who I want to be and who my friends from these multiple constituencies perceive me, allow me, and need me to be. (pp. 92-93)

Thus, when interacting on SNS users are constantly considering their public image, and what to post and avoid posting in order to build or maintain that image. Indeed, because these interfaces are streamlined and rarely change, their presence becomes engrained and users focus on the posts as self-representation instead of using the interface for self-expression, thus, "You are what you post and what others post about you" (Arola, 2010, p. 9). As such, it is vital that we as students, pedagogues, and citizens are aware of what, how, and why we post and interact on SNS.

Rhetorical Audience/Awareness

Another primary topic regarding the use of SNS is its impact on users' awareness of rhetorical strategies and considerations of audience in personal, professional, social, and civic situations. So often, the level of overlap between these realms on SNS surprises students, and calling attention to how and what they post about a party they attended over the weekend can play a role in their future social and professional lives is tremendously important. It is vital that students understand just how many different people can interact with them in SNS spaces. Indeed, Maranto and Barton (2010) state that SNS can produce significant opportunities for users to engage and rhetorically interact with a vast multitude of other users with myriad contexts and stakes.

In fact, according to Maranto and Barton (2010), "Users can search for others who share their labels or interests, and request to add them as 'friends,'" and "the most popular users are hubs for millions of others—swirling vortexes of shared interests and common goals" (p. 43). However, if students in an FYC classroom are unaware of how to interact within these "hubs" based on various situational contexts, they will be at a disadvantage compared to those who do.

Another potential concern regarding rhetorical and audience awareness is the possibility for limited connection with individuals and ideas with which users may not already be familiar. DeAndra, Shaw, and Levine (2010) assert that the primary function of SNS, like Facebook, is to "aide users in maintaining their already existing relationships" (p. 430), and ongoing changes to SNS make such sites less likely to produce unique connections that provide users with opportunities to fully develop their rhetorical and audience awareness.

For instance, Google+ disrupts making unique connections by offering an addition to the Facebook friends list, which is called "circles." With circles, an individual is able to place each of his/her friends in separate groups of people that share a particular interest or bond in association with the original user (e.g. family, friends, work associates, etc.). After a user's circles are established, the user is able to post information to individual circles, which can only be viewed by people within the posted-to circle, which further limits the chance of exposure to new people and ideas. Marwick and boyd (2010) claim, "Twitter flattens multiple audiences into one – a phenomenon known as 'context collapse'. The requirement to present a verifiable, singular identity makes it impossible to differ self-presentation strategies, creating tension as diverse groups of people flock to social network sites" (p. 122). However, with the advent of Google+' "circles," this "content collapse" is mitigated as people are able to control what content is viewed by which people; thus removing most tension that would have been present, and creating a series of more homogenous environments.

Graff (2003) discusses the importance of entering the rhetorical conversation by considering potential audiences who may differ from us. He states, "in order to write a conversation into her text, Ellen needs to do something that can be hard for everyone but especially hard for young people: to imagine a person whose beliefs are different from her own" (Graff, 2003, p.160). However, for individuals to understand how to imagine and work with/around those with differing views, they must first be made aware that such situations and individuals exist in order to create such a "rhetorical situation" (Bitzer, 1968, p. 6). Yet, if students are constantly interacting only with those with whom they agree or share common beliefs, fewer such situations present themselves, and students will likely have a more difficult time honing the skills needed for effective rhetorical expression.

Civic Engagement

Another topic of importance, when considering the SNS use and the reach of that use on a world scale, is that of civic engagement through SNS. For the purposes of this chapter, I mean civic engagement through SNS to represent engagement in activities and interaction on SNS for the purpose of activism beyond simple social interaction. In other words, posting about one's recent personal experiences, or liking/favoriting another person's post is not likely to engage others in a cause or inspire much social change. On the other hand, a phenomenon such as the ALS ice bucket challenge in the summer of 2014, where individuals posted videos raised awareness for ALS and helped raise $100 million in thirty days, according to the ALS Association (2014), is an example of such promotion.

One major consideration regarding this topic is that despite the potential use of SNS for civic engagement (as demonstrated with movements such as Occupy Wall Street, the Arab Spring and #BlackLivesMatter), teachers cannot expect increasing student use of technology and SNS to equate with an enhanced desire or ability to actively participate in civic activities. Indeed, Livingstone, Couldry, and Markham (2007) assert that "young people's motivation to pursue civic interests depends on their background and their socialization, and it is not greatly affected by the amounts of time spent or levels of expertise online" (p. 24). Unfortunately, it seems that the inequalities that exist in our offline cultures continue to play a large role in on-line civic engagement. In fact, Mesch and Coleman (2007) state that "socioeconomic and gender differences observed in offline participation seem to be reflected and reproduced in the low level of election-related Internet use by females and less-educated individuals" (p. 46). Thus, "The internet instead provides a route to pursue already existing civic interests. And these already existing interests, it seems, may derive from social capital, and social expectations—in short, from opportunity structures of people's everyday lives" (Livingstone, et al, p. 26).

Perhaps as a result of this apparent echoing of offline civic engagement, boyd (2008b) asserts that we should think of SNS more as locations for analysis to better understand how/where change is occurring (p. 244). She contends that:

Rather than fantasizing about how social network sites will be a cultural Panacea, perhaps we need to focus more directly on the causes of a alienation and disillusionment. SNS are not going to make people engage, but they can make visible whether or not political operatives are succeeding in getting their message across. (Boyd, 2008b, p. 244)

Furthermore, some argue that many students are actively engaged civically and politically, but the face of engagement is changing as the use of the Internet changes the way we engage with one another at large. According to Gerodimos and Ward (2007), "Both politics and the way we participate in public affairs are changing, and this change is partly due to the nature of new media and online communication" (p. 114). And, as Watkins (2009) claims, "Social-network sites are not merely a source of communication among the young and the digital; they are *the* source of communication" (p. 89). Gerodimos and Ward (2007) claim that, "Our analysis of online political content needs to adapt, especially when it comes to observing the younger generation [because] these young people, through practices such as sampling and remixing, are building their own culture online" (pp. 114-16). Thus, it is important for composition educators to consider ways of implementing SNS in the classroom as a means of helping students build these cultures in a productive and responsible way. But, in order to do that, we must have a better idea of how students view such interaction and engagement via their SNS.

Unfortunately, "young people are often positioned by even the most well-meaning public sectors sites not as citizens but as citizens-in-waiting [...] and, it seems that while they wait to become fully fledged citizens, young people think of better things to do with their time" (Livingstone, et al, 2007, p. 25). And with over five hours a day spent online (Emarketer INC, 2013), and 27% of that online time devoted to social networking (Marketing Profs, 2013), failing to better teach students how SNS can be tools for civic engagement is a grievously missed opportunity.

Privacy

Another consideration that relates to the concept of audience awareness is that of Internet tracking and data mining. Because of enhanced digital technologies, it is becoming simpler for individuals and companies to track details about our lives when we engage online, particularly in SNS spaces. As Mayer-Schonenberger and Cukier (2013) assert:

The Internet has made tracking easier, cheaper, and more useful [...] Amazon monitors our shopping preferences and Google our browsing habits, while twitter knows what's on our minds. Facebook seems to catch all that information too, along with our social relationships. (pp. 150-51)

This kind of information is highly valuable to those who hold it. As Pariser (2011) states:

It'd be one thing if we all knew everything about each other. It's another when centralized entities know a lot more about us than we know about each other—and sometimes, more than we know about ourselves. If knowledge is power, then asymmetries in knowledge are asymmetries in power. (p. 147)

As a result, issues of privacy could be the most important matter for users when considering audience, since the audiences many users may not consider—the websites and their corporate interests—may be the ones with the most power to impact users in the future. In this way, it is important to gain a better understanding of students' knowledge of and views on internet tracking and data mining as it relates to what they do and do not post, and how they interact on SNS.

Selfe (1999) discusses two issues regarding human understanding of technology when she states:

First it encourages us to understand and experience the world as a series of problems amenable to technological fixes [and this view] encourages the intellectual habit of perceiving everything around us. ... as a 'standing reserve' of resources that can be used to create, design, and manufacture technologies. (p. 141)

I would add a third problem, which is that when we focus on technology as a perpetual solution, it deters us from seeing it as a potential problem that could be stripping us of rights, such as privacy, and skills, such as critical thinking.

SNS IN THE (COMPOSITION) CLASSROOM

Of course, at the end of all these important considerations about the impact of SNS on its users, a final guiding consideration for this project is how teachers can responsibly and effectively use SNS in the composition classroom. Vie (2008) argues that there is a divide between teachers and students with regard to SNS and that it is important for educators to become better educated about SNS in order to better educate their composition students about the importance of SNS and best practices for using such sites. She argues that, "Despite the challenges of using social networking sites in the classroom, they can provide many teachable moments for instructors who wish to talk with students about audience, discourse communities, intellectual property, and tensions between public and private viewing" (Vie, 2008, p. 21). Given the potential myriad ways SNS can significantly affect their users' personally, socially, and professionally, it is important to consider the ways SNS can be used to enhance students' understanding of their world, without overemphasizing the need to use such sites and potentially causing students to engage online when they are ill equipped to do so.

One major pedagogical issue that is often cited in the interdisciplinary literature regarding SNS is that there is a danger of creating false, or *unreal* identities/communities among students. boyd (2008a) argues that:

Teens often fabricate key identifying information like name, age, and location to protect themselves... While parents' groups often encourage this deception to protect teens from strangers [,] many teens actually engage in this practice to protect themselves from the watchful eye of parent. (p. 131)

Boon and Christine (2009) expand on this by saying students do this to avoid both parents *and* teachers when they contend, "It has been recorded that students do not like teachers or parents in 'their' space, especially if they are making embarrassing attempts to be cool. Control is also an issue of some import" (p. 102). This of course presents obvious problems when one considers the use of such sites in the classroom, but the problem goes deeper, as Boon and Sinclair (2009) make clear in their assertion that:

Indeed, Facebook seems to encourage us to create essentially false communities of superficial relationships. That is not to say that the medium is never used to maintain strong communities of meaningful relationships, but rather that these seem to be in the minority. (p.104)

Considering SNS are already being primarily used for maintaining social relationships and entertainment—versus for informational or educational purposes—(Maranto and Barton, 2010), this begins to raise ethical dilemmas as one must consider what sort of identity/community-building one promotes through the use of such sites in the composition classroom.

On the other hand, it has been shown that using SNS in the composition classroom can be an effective method of enhancing engagement and success in the classroom. Fernandes, Giucanu, Bowers, and Neely (2010) found that when students engage in groups that are focused on particular goals (i.e. following and promoting the election of their candidate of choice), their interaction on Facebook switched from a focus on social networking and interaction, to that of political action, and the direct promotion of their candidate and political beliefs. This seems to indicate that, when given direction in SNS spaces, students are willing and able to focus their attention on achieving a non-social goal, or as Fernandes, et al (2010) assert, "Facebook [can be] used as venue where supporters can organize on a local level and exhibit their support for their candidate as well as frustrations they have with the opposing candidate" (p. 671).

Junco, Heiberger and Loken (2011) similarly found that students are capable of focusing their use of SNS for less social purposes, when they discuss findings from research regarding the use of Twitter in the classroom. In the study, students were divided into a study group as students of Twitter-framed courses, and a control group of students in courses where twitter was not implemented, to test for student engagement and performance. At the end of the study, it was found that the students in the Twitter group were significantly more engaged, and had higher GPAs than their control-group peers (Junco et al, 2011, p.128).

Furthermore, Fife (2010) discusses how Facebook can be an important tool for teaching student critical analysis skills. Indeed, Fife asserts that since:

Facebook profiles are representations of the self, most features that can be seen as appeals to logos or pathos also have a strong reflection on the writer's ethos. Even comments written by someone else on one's wall gain a tacit endorsement by the profile owner if they are left instead of deleted. (p. 558)

She continues by stating that analyzing such SNS interaction, "helps [students] to develop a more critical stance toward a popular literacy they encounter regularly and to appreciate its complexity" (Fife, 2010, p. 561). Thus, Fife sees SNS as new venues for critical thinking, rhetorical analysis, and the building of metacognitive skills. Similarly, Sabatino (2014) discusses how many of the skills and practices that are required of participating in games on Facebook can be incorporated in the composition classroom to positively impact composition skills and considerations. Sabatino (2014) asserts, "Facebook and its games are providing composition with an outlet to reach students in a new way and provide them with practices to see how these digital literacies inform composition literacies" (p. 43).

As Gergitis and Schramer (1994) claim, students "are not 'blank slates' with no-experience; they are not open to any and all instruction [...] their complex lives and beliefs color and sometimes impede whatever they learn" (p. 190). They go on to state that:

Indeed, fruitful collaboration often starts with the recognition that difference is essential if a group wishes to generate truly original ideas rather than to rely on made-to-order compromises that satisfy no one. The problem lies not so much in views openly and then deal with them productively. (p. 190)

Therefore, instead of simply having FYC students sign on to a social networking site as a novel location for posting homework assignments and responses, we can begin to have students interact with one another to learn about, and embrace, one another's interests, beliefs, etc. Such beliefs will more likely than not be quite different from student to student, thus expanding their networks to those with beliefs that differ from their own.

Best Practices

Based on the analysis of the research and my personal experience in the composition classroom, it seems that, regardless how much instructors plan on using SNS in the composition classroom, there are certain basic considerations instructors should hold if they wish to incorporate SNS as pedagogical tools to enhance composition and rhetorical skills, and create a greater sense of audience awareness within their students:

- Talk with students about which SNS they are comfortable using in a classroom setting.
- Provide opportunities for students to write about and discuss their personal SNS uses and views.
- Set guidelines for appropriate interaction between the instructor and students, as well as guidelines for appropriate interaction among students while using SNS in and for the class.
- Introduce SNS use with a detailed discussion of the privacy settings and guidelines associated with the SNS to be used in the class.

- Collaborate with students to determine criteria for determining how to productively use SNS in the class.
- Talk with students about positive self-representation on SNS.
- Discuss how activities/assignments utilizing SNS have a direct positive connection to students' personal, social, professional, and/or civic lives and composition practices.
- If it is possible, consider creating closed groups within the SNS to provide students space in the SNS to practice engagement without concern over how their personal interaction outside of the classroom will be affected.
- Do not assume all students are familiar using any SNS (except, perhaps, Facebook), and be prepared to introduce students to basic applications of SNS use meant for classroom activity.

While this list is not meant to be comprehensive, it is meant to act as a starting point for instructors who have not yet attempted, or do not feel confident, using SNS in their composition classroom.

SNS ACTIVITIES FOR THE COMPOSITION CLASSROOM

The following is a list of classroom activities that could be implemented as early uses of SNS as rhetorical and/or compositional tools. Much like the previous list of best practices, this is not (intended to be) a comprehensive set of activities, but a starting point for instructors who are interested in SNS use in the composition classroom. It is worth noting that different populations of students may benefit from engaging in various other potential projects and activities since the skills, understanding, and rhetorical considerations of SNS will be as varied as the number of courses and students an instructor teaches.

Close Reading of SNS User Agreements

Perhaps one of the most important goals instructors can have for the implementation of SNS as pedagogical tools in the composition classroom is to help students understand the real-world implications of their online composition, interaction, and persona-building. One way to begin creating a sense of the potential consequences associated with SNS use is to have students perform a close-reading and analysis of the user agreement for their most-used SNS, or the SNS that will be used by all of the students for an upcoming assignment/activity.

For this activity, the instructor can ask students to read the user agreement of the SNS in its entirety, explaining that with many of the larger SNS there are multiple subsequent links that provide more information about privacy, user data, or monetary transactions that are not discussed in detail on the primary user agreement page. Ask students to take notes on the entire reading, but to pay attention to language used, repeated words, sentence length, visual presentation of information, and which information is present on the primary page compared to the information that is linked to separate pages. Have students list anything they found surprising, troubling, or helpful, and have them list and answer any questions they had during their reading.

Upon completion of the reading, students could be asked to write an analysis of the user agreement in which they discuss the significance of aspects in the agreement they were asked to take notes on and present their interpretation of why the authors of the user agreement present information the way they do.

Another option, or a supplemental option following the close reading, is to have an in-class discussion of the students' findings, and compare and contrast student interpretations of the same user agreements.

An alternative option could be to split students into groups and task each group with performing a close reading of the user agreement for a different SNS. Then compare and contrast each group's findings and discuss reasons for any similarities and differences based on the perceived goals of each SNS.

This activity not only provides students with a new genre in which to perform a close-reading, but it also gives students the opportunity to truly read the fine print of the user agreement for a SNS they have likely already signed up for and have been using for years without reading said user-agreement. This will likely provide many students with a new perspective on the goals of the SNS creators and force students to reconsider the ways they engage and compose on their SNS.

Close Reading of SNS Timeline

Another way to have students look at their use of SNS is to follow the lead of Fife (2010) and have student perform a rhetorical analysis of their SNS. Such an activity requires students to critically consider rhetorical choices made when engaging on SNS and the impact their SNS composition has on their online, and offline, personas. For this activity, students could be asked to read through the public information and interaction presented by a single individual on a single SNS. Instructors could then ask students to take notes on the specific information the individual chooses to share on his/her profile page (e.g. interests, likes, dislikes, family, etc), and keep track of the topics the person posts about and comments on, time of day the person engages on the SNS most, and how frequently the individual engages on the SNS.

Students might perform such a reading of an individual's timeline over the course of a day or a week, then compose a SNS personality profile in which the students write about the type of person the individual appears to be based solely on his/her single SNS profile and interaction. As a companion activity to this initial profile close-read, once students have performed the first close-reading and have a sense of what information to look for and how, instructors could then ask students to perform a similar close reading of their own profile and interaction on their SNS from a month or year before and compose a similar personality profile of themselves.

Such activities speak to a number of ideas that enhance students' critical thinking about SNS engagement and rhetorical composition. First, they could help reinforce the importance of privacy settings on individuals' SNS, as many students will like be surprised by how much information they are able to find about an individual, and themselves, based solely on profile information and timeline engagement, which each individual gives freely when s/he composes in such spaces. Second, performing such tasks could help students see how easily others can form opinions about others based on their SNS interaction. Students will likely be particularly surprised by the kind of interaction they partook in a month or a year before compared to their more recent engagement on SNS. Finally, as Fife (2010) asserts, these kinds of activities have "the added benefit of teaching teachers about an important literacy practice of college students that can easily be written off as a waste of time by those outside the social network" (p. 561). Indeed, such activities provide instructors more insight into the composing practices and rhetorical considerations of their students in the online environments that are often most important to students.

It is important to note that if instructors choose to assign this activity to their students, they should make sure to clarify that students must choose to analyze someone with a public profile and that students should create a pseudonym for the individual the student is analyzing in order to protect the desired privacy of that individual. Students should be aware that sharing information given on a users' private profile is often a violation of most SNS terms of service. If the instructor or students are not comfortable performing such an analysis of another individual the instructor may choose to have students move directly into only performing a self-analysis of students' own profiles and interactions.

SNS Historical Figure Profile Creation

For this task, an instructor asks students to perform research on a historical figure who lived before the advent of SNS and attempt to create a fake profile page for that person, based on their research. Students could begin by engaging in a research project of the historical figure by finding out major activities the figure was involved in, the personal, political, social, and civic views and events the person was interested in, as well as the temperament and public/private engagement tendencies of the figure. Following this research, students could be tasked with creating a fake profile page of the historical figure, then spending a week engaging on a fake SNS as they believe their chosen historical figure would if s/he were still alive today. Students could be asked to spend a week posting about, liking, sharing, and commenting on topics the historical figure would have found interesting today. Then, after a week of such interaction, the students could write an essay describing and defending the rhetorical choices made when the student chose to interact in certain ways on behalf of the historical figure.

By having students spend a week interacting on a SNS as an historical figure, students see their own interaction on SNS from a new perspective. By critically thinking about the rhetorical decisions that would have gone into the engagement choices of another person, students may walk away with a better understanding of the rhetorical considerations that go into their own SNS composition practices, and subsequently, look at their other composition practices through a more critical lens. Specifically, because students would likely be posting on behalf of their selected figure to an imagined group of followers who would be different than those who follow the actual student's account(s), this activity could provide an enhanced opportunity for considerations of audience awareness.

Another benefit of this kind of activity is demonstrating to the students the various composing options at their disposal through SNS. DeVoss (2013) expresses to her reader, "With your purpose in mind and your audience profile under way, you are ready to think about the best way to connect with your audience. The benefit of composing multimodally is that you have options for communicating your message" (p. MM-58). Of course, maintaining the profile page of an historical figure is not inherently multimodal. However, because the students' historical figures would not have engaged in SNS interaction, having students reappropriate various forms of SNS interaction and compositions to fit the public interaction styles of their figure could stretch students into playing with multimodal composition.

For instance, if a student were to create a faux-profile for a well-known public figure such as Dr. Martin Luther King Jr., the student could take into account the fact that Dr. King would often travel to various locations in order to deliver speeches and sermons. Thus, if the student created a Twitter account for Dr. King and linked it to Vine, the student could tweet Vine videos of people marching for a civil rights cause and caption the vine with an appropriate 140 quote from one of King's speeches. In this way, the student would be able to present a single textual and audio-visual composition in order to spread Dr. King's message, all while using the location feature to advertise where the next demonstration would be taking place in order to further engage the audience. Such experiences could give students a deeper understanding of the potential of SNS and cause them to reflect on their own SNS composing habits and rhetorical choices as a result.

Finding Common Ground among Fellow Students

With a similar goal of having students try to reach a better understanding of friends, family, or followers with whom they may not normally agree, instructors could give students an assignment in which they must find a number of commonalities with an individual who holds differing views on issues that are important to each student. In this assignment, students would need to first find a fellow student within the class with whom they strongly disagree on a single issue that each student finds important, or with whom they generally disagree on a number of issues. After finding such a partner, the students would then need to read through their partner's profile and posts in order to find a number of interests or posts that the student agrees with or to find nuances within the issue(s) of disagreement that allow for some common ground to be reached.

Finally, the student would need to either engage the individual in a SNS conversation or compose a mock SNS conversation in which the student and individual discuss the issue(s) until common ground is reached. If the students engaged in an actual SNS discussion, they could then collaboratively write a follow-up essay in which they discuss the various points of disagreement and common ground as well as the methods they used for finally reaching a point of common ground on the topic(s). If students instead decided to compose mock conversations, they could then come together and share their conversations with one another to compare and contrast how each believed the conversation would go, then work together to collaboratively compose an analysis of the two mock conversations.

The potential benefits of such an assignment are numerous. First, this assignment could provide students with a low stakes opportunity to engage in friendly disagreement on SNS, as being friendly and respectful would be one of the first rules of interaction during such an activity. It would get them used to the idea that such conversations can take place on SNS instead of seeing SNS debates as extreme and negative interactions that should be avoided. Second, such an activity would require that students know how to effectively present their position within the confines of the chosen SNS, each of which has distinct engagement characteristics (e.g. Twitter's 140-character limit).

Starkey (2012) states that,

Learners in the digital age are able to connect and collaborate with people beyond their physical environment. They can connect a range of information or data and draw on a range of perspectives to collaboratively generate and critique new ideas. (p. 24)

With the idea of using a range of perspectives for collaborative generation of ideas in mind, this activity would also be beneficial in that it could provide students the opportunity to engage in a collaborative post-discussion analysis of the conversation, or mock conversation. This could provide them greater insight into their own rhetorical choices as well as provide them with a greater understanding that there are real people behind the online personas of people with whom they interact on SNS.

Viral Breakdown

Another activity that promotes building audience awareness and applying it to rhetorical considerations of composition asks students to perform a rhetorical analysis of viral SNS content. Students could be broken into small groups (three to four), and each group could find a piece of viral content on SNS, and try to determine the factors that led to it going viral. Groups could analyze popular videos on YouTube, memes on Tumblr or Facebook, an extremely popular Vine post, or a tweet with a massive number of retweets. After breaking down the content, groups could be tasked with finding a piece of similar content (within the same genre) that was not able to go viral and compare the two pieces to determine if there are any factors that led to one going viral while the other did not. Following the groups' analyses of their content, the groups could then present their findings to the class in order to determine if there were any commonalities between the content that went viral versus those that did not.

First, students could be drawn to this activity because they are likely seeing and engaging with viral content on a regular basis if they are regularly interacting on SNS, so the concept of viral content should be familiar and relatively interesting to them. As Hocks (2008) claims, there is a call for:

Redefining literacy practice and attending to the political and social impact made possible by technologies as complex artifacts that can help transform our lived experience. Their approach to pedagogy suggests that students can work from within their diverse cultures and multiple identities using their own languages as well as their everyday lived experiences to design new kinds of knowledge. (p. 351)

Such an activity could be an attempt to redefine what knowledge students bring to the classroom, and this kind of assignment allows students to bring in their own experiences and expertise as consumers, and perhaps producers, of viral content, to assist in developing rhetorical analysis criteria for such content.

Such an assignment is also potentially productive because it asks students to go beyond simply being entertained by such content and to critically consider what may have made content so popular, from rhetorical considerations of the author of the content, to the kairotic moment that made space for the content to become so popular. Furthermore, having students engage in this kind of critical thinking about other people's content on SNS provides an opportunity to begin discussion about the rhetorical decisions they can make regarding their own compositions, both on SNS and in their academic and professional lives, in order to make them as appealing as possible to their intended audience.

Tweeting Summaries

The last kind of activity discussed here is potentially a course-long activity that asks students to share their thoughts on in-class work on their SNS throughout the semester. For example, if a course were to utilize Twitter over the course of the semester, the instructor could ask students to begin posting single-Tweet summaries, which utilize a course hashtag (e.g. #eng2070), about the reading they have to perform for homework in class. This kind of assignment could be performed as an alternative to using a discussion board in class, and the teacher could further ask students to reply to (and potentially, if all have agreed to favorite or retweet) other students' tweeted summaries so many times per week or within the semester.

This is another assignment with a number of potential benefits. First, if students are indeed using Twitter for such an assignment, composing sufficient summaries within the confines of a 140-character tweet is no easy task. Students must determine the most essential information to share about the reading as well as how to present that information in order to convey its importance within the character limit. Students will have to demonstrate a strong understanding of the material as well as work on rhetorical decisions to remain concise in conveying their understanding.

The second potential benefit is that students are more likely to engage daily on SNS to present information and discuss topics outside of the classroom than they are to engage in such interaction on discussion boards. As Krause (2008) states, "Students (or anyone else) don't just want to write, and certainly not in a blog space" (p. 329). Krause (2008) also discusses the notion of focusing on "fostering and nurturing an atmosphere where students can 'learn' instead of being 'taught,' where students can write not because they are being *required* to do so by some sort of 'teacherly' assignment but because they want to write" (p. 329). Of course, today, students do want to write. They simply want to write on SNS, and perhaps having students participate in this activity could provide them with more incentive to write in the classroom by giving them opportunities to practice participating in activities they are likely to engage in outside the classroom.

Lastly, by creating an activity in which students are engaging academically in composition for their SNS, instructors can begin making students comfortable with the idea of SNS as spaces for academic and professional writing and engagement. In order to remove the stigma of SNS as non-academic disruptions of the classroom, instructors must provide numerous examples of SNS as spaces for academic engagement, and such assignments provide students with daily or weekly reminders of the academically productive potential of SNS in and out of the classroom.

It should be noted that if students are concerned with making academic posts on personal SNS accounts, such as Twitter, the instructor could consider asking students to create a student profile to interact only with those in the classroom and/or others outside the class who have more academic/professional SNS goals.

CONCLUSION

The conversation regarding SNS and their impact on the field of composition is clearly larger than the scope of the ideas and individuals discussed in this chapter. As stated at the onset, the goal of this chapter is to act as a small primer for others who may be engaging in the conversation for the first time in an attempt to orient such individuals in an increasingly pervasive area of academic, professional, and social life. Furthermore, the conversation about SNS should remain in a constant state of change and growth in order to maintain understanding of the views and uses of SNS in and out of the composition classroom, which are also in a state of constant flux.

Thus, continued research that focuses on the students is necessary for a better understanding of how teachers can effectively and ethically implement SNS in the composition classroom. With more studies, such as surveys, interviews, and case studies of the student populations, scholars and teachers can continue to gain an understanding of whether or not students see the classroom as a space that is appropriate for SNS use, why/why not, and, if so, how they would prefer to use SNS as potential learning and rhetorical tools.

Moreover, continued research should focus on the ways students are already effectively using SNS as scholarly, professional, and civic-centered tools, so that teachers may learn from students and work with them to share their successful strategies with others. Alexander (2006) contends that youth are writing on the web "in ways that are creative, dynamic, and boundary-pushing. The question is, are we paying attention? And what can we learn from the literacies with which such digital youth are playing on the web" (p.10)?

Since this conversation about SNS will continue to develop for the foreseeable future, it should be our goal to confidently answer Alexander's (2006) question in the affirmative and to collaborate with all those who have a stake in the successful use of SNS in and out of the composition classroom.

REFERENCES

Alexander, J. (2006). *Digital youth: Emerging literacies on the World Wide Web*. Cresskill, NJ: Hampton Press.

Arola, K. (2010). The design of web 2.0: The rise of the template, the fall of design. *Computers and Composition, 27*(1), 4–14. doi:10.1016/j.compcom.2009.11.004

Association, A. L. S. (2014). The ALS Association extends 'thank you' in new message [Press release]. Retrieved from www.alsa.org/news/archive/als-association-thankyou-video.html

Baron, D. (2009). *A better pencil: Readers, writers, and the digital revolution*. New York, NY: Oxford University Press.

Bitzer, L. F. (1968). The rhetorical situation. *Philosophy & Rhetoric, 1*, 1–14.

Boon, S., & Sinclair, C. (2009). A world I don't inhabit: Disquiet and identity in Second Life and Facebook. *Educational Media International, 46*(2), 99–110. doi:10.1080/09523980902933565

boyd, d. (2008a). Why youth [heart] social network sites: The role of networked publics in teenage social life. In D. Buckingham (Ed.), *Youth, identity, and social media* (pp. 119-142). Cambridge, MA: The MIT Press.

boyd, d. (2008b). Can social network sites enable political action? *International Journal of Media and Cultural Politics, 4*(2), 241-44.

Consigny, S. (1974). Rhetoric and its situations. *Philosophy & Rhetoric, 7*, 175–186.

DeAndrea, D. C., Shaw, A., & Levine, T. R. (2010). Online language: The role of culture in self-expression and self-construal on Facebook. *Journal of Language and Social Psychology, 29*(4), 425–442. doi:10.1177/0261927X10377989

DeVoss, D. N. (2013). *Understanding and composing multimodal projects*. New York, NY. Bedford: St. Martin's.

Emarketer Inc. (2013). Digital set to surpass TV in time spent with US media: Mobile helps propel digital time spent [Press release]. Retrieved from http://www.emarketer.com/Article/Digital-Set-Surpass-TV-Time-Spent-with-US-Media/1010096

Fernandes, J., Giurcanu, M., Bowers, K. W., & Neely, J. C. (2010). The writing on the wall: A content analysis of college students' Facebook groups for the 2008 presidential election. *Mass Communication & Society, 13*(5), 653–675. doi:10.1080/15205436.2010.516865

Fife, J. M. (2010). Using Facebook to teach rhetorical analysis. *Pedagogy, 10*(3), 555–562. doi:10.1215/15314200-2010-007

Gergitis, J. M., & Schramer, J. J. (1994). The collaborative classroom as the site of difference. *JAC, 14*(1), 187–202.

Gerodimos, R., & Ward, J. (2007). Rethinking online youth civic engagement: Reflections on web content analysis. In B. D. Loader (Ed.), *Young citizens in the digital age: Political engagement and new media* (pp. 114–126). New York, NY: Routledge.

Graff, G. (2003). *Clueless in academe: How schooling obscures the life of the mind*. New Haven, CT: Yale University Press.

Hocks, M. E. (2008). Understanding visual rhetorics in digital writing environments. In T. R. Johnson (Ed.), *Teaching composition: background readings* (pp. 337–362). New York, NY: Bedford St Martin's.

Junco, R., Heiberger, G., & Loken, E. (2011). The effect of Twitter on college student engagement and grades. *Journal of Computer Assisted Learning, 27*(2), 119–132. doi:10.1111/j.1365-2729.2010.00387.x

Krause, S. D. (2008). When blogging goes bad: a Cautionary tale about blogs, email lists, discussion, and interaction. In T. R. Johnson (Ed.), *Teaching composition: background readings* (pp. 325–336). New York, NY: Bedford St Martin's.

Livinstone, S., Couldry, N., & Markham, T. (2007). Youthful steps towards civic participation: Does the Internet help? In B. D. Loader (Ed.), *Young citizens in the digital age: Political engagement and new media* (pp. 21–34). New York, NY: Routledge.

Maranto, G., & Barton, M. (2010). Paradox and promise: MySpace, Facebook, and the sociopolitics of social networking in the writing classroom. *Computers and Composition, 27*(1), 36–47. doi:10.1016/j.compcom.2009.11.003

MarketingProfs. (2013). Social takes up 27% of time spent online. Retrieved from http://www.marketingprofs.com/charts/2013/10582/social-takes-up-27-of-time-spent-online

Marwick, A. E., & boyd, . (2010). I tweet honestly, I tweet passionately: Twitter users, content collapse and imagined audience. *New Media & Society, 13*(1), 114–133. doi:10.1177/1461444810365313

Mayer-Schonenberger, V., & Cukier, K. (2013). *Big data: A revolution that will transform how we live, work, and think*. New York, NY: Houghton Mifflin.

Mesch, G. S., & Coleman, S. (2007). New media and new voters: young people, the Internet and the 2005 UK election campaign. In B. D. Loader (Ed.), *Young citizens in the digital age: Political engagement and new media* (pp. 35–47). New York, NY: Routledge.

Pariser, E. (2011). *The filter bubble: How the new personalized web is changing the way we read and how we think*. New York, NY: Penguin.

Pew Research Center. (2014). Social networking fact sheet. Retrieved from http://www.pewinternet.org/fact-sheets/social-networking-fact-sheet/

Pingdom, A. B. (2012). Report: Social network demographics in 2012. Retrieved from http://royal.pingdom.com/2012/08/21/report-social-network-demographics-in-2012/

Sabatino, L. (2014). Improving writing literacies through digital gaming literacies: Facebook gaming in the composition classroom. *Computers and Composition, 32*, 41–53. doi:10.1016/j.compcom.2014.04.005

Selfe, C. (1999). *Technology and literacy in the twenty-first century: The importance of paying attention. Carbondale and Edwardsville*. IL: Southern Illinois University Press.

Starkey, L. (2012). *Teaching and learning in the digital age*. New York, NY: Routledge.

Thomas, M. (2011). *Deconstructing digital natives: Young people, technology, and the new literacies*. New York, NY: Routledge.

Vatz, R. E. (1973). The myth of the rhetorical situation. *Philosophy & Rhetoric, 6*(3), 154–161.

Vie, S. (2008). Digital divide 2.0: "Generation m" and the online social networking sites in the composition classroom. *Computers and Composition, 25*(1), 9–23. doi:10.1016/j.compcom.2007.09.004

Wandel, T., & Beavers, A. (2010). Playing around with identity. In S. C. Wittkower (Ed.), *Facebook and philosophy* (pp. 89–96). Chicago, IL: Open Court.

Watkins, S. C. (2009). *The young and the digital: What the migration to social-network sites, games, and anytime, anywhere media means for our future*. Boston, MA: Beacon.

Chapter 9
Creating Meaning for Millennials:
Bakhtin, Rosenblatt, and the Use of Social Media in the Composition Classroom

Erin Trauth
University of South Florida, USA

ABSTRACT

Despite the Millennial's growing attraction to social media technologies, composition instruction has yet to fully explore the potential of these technologies as resources rather than hindrances to instruction. As instructors of composition, then, it seems logical to apply what we know about these dominant rhetorical and pedagogical theories of the 20th century to the prospective use of social media to better our own pedagogies. Employing the ideas of Mikhail Bakhtin's social construction of knowledge and Louise Rosenblatt's student-centered pedagogy, the author explores the many complementary uses of social media technologies such as Facebook and Twitter in the composition classroom in order to generate a new model of instruction – one which challenges traditional, unilateral exchanges of knowledge and centers on a dialogical, student-centered model of composition instruction.

INTRODUCTION

As a society grounded in rhetoric, the ways in which we understand how to most effectively use discourse to build knowledge in the university setting are in constant flux with rhetorical epistemic shifts. It does seem somewhat certain, however, that as technology use becomes more frequent, and college students become even more connected in their discourse through the use of these technologies, University instruction will likely follow suit. Composition instructors often attempt to meet the needs of changing groups of students, and the use of social media sites, particularly Facebook and Twitter, can help composition instructors best meet the writing abilities of Millennial students.

Most recently, instructors have sought to serve the unique requirements of students of the "Millennial" generation – those born between 1982 and 2000, according to the Pew Research Center (2015).

DOI: 10.4018/978-1-5225-0562-4.ch009

Despite efforts by composition instructors, however, students of the Millennial generation often find the composition course, in its most basic form, difficult to construct personal meaning from. In his essay "Language, Power, and Consciousness: A Writing Experiment at the University of Toronto," Guy Allen (2008) writes that over a span of 15 years of surveying, nearly 95 percent of students have a negative view of writing in a school setting (p. 72). In her 2008 dissertation, "I hate to write. I can't do it.": *First-Year Composition and the Resistant Student Writer*, Heather Urbanaski explains that resistant writers in the composition classroom "don't just struggle with writing; they actively resist the task and the course because both seem incompatible with their strengths and affinities" (p. 1).

So, one might ask then: *What are the Millennial students' strengths as writers, and how can composition instructors use what they may already know about rhetorical theories and pedagogies to better connect with this distinctive generation?*

Members of the Millennial generation, many of whom are now of traditional college age, are known for their constant connectivity and use of multi-modal technologies. "Social Media & Mobile Internet Use among Teens and Young Adults," a 2010 study conducted by the Pew Internet and American Life Project, found that 73% of United States people ages 18-24 use social networking sites; 45% of them use the sites daily. Whether through the Internet, cell phones, or social media sites, today's average college student is constantly connected to a circle of friends, family, and–potentially–to hundreds or even thousands of other people, and they interact quite frequently with these groups. As Greg Heiberger and Ruth Harper assert in their 2008 article, "Have You Facebooked Astin Lately? Using Technology to Increase Student Involvement," Millennial students "network with each other using technology as much as, if not more than, face-to-face communication" (2). The millennial students' strengths, therefore, are in fact inherently situated in their ability to communicate.

According to an Ipsos Millenial Social Influence Study (2014), 71 percent of Millenials connect on social media sites daily. Social media sites are where a large majority of Millennial students do their writing; these sites are where students discuss, argue, and question topics relevant to their lives. Millennial students hold entire arguments on Facebook, they work through problems on blog posts, they text message their parents for life advice, and they Twitter their friends regarding their relationship woes.

Composition teachers might meet the Millennial generation's unique communication skill sets, then, through the many potential uses of social media sites in the classroom. The writing proficiency of the incoming Millennial college student is often framed by the use of the Internet and online technologies; as such, the use of interactive social media sites such as Facebook and Twitter in the classroom is a significant and promising trend to examine for how composition instructors might facilitate greater student interest, participation, connectivity, collaboration, and community to subsequently generate optimal knowledge-building. Further, employing social media tools in the composition classroom might generate a new model for composition instruction which empowers the student-learner in ways not as synonymous with the traditional, unilateral transfer of knowledge often found in college-level classrooms.

Using Twitter and Facebook in the classroom may be new to some teachers; however, integrating Twitter and Facebook into the traditional classroom is not a new concept: Communications, media studies, anthropology, social sciences, and several other college disciplines have found useful ways to incorporate social media into the classroom. In fact, major studies touting the benefits of employing social media in the classroom are now beginning to emerge: in a 2010 study published in the *Journal of Computer Assisted Learning*, researchers found that Twitter in the college classroom can lead to greater student engagement: Two college classrooms for a first-year seminar course consisting of 125 students (one employing Twitter as a teaching tool, one using traditional methods only), were studied. In the 14-week study, seven sections of a first-year seminar utilized Twitter for academic discussion, including tweets continuing in-class discussions, tweets focused on class questions, book discussions, class reminders and organization of student service learning projects. The results concluded that "both student and educator engagement was significantly higher in the class using Twitter. The Twitter group also averaged about half a point higher in their GPAs than the control group" (Junco et al., 2010).

However, while the Internet is rife with the potential benefits of employing social media technologies in the classroom, for possible reasons of resistance to potentially "distracting" technologies or perhaps a simple lack of understanding how composition instructors might meet their students' needs through social media sites, published work on how social media usage in the composition classroom might enhance and embody the very rhetorical theories we study as compositionists is only just emerging. Despite the Millennial's growing attraction to social media technologies, composition instruction has yet to fully explore the potential of these technologies as resources rather than hindrances to instruction. However, as I will discuss in the remainder of this chapter, many of the predominant 20th century rhetorical theories seem to support the type of instruction social media technologies might encourage.

As composition instructors, then, it seems logical to apply what we know about these dominant rhetorical and pedagogical theories of the 20th century to the prospective use of social media to better our own pedagogies. Employing the ideas of Mikhail Bakhtin's social construction of knowledge and Louise Rosenblatt's student-centered pedagogy, I will explore the many complementary uses of social media technologies such as Facebook and Twitter in the composition classroom in order to generate a new model of instruction – one which challenges traditional, unilateral exchanges of knowledge and centers on a dialogical, student-centered model of composition instruction.

THEORETICAL FRAMEWORK

Mikhail Bakhtin: No Experience without the Social

Many rhetoricians of the 20th century afford great focus on language's meaning itself; in this episteme, we can observe a concentration of the socially-constructed and contextual function of language. For most 20th century rhetoricians, "truth" or "knowledge" is merely a social construction –a language construct derived from social concourse (Bizzell & Herzberg, 2000, p. 1210). Theories of language as social constructions, such as those of Bakhtin, posit that "without some kind of evaluative social orientation, there is no experience," and thus language "means nothing unless it's a social act" (as cited in Bizzell and Herzberg, 2000, p. 1213). For Bakhtin, all language (and perhaps all thought) interaction centers on a dialogic, and a conversation between speaker and addressee must happen for true meaning to generate. Every statement made, then, always exists in relation to another statement made before it, and all language and ideas are dynamic and interrelational. Bakhtin even goes so far as to suggest that without social interaction, there is no perception: "Consciousness becomes consciousness only once it has been filled with ideological (semiotic) content, consequently, only in the process of social interaction" (as cited in Bizzell & Herzberg, 2000, p. 1212).

Bakhtin, Twitter, and Facebook

In many ways, Bakhtin's focus on the dialogic is embodied by social media sites such as Twitter and Facebook. On these sites, most every utterance is made in relation to another person; tags and posts are made in direct relation to an audience of at least one or perhaps hundreds of other people. With hundreds of millions of users each, Facebook and Twitter provide users direct access to a complex network of relationships established and supported by a continual discourse and conversation with one another; essentially, the sites illuminate the very nature of Bakhtin's dialogic theory of language and are embedded in rhetorical theories centered on the social orientation and construction of knowledge.

Bakhtin's rhetorical theories of the social nature of knowledge and language, then, might extend to and support the use of social media technologies in the composition classroom. Researchers James P. Zappen, Laura J. Gurak, and Stephen Doheny-Farina assert in their 1997 article, "Rhetoric, Community, and Cyberspace," that online environments, when used for educational purposes, could distinctly "resemble characteristics of contemporary rhetorical communities" (p. 401). In line with this idea, Bakhtin's notions that a true conversation must take place for there to be an actual experience support that the composition course should do all it can to purposefully extend conversations in and outside of the classroom to allow previously-isolated dialogues to become a real-world act of conversing with a constant and wide-reaching audience on social media sites. Yet, for many composition courses, this conversation extension is not yet the case.

Assignments are usually written for an isolated context and audience – namely, the instructor and possibly a grader, teaching assistant, and perhaps some classroom peers. If social media is brought into the picture, either through topic-building and brainstorming activities or the sharing of ideas and partial (or even whole) written works through Facebook posts and notes or Twitter tweets, however, this situation might allow for students to potentially bring personal experiences, life stories and multi-modal contexts in to the conversation. Further, as Zapen et al. (1997) assert, online environments allow for an ideal forum in which "beliefs and values can be articulated and negotiated" (par.1).

On the basis that composition typically advocates a writing process derived from the inner self (yet, in Bakhtinian terms, only becomes real when shared with an addressee), if instructors asked students to share their topics or themes present in their writing assignments, students could potentially share pictures, links, and posts relevant to the conversation at hand with the click of a button, thus adding a multi-modal element to their work in a dialogic framework integral to 21st-century learning. In simply sharing topics and allowing for feedback afforded by social media platforms, the students, therefore, might learn just as much from the conversation as they do the writing and composing process, and thus, Bakhtin's dialogic might be put to work in a practical, Millennial-student-centered-manner.

Public writing acts through Facebook or Twitter can also allow for the composition students' knowledge-building process to extend far beyond the writing classroom to greater social contexts, which places importance and a needed weight on the writing work students might sometimes seem as "pointless" if only presented and evaluated in the isolated classroom environment. Engaging the Millennial student can be a tricky task – with their constant connectivity and familiarity with lightning-fast technologies, composition instructors should seek to merge academic work with personal connections; social media technologies might provide the perfect storm to support student engagement and motivation.

If certain writing assignments take place in a public sphere, the students' community can plausibly become involved with their work in the classroom. The students' parents, peers, and friends, are then able to respond to their public work, and, further, conversations about relevant topics can extend far beyond the constrictions of class time. Michael C. Elavsky, an assistant professor of communication at Penn State University, asserts (2010), "All of these technologies produce an empirical record for future analysis, consideration, and conversations extending beyond the time/space constraints (i.e. 'outsiders' have contributed tweets) of the classroom" (p. 1). Greg Ferenstein, a freelance technology journalist and author of the article, "How Twitter in the Classroom is Boosting Classroom Engagement," explains (2010) that "the dynamic of an intellectual ecosystem, where students dive deep into class readings and argue contentious issues outside of class, is difficult to create if discussion ends when class is over. Fortunately, Twitter has no time limit" (par. 2). This sort of public sharing of work not only echoes Bakhtin's emphasis on the dialogic nature of utterances, but it also can provide valuable teaching moments for negotiating language acts in a highly-public, technology-based, 21st-century workforce students will soon likely enter. Further, this sort of "learning ecology" promotes academic content which inherently becomes integrated with individual and social interests, thus engaging students in a highly-personal manner.

Social Media and Classroom Discussions

Social media sites might also promote in-class discussions for hesitant speakers in the composition classroom. As Bakhtin would likely assert, because knowledge is socially constructed and is a product of contexts, classroom discussions are a necessarily important part of the learning process. The problem of voiceless students is a familiar one for instructors, as Ferenstein (2010) asserts that "...classroom shyness is like a black hole: Once silence takes over, it never lets go. In my own experience, in a class of hundreds, the fraction of students who speak up is small, and a still tinier fraction contributes regularly" (p. 3). This problem is further augmented when one considers that composition at the college level is now often taught with a level of anonymity derived from institutional emphases on objective, anonymous grading methods and increasingly large class sizes. Therefore, employing social media such as Facebook and Twitter as an in-class response option offers instructors the chance to give these students another venue for a "voice."

Using sites to enhance in-class conversations is further supported by notions that online dialogues might also "provide a powerful vehicle for all students to participate in class discussions, regardless of race, gender, or personality" (Dorwick, 1996, p. 23). Not only might some students be more open and direct in their in-class opinions when given the opportunity to speak through the online avatar they so commonly interact with outside of the academic world, social media platforms can allow for "more extended, inclusive, and multi-faceted conversations to occur in class (and beyond), linking course content and insights more effectively to the real world experiences and the diverse perspectives the students bring to the course" (Elavsky 20). Further, grounded in Bakhtin's notion that "the individualistic confidence in oneself, one's sense of personal value, is drawn not from within, not from the depths of one's personality, but from the outside world" (as cited in Bizzell & Herzberg, 2000, p. 1217), if students (as they so often are) are under-confident speaking in a classroom setting, discussing via social media sites might afford them the opportunity to flourish in ways not possible for them in a traditional classroom setting.

Bakhtin's main theories emphasize the social construction of knowledge and the contextual nature of language, and social media sites such as Facebook and Twitter might allow for composition instructors to explore with their students the benefits of socially-enhanced brainstorming, reviewing, and discussion-building via platforms with which students already spend a great deal of time. If, for Bakhtin, all language and thought centers on a dialogic, social media sites provide a simple, free, and readily-available means to explore the nature of his argument. Facebook and Twitter use in the classroom could easily elucidate

Bakhtin's assertion that "all words have a 'taste' of a profession, a genre, a tendency, a party, a particular work, a particular person, a generation, an age group, the day and hour" ("Discourse," p. 293), and use of these sites in the writing classroom setting would allow for optimum exemplification of this notion about the construction of language acts. Further, for Millennial students who struggle to connect with the writing process as taught in traditional composition course models or remain "voiceless" for a variety of other institutionally-imposed reasons, in class Facebook and Twitter use might enhance the course (and, subsequently, the knowledge-building process) experience for this group.

Louise Rosenblatt: Meeting Students in Their Own Spaces through Social Media

Moving beyond how social media technologies might exemplify Bakhtin's ideas of the social construction of knowledge in the composition classroom, considering the unique process of the student learning experience, as many might struggle to generate personal meaning from the writing process as presented in the composition classroom, is equally important. Louise Rosenblatt, an early 20th-century teacher and rhetorician, was one of the first to argue that college-level English instructors should understand and employ pedagogies which work to reach students and their specific needs in order to create meaning for their education.

Rosenblatt wrote much of her work in response to the notion that "literary education tended to treat students' contributions—their personal responses to literature—with skepticism" (Hallin, 2004, p. 290). Conversely, Rosenblatt emphasized students' personal reaction to works; in her pedagogy, the primary goal of English study was to stimulate a students' individual engagement with a text (Hallin, 2004, p. 286). Thus, Rosenblatt advocated for students to bring personal meaning to their educational experiences in order to most effectively generate new meanings from the material presented in courses.

She also understood that the study of English was greater than interpreting and writing about literary works:

Central to Rosenblatt's work was the idea that our perception of literary works cannot be separated from everyday discourse, and that, ultimately, literary education ought to help students integrate their linguistic competence with who they are as persons. (Hallin, 2004, 286)

Extending literary education to the composition classroom, use of social media technologies in the classroom becomes a natural answer to Rosenblatt's central ideas about pedagogy. If Facebook and Twitter are the "everyday discourse" context that the Millennial students converse within, writing skills learned in the classroom should work in tandem with these sites. Further, if "linguistic competence" should be integrated with "who they are as persons," it makes sense to bridge these students' online and in-person personas.

For example, if the average college student spends an equal amount of hours online and in class per day, their lives in social media contexts will intrinsically shape them as persons in classroom environments (and vice versa). As composition instructors, we should meet students "in the middle"—in the places they actually do their writing—to have an optimal effect on student writing.

Rosenblatt's ideas about pedagogy also advocate for student agency and thus the de-emphasizing of the unilateral classroom model. Facebook and Twitter use in the composition classroom might promote student agency and allow students a voice, subsequently renegotiating the traditional power structure of the classroom and promoting an egalitarian model. In "Computer Conferences and Learning: Authority, Resistance, and Internally Persuasive Discourse," Marilyn Cooper and Cynthia Selfe (1990) assert that various modes of online dialogues used to supplement classroom instruction can help students resist unilateral patterns of face-to-face classroom dialogue. They assert that, through online dialogues, "our students are learning how to resist—how to resist the interpretation of facts we present in classroom discussion, how to form their own opinions of the experts we introduce them to in the course, and how to dissent even against the traditionally accepted conventions of a university education" (p. 853). Zapen et al. (1997) further posit that computer-mediated social rhetorical communities might promote "increased democratization" (par. 3). Allowing students to chime in on topics originating from a space which is comfortable, easy, and personal during in-class discussions or even out-of-class assignments allows students a voice and valued perspective which might invoke greater meaning for the said activities.

When students have the opportunity to contribute to class from the context of a source as personal as a Facebook profile or Twitter page, the activity might also invoke feelings of self-worth and pride in the classroom. Voicing opinions with a face to the post might allow for greater personalization of course content, and the unique milieu of students contributed in the form of images, links, and personal profiles might provide valuable insights to personal strengths, backgrounds, and preferences--all of which can enhance the students' agency and course input. In turn, this act might decentralize the power structure of the traditional, unilateral classroom model.

Even if the information brought in from students in social media contexts does not fit the "model" the instructor expects for a certain response, the contribution, by any model of social constructions of knowledge, becomes a valuable part of the learning process and thus contributes to true *meaning*.

As Rosenblatt (1983) asserts:

Only by beginning with personal reactions, even those emphasizing personal obsessions, chance associations, and irrelevant conventional opinions...and then testing and developing these reactions—can a teaching method bring readers to come to terms with their responses to texts. (p. 64)

If students are connected to course content through social media sites, previous and current postings of links, videos, images, web sites can all be shared in the classroom context to help build upon the information at hand. In the 21st century, when Millennial students learn much about the world around them through various social media programs, Facebook and Twitter seem ideal vehicles for students to try out their personal reactions and "personal obsessions and chance associations" in a writing setting that seems "safe" from their perspective. Rosenblatt's pedagogy also promotes a classroom community of communal esteem and consideration between members, and, as Zappen et al. assert "New computer-mediated communication environments have the potential to become contemporary rhetorical communities – within which limited or local communities and individuals can develop mutual respect and understanding" (p. 1). Rosenblatt (1983) also advocates students as critical beings: "An important overall goal in education—is to develop individuals who will function less as automatic bundles of habits and more as flexible, discriminating personalities" (p. 105). If, as Rosenblatt posits, a student-reader should construct the text, this idea can extend to the notion that the student-reader, or course participant, should also help construct the course experience. Enabling students to give course feedback via social media platforms provides an interactive, socially-constructed venue for students to take an active role in the course experience. Using Facebook and Twitter in the composition classroom might afford students the opportunity to provide real time feedback and thus enhance their critical language functions. Elavsky

(2010) asserts that "by monitoring this conversational stream and contributing input regularly, the course instructor has the opportunity to generate and expand the classroom dialogue, foster more personalized engagement with students in general, and assess the "pulse" of the class to see what is and isn't working in terms of developing course objectives" (p. 3).

Because it can grant students a stronger voice in the classroom, use of social media programs might "actually foster an environment for collaborative, self-directed learning in the ways they provide specific avenues by which student input can inform the course design" (4). As opposed to the nature of a remote course survey, allowing students to provide simultaneous course feedback in an open environment through social media sites might enable the students to, as Evalsky (2010) asserts, "take ownership of the knowledge parameters of the course and develop their critical literacy as well as skill sets in relation to these technologies in ways which have real-world applications well beyond the course" (p. 1). Should course feedback ever become inappropriate or too off-topic (as some opposed to this idea might predict), this situation may offer composition teachers fruitful opportunities to teach audience awareness.

Rosenblatt, like Bahktin, emphasizes expressive acts as shared acts between the speaker and the addressee, and thus expressive acts require a high level of audience awareness for messages to work appropriately. Using social media programs such as Facebook and Twitter in a classroom environment is an optimum way to teach students audience awareness. Lessons on creating posts, notes, or tweets catered to the needs of an academic audience versus a personal audience could be fruitful; additionally, reviewing case studies of people losing jobs over derogatory posts on Facebook can provide students with an important lesson in considering audiences when engaging in public writing related to the workplace.

Facebook and Twitter in the composition classroom might also embody Rosenblatt's (1983) argument for students to become consummate in language in diverse ways. Facebook and Twitter offer multimodal exemplifications of language and discourse in the 21st century; if the Internet is where students of the Millennial generation spend a great portion of their time, it only makes sense to incorporate these spaces as legitimate modes of discourse exchange in the context of writing.

This idea echoes Rosenblatt's early thoughts on a multi-modal English education:

Rosenblatt...felt that the legitimate aim of teaching English was to 'help people acquire the capacity to use language in all its modes, to organize their sense of their worlds, to communicate it to others, and to participate in the experiences and ideas of others' Ultimately, the purpose of scholarly expertise in the 'disciplines' of discourse was not simply to advance specific kinds of knowledge but to give students opportunities to become accomplished with language in varied ways. (Hallin, 2004, p. 286)

Using language "in varied ways" can translate quite clearly to teaching composition students to effectively use language in technologically-based environments. Much like discussions of audience awareness, in becoming adept in the varying modes of language as framed by new social situations and knowledge-generation in technological and social network contexts, composition students can grow to understand the new communication and writing venues they will be faced with in the workplace and beyond.

Rosenblatt's theories about pedagogy, like Bahktin's of knowledge, emphasize the social experience of language, discourse, and knowledge in that they emphasize the contribution of personal experiences and reactions. Rosenblatt's ideas seem to promote a sort of empowerment and greater consideration of students. It becomes obvious that if composition instructors hope to meet the unique needs of the Millennial student, they must experiment with social media technologies in the classroom. Social media sites such as Facebook and Twitter provide valuable opportunities to meet students halfway in their writing life; in addition, the sites embody ideas of better appropriating power in the classroom and the social construction of knowledge.

DISCUSSION

Possible Resistance to Social Media in the Composition Classroom

Though these discussions are limited for the context of this essay, it seems that many rhetorical and pedagogical stances of the 20th century support the potential use of social media in the composition classroom. This idea, however, does not come without resistance. The greatest potential conflict to employing social technologies in the composition classroom lies in the fact that many instructors might view social media as a "distraction" to real instruction. However, there are many retorts to this opposition. The first response is situated in the inherent learning differences of the Millennial students.

Millennial students have grown up as multi-taskers: they switch between Facebook and homework, Twitter posts and Blackboard entries. They text while they study, and they read while they listen to music on their iPods. In a 2005 *Chronicle of Higher Education* article entitled "The Net Generation Goes to College," Richard T. Sweeney, university librarian at the New Jersey Institute of Technology, explains, "Raised amid a barrage of information, [students] are able to juggle a conversation on Instant Messenger, a Web-surfing session, and an iTunes playlist while reading Twelfth Night for homework" (p. 1). Many students, however, might in fact learn better in this manner; says Ophir et al. (2009) in "From the Cover: Cognitive control in Media Multitaskers: "There is evidence that high media users and multi-taskers have different [yet intrinsically faster] information processing styles than low users" (p. 2).

In his work, "Faculty perceptions of the impact of student laptop use in a wireless Internet environment on the classroom learning environment and teaching," Aaron T. Brubaker (2006) presents survey responses in which 70% of writing professors agreed that Millennial students need to be taught differently than students 10 years ago. Brubaker (2006) also reports on the Millennial students' penchant for multitasking, visual orientation, and need for immediacy. Thus, while for many instructors, social media may seem a potential issue of distraction, Sweeney argues that instructors should absolutely "change [their] teaching styles. Make blogs, iPods, and video games part of [their] pedagogy. And learn to accept divided attention spans. A new generation of students has arrived" (p. 1).

For these students, "attention" is entirely different than for generations past. Like discourse, what constitutes "attention" versus "distraction" in a classroom is a socially-constructed notion (as Bakhtin would assert); the line between these two cognitive states might mean one idea to an instructor, stagnant in his or her thinking about what student attention entails, and an entirely different thought to the Millennial student who only learns through layered technological literacies.

A final response to the distraction issue echoes Rosenblatt's theories of a pedagogy that meets students in the "middle." As I have argued, Millennial students are in fact different from past learners. Good instructors who wish to use every resource available to reach their students, then, ought to meet students where they are learning and interested. If a student spends hours of his or her day on Facebook and Twitter, for example, we ought not to find this a distraction but instead a potential learning opportunity.

Preferably, we should ask ourselves: how might we make these social media technologies work for us and more closely replicate the skills we wish to unearth in this group of multi-modal, 21st-century learners?

Others opposed to social media in the classroom have argued that use of the programs such as Facebook and Twitter may undermine current teaching practices of the teacher as center. In the classroom, learning can easily take place in a controlled situation in which the teacher transfers knowledge to students. In social media environments, however, knowledge is built in a less controlled way. The instructor can act as a facilitator of discussion, but traditional pedagogies are thus altered in ways that make grading and controlled learning more difficult from the instructor's end. For some, this model of impaired control may undercut "traditional" academic models. However, as today's student changes, pedagogy must change. Millennial students learn in multiple literacies, and they are generally familiar with constructing knowledge through Internet use. Why, then, as Rosenblatt argues through her pedagogical theories, should we not fulfill this need?

The traditional teaching model may allow for some construction of knowledge in a classroom environment, but integrating social media, could potentially allow for the greatest construction of knowledge possible – a framework Bakhtin would likely support. Arguably, some may also claim that requiring social media in an academic environment undermines the very personal nature of social networks – that by requiring its use, we cross a clear-cut line between students' social and academic lives. However, if the model of the teacher changes from "center" to "facilitator of knowledge" to fit the use of social media in the classroom, most likely, students will recognize their "granted" voice and will be more apt to share in the classroom?

While more research is necessary to posit exactly how this new model might function, it seems that Rosenblatt's ideas on pedagogy, Bakhtin's rhetorical theories, and the facts present about Millennial students' learning styles all support that, through social media, writing, language, and discourse might be a more personal act and thus become more meaningful to the students' life.

CONCLUSION

As Bakhtin argues, there is no meaning to knowledge or language without some sort of social orientation, and all understandings of awareness and discourse are socially constructed. Likewise, as Rosenblatt would assert, students' responses are integral to a successful English course, and allowing students to construct meaning though personal reactions and "everyday discourse" is essential to success. Millennial student are multi-taskers different from any previous generation of university students. If traditional, unilateral models of education do not reach the Millennial student in ways these models may have reached students in the past, social media programs like Facebook and Twitter seem appealing for their ability to help instructors better reach students in course discussions, allow course input from varying contexts, teaching audience awareness, enable course feedback in real-time environments, post relevant medias related to course topics, and prepare students to communicate in a highly-technological world.

Composition courses can do even more to incorporate such resources into the curriculum. In this sense, we have a promising opportunity here, and it seems now is the time to explore the benefits of engaging what Zappen et al. deem a "contemporary rhetorical community in cyberspace" for use in the composition classroom. Social media programs seem a natural vehicle to meet this charge. The possibilities of social media programs in the composition classroom are fruitful, and therefore, should be considered for those composition instructors wishing to most effectively meet the needs of and further generate meaning for the Millennial student.

REFERENCES

Allen, G. (2008). *Language, Power, and Consciousness: A Writing Experiment at the University of Toronto. Teaching Composition: Background Readings* (T. R. Johnson, Ed.). New York: Bedford St. Martin's.

Association for Education in Journalism and Mass Communication. (2010). AEJMC: Social Media in the Classroom.

Bakhtin, M. (2001). Marxism and the Philosophy of Language. In Bizzell & Herzberg (Eds.), The Rhetorical Tradition: Readings from Classical Times to the Present (pp. 1206-1245). Bedford St. Martin's.

Bizzell & Herzberg (Ed.), (2001). *The Rhetorical Tradition: Readings from Classical Times to the Present. New York*. Bedford: St. Martin's.

Brubaker, A. T. (2006). Faculty perceptions of the impact of student laptop use in a wireless Internet environment on the classroom learning environment and teaching.

Carlson, S. (2010). The Net Generation Goes to College. *The Chronicle of Higher Education*: Information Technology, A34.

Coogan, D. (1998). Email 'tutoring' as collaborative writing. In *Wiring the Writing Center*. Logan, UT: Utah State University Press.

Cooper, M. M., & Selfe, C. L. (1990). Computer conferences and learning: Authority, resistance, and internally persuasive discourse. *College English*, 1990, 849–869.

Dorwick, K. (1996). Rethinking the Academy: Problems and Possibilities of Teaching, Scholarship, Authority, and Power in Electronic Environments. *Kairos*.

EDUCAUSE Center for Applied Research. (2008). ECAR Study of Undergraduate Students and Information Technology.

Elavsky, M. C. (2010). Social Media in the Classroom.

Hallin, A. (2004). A Rhetoric for Audiences: Louise Rosenblatt on Reading and Action. Lunsford, A. (Ed.), Reclaiming Rhetorica: Women in the Rhetorical Tradition (pp. 285-303). Pittsburg: University of Pittsburg Press.

Heiberger, G., & Harper, R. (2008). Have You Facebooked Astin Lately? Using Technology to Increase Student Involvement. *New Directions for Student Services*, 2008, 3–25.

Ipsos (2014). Ipsos Millenial Social Influence Study. Retrieved from http://corp.crowdtap.com/socialinfluence

Junco, R., Heiberger, G., & Loken, E. (2010). The effect of Twitter on college student engagement and grades. *Journal of Computer Assisted Learning*.

Kemp, F. (2010). *Introduction to Rhetorical Theory Course*. Texas Tech University.

Ophir, E., Nass, C., & Wagner, A. D. (2009). From the Cover: Cognitive control in media multitaskers. *Proceedings of the National Academy of Science.*

Pew Internet and American Life Project. (2010). Social Media & Mobile Internet Use among Teens and Young Adults.

Rosenblatt, L. (1977). What We Have Learned: Reminiscences of the NCTE. *English Journal, 66*(8), 88–90.

Rosenblatt, L. (1983). Literature As Exploration (4th ed.). New York: MLA.

Urbanaski, H. (2008). *"I hate to write. I can't do it.": First-Year Composition and the Resistant Student Writer* [Dissertation]. Lehigh University.

Zappen, J. P., Gurak, L. J., & Doheny-Farina, S. (1997). Rhetoric, Community, and Cyberspace. *Rhetoric Review, 15*(2), 400–419. doi:10.1080/07350199709359226

Chapter 10
Slacktivism, Supervision, and #Selfies:
Illuminating Social Media Composition through Reception Theory

Elisabeth H. Buck
University of Massachusetts Dartmouth, USA

ABSTRACT

Since its original development for use in literary studies by German scholar Hans Robert Jauss in the late 1960s, reception theory has been successfully applied to fields as diverse as media studies, communications, and art history; its efficacy within rhetoric and composition pedagogy, however, has been less fully explored. I argue in this essay that reception theory can provide a meaningful way to understand and discuss social media composing practices, especially as a lens for thinking about why and how we participate in social media as both readers and writers in the 21st century. This essay thus examines the three "aesthetic experiences" of Jauss's reception theory—catharsis, aisthesis, and poiesis— which describe the ways that audiences derive satisfaction from engaging with texts. I apply each aesthetic concept to a corresponding mode of social media composition: practices of social media-based activism, regulation of content on social media, as well as the act of creating "selfies." These applications stand as potential entry points for classroom discussion about how social media draws its users into producing a response. The "aesthetic experiences" represent ways to look at composing practices on social media cohesively, but they also give language to how individual social media users gain enjoyment from participating with these sites. I offer specific strategies for incorporating reception theory in a classroom context, and conclude that this approach helps students think more specifically about the intricacies and limitations of audience(s)—important recognitions for anyone who produces content in social media environments.

DOI: 10.4018/978-1-5225-0562-4.ch010

INTRODUCTION

On March 2nd, 2014—the night of the 86th annual Academy Awards—host Ellen DeGeneres broke Twitter. During an interlude in the awards ceremony, DeGeneres asked actress Meryl Streep to pose with her for a selfie and commemorate her record-breaking eighteenth Oscar nomination by "[trying] to break another record right now, with the most retweets of a photo." In a moment of ostensible spontaneity, DeGeneres solicited several other celebrities—including Brad Pitt, Angelina Jolie, Jennifer Lawrence, Julia Roberts, and Kevin Spacey—to join her and Streep for a picture that ultimately showcased a coterie of Hollywood A-listers. Within forty minutes of DeGeneres's uploading the photo to her Twitter account, the "Oscar selfie" became the most retweeted item ever posted on the social media site, causing Twitter to crash momentarily. DeGeneres's photo broke the record previously held by Barack Obama's picture celebrating his 2012 reelection to the presidency. This picture has since been retweeted over three-and-a-half million times, a number that continues to grow despite claims that the epic selfie was actually a planned product placement for awards sponsor Samsung (Guynn, 2014). Whatever the true intent behind the post was, the fact remains that in this instance, DeGeneres directly solicited a response from the over forty million individuals tuned into the ceremony, and respond they did—in a number roughly equivalent to the combined populations of South Dakota, Alaska, North Dakota, Vermont, and Wyoming.

There are many ways that individuals can compose on and through social media, yet retweeting a post requires a comparatively high level of investment. In contrast to "favoriting" another user's tweet—an act that implies mere tacit approval of that content—retweeting publically announces to followers a desire for the content to be shared. Perhaps more significantly, because the retweeted post appears on the user's profile page, it becomes a part of that person's collective Twitter identity, helping to form the narrative that will shape how individuals read a user's profile. Retweeting DeGeneres's selfie implies a desire to perpetuate and engage in the act of collective reading—it is an acknowledgement that one receives pleasure from participating in this historical moment, and, in consequence, marks the user as inevitably cognizant of the post's significance.

This Oscars anecdote stands as emblematic of the kind of meaningful discourses that can emerge when considering how audiences function collectively as composers and recipients of social media content—key to understanding reception theory's applications. At its most essential level, reception theory is a lens often applied to literature, communication, and art history that views the interpretation of texts "as dependent on the reading public's horizon of expectations in a given period" (Chandler & Munday, 2011). This concept of "horizon of expectations" is a key principle within reception theory, and it can be understood as a "shared 'mental set' or framework within which those of a particular generation in a culture understand, interpret, and evaluate a text or an artwork." These shared qualities—which reinforce an ideology of a collective audience—include "knowledge of conventions and expectations (e.g. regarding genre and style), and social knowledge (e.g. of moral codes)" (Chandler & Munday, 2011). In the case then of the Oscar selfie, the three-and-a-half million individuals who retweeted the post demonstrated the "shared mental set" of the social media-saturated generation, in which the act of retweeting signifies a collective understanding of how to read and participate with that text. This chapter consequently explores the use of reception theory to discuss social media, and also includes practical, accessible activities for classroom application. For 21st century teachers of writing, this model can provide a helpful framework for theorizing social media and understanding its broader implications, especially because it places emphasis on the importance of audience and context.

Reception theory differs meaningfully and significantly from rhetorical analysis and reader-response theory, however, by also emphasizing how individuals gain pleasure from the act of reading. In this chapter, I argue that applying reception theory to acts of composing on social media presents new and interesting ways to think about the complexities of collective audiences. To illustrate this application, I will read the three categories of "aesthetic experience" illuminated by reception theory—*catharsis*, *aisthesis*, and *poiesis*—and relate them specifically to ways that collective audiences respond on social media using the concepts of social-media-based "activism," regulation of content, and selfies. I then offer suggestions for discussing and applying these concepts in writing-intensive classrooms. Ultimately, incorporating reception theory pedagogically helps students think more specifically about the intricacies and limitations of audience(s)—important recognitions for individuals who already produce or will be expected to generate content on a digital platform.

BACKGROUND

Like all theoretical approaches, the concept of reception theory is not wholly cohesive: a number of scholars and critiques problematize and interrogate this epistemology. For the purposes of this discussion, I will consider reception theory as it was originally conceptualized by German scholar Hans Robert Jauss.[11] In his 1969 essay, "The Change in the Paradigm of Literary Scholarship," Jauss argues for a new approach to literary studies that calls for a more particular attention to the aesthetics of literary work, suggesting that, "the increasing importance of mass media compels any prospective paradigm to incorporate methods for dealing adequately with an entire range of hitherto unforeseen 'aesthetic and quasi-aesthetic' effects" (Holub, 1984, p. 4).

This essay had a profound impact on studies of literature and art, especially as a way to facilitate re-evaluation of canonical works. Jauss's goal was to think about these texts in relation to their context by placing emphasis not just on the production of texts, but on how they would be received by audiences within their particular historical setting. This reception depends on the principle of "horizon of expectations." While Robert Holub (1984) notes that even Jauss's use of this term is rather "nebulous," he suggests that he primarily understands "horizon of expectations" as "[referring] to an intersubjective system or structure of expectations, a 'system of references' or a mind-set that a hypothetical individual might bring to any text" (p. 59). The emphasis is thus placed on the shared experiences of a text that are dictated by contextualized notions—referring back to Chandler and Munday's definition of "horizons"— of conventions and expectations pertaining to genre/style as well as social knowledge. "Aesthetic experience" is important to determining what specifically motivates an audience's response. In simplified terms, aesthetic experience refers to the ways that audiences derive pleasure from a text or object.

Jauss hypothesized that there are three ways of describing these aesthetic experiences, encompassed by the Greek ideas of *catharsis*, *aisthesis*, and *poiesis*. Later in the chapter, I will explore the specific meanings of each of these terms in relation to the specific social media phenomenon that they help to elucidate, but, considering the value of aesthetic experiences more broadly, the primary goal is to think about the pleasurable relationship between the viewer and the text: "Jauss wants to emphasize not only the back-and-forth movement between subject and object, but also the 'primary unity of understanding enjoyment and enjoying understanding.' Pleasure…should not be separated from its cognitive or praxis-oriented functions" (Holub, 1984, p. 75). The concepts of *catharsis, aisthesis, and poiesis*, therefore, describe the thought processes and actions that occur when an individual receives pleasure as a result of his or her experience with the text.

To reiterate why using reception theory might provide valuable insight into social media composing practices: 1) the concept of "horizons of expectations" suggests that there is a collective understanding of genre conventions and moral codes that will dictate how an audience within a particular historical context responds to a text/object; and 2) as explained by *catharsis, aisthesis, and poiesis*, these reactions will be based on how the audience (collectively) derives pleasure from the act of responding. All actions conducted publically or semi-publically on social media are texts that are subject to interpretation by numerous audiences—sometimes these audiences are specifically defined (i.e., an audience of one's Facebook "friends") but, in many cases, they are not. The use of reception theory can consequently give greater meaning to the ways that these ambiguous collective audiences work together to make meaning of social media interactions.

Catharsis: Communicative Aesthetic Experience

Jauss's understanding of *catharsis* is not necessarily the way that the term is typically understood in relation to its original Greek iteration— i.e., the concept that a person receives pleasure and release from viewing the tragic misfortune of others. While this is one of the ways that pleasure from a text can be obtained, Jauss defines *catharsis* more broadly, suggesting that it encompasses "communicative aesthetic experiences." He also argues that, "an important aspect of communication takes place in transmitting role models of behavior, and *catharsis* can consequently be examined through an analysis of aesthetic identification" (Holub, 1984, p.78). Aesthetic identification refers to the ways that individuals align themselves with a character or event, thus receiving pleasure from that alignment. Jauss claims that there are five kinds of alignment in relation to types of role models or "heroes": associative ("placing oneself in the roles of all other participants"), admiring (the perfect hero), sympathetic (the imperfect/everyday hero), cathartic (the suffering/hard-pressed hero), and ironic (the missing hero or anti-hero) (Holub, 1984, p. 80). I want to think about *catharsis* in relation to two forms of "activism" on social media—slacktivism and hacktivism. In each of these instances, groups of individuals align themselves with a cause on social media, therefore resulting in an "aesthetic identification" with that cause. While these are not necessarily positive or entirely effective forms of activism, they demonstrate a very important aspect of how collective audiences work together on social media to support a particular "hero." Slacktivism and hacktivism then exist as ways to illuminate the concept of *catharsis*.

To illustrate this concept of slacktivism, Vie (2014), in "In Defense of 'Slactivism': The Human Rights Campaign Facebook Logo as Digital Activism," provides an effective overview both of a specific instance of slacktivism as well as a demonstration of how this illuminates the significance of collective audience activity. Quoting Neumayer and Schoßböck's understanding of social media-based forms of activism, Vie notes that the concept of slacktivism, "can be defined as 'having done something good for society without actively engaging in politics, protest, or civil disobedience, or spending or raising money.' Thus slacktivism is critiqued as an easy–to–engage–in effort that makes little difference in the world" (p. 9). Vie traces the development of the 2013 "slacktivist" campaign of individuals using the Human Rights Campaign's logo as a profile picture on social media to demonstrate their support of LGBT rights, which was particularly significant given the arguments on the legality of gay marriage about to be delivered in the US Supreme Court.

Vie comments on the remarkable visibility generated by this logo (see Figure 1), noting that the movement received coverage from major news outlets and that "overall, the HRC logo appeared over 18 million times in Facebook's News Feed, and the HRC's nine separate Facebook posts over a five–day span in March 2013 garnered more than 50 million impressions, which resulted in record traffic to the HRC's Web site, HRC.org" (p. 2). Rather than viewing slacktivism as ultimately having very little impact, Vie concentrates on how seeing these images of support on social media can be an effective way to combat microaggressions against the LGBT population—that viewing a user's public display of the equality symbol, especially in a collective capacity, can help individuals align with a virtual community. She ultimately takes a more positive stance on the potential for social media-based slacktivism to shape off-line discourses, noting that "in examining the potential power of Internet memes, then, looking to an example like the Human Rights Campaign logo allows us to see how memes spread within kairotic cultural ecologies. They draw on both individual and group identities and they allow for rapid visual representation of alignment with a cause" (p.10). This concept of slacktivism as a means of bringing together these "identities" stands as an important iteration of the way that social media can facilitate group interactions.

To further illustrate how social media can be used to rally individuals toward activist intent, Penney & Dadas (2014) describe how Twitter was used to generate support for the 2011 Occupy Wall Street movement. While this instance is perhaps less "slacktivist" because it did often inspire real-world (not

Figure 1. The original 2013 "call to action" on the HRC Facebook page
Vie, 2014.

just digital) engagement with this issue, Penney & Dadas's intent is to "call attention to circulation as a major consideration in how users capitalize on the affordances of Twitter, how the OWS movement has become so dispersed and has grown so quickly, and how the OWS network on Twitter functions as a counterpublic" (p. 77). By conducting interviews with seventeen individuals involved in the Occupy Wall Street movement, which sought, broadly to draw attention to the ways that corporate America functions repressively, the authors ultimately describe how Twitter became an effective communicative platform to bring disparate audiences to the cause, especially as a way to report face-to-face protests and distribute/circulate information.

Importantly, Penney & Dadas also examine the ways that non-affiliated audiences could regulate content distribution, as some of their participants expressed concern that Twitter itself did not allow Occupy-related hashtags to "trend" and that government entities might be monitoring the posts in order to curb illegal protests (pp. 86-88). Penney & Dadas ultimately conclude that using Twitter to generate support for the Occupy movement was effective because "Twitter's technical specifics are not only amenable to the intensive textual circulation necessary for building and sustaining a counterpublic, but may in fact foster such processes through the aggregated tweeting and retweeting activities of individual users" (p. 89). In this case, aggregation demonstrates how users can both individually affiliate with a cause that—like retweeting the Oscar selfie—eventually creates an event that has collective significance and purpose.

The perpetuation of the HRC logo and the Twitter–mediated collaboration of users supporting the Occupy movement demonstrate the associative iteration of *catharsis*. By participating in these slacktivist/ activist causes, the user generates pleasure from his or her identification *with* that cause. If no pleasure is derived, individuals would simply not participate in that act. In isolation, however, these individual acts of identification (i.e., one Facebook user's decision to make the HRC logo her profile picture) do not have significance until they are grouped together with similar behaviors. The collaboration consequently signifies a mutual understanding of how to "read" a user's involvement with that movement, making such an event legible even for those who do not directly participate. For instance, a user did not necessarily have to make the HRC logo a profile picture in order to "like," support, and/or understand that choice. Social media platforms have even recently facilitated these actions, as, for example, Facebook made available to users a French flag profile picture overlay to show solidarity with victims of the November 2015 Paris terrorist attacks. The collective participation is ultimately what makes each of these actions more universally legible, thereby strengthening the cohesiveness of the movement as a whole.

It is important to note that not all ways of collaborative activism are necessarily associative. Hacktivism, which the *Oxford* dictionary defines as, "a computer hacker whose activity is aimed at a social or political cause," is often conducted with a more cathartic or ironic intent. To briefly illustrate an instance of social media-orientated hacktivism in which the goal was certainly not to associate with the cause of the "hero," but instead to gain collective pleasure from seeing an individual's fall, a particularly useful anecdote is that of Alicia Ann Lynch.

In October 2013, Lynch shared images of her Halloween costume (see Figure 2) on her public social media accounts: she dressed up as a victim of the 2013 Boston Marathon bombings. According to the *New York Daily News*, to punish Lynch for her "distasteful" post, "Internet vigilantes raided Lynch's social media accounts, pulling out nude pics and a partial photo of her driver's license, which included personal details such as her family's address in Fairgrove, Mich" (Murphy, 2013, para. 6).

Lynch was ultimately fired from her job, and she and her family received threats of varying severity; as the *News* article notes, "The rape threats hit the hardest, Lynch said. She claimed she was raped last

Figure 2. Lynch's unfortunate choice of Halloween costume
Murphy, 2013.

Thanksgiving" (para. 10). While many others decried the hacktivist harassment as far more reprehensible than Lynch's initial post, this instance certainly demonstrates a collective desire to receive pleasure by causing "anti-hero" Lynch to suffer tangible repercussions for her actions—the majority of which were implemented on and through social media.

Many of the social media hacktivists in the Lynch circumstance were anonymous, but collective hacktivism with a similar intent to bring down an "anti-hero" can still occur when participants are much more specific. To illustrate: during the particularly painful January days of the 2014 polar vortex, when temperatures across the Midwest and eastern regions of the country plunged well below zero, University of Illinois at Urbana-Champaign chancellor Phyllis Wise distributed an email informing students that, despite the frigid temperatures and wind chill, classes that Monday would be held as scheduled. Students at Illinois subsequently took to Twitter to verbally bash Wise, who they largely held as singularly responsible for the university's decision not to cancel classes.

According to *Inside Higher Ed*'s Jaschik (2014), "That some students would take to Twitter to gripe is not shocking. But a flurry of comments focused either on Wise's status as a woman, as an Asian-American, or both. The hashtag of choice: #fuckphyllis" (para. 2). Because of the particular vitriol, misogyny, racism, and sheer number of the social media posts, this case drew national attention as particularly emblematic of how general displeasure over an event can quickly devolve into ad hominem attacks against a figurehead. This instance also led to speculation about the collective mentality of Illinois students. According to Jaschik, "[T]his is the same university where some alumni made harsh attacks on officials who wanted to retire a Native American mascot…One blog post talked about 'a culture of complacency' in which wealthy, white students (or some of them) feel entitled to take down those with whom they disagree" (para. 7). This instance functions then not just as a particularly regrettable isolated incident, but one that could have larger implications for defining group mentalities—again, attitudes that are revealed through the cohesive social media composing practices of a specific population.

Thinking then about both slacktivism and hacktivism in relation to *catharsis* and reception theory, it is important to emphasize that historical context dictates all the aforementioned instances. Without an understanding of this context, there would be no reason for a collective response. For instance, without the knowledge that Lynch's costume was intended to evoke the tragic bombing that occurred months before Halloween in the year 2013, to look merely at the picture as it "exists," it is likely that the immediate reaction would be one of confusion, not abhorrence (i.e., Why is this young woman dressed in running clothes when she is clearly neither outside nor at a gym? And why is she smiling at the camera when she is obviously bleeding?) When considering writing produced on social media platforms, where content is quickly and infinitely distributed to multiple audiences, having an understanding of this context in order to ascertain the possible "horizons" of response is critical. Otherwise, a picture with an obviously offensive connotation becomes merely an image of a woman who is seemingly impervious to pain and/ or who lacks an understanding of what constitutes "appropriate" office attire.

Applying *Catharsis* to the Classroom: Suggested Pedagogical Activity

Have students research and select an event that demonstrates either a slacktivist or hacktivist mentality, making sure to guide them into an incident where a group of social media users acted collectively with a particular purpose (again, the distribution of the HRC logo, #OccupyWallStreet, the Lynch incident, and the Illinois students' responses to Chancellor Wise are useful examples of this). Students can research these events either individually or in small groups. When they discuss or write about these events, have them think about the following questions:

1. What, ultimately, was the goal of the social media users' actions?
2. On which social media platform(s) did these actions take place? Why do you think that these platforms permitted or facilitated these actions?
3. Define the role of context in this event: what background information do you need in order to be able to understand its significance?
4. What might be the lasting effects of this event in terms of its impact on a particular individual, group, or community?
5. How do social networking sites particularly enable large-scale activism? In what ways might social media be a more effective tool for such activism?

Aisthesis: Aesthetic Perception

As with *catharsis*, the "horizons" also become very important to the concept of *aisthesis*, which Jauss understands as "the receptive side of aesthetic experience" (Holub, 1984, p.76). If aesthetic experience can be understood as how individuals gain pleasure from the act of engaging with a text/object, then *aisthesis* refers to the particular ways that individuals receive this pleasure through both their sensory and perceptory experiences. An individual's morality and understanding of social codes become key in discussions of *aisthesis*, as these attitudes affect the ways that an object will be assessed, beyond just how it looks/smells/tastes/sounds.

Where the concept of *aisthesis* becomes most relevant to social media composing practices is in the complicated process of regulation and supervision. Every social media site has a set of conventions that dictate what users comprehensively can and cannot post. Individual users, however, have very different notions of what constitutes "offensive" content. For some, a post is worthy of censure when it fails to respond to the particular genre conventions of a site—such as when a person on Facebook types a name into the "status update" portion of the page instead of the search bar. Other posts that have violent or overly suggestive content might be more universally prone to reprimand. Even large companies periodically misinterpret what constitutes appropriate behavior on social media.

For instance, in 2013 UK grocery store chain Tesco was criticized for selling beef products that contained significant quantities of horsemeat. Soon after this scandal came to light, the official Tesco Twitter account failed to stop a hilariously inappropriate pre-scheduled tweet: "It's sleepy time so we're off to hit the hay. See you at 8am for more #TescoTweets" (Curtis, 2013, para. 4). It is evident that, just as in the discussion of *catharsis*, the concepts of collective knowledge and context are important here. The Tesco tweet in particular, had it not so immediately followed the horsemeat incident, would have been entirely innocuous, but the use of "hit the hay" made the tweet (literally) distasteful. The challenge for any entity charged with regulating content on social media is to both fully understand context and transcend individual notions of what is "offensive" into content that should be comprehensively banned. Thinking about this in relation to *aisthesis* enables more specific discussion of how important collective perception is to this process.

Facebook maintains a page of community standards that is designed to illustrate content that is not allowed on the site. In vague language that hints at the complexities of interpretation for their audience of over one billion users, Facebook claims that in order "to balance the needs and interests of a global population" these standards exist to help individuals "understand what type of expression is acceptable and what type of content may be reported and removed" ("Facebook Community Standards").

There are eleven categories, each with an accompanying explanatory paragraph, that describe content that could be banned: violence and threats, self-harm, bullying and harassment, hate speech, graphic content, nudity and pornography, identity and privacy, intellectual property, regulated goods, phishing and spam, and security. The problem with the accompanying paragraphs offering explanation of these categories is that the language is necessarily vague: it must be broad enough, of course, to cover anything that could possibly fall under that category, but it cannot be so specific that it rules anything out. For instance, the paragraph discussing graphic content—probably the most hazy of the categorical labels—notes:

Facebook has long been a place where people turn to share their experiences and raise awareness about issues important to them. Sometimes, those experiences and issues involve graphic content that is of public interest or concern, such as human right abuses or acts of terrorism. In many instances, when people share this type of content, it is to condemn it. However, graphic images shared for sadistic effect or to celebrate or glorify violence have no place on our site. ("Facebook Community Standards")

It later continues to indicate that if users decide to post graphic videos, they should "warn their audience about the nature of the content in the video so that their audience can make an informed choice about whether to watch it." A specific incident that illustrates the complexities of this graphic content policy occurred in 2013 when Facebook reversed its ban on videos with violent content—including videos depicting decapitation—with the condition that the user make clear that the video condemns violence and does not celebrate it. Yet, as Bianca Bosker (2013) of *The Huffington Post* points out, "The decision prompted immediate backlash from critics who highlighted the hypocrisy of Facebook allowing violent content, while banning breasts. (Facebook routinely censors breastfeeding photos.)" ("Beheadings Belong on Facebook," para. 3). Even though Bosker ultimately concludes that these videos should be allowed since activists might not have the sanction to disseminate this content elsewhere, she also posits whether or not coming across these videos unintentionally might have detrimental manifestations for sensitive or vulnerable individuals. Implicit in this claim is the unlikelihood that a photo of a mother breastfeeding would raise similar psychological concerns.

Also important to this discussion is who *specifically* applies these broad-based policies toward individual posts that users flag as offensive. If the process of comprehending the particular categories of offensive content is confusing, perhaps even more perplexing is the procedure a post goes through once it has been flagged by a user. Facebook publishes a complex infographic, available on their "What Happens After You Click 'Report'" page, that explains the reporting process. This infographic indicates that there are certain protocols that occur depending on how a post is marked by a user. In some instances, such as when something is marked by a user as "I don't like this post" or the post is "harassing me/a friend," regulation of the content becomes the responsibility of the user, and he or she is either prompted to send the user a message or block/unfriend that individual.

Facebook also has a "social reporting" system in place, where users, intriguingly, "can use the tool to reach out to a trusted friend who may understand the offline context of the situation." This is especially compelling because this demonstrates Facebook's awareness of the importance of context to a user's interpretation of a specific event, although it would be interesting to see how this is accomplished in practical terms. Further, there are also four specific groups of Facebook employees—the safety, hate and harassment, abusive content, and access teams—that have the power to warn the user, disable the user's page, ask for an identification check, or, in some instances, report the behavior to law enforcement. Facebook's infographic notes that "hundreds" of individuals make up these teams, they are versed in twenty-four languages, and are based in Menlo Park, Austin, Dublin, and Hyderabad (India). This is, overall, a very intricate diagram, and one that hints at the complexities involved in the reporting process.

When examining this chart further, however, there are some apparent gaps in this system—the most obvious of which is that there are certainly more than twenty-four languages spoken around the world. This infographic does not explain what happens when a team member encounters text outside of his or her designated language(s). This potential for miscommunication is something that Bosker (2013) suggests is problematic as well, and she comments, "Facebook's moderators often lack the knowledge of a region's politics that is necessary to arbitrate, or may be lacking the language skills to determine the context for a graphic video, analysts note. Others say Facebook's staff reviews reports too quickly, meaning that innocent posts are deleted erroneously" (para. 16). So it is interesting that, on one hand, Facebook emphasizes the importance of context to "social reporting," but, on the other hand, may lack this context within its own internal reporting protocols.

What *aisthesis* can consequently add to this reading is a way to think about how collective moral codes and perceptory experiences complicate the way that both individuals and entities regulate social media content. What one user might consider offensive, another might think is humorous. Because of the huge variety and number of social media posts that circulate on these sites, ascertaining what is *collectively* offensive enough to be banned becomes difficult. And, certainly, Facebook (and other social media sites) often makes mistakes. For instance, materials promoting Kirk Cameron's 2013 Christian-oriented film *Unstoppable* were temporarily banned on Facebook, until the site realized its mistake, as the film features no graphic content, profanity, and/or other material that would be considered offensive under Facebook's community standards.

Fox News commentator Starnes (n.d.) discussed Facebook's improper ban of Cameron's film, noting, "The religious nature of the film led Cameron to speculate that perhaps the Christian content might have led to the block" (para. 13). Starnes further commented, "In recent months, the social networking website has come under criticism from conservatives and Christians who said their pages have been either blocked or banned because of 'abusive' content" (para. 18.). Implicit here is the idea that individual users, in numbers great enough to warrant the initial ban, did find Cameron's film offensive—but not in the way that the community standards page is designed to account for. What *aisthesis* consequently illuminates within this conversation is how context and collective perceptory experiences inevitably shape social media composition—as well as the fact that a great number of people apparently derived pleasure from labeling a former *Growing Pains* star "offensive."

Applying *Aisthesis* to the Classroom: Suggested Pedagogical Activity

Put students in groups and give them copies of the reporting policies and/or community standards pages of a social networking site. Provide them with several mock examples of content that users have "reported" (e.g., a video depicting and condemning a beheading by a terrorist group, a non-explicit picture of a woman breastfeeding, a threatening tweet from a male Twitter user directed at a female Twitter user). Indicate that, using the policies as guidelines, they must make a decision about what—if any—of this content is permitted on the site. As a group, they must be able to justify their decisions based on the policies. Following this activity, discuss these questions:

1.   Which of the sample posts that you were given was the most difficult to determine what to do with? Why?
2.   How effective do you think the policies are at regulating the content on social media sites? To what extent do you agree with the language of these policies (in other words, do you think there might be a way to make them more useful or specific?)
3.   Perform a quick search on how a social networking site actually responded to one of your sample posts (or a circumstance similar to the one indicated in your sample post). To what extent do agree with how the platform handled this?
4.   What did this activity demonstrate to you about the importance of context and audience?

Poiesis: Productive Aesthetic Experience

"Selfie" was the 2013 *Oxford Dictionary* word of the year, which it defined as, "a photograph that one has taken of oneself, typically one taken with a smartphone or webcam and uploaded to a social media website." While thinking about selfies in relation to collective audiences is seemingly counterintuitive, the concept of selfies illustrate Jauss's third category of aesthetic experience, *poiesis*. This is "the pleasure that stems from the application of one's own creative abilities" (Holub, 1984, p. 75). Also important to *poiesis* is the idea that "[i]nstead of referring to the ability to imitate a pre-existing perfection, [*poiesis*] gradually became identified with creating a work itself that would bring forth perfection, or at least the beautiful appearance of completion" (Holub, 1984, p. 75). This notion of *poiesis*—in which pleasure is obtained by applying one's own creative abilities in the attempt to make something beautiful—is thus apropos to the concept of selfies.

The goal of a selfie, after all, is generally to demonstrate one's own photographic skills (aided sometimes by particular applications and filters) in an attempt to create a flattering self-portrait. Once the selfie is uploaded to social media, the user can gauge the selfie's success—and obtain pleasure—based on the number of likes or comments it receives. What makes this activity perhaps more interesting is the collective understanding of what constitutes a selfie and the genre conventions that dictate that act of composition. This is something that The Chainsmokers's 2014 Billboard #1 hit "#Selfie" satirizes brilliantly. This song features electronic dance beats interspersed between spoken verses, in which a young woman discusses the night's events and comments on the act of taking a selfie. Here are the lyrics to the song's second verse:

Can you guys help me pick a filter?

I don't know if I should go with XX Pro or Valencia:

I wanna look tan.

What should my caption be? I want it to be clever.

How about, "Livin' with my bitches, #live?"

I only got 10 likes in the last 5 minutes.

Do you think I should take it down?

Let me take another selfie. ("#Selfie," 2014)

In this verse, the speaker comments both on the composition of the selfie and her desire for perfection (using a filter to make her look "tan") as well as the failure of the selfie to produce a fully pleasurable result (only achieving ten likes). This consequently spurs her desire to re-create that act of composition in order to possibly derive additional pleasure from a more "perfect" attempt—all practices described by *poiesis*. The Chainsmokers's music video for the song also stands as a showcase for selfies, including user-submitted pictures as well as those featuring celebrities as disparate as David Hasslehoff and Darth Vader.

If there is a cohesive goal for a selfie, it is that such a picture, when posted on social media, always represents an explicit or implicit attempt to generate some sort of response. But a picture need not just include pictures of the self to still fall under the "selfie" designation, as DeGeneres's Oscar rendition demonstrates. *The Atlantic's*LaFrance (2014) comments on the Oscar photo in relation to the tendency to deem this picture a "selfie" despite the fact that this label is a clear misnomer. LaFrance notes, "At first glance, it seems it may be turning into what linguist Ben Zimmer calls an 'anachronym,' a word or phrase that remains in usage even as behaviors change. 'The accumulated cultural knowledge of past technologies ends up powerfully shaping the way we talk about new technologies,' Zimmer told me"

("When Did Group Pictures Become 'Selfies'?," para. 6-7). LaFrance argues that the shift of meaning of "selfie" from its dictionary definition to something with a more complex connotation is important, and it marks a way that we communicate shared cultural information. She concludes that "selfies are a way of communicating narrative autonomy" where "a selfie isn't fundamentally about the photographer's relationship with the camera, it's about the photographer's relationship with an audience. In other words, selfies are more parts communication than self-admiration (though there's a healthy does of that, too)" (para. 22).

Selfies that provide a way to connect with an audience through self-composition—an act that transcends merely taking a picture—is thus a direct example of what reception theory can make meaningful in terms of explaining why and how audiences communicate with texts. The act of creating a selfie is generative: selfies spawn more selfies, as users seek to build upon both their own work (e.g., to capture their "best" selfie) and to duplicate positive reactions to others' selfie compositions. Reality star Kim Kardashian's 2015 text *Selfish*—a photography book in which, as the text's Amazon blurb notes, Kardashian exclusively demonstrates "the art of taking flattering and highly personal photos of oneself" —perhaps stands as the apotheosis of this mentality. As *poiesis* illustrates, pleasure emerges from the viewer's recognition of his or her own creative potential to generate a text, which always seeks to be read—even if only to determine which filter makes someone look more tan.

Applying *Poiesis* to the Classroom: Suggested Pedagogical Activity

This activity can be a way to incorporate a discussion on multimodality into the classroom, as well as encourage students to think about audience in relation to image-based forms of social media composition. Without providing any context, tell students to use their available technology (phone, computer) to attempt to take the "perfect" selfie in five minutes (give them the option of leaving the classroom to complete this task, as some students might be uncomfortable taking pictures in front of others). In a short journaling activity, have them describe the various ways that they altered their pictures in order to create this "perfect" image (e.g., changing poses or expressions, using filters or photo editing tools, altering backgrounds). At the end of this activity, ask students to indicate how many attempts they needed before they achieved a version of a picture they believe is closest to "perfect." In a class discussion, have them think about the following questions:

1. What do selfies reveal about the human compulsion to capture their own image?
2. What are some of the universal features of or expectations for taking selfies?
3. When you see a friend's selfie on a social networking site, what do you imagine is the response that your friend hopes to receive on this post?
4. Do you think it is possible to ever take a "perfect" selfie? Why or why not?

CONCLUSION

Why Reception Theory Matters to Composition Pedagogy

Many discussions about the use of social media in a pedagogical context focus on the ways that these networks might help students develop their understanding of audience. Swartz, in a piece for the *Kairos* praxis wiki, suggests, for instance, that she asks her students to think about social media in relation to how individuals might react to posts: "As with all forms of communication, the message we intend to convey might not be the message that is received. Moreover, the ways in which we imagine an audience might not be consistent with the reality of that audience, since those who peruse our profiles are very often not the ones whom we envision will be doing so" ("MySpace, Facebook, and Multimodal Literacy in the Writing Classroom," 2010, para. 5). Even when writing a status on Facebook on a private account—one that only "friends" have access to—it is impossible to anticipate the reactions of *every* friend to that post.

When someone posts on a public account or on a friend's profile, these reactions become even more difficult to anticipate, since it will be impossible to ascertain who specifically has access to that content. The different audiences that students conceive for these sites might dictate the ways that they compose on social media, especially if they operate profiles on more than one social network. For instance, composition scholar Lunsford (2015) argues that, "the digital age has brought with it the need for even closer considerations of audiences…the advent of digital and online literacies has blurred the boundaries between writer and audience significantly: the points of the once-stable rhetorical triangle seem to be twirling and shifting and shading into one another" (p. 21). She argues then that, "When consumers of information can, quite suddenly, become producers as well, then it's hard to tell who is the writer, who the audience" (p. 21). This suggests that there are important changes occurring in how students perceive the nebulous concept of audience in relation to their various online activities. As both readers and composers, students must begin to think critically about the ways that social media participation exists as a significant iteration of digital communication.

For this reason, it is critical that instructors provide students with a framework to discuss both their own and others' social media compositions. Asserting the value of incorporating social media into the classroom, Vie (2008) proposes that "compositionists [should] begin looking at online social networking sites through an academic lens to examine the complexities these sites showcase and what ramifications they may hold for our pedagogies and our field" (p. 21). Reception theory is certainly an academic lens—one that has been adopted to and within many disciplines—but its viability as a framework for the teaching of writing has not yet been thoroughly explored.

I believe, however, that reception theory offers a particularly unique and useful structure for thinking about acts of social media composition, especially as a way to put language to the complexities of audience brought about by any act of such composition. The concept of "horizon of expectations" can help students contemplate both the historical context in which a post was produced, as well as the ways that individuals might respond differently when they do or do not have access to that context. Reception theory can also help students think about the importance of genre conventions and social knowledge, as well as the ways that "group mentalities"—as demonstrated through acts of slacktivism and hacktivism—are made visible through collective social media composition practices. The "aesthetic experiences" represent ways to look at composing practices on social media cohesively, but they also illuminate how individual social media users seek to gain pleasure from participating with the sites. Reception theory ultimately helps elucidate why we participate in social media as both authors and readers.

While I have presented only a few applications of reception theory to social media artifacts, I believe that it could stand as an appropriate framework for interpreting possible responses to all acts of social media composition, both collectively and as generated by individuals. I have taught using reception theory in my own courses, and I have found that it is particularly beneficial because it resists temporal limitations: social media technologies—like nearly all innovations—are fleeting. Thus, even when Facebook is no longer the most en vogue platform, reception theory will still be an applicable lens for interpreting how participants and spectators interact with social media. If understanding audience is one of the most important aspects of the writing process, reception theory can provide students with insight into just how complex these audiences can be—especially within the limitless and inexhaustible space of the Internet.

REFERENCES

Bosker, B. (2013, October 22). Beheadings belong on Facebook. *The Huffington Post.* Retrieved from http://www.huffingtonpost.com/2013/10/22/facebook-beheading-videos_n_4144886.html

Buck, A. (2012). Examining digital literacy practices on social network sites. *Research in the Teaching of English, 41*, 9–38.

Chandler, D., & Munday, R. (2011). Horizon of expectations. Oxford Dictionary of Media and Communication. Oxford: Oxford University Press. Retrieved from http://www.oxfordreference.com.proxy.bsu.edu/view/10.1093/acref/9780199568758.001.0001/acref-9780199568758-e-1217 doi:10.1093/acref/9780199568758.001.0001

Chandler, D., & Munday, R. (2011). Reception theory. The Oxford Dictionary of Media and Communication. Oxford: Oxford University Press. Retrieved from http://www.oxfordreference.com.proxy.bsu.edu/view/10.1093/acref/9780199568758.001.0001/acref-9780199568758-e-2265# doi:10.1093/acref/9780199568758.001.0001

Curtis, S. (2013, August 19). Five biggest social media blunders of 2013. *The Telegraph.* Retrieved from http://www.telegraph.co.uk/technology/social-media/10252609/Five-biggest-social-media-blunders-of-2013.html

Facebook. (n. d.). *Facebook community standards.* Retrieved from https://www.facebook.com/communitystandards

Facebook. (n. d.). *What happens after you click 'report.'* Retrieved from https://www.facebook.com/notes/facebook-safety/what-happens-after-you-click-report/432670926753695

Guynn, J. (2014, March 03). Ellen DeGeneres selfie on Twitter is Oscar gold for Samsung. *Los Angeles Times.* Retrieved from http://articles.latimes.com/2014/mar/03/business/la-fi-tn-ellen-degeneres-selfie-twitter-oscars-samsung-20140303

Hacktivist [Def. 1]). (n. d.). *Oxford Dictionaries.* Retrieved from http://www.oxforddictionaries.com/us/definition/american_english/hacktivist

Holub, R. C. (1984). *Reception theory: A critical introduction.* London: Methuen.

Jaschik, S. (2014, January 28). Snow hate. *Inside Higher Ed.* Retrieved from https://www.insidehighered.com/news/2014/01/28/u-illinois-decision-keep-classes-going-leads-racist-and-sexist-twitter-attacks

LaFrance, A. (2014, March 25). When did group pictures become 'selfies'? *The Atlantic.* Retrieved from http://www.theatlantic.com/technology/archive/2014/03/when-did-group-pictures-become-selfies/359556/

Lunsford, A. A. (2015). Writing addresses, invokes, and/or creates audiences. In L. Adler-Kassner & E. Wardle (Eds.), Naming what we know: Threshold concepts of writing studies (pp. 20-21). Boulder: Utah State University Press.

Murphy, D. (2013, November 6). Woman behind Boston marathon bombing costume blasts critics. *NY Daily News*. Retrieved from http://www.nydailynews.com/news/national/woman-behind-boston-marathon-bombing-costume-blasts-critics-article-1.1508156

Penney, J., & Dadas, C. (2014). (Re)Tweeting in the service of protest: Digital composition and circulation in the occupy Wall Street movement. *New Media & Society, 16*(1), 74–90. doi:10.1177/1461444813479593

Selfie [Def 1]. (n. d.). *Oxford Dictionaries*. Retrieved from http://www.oxforddictionaries.com/us/definition/american_english/selfie

Starnes, T. (n. d.). Facebook explains why they blocked Kirk Cameron. *Fox News*. Retrieved from http://radio.foxnews.com/toddstarnes/top-stories/facebook-explains-why-they-blocked-kirk-cameron.html

Swartz, J. (2010). MySpace, Facebook, and multimodal literacy in the writing classroom. *PraxisWiki: Kairos: A Journal of Rhetoric, Technology, and Pedagogy*. Retrieved from http://kairos.technorhetoric.net/praxis/tiki-index.php?page=Multimodal_Literacy

Taggart, D., & Pall, A. (2014). #Selfie. [Recorded by The Chainsmokers]. On The Chainsmokers [digital download]. Los Angeles: Dim Mak Records.

Vie, S. (2008). Digital divide 2.0: "Generation M" and online social networking sites in the composition classroom. *Computers and Composition, 25*(1), 9–23. doi:10.1016/j.compcom.2007.09.004

Vie, S. (2014). In defense of 'slacktivism': The Human Rights Campaign Facebook logo as digital activism. *First Monday, 19*(4-7). Retrieved from http://firstmonday.org/article/view/4961/3868

Chapter 11
The Blogging Method:
Improving Traditional Student Writing Practices

Christine Fiore
Independent Scholar, USA

ABSTRACT

Why are there more than 450 million blogs on the Internet? The answer is simple: blogging is easy, free, and fun. People have opinions they want to share with the world, and blogging is a form of social media that best allows them to do so at length. This chapter examines how blogging can be used as a way to enhance instruction on expository writing. As with any form of social media, using blogs as a teaching tool can be a daunting proposition. Therefore, this chapter provides its readers practical instruction and ideas about how to integrate blogging practices into a composition classroom. Because blogging closely mirrors traditional writing practices, this chapter invites readers to consider blogging as a 21st century model for a 20th century practice.

INTRODUCTION

Getting students to write well has been the goal of English composition classes for countless decades. Over the years, the proposed means to accomplish this goal have changed, but one thing that has been consistent is frustration with both the process and the results. A Modern Language Association report on English composition teaching published in 1910 complained that "the results of English composition teaching in almost all schools are unsatisfactory" and that too much emphasis was placed on spelling and punctuation and too little on general structure, and artistic and personal qualities (Modern Language Association, 1910, p.1).

An article published in 1943 by the Institute of General Semantics bemoaned the fact that the English teacher pays too much attention to grammar and "appears to attempt to place the emphasis upon writing, rather than writing-about-something-for-someone." According to the author, "Although one may have learned how to write with mechanical correctness, one may still have to learn how to write with significance and validity" (Johnson 1943, p. 26).

DOI: 10.4018/978-1-5225-0562-4.ch011

Ideas about teaching writing finally changed with the Process Movement of the 1960s. One of its primary tenets was that freewriting was the best way to develop writing skills. In the words of Peter Elbow, "'Trying to write well' for most people means constantly stopping, pondering, and searching for better words. If this is true of you, then stop 'trying to write well.' Otherwise you will never write well" (Elbow, 1973, p. 25).

The Process Movement took place at a time when pens and typewriters were still the main tools of writing; since then, technology has made a big impact on how we write and has the potential to impact how we teach writing. By the late 1980s and early 1990s, instructors were looking at the benefits of classroom collaboration among students, sharing or publication of student writing, and the potential of the computer as an editorial tool (Lehr, 1995). The Millennial generation (born between 1982 and 2000) came of age as computers became ubiquitous and the Internet blossomed, and thus quite easily assimilated technology (McNeill, 2011).

Technology makes writing easy. It has changed the way we relate to each other in that it has encouraged average people to write, and to write a lot. Email, smart phones, and social media quickly increased the number of students who used written communication on a regular basis. With some rapid thumb movements or the swipe of a finger, paragraphs get composed quite quickly and effortlessly. As a result, people "talk" more on their phones via text messages than actually making a phone call.

New forms of social media are constantly emerging, each one offering ample opportunities for writing. Each of these forms offers very different writing experiences and opportunities. In this chapter, I will look at how instructors can use social media, specifically blogging, to help students find their voice and become better expository writers—without the pangs often associated with classroom writing tasks.

THEORETICAL FRAMEWORK

21st Century Academic Writing

For students to achieve even a mediocre grade of C, they must meet certain standards in order to be deemed "satisfactory." The University of Maryland Freshman Writing Program and the Center for Teaching Excellence Guidelines on Grading Student Papers, for example, deems that a C paper must present "a sound central idea supported by relevant material" and that "the argument is appropriately supported with evidence, and the reasoning used in the argument is clear and makes sense" that the paper has "a discernible and logical plan" and the "entire essay is unified in support of the central idea; individual paragraphs are similarly unified in support of subordinate points" and finally notes that "the C paper is written in clear English" ("Grading Student Papers," 2002, p. 8).

Many of today's young people are poor expository writers. A 2011 United States Department of Education study of 28,100 American eighth and twelfth graders showed that only 24% of students at each of the two grade levels perform at a writing level of "Proficient" and just 3% perform at a level of "Advanced" (National Center for Educational Statistics, 2011).

According to a 2012 Pew Research Center survey of 2,067 teachers, 33% rate their students as "fair" or "poor" in effectively organizing writing assignments; 44% rate their students as "fair" or "poor" at using tone and style appropriate for their intended audience; and 49% rate their students as "fair" or "poor" in their ability to construct a strong argument (Purcell, Buchanan, & Friedrich, 2013).

With all the writing that is fostered by today's technology, it would seem at first glance that students should be more proficient at writing than ever. Why is this not the case?

Effects of Technology and Social Media on Writing

The first opportunity for increased written communication afforded by the Internet came decades ago with the advent of email. This form of communication held early promise as a teaching tool. It allows students to instantly send messages to anyone in the world, to communicate with each other and with their professors (Hassett, Spuches & Webster, 1995). Email was soon supplanted among young people by text messaging and social media as a means of communication. Between 2009 and 2010, one study showed that email usage among teens ages 12 to 17 dropped 59% (ComScore, 2011). A 2011 Pew Research Center study of teens and technology found that only 6% exchanged emails daily. A 2013 survey of smartphone users found that more than half of those ages 18-24 sent or received text messages every hour between 8 am and midnight, daily (Experian, 2013). A 2015 survey found that 91% of teens ages 13-17 use text messaging (Lenhart, 2015).

Technology is so prevalent for today's young people that it has become an integral part of their identities. 92% of teens between the ages of 13-17 go online daily, and 71% of teens use more than one social network site (Lenhart, 2015). The majority of digital communication caters toward and fosters short spans of attention and encourages brevity in writing. Between texting in constant shorthand with a complete lack of proper grammar, and tweeting while being more concerned about brevity and hashtags than content, how can anyone be expected to write at length in a proper and effective manner? Between the extremes of regulated school writing assignments and unregulated writing within the various social media outlets, many students do not get a chance to find their writing voice or hone their writing skills.

Students today find themselves between teacher-driven writing that must follow strict, rigid rules with little freedom and letting loose on social media with no rules or expectations for clear, concise writing. This back and forth can take its toll on their academic writing. Most forms of social media, while encouraging them to write all day long, do not help them find their writer's voice and become better expository writers. According to a Pew Internet and American Life Project study, 64% of teenagers admit to using informal styles from their text and social media communications in school writing (Lenhart, Arafeh, Smith, & Macgill, 2008).

Many forms of social media encourage creativity and writing, but are not helpful in promoting expository writing skills. According to the authors of *Writing, Technology and Teens* for the Pew Internet and American Life Project, "Most teenagers spend a considerable amount of their life composing texts, but they do not think that a lot of the material they create electronically is real writing." At the same time, students believe that writing well is necessary to achieve success in life (Lenhart et al, 2008, p. i).

Texting, less formal than email and geared toward quick, spontaneous communication, spawned a whole new dialect of language, replete with a wide variety of abbreviations, everything from *lol* and *brb* to *ikr* and *omg*. Twitter, with its 140-character limit, encourages clever, concise writing, but certainly does not help anyone become a better expository writer. Facebook allows users to share their thoughts and feelings with a wide variety of people, their "friends"–whether in their own "status" or as a comment on someone else's post. Facebook encourages more complete thoughts and creativity than texting, but its informal nature does not necessarily encourage intelligence or hone writing skills.

Blogs, a more public form of social interaction, are generally the most thoughtful and well composed form of social media writing, and thus have great potential as a teaching tool. Blogging can help students learn to become better researchers, write effectively, and interact with others in the process (Ferdig and Trammell, 2004). Blogging can serve as a bridge between writing students perceive as fun (social media and digital communication) and writing that they consider to be work (academic assignments). The circular nature of the blogging process mirrors the writing process that instructors seek to instill in students. This chapter will discuss how blogs can best be used to help students become better expository writers.

The Blog as Teaching Tool

Writing for school can be a tedious experience for students, especially when instructors assign essays with rigid formats that leave little room for student writers to break out and follow their own paths, forcing them to focus solely on meeting the rubric for the assignment rather than explore ways in which they can blossom as writers.

According to a University of Pittsburgh study on writing published in 2009, high on the list of what matters most to College of Arts and Sciences students is "the opportunity to write about something that matters to them" (University of Pittsburgh, 2009, p. 22). A study among professors of first year writing students at 15 different Iowa colleges and universities revealed that they place importance on student curiosity, lines of authentic inquiry (the ability to find topics and angles that interest them), and the ability to evaluate sources properly (Donham, 2014). Blogging offers a way to satisfy the needs of both students and professors.

Blogging can be an effective classroom teaching tool. Unlike other forms of social media, blogs instill a sense of authorship, and empower students and encourage them to become better critical thinkers (Oravec, 2002). While an average blog entry may only be read by a handful of people, knowing there is a potential audience of millions can be motivation to bring out the best in a writer. While much writing in a composition classroom is usually shared in some form, the potential of a larger audience can be a motivational tool to student writers.

Simply having students start and maintain an unrestricted journal-type blog throughout the duration of a semester (or contribute to a shared "classroom blog") can help them learn how to express themselves at length, and write for and interact with an audience, but in and of itself does not necessarily show them how to become more effective expository writers (Leslie and Murphy, 2008). In addition, studies show that Millennial students are more likely to respond well to assignments that are clearly defined and that allow for student choice and participation in developing assignment parameters (Wilson & Gerber, 2008).

Similarly, blogs used strictly as an easier and more interactive method for completing and sharing class assignments may not create better writers or thinkers. In a study of classroom assignment blog use by 350 college students in New Zealand, there was no consensus among them on whether their blogging helped them become better writers or increased their interest in learning (Ali & Byard, 2013).

Incorporating new technology into the twenty-first century classroom is the easy part; it is learning how to best leverage that technology in the classroom setting that is critical for student success (Lambert & Cuper, 2008).

Perhaps classroom assignment blogging is too far along the "bridge" toward the academic side. Students need to experience writing on a subject about which they are passionate. In doing so, will they veer from the typically prescribed and rigid path of rules and grammar? Blogging can be a comfortable setting in which to write, but it can also be a little bit too comfortable. As one professor notes: "While blogging may be a more comfortable format for the students—like writing in your favorite slippers at home instead of putting on your suit and going to the office—it is not always the most productive" (Haefeli, 2013, p. 47).

Blogging in an academic setting has a great many purposes and benefits, but it is not a given that professors will see improved writing skills. A table in Leslie and Murphy (2008) summarizes 41 distinct purposes of classroom blogging gathered from over 20 sources, but only a scant few pertain directly to writing, while the rest are related to communication, socialization, and collaboration. The key to using blogging as an effective tool to teach expository writing lies in the details of the content and process. Ideally, blogging should help students learn to write effectively for real life situations. Isn't that what we are preparing them for when we teach writing? We are readying them to go off into the world, with the confidence to express themselves in any situation, whether spoken or written, right?

I believe that there are two critical steps to helping young people learn how to write more effectively through blogging:

1. Reading others' posts and identifying what defines a well written blog; and
2. Utilizing the steps within the blogging process itself to foster better expository writing.

In the pages that follow, I will explore these steps from my unique blogger's perspective.

PEDAGOGICAL PRACTICES: THE BLOGGING PROCESS

Evaluating "Good" Blogs

A good fiction writer reads novels. A good actor watches others perform. A good musician listens to music. It thus makes sense that to understand the basics of good blogging and become a good blogger, one needs to seek out and peruse some of the best examples. This is by no means an easy task. The quality of blogs runs the gamut from awfully written to highly entertaining and informative. So what makes a good blog? Opinions vary, but a lesson plan on blogging on the Education World web site sums it up succinctly: "At a minimum, a blog post should have a focused topic, be informative and engaging, and include some form of backed-up opinion. Posts should be provocative, yet respectful" (Tomaszewski, 2011).

The best way for students to determine if a blog is well written is for them to hear it read out loud. This eliminates any potential for a skewed reaction based on pretty graphics or fonts and layouts. Hearing it read strips the blog to its basics.

Students should note their initial, gut reactions to what they have heard and then try to ascertain what they liked or disliked. If one reads a few different blog entries from random bloggers, a difference in the quality of writing will quickly become evident. Reading a good writer should be as interesting and rewarding as hearing a good speaker——whether a politician making an inspiring speech, or a comedian telling a funny story.

While students could accomplish this at home with a partner, it would be most useful to take this idea and apply it on a classroom-wide scale. Listed below are some examples of blog posts to explore with students.

* http://www.opinionista.us/the-importance-of-common-sense/
* http://lifeloveandhiccups.blogspot.com/
* http://www.goodgollyholly.com/2014/01/child-care-or-stay-at-home/
* http://saramcgrath.blogspot.com/2011/07/feeling-alone-repost.html
* http://chasingcinema.com/rogue-nation/#more-3485

- http://pjmedia.com/parenting/2015/09/02/nope-your-kids-school-supplies-are-not-toxic/
- http://www.negharfonooni.com/2015/08/20/bro-do-you-even-floss/
- http://www.nicoleleighshaw.com/2015/06/aint-no-awkward-like-middleschoolawkward.html

These (or other examples) should be read out loud to the entire class. Create a survey sheet for each sample blog with the title of the blog at top, and the following questions in list format (and/or additional questions as desired) to be answered on a Likert scale of 1 (strongly disagree) to 5 (strongly agree).

1. Is this blog well written?
2. Does the blog target too specific of a topic or audience for me to enjoy it?
3. Was I immediately interested and drawn in?
4. Is there a distinct beginning, middle, and end?
5. Is the viewpoint interesting?
6. Is the tone friendly and inviting?
7. Are the arguments logical?
8. Do I get a sense of who the author is and feel that I know something about them?
9. Am I following along and understanding what they are trying to convey?
10. Does the author sound intelligent?
11. Is the conclusion powerful?
12. Would I want to read more from this author?

Score the results for each blog, rank each one, and share them with the class. Trends will certainly emerge. There will be a general consensus on which blogs work, which do not, and why. Reread or call onto the smartboard the best rated and not so highly rated blog entries to the class, and discuss some of the reasons they voted the way they did, including some of the specific negatives and positives within each blog.

Following this classroom exercise, as a homework assignment, students should be encouraged to locate and print out their own examples of well written and poorly written blogs, and write a short explanation of their reasoning to hand in along with the printouts. Another option would be to have students use a yellow highlighter pen to highlight sentences or paragraphs that they really liked and felt were very well written within each blog. They could also use an orange highlighter to mark sections they really disliked and/or that were poorly written.

After the in-class and homework exercises, students should be able to better understand the difference between having a strong opinion and being able to express that opinion well. Good blogs make readers feel like they are part of an interesting conversation, even if only listening in; bad ones make them feel lectured to or spoken at, and they definitely are not a part of anything but a painful amount of verbose, grammatically incorrect chest pounding.

Freewriting: The Blogger's Authentic Voice

Blogging offers students a chance to locate the voice within and express it in a way that resonates, inspires, and may even hit a nerve. Having their own blog space gives students a place to put thoughts into words and allows them to practice their writing skills. An instructor who uses blogging in the classroom might choose to focus on the blogging experience as a way to encourage analytical thinking and public discourse, or perhaps prefer to focus solely on freewriting, using the blog as a sort of unedited, online journal. While both of these approaches are useful, as a blogger, I believe that the blogging process itself is a critical part of teaching students how to become better expository writers and should be addressed when teaching this method.

Based upon my travels through the blogosphere, I realize that there are plenty of bloggers who use their blogs simply as online journals, a variety of blogging that requires little to no planning, and no research. In fact, the very concept of the blog was born as the weblog, an electronic log of journal-like entries that are published and shared to the Internet. While freewriting may be helpful in getting students to write often and in greater quantity, following a process (and culling some exercises from the steps within the process) may be more useful in honing students' expository writing abilities and can serve as that bridge between the two types of writing, as mentioned earlier.

Notetaking: The Blogger's Notebook

A familiar axiom says, "Write what you know." Thankfully, what we know is not static. Human beings are capable of learning and experiencing new concepts our whole lives. Often, this simply means opening our minds and paying attention to details. As a teacher of young children, I observe how they tend to notice the smallest details around them, how acutely aware they are of their environment. As we grow up, we tend to turn off that attention to details, to shut them out because we are too involved in our own lives to notice anything else. Writers need to pay attention, and the best way to do so is by taking notes.

The concept of a writer's notebook is certainly not a new one. It is no coincidence that some of the most prolific writers through the ages have also been the most prolific at keeping notebooks. Ralph Waldo Emerson filled 263 notebooks with observations. Mark Twain filled nearly 50 notebooks over the course of his writing life. Leonardo da Vinci, Ernest Hemingway, Charles Darwin, Benjamin Franklin, and Isaac Newton all kept extensive notebooks, as did countless other great minds over the centuries (McKay & McKay, 2010). The use of writer's notebooks in an academic setting certainly predates the advent of the Internet, but the ideas of old can be applied to the Millennial student.

Observations are an excellent way for writers to both gather ideas and gather context and details (Oleson, 1999). Someone who blogs regularly will wind up writing a great deal over the course of a year. Three blog entries of 500 words each per week amounts to 78,000 words annually. It would thus serve student bloggers well to keep a running journal of observations and thoughts, at least a few every day—writing them in the moment. Students should carry a pocket-sized notebook with them, jotting down various observations about what they see in the world around them. It is true that with today's available technology, smart devices can be used to record notes in lieu of a paper notebook; that could be an option as well, though I personally favor a traditional paper notebook. Nevertheless, give students strict guidelines to start with, and hopefully, once they complete the assignment, they will realize the value of making notes and continue the practice even after the semester has ended. In-class exercises involving writing notebooks can include starting or ending class with five minutes of notebook freewriting time, as well as interrupting class for a quick notebook writing break (Fulwiler, 1982).

In addition to this in-class journaling time, students must be encouraged to use their notebooks out of the classroom. Instructors should have students record a minimum of five observations per day in their notebooks. Explain to them they can observe anything—animate or inanimate—so long as they really notice the details, and then write down what they see. These observations can be as barebones or as detailed as they wish, as long as each one records some detail they have seen. For example, "A black bird, perched on an oak tree branch" or "A large black bird perched at the end of an oak tree branch twenty feet above jerks its head, hearing some noise not perceptible to my human ears." Over time, students should find that they are recording more detail as they learn to pay more attention.

Make classroom time for students to share these observations. This will further encourage them to make their observations interesting. After two weeks of observations, conduct a test to show them why observing is important. By this point they should have written down 70 observations in their notebooks. Ask them, notebooks closed, to list 20 details they have journaled. Hopefully most will be able to do so. By being fully aware, by closely observing and then recording in the moment, they have left permanent impressions, and this growing database of details can be called upon in future writing. In fact, another exercise toward the end of the semester could involve having the students write a story or essay using their notebooks and incorporating at least 20 of the details they have recorded over the course of the class. In rereading their notes, they may remember the moment in great detail and be able to reconstitute it beyond the few words they jotted down. That is precisely the point of this exercise. In observing and recording they create sensory memory of a moment, and their notes are the recipe to reconstruct it.

In addition to recording details, students they should keep a running list of observations, issues, topics, ideas, gripes in their notebooks, adding to it every day, if possible. These are their "hot buttons," topics that cause them to be emotional, agitated, deeply curious—the topics that will result in passionate writing. This kind of list is indispensable to a blogger, and should include stories seen on television or read online. Students should try to make note of where they heard or read about a particularly interesting topic so they can find it again later. Students should also take note of what they find themselves talking about with friends or family. What topics do they bring up or riff on for what seems like an endless amount of time?

Understanding what issues are most important to students can help inform and hone their observation of details, too. For example, those who care about the environment might make a point to observe nature. Art majors might be interested in architectural details, and sociology or psychology majors might find themselves closely observing people.

Selecting and Researching Topics

Armed with some understanding about what makes a good blog, and strapped with a journal filled with observations and potential topics, students are ready to begin writing their own blog. I will not address the details of blog set-up here, but suffice it to say that instructors should select a platform that works best for their classroom, based on class size, their personal preferences, and the availability of institutional access to technology. Wordpress.com, blogspot.com, blogger.com, and wix.com are free blogging sites that may serve as points of departure. The first step for students when ready to write their first blog entry is for them to look over their list of topics and observations and see if any themes emerge. Are there common threads that can be combined into an overarching topic?

One way I select a topic is by scanning my notebook for a topic or issue that has been burning a hole in my head for some time. Usually, it is something that has set me off on a raging scream fest, battering the listener with my opinion and why it is the only and right one. To the average person, this may seem slightly psychotic, but to me and those close to me, it is a normal part of my writing process. If I don't feel passionate enough about an issue, I simply won't write about it. Should something not hold my interest, how can I hold the reader's interest? Students may not always have the ability to choose a topic in this fashion. That does not preclude them from feeling passionate about an assigned topic.

As I mentioned earlier, students should be encouraged to keep a running list of topics and ideas that interest them; subjects they might want to riff about or topics they have actually written about, whether in a blog or in other social media. This list can be referred to any time a new essay is assigned, as an aid to helping them look for possible angles. Many topics can be infused into an assignment to make it worthy of excitement, hence, creating a highly interesting piece to read. It is all about finding angles.

Students should remember that a good blog or essay will not just be one-sided. In the interest of being thorough (and more powerful), students should look at an issue from the other side of the fence before tackling, and demolishing, the "opposing" viewpoint. What I propose is a modified version of the Rogerian Argument. While students should discuss the key points of the opposing viewpoint, neutrality and compromise between the two views is not necessary. For example, rather than just saying – I hate crickets; they are noisy and ugly, and they get into your house, and they are hard to catch, students could say, "Cricket supporters may think they eat other bugs and are an essential part of the food chain and that their sounds are a soothing and natural part of summer…" and then insert the "but" and proceed to knock down and poke holes in cricket supporters' case.

Researching the topic to find sources that support my argument is crucial to my writing. Spouting what amounts to strictly unfounded opinions is no way to write about any topic. Not only is it important to have supportive citations, it is enjoyable to see what others are saying regarding the topic about which I am writing. Getting a feel for existing literature on a particular subject helps the blogger determine whether he or she is supporting other writers or presenting a fresh new perspective. Either way, this gets my mind prepped with a definite direction and a renewed excitement for my topic, which inspires me to write, and write well. While I am researching, I am saving sites, links, and quotes for use in my blog. This is time consuming, admittedly, but it pays off when writing the essay/blog. Sometimes, my research brings to light an idea or some piece of information I had not considered, and it gives me an entirely new perspective or just adds fuel to my fire.

Speaking with authority on any subject requires a combination of forceful, powerful writing, with facts and sources as back-up. Even the most moving and convincing political speech will ultimately be torn to shreds, if the arguments are not grounded in fact. While opinions matter, they must be supported by others, those seen to be experts or possessing convincing statistics, to make a stronger case. The beauty of the Internet is that there are always statistics to support any side of any topic.

While academic essays require sources, blogs do not. Nonetheless, it behooves bloggers to do research and find supporting arguments and background information, even if they are not providing links or naming sources. Expository writing will often, by nature, be somewhat speculative. Though a writer needs to have theories and ideas to throw out there, these must be supported by credible sources. What can happen in an essay or a blog is a lot of sheer speculation; instead of showing evidence, the writer winds up saying "perhaps" and then rambling into could have, would have, and should have scenarios. These are basically space fillers created either by someone with no sources or facts to back him up, or someone who is too lazy to bother putting in the effort to research. Clear and concise is the way to go. Each sentence should not only inform; it should lead toward an eventual conclusion.

When I research a topic, I am usually looking for a credentialed person or institution with facts that prove my point or information that I lack. Student writers should be doing this, as well. Solid, fact-based sources are the ones that shore up writing, creating a firm foundation on which to base an essay. According to Blood (2002, p. 12), the "great task of the future will not be to gain access to more information, but to develop avenues to information that genuinely enhances our understanding, and to screen out the rest." Historical societies, government websites, scientific journals, newspaper articles, and issue-specific institutions can all provide the back-up and cold, hard facts needed to defend a position. Once in a great while, I'll look for the writings of an average person (perhaps another blogger), someone who simply shares my opinion, to pad mine and make me seem timely. But nine times out of ten, I am seeking solid sources because the truth cannot be refuted the same way opinions can.

Blogging is a way for students to discover how to look for unique perspectives from which to write about topics, a skill that will also be useful in essay writing. Any essay can be enhanced by a unique and different perspective. Students can actually become excited about a supposedly uninteresting topic by looking at it from an angle that speaks to them. Someone who is fascinated with gambling and has written or read several blog posts on the topic, for example, might be assigned an essay about General Ulysses Grant's war strategies, and could look at it from the angle of his poker playing as a metaphor for his approach to warfare. The Internet makes it easy to find a multitude of angles on almost any subject, so that, like a blogger, a student can latch onto some aspect of a topic that is of personal interest to them. My notebook of potentially interesting blog topics, which contains notes about news stories and current issues I have come across in the course of my daily life (whether on the street, in a store or restaurant, or on television), or ideas that just happen to cross my mind, has become my bible, my go-to source for writing inspiration.

As a blogger, I have found that that my most popular posts are the ones that come from my own personal experiences, that have the most meaning for me, and about which I know the most (my posts about perimenopause and about the Italian-American experience). When I am closely connected to the topic about which I am writing, I can write more forcefully and powerfully, making my words resonate with the reader. My message touches a certain group of readers because they feel a bond with me.

Of course, with knowledge comes responsibility, the responsibility to support this wisdom with actual facts. Even though I am Italian, grew up in a predominantly Italian family, and am from New York, this doesn't preclude me from researching the proper spelling of Italian words and the history behind certain traditions and sayings before I start writing a post about Queens-Italian English. Anecdotes are a fantastic way to engage the reader, but supporting them with hard facts makes the writing more powerful. For instance, I am currently writing blog posts about perimenopause. While I am personally going through perimenopause, and my experience alone may appeal to other women in my situation, I must still research perimenopause using several reputable medical sites, such as *Mayo Clinic* and *WebMD*, to find supportive information that strengthens my blog post.

Outlining

Once students have settled on a topic, they should outline any subtopics that may fit into the overall theme, and more generally, outline how they will connect and organize their ideas. *What is the point of the argument they want to present?* If, for example, a student has settled on the topic of anti-vaxxers, that's fine, but what about them? Students will likely have a stance on the issues they have recorded in their notebooks, but they should still organize their thoughts before writing. A stance alone does not make a blog. *How will their argument flow? Where are they going with their topics?*

Without determining an approximate path for a blog, it may become nothing more than a rambling, hard to follow bunch of nonsense. That said, it is fine to reiterate points that have already been made, so long as other points are made in between and the blogger circles back to prove, even more strongly, why what was written earlier was relevant.

Have students draw out a blog flowchart to show some of the ideas they intend to talk about, and to reveal the rough sequence and flow of the thought progression from start to end. An example for anti-vaxxers could go something like this:

Introduction/My stance on anti-vaxxers -> Brief history of vaccination -> Emergence of anti-vaxxers -> Reasons anti-vaxxers are wrong/dangerous -> Summary/circle back to beginning and repeat stance on anti-vaxxers.

The blog outline flow chart should in effect be a circle, with the closing leading back to the opening statement of point. An issue properly argued will be like a circle, a powerful and strong closed loop.

Once I have my blog flow and have coaxed out the topic and its main subtopics, jotting down ideas that I feel are connected to each, I reread them and add little notes or words that jump into my head. This gives me more roads to follow once I actually begin writing. Students should do this with their basic outlines, adding flesh to the basic bones of the outline (Figure 1).

That said, a blog outline is not a formal, academic outline, like the ones I was taught to churn out when I was in school. The most important purpose of a blog outline is to help students ensure that they touch upon all the main concepts they want to convey to the reader. What may seem logical order in their outline may not turn out to be practical or logical once they begin writing, and this is fine. They should be encouraged to return to the outline even while in the midst of the blog post if something they write gives birth to another section for exploration, or to a new idea to discuss under one of the subtopics they will get to later—or perhaps will develop into a new, future blog post.

Ideas flow naturally and cannot be always forced into a neat little format such as the jail cell of a predetermined outline. They need to be recognized as independent of form and nurtured and addressed as they present themselves. That is not to say blog posts should have no structure or organization. Quite the opposite—the words, sentences, and paragraphs must flow. If I have achieved a logical flow, then I know my writing is well organized. I consider the blog flow outline to be the road I will take, and the details of my arguments the vehicle I use to get there.

Figure 1. Ideas notebook

Finding the Hook

With any form of expository writing, the best pieces are the ones that draw readers in. A piece can flow well, be logical, clear and concise, and still make readers yawn. A writer needs a hook, something to grab hold of readers, pull them in, and carry them through the rest of the blog. The first sentence of a blog should both set the tone and be an attention grabber. Here are a few of my first sentences from past blog entries:

- Only a fool would believe everything they read.
- You'd think at my age, I'd be able to tune out most of life's little annoyances.
- Before you tell me that I've ranted about this before, let me stop you in your tracks.
- When I was a teenager, I had an intense love affair with the phone.

Many bloggers are quite good at creating that hook early on, grabbing the reader and not letting go. An essay writer needs to create a hook as well, no matter what the topic. Whatever the blog or essay topic, an interesting fact or statement can reel in readers and keep them hooked.

In reading blogs, students should look for that hook. Is there a hook? Where does the blogger drop it? Is it the first few sentences? How does the blogger take the interest generated by the hook and carry it through the whole blog entry? How interesting are blogs with no real hook?

There are a few different types of opening hooks, and each one has the potential to both grab a reader's attention. The nature of each hook (and how much it reveals) also helps determine the flow of the writing that follows. Here are some examples of different hooks for a blog topic about the legalization of marijuana.

1. **An Interesting or Shocking Statistic:** In the United States, medical marijuana is legal in almost half the country, with 23 states having legalized it.
2. **A Blunt Statement of Position:** I fully support the legalization of medical marijuana in all 50 US states.
3. **A Statement Grabbed from the Headlines:** Lawmakers are pushing to legalize medical marijuana in Virginia, according the Richmond-Times Dispatch.
4. **A Description of a Person, Place, or Thing:** Harborside Health Center in Oakland is not only a medical marijuana dispensary, it is a haven for patients to have their bodies and souls nurtured, offering yoga classes and massage therapy.
5. **A Personal Memory that Connects with the Topic:** As a teenager, I thought marijuana/weed was for stoners and people my age who didn't care about success. As an adult, I see the benefits that medical marijuana has for older people suffering from diseases like cancer and glaucoma.
6. **A Question:** Who does legal access to medical marijuana benefit?
7. **An Enticingly Vague Statement:** Will the US unite over this patient-friendly prescription?

Sometimes the pressure of writing a good first sentence can be overwhelming. Even copious note taking and research and a mind full of ideas and opinions can leave students at a loss as to how to begin. The answer is simple: They should start writing. The Writing Center at the Georgetown University Law Center advises its students who find themselves stuck to jump right in, acknowledging "some people sit down, start with their introduction, and the paper flows sequentially from there, but these people are the exception rather than rule" (Pitts and Bennett, 2011, pp. 3-4).

Instructors should have students write 250-word blog entries on the same topic using each of these different opening hooks. Have students read each series of blogs written by their classmates and determine which one is the most interesting lead-in and holds their attention the best. Are there any trends as to which type of hook works best? It may well depend on both the topic and the blogger's viewpoint on that subject. Reading over classmates' examples will help students understand which hooks work best in which circumstances.

Multi-Tasking and the Writing Process

Many students may be all too familiar with the temptation of stopping to do something else while in the midst of writing. A recent study found that 87.5% of teenagers are moderate to high media multitaskers (Ulmer & Caulfield, 2014) and another found that 12.2% of teens have ADHD ("Summary Health Statistics for U.S. Children," 2009). Multitasking and distractions are second nature for so many of today's students. Are these breaks productive in providing further ideas and inspiration for one's actual writing, or are they counterproductive?

As explained in *Because Digital Writing Matters*: "By making a host of individual tasks easier, computers have dramatically expanded options for writers and have probably made writing, and learning to write, more complex" (National Writing Project, DeVoss, Eidman-Aadahl, & Hicks, 2010, p. 21). A study of 685 K-12 teachers found that 71% of the teachers felt use of entertainment media and social media is decreasing the attention span of young people (Rideout, 2012). Yet teachers in that study also said media use made it easier for students to find information and helped their ability to multitask. The key to getting students to become better expository writers is to harness their restless energy in a positive manner, encouraging them to explore the vast array of information that is just a click away.

The old concept of writing in a vacuum is no longer applicable, hard as we may try to shut out the world. As I am writing my blog, in addition to the research I have already done prior to beginning, I am frequently stopping to scan the Internet for something that supports what I am saying, or just for more facts and details that I feel are missing. When the words "I wonder" enter my mind, that is usually my cue to go off on an Internet research tangent, looking for more answers to satisfy my curiosity and bolster my blog entry. This happens throughout the entire writing process and doesn't stop until I am actually writing my final paragraph, closing out the blog, and dropping in my tag line.

Google is a blog writer's best friend and can become the essay writer's, too. Simply typing in a keyword that a blogger is interested in, yet does not have enough information about, can open up a world of facts, figures, images, and quotes. Keywords, questions about a topic, people associated with that topic, articles for and against the blogger's standpoint, all can be easily found using Google (and even more specifically, Google Books, Google Scholar, and Google News). Of course, if students are already familiar with certain specific sites that help them find information, such as the school library, which holds the key to an endless supply of scholarly articles, then they should jump right in and use them.

I consider what I have described above to be an iterative and continuous multitasking research process. In addition to those purposeful breaks from writing, I also take actual breaks. Even these can be useful to my process. I will often leave my blog to take a quick hop around the various social media sites, including Twitter and Instagram, as well as take a scroll through Facebook. That particular social media site is a fountain of inspiration for my personal writing. Sometimes I will find something germane to my topic and jump for joy as I turn someone's status into a note in my book for touching upon when I get back to writing (see Figure 2).

Figure 2. Author's time allocation while writing an average blog post

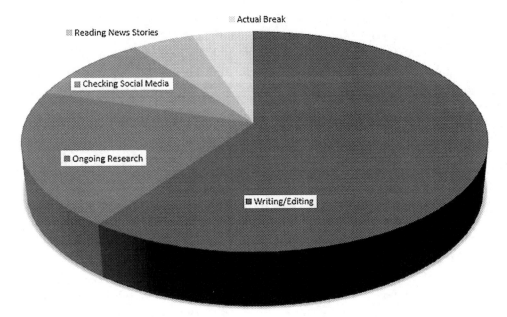

On occasion, I will walk away from my laptop and do something else for a few minutes, something completely unrelated to writing—laundry, straightening up, or cat cuddling. Then, I dive back in, ready to attack my subject with even more gusto than when I started. However, the breaks don't necessarily end there. I also take a different kind of break, an even more productive type. These stopping points are purely to read and reread what I've written every three or four paragraphs...out loud. I am my own best audience and my harshest critic, and reading aloud what I see on my screen gives me a new viewpoint from which to critique what I have been saying up to this point. Am I clear? Do I make sense? Have I gone completely off topic and onto a ridiculous tangent from which I can never return? Is this my voice I am hearing, or do I sound awkward and unpolished? Editing as I go along is just as much a part of the blog as the actual writing (see Figure 3).

Conversely, students can have a friend or classmate read their blog post aloud to them. Hearing it spoken by someone else can provide a different perspective regarding how it sounds and how it translates to others. Their inflection and intonation can allow students to hear their words in a new light and help them pick it apart further, checking for flow, clarity, and continuity. *Is the point being effectively communicated?* Readers should offer suggestions, too. *Was anything missing? What did they want to hear more about or less about?* These face to face comments are more instructive than written comments on a blog post. They also give students a launching pad for further editing. Constant tweaking, adding, and relocating sentences and paragraphs are what turn an already good essay into a fantastic piece of writing.

Writing Conclusions: Ending Well

Wrapping it up can be a challenge for many young writers, and dare I say, writers of all ages. From not being able to stop writing to being unable to find a natural ending point, the conclusion of any piece of writing can be the hardest part to conquer. The fact that a blog isn't a story, and therefore has no ending

Figure 3. Blogging process

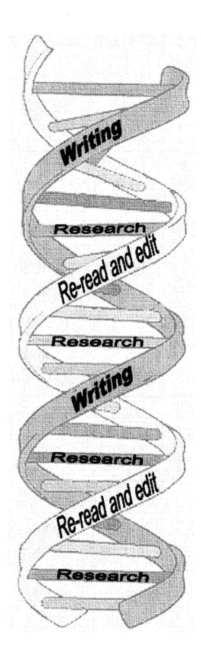

in the true sense of the word, puts the onus on the writer to close out the work. Hence, I am going to refer to the circular nature of my process, which could seem more like an elaborate swirl, since I return to each part of the blog repeatedly throughout my writing. As mentioned earlier, a basic blog outline should be circular. Coming full circle is what allows a blogger to wrap up a blog or essay by reiterating the main point and how it has been proven beyond the shadow of a doubt, citing a few reasons why.

A blog conclusion should restate the point(s) originally made in the introduction, neatly summarizing the arguments that have been presented. Students should use their closing paragraph(s) for reiterating their stance, summarizing the facts and arguments they have presented in the body of their blog. In doing so, they will be able to determine whether they actually have enough meat in their writing. If the conclusion does not sound powerful enough, that means they have not presented enough evidence or do not believe in their own argument. But if the conclusion jumps off the page, both fists in the air, the essay has done its job. The circle is closed and the key points have been hammered home, leaving the reader satisfied. A successful writing journey comes to an end.

As with opening lines, there are several ways a blogger can close. The closing lines may depend on what kind of opening was chosen. Referring back to the hook writing exercise regarding legalizing marijuana, here are some examples of ways to close a blog:

1. **Question(s) and an Answer:** Should medical marijuana be legal in all 50 states? Should local politicians come together and do something about this important issue? Absolutely.
2. **A Powerful Statement:** If medical marijuana is not legalized across the board, thousands of people will go to jail needlessly.
3. **A Call to Action:** So many people have chronic pain and the only thing which can ease it is marijuana. These are not drug addicts! They are average citizens. Parents and grandparents! Write your congress people and tell them how you feel!
4. **A Return to a Memory or Description Used in the Opening:** Looking back to my youth, I wish I knew then what I know now about marijuana. Knowledge is power, and taking the negative stigma off of marijuana is the first step in acceptance.
5. **A Statement that Recognizes and then Dismisses the Opposing Viewpoint:** Don't get me wrong. I am the first to condemn dangerous, illicit drug use. But medical marijuana is not a problem; it is a solution!

Considering Audience: Blogging as an Interactive Experience

Students are more likely to create thoughtful work if they know they are writing for an audience (Godwin-Jones, 2003). Blogging as part of an academic curriculum encourages students to engage with each other, which can result in deeper and more meaningful interaction than in strictly individual journaling (Poling, 2005).

Regardless of the setting, blogs tend to generate a lot of commentary. Structured classroom commenting is quite different from the unsolicited comments a blogger receives from strangers. Students should be encouraged to comment on each other's blogs as part of the rubric for the semester; this interaction is an essential part of the blogging experience and helps students feel connected to their peers (VanEpps, 2012). One classroom blogging experiment with 220 students over 12 weeks resulted in an average of 14 comments per blog post, with the students who commented most being the ones most likely to receive the most comments (Farmer, Yue & Brooks, 2008).

Receiving positive feedback and engaging with others is a good experience for students, but can also be deceptive, as readers are prone to hone in on and applaud a message that matches their own viewpoints, regardless of how poorly written the blog entry may be, and attack arguments that oppose their viewpoints, no matter how well written the piece.

Why are some posts more popular than others? I have asked myself this question more times than I care to admit. *Is it that I have written something more effectively and beautifully than my last post? Have I blossomed into a literary genius over time?* What makes a blog post popular likely isn't the quality of the writing. It's the topic, plain and simple (or the blogger's perspective on that topic, to be more precise). This can be incredibly misleading to a young writer.

Many blog readers love what a blog says simply because it is something about which they have strong feelings and the blog makes them feel validated. When I get positive feedback, I understand that it is usually not because I've written a literary masterpiece. Positive comments drive me forward, regardless. Readers feel validated by what I have written and I feel validated by their compliments. A post will be popular if it resonates with a particular group or demographic, if it is timely and relevant. Student bloggers can and should take pride in their most popular posts, but should continue to explore new topics and ideas in future blog posts, and should never let comments or popularity go to their head or mislead them into believing that their writing is perfect. That is one reason why blogging in a classroom setting is important—to keep students grounded and aware of the quality of their writing, not just their prowess as bloggers.

I also get plenty of negative comments! Once again, these comments are not about my writing per se, rather about my stance on a certain topic. There will always be those who don't agree with a blogger's position, even when the most carefully researched facts back it up. Why? Because anyone who looks hard enough, can back any point of view with some "expert" opinion. I've written a blog about not believing everything one reads, with supporting links about fake articles! Negative comments come from people who have read those articles, from people with very staunch viewpoints on hot button topics, or from those who see themselves in a blog post, and not in a very flattering light. This should never stop students from writing or having opinions. Using links or citing sources, or even simply keeping records of sources, can be helpful in politely answering comments that question the validity of a blog post.

CONCLUSION

Social media will continue to grow in importance and prominence, and the explosion of applications and sites that encourage writing will continue. Blogging will continue to be the best and most relatable way to teach students how to write, how to tell a story—not in 140 characters, not to "friends," and not with any other constraints or novelties that may be attached to the social media of the future. As more and more young people take up blogging, working in that format will become second nature for a growing number of eighteen-year-olds. Using writing classes to encourage good blogging methods and habits will become more and more necessary in order to ensure that blogging remains a bridge between personal writing and academic writing.

Blogging is a unique form of social media because it allows students to write at length for a potentially unlimited audience with whom they can interact. The interactive nature of blogging can encourage young people to write more. However, common classroom applications of blogging, which include: 1) freewriting, which encourages unstructured, frequent writing, and 2) using blogs as a space in which to accomplish classroom assignments, in and of themselves are not the most ideal methods for teaching expository writing.

I would like to think my blog writing has, for the most part, been consistently good. Realistically speaking, my writing has improved over time and continues to do so as I write more blog posts. I have located much more of my voice and am able to convey my messages with far more authority and confidence than I used to; students can do the same.

Using my suggested methods, blogging can serve as a true bridge between social media and academic writing. Student bloggers should be encouraged to produce well researched and carefully crafted blog posts on topics of their own choosing that utilize succinct, strongly supported arguments to back up their point of view.

Using a circular process will help student bloggers shore up each section of their writing with credible sources and editing as they go along instead of waiting until the end when it can become a daunting endeavor. This will in turn help them use words more carefully and purposely, rather than just to fill the page and satisfy a requirement. Reading their blogs out loud will help them to hear what they are saying about the topic and judge if they are heading in the right direction or have veered off course. When writing is solely about getting facts on a page, it loses the joy of conveying an interesting message to another person. When writing becomes a vehicle to carry thoughts and opinions, grounded in hard facts, to an audience...even an audience of one, it blossoms into a journey of connection, connecting to another human being by sharing information. Isn't that the purpose of social media?

The blogging process, as I see it, should not be a linear progression from one step to another, but a series of loops that involve continual self-editing, ongoing research, and crafting hooks that capture and carry the reader's attention. The writing loops back one final time and closes at the end of the blog post, with a conclusion that revisits the introduction and draws everything that came between, together into a neat and rousing package. As mentioned earlier, this non-linear process can be quite useful since it is exactly what many instructors want their students to engage when writing essays.

With an open mind, attention to detail, and good researching skills, students can easily apply the principles of the blogging method to writing academic essays. Instead of a stiff, boring repository of facts (on one end of the spectrum), or an unsupported and disorganized rant (on the other end), expository writing that is based on a solid blogging method, becomes a vehicle to express thoughts and opinions that are based on and supported by facts.

REFERENCES

Ali, I., & Byard, K. (2013). Student perceptions on using blogs for reflective learning in higher educational contexts. *AUT University Department of Economics Working Paper Series*, 2013(6).

Blood, R. (2002). *The weblog handbook: Practical advice on creating and maintaining your blog.* Cambridge, Massachusetts: Perseus Books.

Caulfield, S., & Ulmer, A. (2014). Capacity limits of working memory: The impact of media multitasking on cognitive control in the adolescent mind. *American Academy of Pediatrics National Conference & Exhibition.*

Donham, J. (2014). College ready–What can we learn from first-year college assignments? An examination of assignments in Iowa colleges and universities. *School Library Research*, *17*, 1–22.

Elbow, P. (1973). *Writing without teachers.* New York: Oxford University Press.

Farmer, B., Yue, A., & Brooks, C. (2008). Using blogging for higher order learning in large cohort university teaching: A case study. *Australasian Journal of Educational Technology*, *24*(2), 123–136. doi:10.14742/ajet.1215

Ferdig, R., & Trammell, K. (2004). Content delivery in the 'blogosphere.'[Technological Horizons in Education]. *T.H.E. Journal*, *31*(7).

Fulwiler, T. (1982). The personal connection: Journal writing across the curriculum. In T. Fulwiler & A. Young (Eds.), *Writing and reading across the curriculum*. Urbana, Illinois: National Council of Teachers of English.

Godwin-Jones, R. (2003). Emerging technologies: Blog and wikis: Environments for on-line collaboration. *Virginia Commonwealth University. Grading Student Papers: Some guidelines for commenting on and grading students' written work in any discipline*. Retrieved from https://www.cte.umd.edu/teaching/resources/GradingHandbook.pdf

Haefeli, S. (2013). Using blogs for better student writing outcomes. *Journal of Music History Pedagogy*, *4*(1), 39–70.

Hassett, J., Spuches, C., & Webster, S. (1995). Using electronic mail for teaching and learning. *To Improve the Academy*.

Johnson, W. (1943). You can't write writing. *Etc.; a Review of General Semantics*, *1*(1), 25–32.

Lambert, J., & Cuper, P. (2008). Multimedia technologies and familiar spaces: 21st-century teaching for 21st-century learners. *Contemporary Issues in Technology & Teacher Education*, *8*(3), 264–276.

Lehr, F. (1995). Revision in the writing process. *ERIC Digest, ED379664*(1995-00-00). Retrieved from eric.ed.gov

Lenhart, A. (2015). *Teens, social media & technology overview 2015*. Retrieved from http://www.pewinternet.org/2015/04/09/teens-social-media-technology-2015/

Lenhart, A., Arafeh, S., Smith, A., & Macgill, A. (2008). *Writing, Technology and Teens*. Retrieved from http://www.pewinternet.org/2008/04/24/writing-technology-and-teens/

Leslie, P., & Farmer, E. (2008). Post-secondary students' purposes for blogging. *International Review of Research in Open and Distance Learning*, *9*(3).

McKay, B., & McKay, K. (2010). *The pocket notebooks of 20 famous men*. Retrieved from http://www.artofmanliness.com/

McNeill, R., Jr. (2011). Adapting teaching to the millennial generation: A case study of a blended/hybrid course. *International CHRIE Conference-Refereed Track. Paper 3*.

National Writing Project. DeVoss, D., Eidman-Aadahl, E., & Hicks, T. (2010). Because digital writing matters: Improving student writing in online and multimedia environments. San Francisco, California: Jossey-Bass.

Oleson, Frances B. (1999). Is it a diary? A journal? - No, it's a writer's notebook. *Language Arts Journal of Michigan*, *15*(2), 17-22.

Oravec, J. A. (2002). Bookmarking the world: Weblog applications in education. *Journal of Adolescent & Adult Literacy*, *45*(7), 616–621.

Pitts, M., & Bennett, J. (2011). *Just do it: Tips for avoiding procrastination*. Retrieved from http://www.law.georgetown.edu/academics/academic-programs/legal-writing-scholarship/writing-center/usefuldocuments.cfm

Poling, C. (2005). Blog on: Building communication and collaboration among staff and students. *Learning and Leading with Technology*, *32*(6), 12–15.

Preliminary report on English composition teaching by a committee of the English Section of the Central Division of the Modern Language Association. (1910). Bulletin Iowa State College of Agriculture and Mechanic Arts, IX(3).

Purcell, K., Buchanan, J., & Friedrich, L. (2013). *The impact of digital tools on student writing and how writing is taught in schools.* Retrieved from http://www.pewinternet.org/2013/07/16/the-impact-of-digital-tools-on-student-writing-and-how-writing-is-taught-in-schools/

Rideout, V. (2012). *Children, teens, and entertainment media: The view from the classroom a national survey of teachers about the role of entertainment media in students' academic and social development, a Common Sense Media research study.* Retrieved from https://www.commonsensemedia.org/research/

Summary health statistics for U.S. children: National health interview survey, 2007. (2009). *CDC Vital and Health Statistics*, 10(239).

The University of Pittsburgh Study of Writing: A Report on Writing in the School of Arts and Sciences Undergraduate Curriculum (2009). Retrieved from http://www.academic.pitt.edu/assessment/resources.html

Tomaszewski, J. (2011). Writing lesson: Better blogs. *Education World*. Retrieved from http://www.educationworld.com/a_lesson/better-blog-writing.shtml

VanEpps, C. (2012). Blogging as a strategy to support reading comprehension skills. *Education Masters*.

Wilson, M., & Gerber, L. (2008). How generational theory can improve teaching: Strategies for working with the "Millennials." *Currents in Teaching and Learning*, *1*(1), 29–44.

Writing 2011: National assessment of educational progress at grades 8 and 12. (2011). *National Center for Education Statistics*. Retrieved from http://www.nationsreportcard.gov/

KEY TERMS AND DEFINITIONS

Digital Communication: Any of a number of online methods for connecting and conversing with others, including social media.

Expository: A piece of writing that is intended to explain or describe.

Freewriting: Unedited writing that is akin to stream of consciousness.

Hook: An interesting fact or turn of phrase that is intended to grab the reader's attention and interest so that they want to continue reading.

Journaling: Keeping a personal record of occurrences and experiences, on an almost daily basis.

Multitasking: Working on and accomplishing several different tasks at the same time.

Rubric: A guide listing specific criteria for grading or scoring academic papers.

Writer's Voice: An author's unique style of expression and syntax.

Section 4
Integrating Social Media as Professional Development in the Writing Classroom

In this section, chapters explore WordPress, LinkedIn, and Twitter as vehicles for helping writing students compose themselves professionally. In this section, audience is carefully discussed as authors suggest students be aware of their professional audience so that they can write more strategically, and therefore, "curate" a professional online identity that makes them more marketable. This section also includes a chapter Q&A between teacher and students regarding students' responses to using social media in their Technical Writing course.

Chapter 12
Teaching Casual Writing for Professional Success with Twitter:
Digital Small Talk and the New Textese

Amy Rubens
Radford University, USA

ABSTRACT

Using social media to construct a digital, professional presence for the job search is a necessity in today's labor market. Millennials are skilled in using social media for personal purposes but cannot immediately intuit how to use familiar social media outlets in professional contexts. Writing instructors can guide students in enacting an online, professional presence through digitally mediated communication practices that increasingly are seen as valuable in the workplace. Instead of training students away from using "textese," instructors should help students develop an abbreviated writing style that is strategic, consistent, and responsive to the needs of their audience. Twitter is the best social media platform in which to help students achieve these learning goals. This chapter provides readers with a description of a capstone, problem-based learning assignment in which students use Twitter to market their professional selves, network, and improve their digital workplace writing skills.

INTRODUCTION

Ten years ago, when MySpace reigned supreme and Facebook was in its infancy, universities and colleges began advising students to censor their digital selves in order to achieve greater career success after graduation (Bombardieri, 2006; Cummins, 2006; Maitre, 2006; Pope, 2006). Today, students of all ages still are being warned to use social media judiciously (S. Buck, 2012; Donnelly, 2013; Stauts, 2015). At the same time they are being urged to censor their social media footprint, however, they also are hearing something new: that they should have a separate "professional" web presence that would be attractive to employers. Despite millennials' skillful, frequent use (E. Buck, 2015; Grabill et al., 2010) of social media to sustain interpersonal relationships, they cannot immediately intuit how to use social media for professional purposes, like augmenting a job search (Pegrum, 2011).

DOI: 10.4018/978-1-5225-0562-4.ch012

This learning curve first emerges when millennials are tasked with building a professional presence through "digital small talk," or the polite, *online* exchange of career aspirations, observations of the world, and appropriate information about their lives outside of work. "Casual" or "everyday" writing genres overlap with digital small talk. Like digital small talk, digital- or computer-mediated (DCM) casual writing has an important place in and adjacent to workplace communication.[1] In a professional context, casual writing is produced quickly and under pressure. Casual writing genres can encompass email, instant messaging, and mobile phone text messaging. Grabill et al., (2010) has shown that millennials are prolific casual writers who see this material as valuable. However, despite the frequency with which they produce casual writing, and despite the value to which they ascribe it, millennials have difficulty enacting such genres in professional (i.e., non-personal) contexts.

Millennials especially struggle with digital and casual writing at the level *language*. They tend to use "textese," an abbreviated, orthographically and grammatically innovative writing form (Crystal, 2008). On the surface, textese appears to expose a poor grasp of Standard Written English (SWE). Empirical studies demonstrate, though, that textese does not necessarily reflect poor grammatical knowledge or the degradation of a once-adequate understanding of SWE (Crystal, 2008; DeJonge & Kemp, 2012; Kemp, Wood, & Waldron, 2014). Rather, textese partially stems from an inability to "code switch," or recognize that "language varies by context, and…what is appropriate in one setting may not be appropriate in another" (K. Turner, 2009, pp. 61-62). In addition, as Tannen (2013) has shown, textese's repetitions, misspellings, and abbreviations often are not mistakes but rather deliberate attempts to convey "metamessages" or markers of emotional intent.

This essay addresses how instructors, especially those who teach workplace writing, can guide students in constructing an online, professional presence that is expressed through digital small talk, casual writing, and (surprisingly) textese. To help students create a professional persona that anchors their online presence, instructors should capitalize on millennials' existing social media skillset and rhetorical sensibilities. To improve students' online writing skills—that is, the language they use to enact their professional persona—instructors should guide students in code switching, or more mindfully using SWE. Just as importantly, instructors *also* should aid students in what I call "code sliding." Whereas code switching encompasses abandoning textese in favor of SWE, code sliding involves mediating between the conventions of SWE and the inventive, supposedly "deviant" forms of online communication that many millennials already use. Code sliding or intermittently relying on textese is a necessary skill. Many forms of workplace communication require the ability to write quickly. Furthermore, the constraints or "affordances" of electrical or digital technologies sometimes make using textese unavoidable. Thus, rather than train students away from using textese, instructors should teach students how to break the rules of SWE in ways that respect their workplace audiences' needs and expectations.

The social media site Twitter is the best platform on which millennials can (1) establish an online presence as early- or pre-career professionals, (2) engage in digital small talk, and (3) hone their casual writing skills, including their ability to code switch (abandon textese) and code slide (strategically use textese) in a professional context. Twitter facilitates this learning better than other social media sites for several reasons, and one of the most consequential involves its affordances: Because tweets can be no more than 140 characters, some necessarily include textese. Twitter, of course, has long been used in college classrooms, yet most critical analyses do not address using it to help students *write* for workplace audiences; instead, much of the existing scholarship describes how Twitter promotes subject-specific discussion within the classroom and exclusively among students and teachers (Kuznekoff, Munz, & Titsworth, 2015; Marshall, 2015). In this essay, I provide a blueprint for helping students use Twitter to develop a digital presence and interact with a public audience. Specifically, I discuss an assignment in which students create a professional persona for the job search that demonstrates their passion and "fit" within an organization or field; the assignment also encourages students to focus on language use so they can illustrate their workplace digital and casual writing skills.

THEORETICAL FRAMEWORK

Cybervetting and What It Reveals about Potential Employees

A professional, online presence benefits most people in the workforce, and today's college students often may hear this advice from their campus career center (Career Planning, n.d.). Outside of academia, career coaches, recruiting services, and employment websites all tout the need for a digital presence. Consider that a search of the terms "social media" in the "Career Advice" section of Monster.com returns hundreds of articles with titles like: "The Science of [Your] Google Web Presence" and "Revamp Your Online Image" (Search results, n.d.). Surveys of employers and recruiters further legitimize the advice given to job seekers about personal branding on the web (CareerBuilder Survey, 2015; Jobvite Survey, 2014). One survey conducted by CareerBuilder.com, for instance, revealed that 52% of employers and 51% percent of hiring managers investigate job candidates by looking at their social media activities (CareerBuilder Survey, 2015).

A qualitative study by Berkelaar & Buzzanell (2015) produced similar findings regarding "cybervetting," or the assessment of applicants' digital footprints (or lack thereof) during the hiring process. They found that most employers cybervet at all hiring levels despite "ongoing ethical debates and unclear legal precedent regarding online information use for personnel selection" (Berkelaar & Buzzanell, 2015, pp. 85, 96; Brown and Vaughn, 2011). They also noted that most employers "did not exclusively focus on salacious vices or illegal behavior" (Berkelaar & Buzzanell, 2015, p. 97). Rather, employers also used candidates' digital footprints to assess their commitment to the field and profession-specific skills, such as networking prowess (Berkelaar & Buzzannell, 2015). In addition, Berkelaar & Buzzannell (2015) found that social media networks help employers "assess the trustworthiness of applicants' character or reputation" (p. 100). In this way, social media profiles complement traditional methods of checking references.

Most significantly, Berkelaar & Buzzanell (2015) discovered that employers examined "online textual information" about but also *by* prospective employees (p. 97). What job seekers write about online is believed to reflect not only their "passions or drive," but also the degree to which this material complements their stated career goals (Berkelaar & Buzzanell, 2015, p. 99). Cybervetting candidates' online writing also allows employers to evaluate the much more nebulous concept of cultural fit. Cultural fit "is the likelihood that [a potential hire] will reflect and/or be able to adapt to the core beliefs, attitudes, and behaviors" that define an organization or a role within it (Bouton, 2015; Kristof-Brown, 2000). Determining the qualities that define an organization's culture and the extent to which a prospective employee embodies those traits is highly subjective, to be sure (Kristof-Brown, 2000). Despite the fraught nature of assessing fit, it is a ubiquitous part of the hiring process because it is linked to employee retention (Bouton, 2015; Rivera, 2015). For this reason, fit assessment occurs at all stages of employment screening (Berkelaar & Buzzanell, 2015; Kristof-Brown, 2000; Rivera, 2015).

Finally, job candidates' online writing reveals much to employers about writing ability, particularly in terms of "everyday" or "casual" writing skills. These genres encompass short but important forms of correspondence, such as email and SMS text messages, that "dominate many employees' work" (Berkelaar & Buzzanell, 2015, p. 98). Employers *do* use cover letters and resumes to evaluate writing skills, but these documents are "heavily edited" and "subject to extreme impression management" (Berkelaar & Buzzanell, 2015, p. 98). In contrast to resumes and cover letters, sustained attention cannot always be afforded to everyday writing genres. Resumes and cover letters thus present an incomplete portrait of candidates' abilities to write quickly and under pressure (Berkelaar & Buzzanell, 2015, p. 100). Online and social media-based writing fill in this picture.

Digital Small Talk as a Performance and Tool for Job Seekers

College students are aware that their digital footprint is subject to review by employers, and many believe that individuals involved in the hiring process have the right to check [applicants'] social networking profile[s] when evaluating whether or not to hire them" (Vicknair, Elkersh, Yancey, & Budden, 2010, p. 9). Despite these assumptions, college students struggle with constructing a digital presence for the purview of potential employers. One undertaking that proves challenging is enacting a "professional persona" through digital small talk. More than banter, digital small talk is a *performance* of one's passion for and fit within a particular field and a *tool* for building an online network that could have offline value. Importantly, digital small talk can consist of back-and-forth dialogue between a job seeker and other people, but it also can be directed to an imagined audience. Social media marketing texts are helpful in illuminating the types of online utterances that fall under this definition of digital small talk, especially in the context of Twitter. According to Schaefer (2014), sharing relevant, interesting, amusing, and valuable content attracts followers and sparks conversation. To produce such content, one could generate tweets as well as share others' tweets (i.e., "retweet"). Tweeted and retweeted content can include text, images, video, hyperlinks, or combinations thereof. Job seekers thus could demonstrate their passion for and fit within their field by tweeting a link to a blog post or news story about their "business, market, or industry" (Schaefer, 2014, pp. 60-61).

Significantly, Schaefer (2014) argues that Twitter-based digital small talk also should be about "something other than business"; ideally, it should show one's personality (p. 20). Such content could include tweets about community-based events; current events *unrelated* to one's profession (e.g., a sports event on television); something funny; or merely something "human," such as news that one's infant daughter took her first steps (Schaefer, 2014). In defining digital small talk on Twitter, Schaefer also advocates a "mindset of helpfulness" (2014, p. 77). Within Twitter, such helpfulness might include answering questions, signal-boosting (i.e., forwarding or publicizing) others' requests for help, or offering thanks for the assistance one has received (Schafer, 2014).

Taken together, the Twitter strategies that Schaefer (2014) endorses help job seekers craft a productive, digital presence in a several ways. Discussing and sharing industry-specific information could make job seekers seem knowledgeable and excited about their field. Rationally discussing controversial issues within one's field also could underscore applicants' ability to engage in civil debate. By being what Schaefer (2014) calls authentically helpful on Twitter (e.g., signal boosting others' tweets), job applicants can show they are sincere and charitable. To add to this, discussing topics unrelated to one's career allows job candidates to demonstrate that they can be personable yet professional in the workplace.

Importantly, digital small talk on Twitter not only allows job candidates to impress employers; it also assists them in building a professional network. By forging online relationships of sufficient number and quality, especially on social media sites like Twitter, job seekers will be more likely to convert online contacts to strong, offline relationships that "move people to take a concrete action" (Schaefer, 2014, p. 190). For millennials poised to enter the full-time workforce, online networks, including those afforded by Twitter, could produce job leads, referrals, mentorships, and professional development opportunities.

Casual Writing and the New Textese as Vital Skills for Today's Professionals

If employers cybervet job candidates' online writing, then it is conceivable they could look to Twitter to judge fit, passion, and professionalism as well as proficiency in casual writing genres. Indeed, as Sacks & Graves (2012) note, "students who can communicate via informal and formal communication channels are becoming increasingly valuable in organizations" (p. 81). Millennials' online writing, though, may detract from their perceived employability, as it tends to exhibit "a highly distinctive graphic style" whose abbreviations flout conventional uses of "morphology…, syntax, … capitalization, and punctuation" (Wood, Kemp, & Waldron, 2014b, p. 282; Kemp, Wood, & Waldron, 2014, p. 1586). Popular media often portrays these interventions as a "deviant use of language used by a young generation that doesn't care [or know] about standards" of spelling, grammar, and mechanics (Crystal, 2008).[2] Textese is not inherently bad, however. In fact, it has an important, sometimes unavoidable role in workplace communication. Accordingly, just as millennials need guidance in knowing *what* to say online to establish a professional, digital presence, they also need assistance in figuring out *how* to graphically represent it—that is, how to *say* it.

Essentially, millennials who are building an online presence through digital small talk should be more mindful of code switching (K. Turner, 2009), or recognizing the situations in which one should abandon textese in favor of Standard Written English (SWE). On the other hand, millennials also must become proficient in "code sliding," or combining SWE and textese in their online/digital writing. Knowing how to code switch (make a contextually appropriate choice between either textese or SWE) and code slide (combine SWE and textese in consistent, visually appropriate ways) should greatly improve millennials' ability to write online for workplace audiences. As I will show later in this chapter, the social media site Twitter represents an excellent space in which to guide millennials in developing a professional style of textese.

Code switching and sliding are indispensable in creating a digital presence, making digital small talk, and producing casual writing genres. In terms of the former, millennials need training in using SWE more mindfully, especially when building their digital presence with familiar social media sites. After all, textese is laden with assumptions about literacy and education level. Older generations, for instance, are more likely to link textese to the decline of literacy and the degradation of language (Berkelaar & Buzzanell, 2014; Crystal, 2008; Wood, Kemp, & Waldron, 2014b). While this belief has moral undertones (Crystal, 2008; Tannen, 2013), it also stems from the more pragmatic concern that textese *reduces*, as opposed to reflects, one's command of SWE (Lenhart, Arafeh, Smith, & Macgill, 2008). Recent scholarship does not bear out these concerns. For instance, studies measuring "the extent to which the violation of grammatical conventions in text messaging is associated with more conventional grammatical ability" found no correlation between the two among adult populations, even over time (Kemp et al., 2014, pp. 1588, 1600; Wood, Kemp, & Waldron, 2014a, p. 427).[3]

To help millennials build an online presence with Twitter, it is helpful to know why people use textese. Research points to both incidental and intentional motivations for using textese. Time constraints, technological affordances, and lack of concern generally with SWE (which does not necessarily correlate with *knowledge* of SWE) all are associated with use of textese (DeJonge & Kemp, 2012; Wood, Kemp, & Waldron, 2014a). In contrast, Crystal (2008) suggests textese reflects a playful, creative approach to language. Tannen (2013) and Gunraj, et al. (2016) likewise view many of the spelling, grammar, and other typographical errors in textese as calculated devices that convey emotional intent as well as "social information normally communicated through prosody, pauses, gestures, filler words, and eye gaze" (p. 1069). Specifically, in studying the digital and casual writing of millennials, Tannen (2013) found that capitalization and repetition of punctuation marks signified intensity whereas the "reduplication of the word-final letter" (e.g., youuuuuu) indicated sincerity and depth of emotion (p. 107). Digital- and computer-mediated (DMC) writing that lacked these metamessages or markers of intent sometimes were misunderstood by the recipient. As a result, Tannen (2013) concluded that textese is "not…fundamentally different from what has always been done with language in social [face-to-face] interaction" (p. 99).

Instructors can help students minimize the incidental causes of textese and maximize its intentional possibilities by guiding them in formulating their own professional style of textese. This "new" textese would be more legible and visually appealing, as it would reflect *logical* and *consistent* deviations from SWE. In studying the texting habits of high school and college students, De Jonge & Kemp (2012) discovered that within individuals, textese varies widely and even when the "predicative texting" option was enabled on mobile devices and tablets (p. 63). Consistency, they argue, "depends partly on the ability (or decision) to learn and remember one's own previous" inventions (De Jonge & Kemp, 2012, p. 63). It is entirely possible for high school and college students to "reflect on their own texting habits" because they can "reproduce textisms on paper" and in the absence of technology (De Jonge & Kemp, 2012, p. 63). Following De Jonge & Kemp's (2012) findings, writing instructors could encourage students to develop and implement their own textese style guide that addresses non-standard spelling and punctuation; abbreviations; and the deployment of metamessages or graphical markers of emotional intent.

Wheeler's (2008) work on teaching African American K-12 students to code switch from informal ("home") English to formal English in their school-based writing counter-intuitively offers an important framework for "new" textese style guides. In teaching speakers of African American Vernacular (AAV) to write in SWE, Wheeler (2008) advocates against only correcting usage mistakes. Instead, she argues for "build[ing] an explicit, conscious understanding of the differences between" AAV and SWE (Wheeler, 2008, p. 56). The teacher is central in this process: he or she guides students in a "contrastive analysis" where they identify grammar rules in AAV, find similar patterns in SWE, and apply those patterns in their school writing (Wheeler, 2008, p. 56). Textese style guides thus could help students identify various linguistic patterns in their own textese and then logically and consistently employ an equivalent pattern in the "new," workplace-friendly textese.

METHODOLOGY AND PEDAGOGY

Purpose

To help my business and professional writing students build an online presence and develop their digital communication skills, including a "new" textese, I created a capstone, problem-based learning assignment organized around Twitter. In problem-based learning (PBL), students are confronted with a realistic issue that they must resolve by synthesizing prior learning and applying it to a new context; Margetson (1991) calls this an "integration...of knowing *that* with knowing *how*" (p. 38). During this process, students ideally are the agents of their own knowledge acquisition, and the teacher facilitates this process (Savin-Baden & Major, 2004). As a PBL assignment, the Twitter project helped students more independently synthesize and apply their knowledge of business and professional writing skills to digital spaces. In addition, the PBL features of the project encouraged transfer of learning related to the hiring process and the role various writing genres play in it: Immediately before completing the Twitter project, students wrote a resume and cover letter in response to a job advertisement of their choosing.

Sometimes referred to as a "microblogging" site, Twitter's platform allows users to exchange brief "tweets" with one another that are "available for viewing and reply long after they were originally produced" (Zappavigna, 2012, p. 32). Tweets are visible to one's "followers" on the site, but users also can choose to make them publicly visible to anyone on the web. Each tweet can be no more than 140 characters and "can contain text, photos, and videos" as well as hyperlinks, other tweets ("retweets"), or hashtags (Twitter, n.d.a). Hashtags are words or phrases preceded by a pound or hash sign (#). These days, hashtags are used widely across social media, but they were pioneered by Twitter (J. Turner, 2012). In their original and most basic purpose, Twitter hashtags work as an electronic filing system: "clicking on a hashtagged word in any message shows...all other Tweets marked with that keyword" (Twitter, n. d.a).

In comparison to Twitter, LinkedIn may seem like a better social media site for building a professional digital presence: As reportedly the "world's largest professional network," LinkedIn "connect[s] the world's professionals" and provides them "access to people, jobs, news, updates, and insights" (LinkedIn, n.d.). To be sure, LinkedIn is a valuable resource for job seekers. Twitter, though, can augment the job search in ways that other platforms, like LinkedIn or Facebook, cannot. First, consider that Twitter's features and affordances allow tweets to be exchanged more expediently (Sacks & Graves, 2012). Faster digital small talk could foster stronger online relationships—that is, those that may lead to offline opportunities, such as referrals or job leads. Second, along with encouraging rapid dialogue, Twitter permits "asymmetrical relationships, where reciprocation of a follower is not obligatory, nor is non-reciprocation interpreted as a rejection" (Zappavigna, 2012, p. 31). A Twitter user thus chooses the timing and duration of her participation, and these decisions would not necessarily diminish the size and strength of her network. Moreover, as I claimed earlier, even asymmetrical digital small talk with an imagined audience can help one maintain an online presence. Third, Twitter is optimally positioned to help job seekers because it encourages richer digital small talk. Indeed, tweeting can be a multimodal act of composition, and tweets that combine text with images, links, and hashtags can help job seekers demonstrate fit more vibrantly.

Ultimately, Twitter helps millennial job seekers because it can improve their digital writing skills at the level of language. Each tweet's 140-character limit forces students to write concisely while following the rules of Standard Written English. At the same time, the 140-character limit for individual tweets makes breaking the rules of SWE and using textese occasionally unavoidable. Thus, while other social media sites like Facebook allow students to network and write multimodally in a professional context (Decarie, 2010), they cannot facilitate code switching (using SWE) and code sliding (using a professional textese) to the same extent as Twitter. Twitter's unique ability to help students simultaneously code switch and slide further is underscored by the fact that Twitter has its own lexicon (Zappavigna, 2014). In deciding to use this site-specific textese, students gain additional opportunities to code switch and slide in a professional context.[4] Twitter's affordances also groom students to write quickly and carefully before hitting "send." Indeed, tweets cannot be edited (only deleted and, if desired, rewritten), and as of February 2016, tweets appear in news feeds instantly, but not always chronologically (Twitter, n. d.b).

Participants, Setting, and Required Resources

I taught a Twitter-based digital presence project for four semesters at two demographically distinct institutions, and the narrative that follows synthesizes those experiences. I first conceived of the assignment as the capstone for a 300-level Business Writing course at Francis Marion University (FMU), a small, state-sponsored school in South Carolina.[5] The course primarily enrolled students from majors outside of the English Department and was held in a lab where students could sit at computers or tables in small groups. When I transitioned to Radford University (RU), a medium-sized, state institution in Virginia, I also used the Twitter assignment as a capstone for my 300-level Business Writing course. The RU Business Writing course mainly enrolled non-majors, but it met in a traditional classroom. Through my experiences at FMU, I learned that student access to a computer (as opposed to a mobile device) during instruction time was indispensible, so I arranged for my RU Business Writing courses to meet in a computer lab during the Twitter project. In addition to having computer access during class, students used Schaefer's *The Tao of Twitter* (2014) along with the textbook I adopted for the course, Locker and Kienzler's *Business and Administrative Communication* (2015). Shorter readings about hashtags, privacy concerns, and search engine optimization also were assigned.

Before beginning the assignment, I asked students to complete three tasks: Set up a *new* Twitter account; choose between "public" or "private" settings for the new account; and "follow" my classroom account on Twitter, which I set up exclusively for managing the assignment. In the past, I used my own "professional" Twitter account because I felt as if it illustrated the behaviors I wanted students to emulate during the project. However, I discovered that using a dedicated classroom account, as endorsed by Cordell (2012)Jones (2010), makes everyone feel more comfortable. Indeed, as Jones notes, when the instructor uses a dedicated classroom Twitter account, there is "never a sense that [he or she is] trying to elicit information about [students'] lives" (2010). Using my classroom account, I followed students who followed me, and I also placed them on a Twitter "list" to facilitate networking across course sections. The requirement that students set up a new, preferably public Twitter account for the assignment derives from the notion that one should censor *and* cultivate an online presence. Ideally, then, students with existing "personal" Twitter accounts should "protect" or hide them from non-followers. Conversely, students' "professional" Twitter accounts should be visible to anyone on the web.[6] Relatedly, profile and user names associated with students' professional Twitter accounts also should include their full, legal names. Otherwise, when employers use search engines to cybervet applicants, they might not be able to find candidates' professional Twitter accounts, thus rendering their work on the site moot.[7]

Getting Started: Crafting a Persona and Gathering Content

I scaffolded the Twitter project across two weeks: The initial stage of the scaffolding prepared students to tweet while the latter helped them assess their tweets in terms of content and writing. In other words, students did not begin the project by tweeting; instead, they strategized and built a foundation for their Twitter work. To that end, students first crafted a Twitter identity or professional "persona" around their educational and career goals, which were brought into focus by the preceding resume and cover letter assignment. Educational and career goals should comprise only one part of the professional Twitter persona, however. Recall that in *The Tao of Twitter*, Schaefer (2014) suggests sometimes tweeting about topics unrelated to work or business; this advice applies to social media marketers, but also to people marketing themselves for employment. I thus required students' Twitter personas to encompass one or two hobbies or personal interests that they could comfortably share with potential employers. To envision this kind of Twitter persona, students completed an informal writing activity, as seen in Figure 1.

After settling on a professional-yet-personable Twitter persona, students completed their accounts by writing a biography ("bio"), choosing profile and header images, and selecting a color scheme. These elements are the discursive and visual representations of their Twitter persona. In terms of their bios, students wrote with two audiences in mind: (1) potential employers who may use the bio to assess fit, passion, professionalism, and writing ability, and (2) potential followers with whom one could network and engage in digital small talk. Therefore, in their bios, I instructed them to highlight their Twitter persona's primary features by describing their educational achievements, career goals, and personal hobbies/interests in a "70/30" split. As illustrated by Figure 2, this means that 70% of the bio should focus on professional goals and educational accomplishments while 30% of the bio should highlight personal hobbies and interests. Importantly, Twitter only allows for bios of 160 characters or less. This constraint

Figure 1. In an informal writing activity, a student outlines the professional, educational, and personal elements of his Twitter persona and also lists "evergreen" sources of digital content

A. Share relevant "professional" content. Demonstrate with your tweets that you have a passion for and desire to learn about your industry.

List at least three professional and/or school-related interests that you'll tweet about. Then, list reputable websites, news organizations, and blogs that you could mine for content in these areas to share with your followers. (By reputable, I mean materials on the web that are well-written, associated with a reputable organization, published by an expert, and timely.) If these organizations have a Twitter feed, you might want to follow them as well.

Professional Interests	Sites to Mine for Content
Sports Contracts	ESPN
Trades	NBA
Free Agency	Washington Post Sport Section

B. Share relevant "personal" content. Be personable by occasionally tweeting about your personal interests, hobbies, or accomplishments.

List two personal interests that you'll tweet about that an employer would view favorably:

1. **Philadelphia Sports Teams**
2. **School**

afforded students with their first opportunity to develop a professional textese by breaking from both SWE and the textese they would use when writing to friends and family.

Students were supported in their first "code sliding" endeavor. In an in-class activity, I asked them to analyze the Twitter bios of other professionals in their field, paying special attention to how and when incomplete sentences were used. We then discussed their findings as a group. During this conversation, we also revisited the profile and header images students encountered during their study of Twitter bios. Students determined that the most impressive Twitter accounts had engaging, easy-to-read bios as well as profile and header images that complemented the tone of the bio and the user's professional field. Students further observed that individuals in creative fields, such as graphic artists, marketers, and creative writers, had more freedom in the composition and styling of their profile images. This discovery lead to an interesting discussion of "selfies," or photographs one takes of one's self with a camera phone. Ultimately, students concluded that even "tasteful" selfies should be used with caution, as the genre is more appropriate for one's personal social media accounts. Because finding acceptable profile and header images takes time, I asked students to complete this task outside of class. In that same homework

Figure 2. A Twitter bio that discursively illustrates the Twitter persona outlined in Figure 1

Justin ▓▓▓▓▓▓
@▓▓▓▓▓▓▓   FOLLOWS YOU

English major at Radford University.
Aspiring sports lawyer. Huge
Philadelphia sports fan.

Tweet to   Message

activity, I also directed students to choose a color scheme for their Twitter page that matched their profile and header images, looked professional, and aided readability.

With their personas reflected in the basic features of their Twitter accounts, students began gathering "tweetable" or "shareable" content. I reserved class time for students to find newsworthy or interesting material related to the personal and professional features of their Twitter persona. Finding the right content is essential: it is the basis for engaging others in digital small talk, and it implicitly demonstrates one's passion, knowledge, and fit to potential employers. Accordingly, I directed students to find objective and "evergreen," or continual, sources of content. As shown in Figure 1, good sources of such content include news outlets and blogs as well as the social media feeds of organizations and industry leaders.

Doing the Work: Generating, Sharing, and Responding to Tweets

Armed with relevant, timely sources of content, students started tweeting and thus "performing" the professional and personal sides of their Twitter persona. Students' tweets were supposed to attract followers to their network, engage users (followers or not) in conversation, and demonstrate to potential employers that they are knowledgeable professionals who can discuss workplace issues and their personal lives appropriately. I allowed students to tweet in class because it enabled me to provide immediate, one-to-one feedback. I considered issues such as: *Does the tweeted content correlate with the bio, and are professional and personal tweets balanced appropriately* (as in Figure 3)*? Are students responding to tweets about workplace and industry issues? Are they also responding to tweets about light-hearted matters, such as last night's football game or someone's upcoming 5K race* (as in Figure 4)*? Are students following Schaefer's advice in* The Tao of Twitter (2014)*by being helpful (e.g., answering questions, retweeting others' content, etc.)* (as in Figure 5)*?*

Figure 3. Tweets from early in the project; an interdisciplinary studies major shares content related to all dimensions of her Twitter persona. One tweet also uses an expressive hashtag.

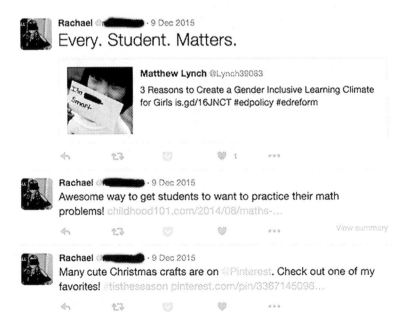

Figure 4. A light-hearted tweet that illustrates the student's interests and approachability

Figure 5. A "helpful" tweet that demonstrates sincerity and builds relationships

I used a subsequent in-class tweeting day for an ad-hoc workshop focusing on engagement with Twitter users. Not every tweet will be met with discussion and dialogue, of course, but students nevertheless needed to be diligent about conversing with others in order to meet the objectives of the assignment. Silver (2009) describes tweets that are more conducive to discussion as "thick." "Thick tweets" have at least two "layers" of information: The first layer may be a piece of content, such as an image or hyperlink. A second layer of information might be a meaningful comment about the first layer; a third layer could be a hashtag or a username (an "@ mention") (Silver, 2009). Because thick tweets are content-rich, they provide multiple entries for engagement in the form of replies, retweets, or rewteets with added commentary. In addition to sparking more conversation, thick tweets may better convey one's professional knowledge and personal interests to prospective employers (see Figure 6). Given the advantages of thick tweets, I asked students to read Silver's blog post (2009) and compose three "thick" tweets. To conclude the workshop, students evaluated their classmates' thick tweets in an informal writing activity.

Refining the Work: Code Switching, Code Sliding, and Hashtags

Thick tweets served as a natural transition to the final stage of project in which students focused on the written mechanics of tweets. Because "thin" tweets contain only one layer of information, I advised students to code switch and use SWE to compose these relatively straightforward messages. By comparison, thick tweets are challenging to write: in order to incorporate a thick tweet's multiple layers in 140 characters or less, students often had to code slide and develop their own textese. The problem-based learning dimensions of the project were useful in helping students meet this learning objective. As shown in Figure 7, students had to independently discover how to consistently and legibly break grammar, spelling, and punctuation rules. To do this, they had to review and apply some of our prior course learning about SWE conventions, such as parallel structure or the difference between semi-colons and colons.

During the final day devoted to the project, we addressed using hashtags. Although they are not exactly related to code sliding and switching, hashtags are ubiquitous in Twitter's native lexicon, and students need guidance in incorporating these linguistic features into their digital small talk. Nearly all of my students previously had used functional hashtags (see Figure 6) on social media (e.g., Instagram)

Figure 6. A thick tweet that includes a link to timely content, the author's thoughts on that content, and a functional hashtag

Figure 7. A student pursuing a career in forensic nursing breaks with SWE so that her entire comment can fit within the reduced character limit of the retweet; her code sliding is successful because it is consistent and does not hamper readability

to topically label their posts, so we focused our energy on the expressive varieties of hashtags. As J. Turner (2012) explains, expressive hashtags

… give the writer the opportunity to comment on his own emotional state, to sarcastically undercut his own tweet, to construct an extra layer of irony, to offer a flash of evocative imagery or to deliver metaphors with striking economy.

I devised an expressive hashtag "scavenger hunt" to give students a broader understanding of this device. Students had a set amount of time to identity various uses of expressive hashtags. Next, they experimented with some of these approaches and then composed a brief, informal analysis of their results. Many remarked that it was acceptable to use hashtags to convey emotions like humor, but hashtag sarcasm should be used with caution, as it can be misinterpreted. Figure 3 shows a student using the hashtag #tistheseason as a whimsical reference to her excitement about making Christmas crafts during the impending semester break.

DATA COLLECTION

Because the project was scaffolded, "low stakes" assignments and informal writing activities were scheduled throughout the project so that students could receive early, ongoing feedback. At the conclusion of the project, students' work on Twitter was evaluated holistically for a grade: I looked at their user and profile names; bio; profile and header images; accounts they followed; and tweet stream. In assessing tweets, I focused on the extent to which tweeted content aligned topically with the Twitter persona, as it was characterized in the bio. I also looked at students' code switching and sliding choices. In relation to the latter, I measured the extent to which their textese broke from SWE in consistent, legible ways. In addition, I evaluated whether students' writing and hashtags were tonally appropriate. Tweet quantity was as important as quality: Students had to tweet a set number of times and also vary the days and times of their tweets.[8] Finally, in the most recent iteration of the assignment, I asked students to write a memo in which they reflected on their successes and challenges throughout the project.

RESULTS AND DISCUSSION

Many students initially were wary of building an online presence despite my insistence that one benefits job seekers. Their skepticism was understandable, given what they likely had heard throughout their educational lives about the necessity of social media censorship (S. Buck, 2012; Donnelly, 2013; Stauts, 2015). To better convince students of my claims, I introduced the most recent version of the Twitter project by discussing much of this chapter's findings about cybervetting. My RU students were surprised to discover that employers who cybervet do not always look for reasons to exclude a candidate but instead use social media platforms to make positive hiring decisions. This knowledge led them to be more open to professionalizing with social media. I think most millennials are receptive to the notion of censoring and cultivating their web presence because they typically already assume multiple online personas (Duggan, Ellison, Lampe, Lenhart, & Madden, 2015). Therefore, they at least can imagine maintaining their current personas on social media while projecting another image of themselves that speaks positively to employers.

Professional and business writing textbooks, including those that I adopted for the courses discussed in this chapter, also assert that a digital presence is essential in today's job market (Bovee &Thill, 2014; Locker & Kienzler, 2015; Markel, 2015). However, they provide few details as to how this can be accomplished, as it is assumed that millennials are social media experts because they are digital natives who have "spent their entire lives surrounded by…the…toys and tools of the digital age" (Prensky, 2001). Although the notion of the "digital native" indeed has been deconstructed (Helsper & Enyon, 2010), we would do well to remember that millennials use social media to maintain friendships and familial bonds in rhetorically savvy ways (E. Buck, 2015). I designed the Twitter project, then, to leverage my millennials students' rhetorical sensibilities. In areas where they might struggle to transform their personal use of social media into a professional one, I use a structured, scaffolded approach and gave students ample time to reflect on their choices.

As I suspected, students' existing social media skills afforded them some early successes. With only minimal guidance from me, for example, students quickly developed rhetorically savvy Twitter personas, as reflected by their bios, which also exhibited an appropriate balance of "professional" and "personal" content (as seen in Figure 2).[9] Along with devising balanced, strategically constructed Twitter personas, students selected appropriate, visually appealing profile and header images—and for good reason. Millennials like my students are active producers and consumers of visual media, especially within social media. Thus, with little prompting beyond our discussion of "selfies," my students were able to choose images for their accounts that clearly communicated their professional "brand" to employers in their field. Ultimately, these early successes bolstered their interest and confidence in the Twitter project as a whole.

The assignment became more complicated for students when they began enacting their Twitter persona through digital small talk. Finding suitable digital small talk topics may be difficult for millennials because they have short or absent work histories. Consequently, they have had few if any opportunities to engage in informal, face-to-face conversation with people in a professional setting, particularly when those individuals are not in their peer group. This was especially true for my students at FMU in northeastern South Carolina where jobs generally were scarce. Digital small talk about workplace topics also may be difficult for millennials because they might not regularly read trade publications that address industry-specific news and developments. My students at FMU and RU struggled to engage actual and imagined audiences in career-related digital small talk for this reason as well.

Having time in class to find "evergreen" sources of content eased these difficulties. Yet, even with an arsenal of content at their fingertips that they could use to implicitly highlight their employability, students did not always choose material that would elicit feedback or interest from their audiences. For instance, during our in-class lab session, I observed many students sharing a static web page (e.g., "Home" or "About" pages) from prominent organizations in their field instead of a blog post or news story about an industry development or specific company issue. Sharing a news item about a company, for instance, shows that one is engaged with ongoing developments in one's field. Tweeting a link to a company's webpage, on the other hand, demonstrates relatively little beyond one's awareness of the company's online home. Addressing this issue in class allowed students to quickly change course. But even as students began tweeting the right kind of content, they still struggled with digital small talk, particularly in terms of using it to network, and as a result, their dialogue with Twitter users who were not enrolled in my courses was sparse.

Tweeting about non-workplace issues, such as hobbies and personal interests, also was difficult for my students, but only because they were fearful of exposing themselves in an unprofessional manner. Given the weight of fit in the hiring process, their nervousness was justified, but only to an extent: Employers *do* evaluate job seekers' online writing to judge overall professionalism. For this reason, and not in spite of it, it is important to show that one can discuss his or her personal life and the world at large appropriately on social media. Doing so speaks volumes about one's ability to do the same in the workplace. To alleviate students' anxieties, I emphasized Schaefer's (2014) view that the Twitter user who is "all business" will have a smaller, less robust network, and as a result, he or she would not fully enjoy the residual benefits that a professional Twitter presence offers to job seekers, such as job leads, referrals, or collaborative opportunities. The assignment's problem-based learning features emerged most noticeably in regards to sharing personal content, as students had to use prior course knowledge to resolve a complex problem with multiple "right" answers: What personal information should the Twitter persona incorporate, given one's employment goals? Interestingly, some students felt liberated in knowing they could tweet about personal interests and hobbies as part of maintaining a professional, digital presence. While the tenor of these conversations often was appropriate, the amount was not. Instead of tweeting about "professional" topics 70% of the time and personal topics 30% of the time, many students did the opposite. Their reversal of the "70/30" rule is understandable, to an extent, because millennials are more familiar with using social media for interpersonal purposes.

My students had mixed results with using Twitter to develop workplace digital writing skills. My theory of a professional style of textese made sense to them, and they eagerly experimented with code sliding by, for example, making their abbreviations and other elisions more uniform (see Figure 7). For some of my students, code sliding also encompassed using fewer metamessages (i.e., graphical markers of intent) than they would when writing to friends. Significantly, when my students avoided hyperbolic graphical metamessages, they instead relied on word choice and tone to convey their tweets' full meaning. Students were well versed in writing with an informal or conversational tone, which is the preferred sound for most business communication situations (Shwom & Snyder, 2012). Nevertheless, some students struggled to consistently implement a conversational tone and instead used stilted, overly formal language in their tweets. Other students used a conversational tone but pushed the boundaries of what might be considered an acceptable demeanor in a professional environment. These students often used too many exclamation points, and as a result, they came across as overly eager or unprofessional. Finally, nearly all of my students fell victim to the habits and incidental circumstances that lead to textese. For instance, apostrophes often seemed to be carelessly dropped (e.g., "Im" instead of "I'm"). Over time, these oversights added up, and their Twitter feed, as a whole, took on a less-than-polished, sloppy look.

LIMITATIONS

Overall, many of my students mentioned that they enjoyed and benefited from developing a digital presence with Twitter. Students' positive perceptions of the project notwithstanding, the assignment has some drawbacks. Its short duration of two weeks limited their ability to build a large, diverse network to engage in digital small talk. In light of this, the project could be assigned during a longer period or even the entire semester, but in its early stages, students would not have learned all the writing and rhetorical skills needed for competency. Most significantly, this project is limited by the extent to which its underlying framework does not acknowledge the ways in which gender, race, ethnicity, and socioeconomic class complicate the reception of one's digital presence. More studies are needed, then, that qualify existing claims about the ways employers interpret the presence and absence of women and minorities' digital footprints.

CONCLUSION

Employers increasingly are evaluating online textual information about but also by job candidates. Accordingly, social media can be a vital tool for performing an online, professional identity, as it can help candidates demonstrate "fit" as well as their ability to communicate digitally in a professional context. Millennials are skilled in using social media for personal purposes but cannot immediately intuit how to use familiar social media outlets to achieve these goals. Twitter allows writing instructors to guide students in enacting a professional presence through small talk and other digital communication practices that are valuable in the workplace. Most significantly, this means that instead of training students away from using "textese," instructors can use Twitter to help students develop a professional style of textese—one that strategically and consistently breaks the rules of SWE. Twitter's asymmetrical, chat-like features as well as its 140-character tweet limit especially help students code switch and slide. Hopefully, by designing a Twitter project with problem-based learning features, scaffolding, and metacognition activities, I enabled students to transfer their Twitter-based writing practices to other workplace digital genres in which efficient, abbreviated discourse is valued.

REFERENCES

Berkelaar, B., & Buzzanell, P. (2015). Online employment screening and digital career capital: Exploring employers' use of online information for personnel selection. *Management Communication Quarterly*, *29*(1), 84–113. doi:10.1177/0893318914554657

Bombardieri, M. (2006, July 9). Life away from home 101: Orientations warn students of drugs, Facebook, Texas Hold'em. *The Boston Globe*. Retrieved from http://www.boston.com/news/education/higher/articles/2006/07/09/life_away_from_home_101/?page=full

Bouton, K. (2015, July 17). Recruiting for cultural fit. *Harvard Business Review*. Retrieved from www.hbr.org

Bovee, C., & Thill, J. (2014). Business communication today (12th ed.). Boston: Pearson.

Brown, V., & Vaughn, E. D. (2011). The writing on the (Facebook) wall: The use of social networking sites in hiring decisions. *Journal of Business and Psychology*, *26*(2), 219–225. doi:10.1007/s10869-011-9221-x

Buck, A. (2012). Examining digital literacy practices on social network sites. *Research in the Teaching of English*, *47*(1), 9–38. Retrieved from http://www.ncte.org/library/NCTEFiles/Resources/Journals/RTE/0471-aug2012/RTE0471Examining.pdf

Buck, E. (2015). Assessing the efficacy of the rhetorical composing situation with FYC students as advanced social media practitioners. *Kairos: A Journal of Rhetoric, Technology, and Pedagogy*, 19(3). Retrieved from http://kairos.technorhetoric.net/

Buck, S. (2012, September 4). 12 things students should never do on social media. *Mashable*. Retrieved from http://mashable.com/2012/09/04/students-social-media-warnings/

CareerBuilder Survey. (2015). Thirty-five percent of employers less likely to interview [Press release]. Retrieved from http://www.careerbuilder.com/share/aboutus/pressreleasesdetail.aspx?sd=5%2f14%2f2015&siteid=cbpr&sc_cmp1=cb_pr893_&id=pr893&ed=12%2f31%2f2015

Cordell, R. (2010, May 28). Disposable Twitter accounts for classroom use [Blog post]. http://chronicle.com/blogs/profhacker/disposable-twitter-accounts-for-classroom-use/40145

Crystal, D. (2008). *Txtng: The Gr8 Db8*. Oxford: Oxford University Press.

Cummins, H. J. (2006, March 30). Students' Facebook faces adult invasion; Facebook, a web world for college students, now gets visits from prospective employers. *Star Tribune*. Retrieved from http://www.highbeam.com/doc/1G1-143881218.html

De Jonge, S., & Kemp, N. (2012). Text message abbreviations and language skills in high school and university students. *Journal of Research in Reading*, 35, 49–68. doi:10.1111/j.1467-9817.2010.01466.x

Decarie, C. (2010). Facebook: Challenges and opportunities for business communication students. *Business Communication Quarterly*, 73(4), 449–452. doi:10.1177/1080569910385383

Donnelly, K. (2013, September 20). Graduates could be 'Googled' out of jobs over online posts. *Irish Independent*. Retrieved from www.independent.ie

Duggan, M., Ellison, N., Lampe, C., Lenhart, A., & Madden, M. (2015, January 9). Social Media Update 2014. *Pew Research Center*. Retrieved from http://www.pewinternet.org/2015/01/09/social-media-update-2014/

Grabill, J., Hart-Davidson, W., Pigg, S., Curran, P., McLeod, M., Moore, J., . . . Peeples, T. … Brunk-Chavez, B. (2010, September 7). *The Writing Lives of College Students*. Retrieved from http://www2.matrix.msu.edu/wp-content/uploads/2013/08/WIDE_writinglives_whitepaper.pdf

Gunraj, D., Drumm-Hewitt, A., Dashow, E., Upadhyay, S., & Klin, C. (2016). Texting insincerely: The role of the period in text messaging. *Computers in Human Behavior*, 55, 1067–1075. doi:10.1016/j.chb.2015.11.003

Helsper, E., & Enyon, R. (2010). Digital natives: Where is the evidence? *British Educational Research Journal*, 36(3), 503–520. doi:10.1080/01411920902989227

Jobvite Survey. (2014). Social recruiting survey (Press release). Retrieved from https://www.jobvite.com/wp-content/uploads/2014/10/Jobvite_SocialRecruiting_Survey2014.pdf

Jones, J. (2010, March 9). The creepy treehouse problem (Blog post). Retrieved from: http://chronicle.com/blogs/profhacker/the-creepy-treehouse-problem/23027

Kemp, N., Wood, C., & Waldron, S. (2014). do i know its wrong: Children's and adults' use of unconventional grammar in text messaging. *Reading and Writing: An Interdisciplinary Journal, 27*(9), 1585–1602. doi:10.1007/s11145-014-9508-1

Kristof-Brown, A. (2000). Perceived applicant fit: Distinguishing between recruiters' perceptions of person-job and person-organization fit. *Personnel Psychology, 53*(3), 643–671. doi:10.1111/j.1744-6570.2000.tb00217.x

Kuznekoff, J., Munz, S., & Titsworth, S. (2015). Mobile phones in the classroom: Examining the effects of texting, twitter, and message content on student learning. *Communication Education, 63*(3), 344–365. doi:10.1080/03634523.2015.1038727

LinkedIn. (n. d.). About Us. Retrieved from: https://www.linkedin.com/about-us

Locker, K., & Kienzler, D. (2015). *Business and administrative communication* (11th ed.). Boston: McGraw-Hill.

Maitre, M. (2006, August 22). Myspace 101: Colleges urge caution. *Inside Bay Area.* Retrieved from http://www.insidebayarea.com/dailyreview/localnews/ci_4218247

Margetson, D. (1991). Why is problem-based learning a challenge? In D. Boud & G. Feletti (Eds.), The Challenge of Problem Based Learning (pp. 36-44). London: Kogan.

Markel, M. (2014). *Technical communication* (11th ed.). Boston: Bedford/St. Martin's.

Marshall, K. (2015, June 1). Rethinking Twitter in the classroom. *Chronicle Vitae.* Retrieved from https://chroniclevitae.com/news/1021-rethinking-twitter-in-the-classroom

Monster.com. (n. d.). Search results. Retrieved from: http://career-advice.monster.com/searchresult/employment.aspx

Pegrum, M. (2011). Modified, multipled, and (re-)mixed: Social media and digital literacies. In M. Thomas (Ed.), *Digital education: Opportunities for social collaboration* (pp. 9–36). New York: Palgrave Macmillan.

Planning, C. (n. d.). Radford University. Retrieved from http://www.radford.edu/content/career-services/home/students.html

Pope, J. (2006, Aug 2). Students warned about networking sites. *USA Today.* Retrieved from http://usatoday30.usatoday.com/tech/news/internetprivacy/2006-08-02-facebook-orientations_x.htm

Prensky, M. (2001). Digital natives, digital Immigrants. Retrieved from http://www.marcprensky.com/writing/Prensky%20-%20Digital%20Natives,%20Digital%20Immigrants%20-%20Part1.pdf

Rivera, L. (2015, May 30). Guess who doesn't fit in at work. *The New York Times.* Retrieved from: http://nyti.ms/1d61kMt

Sacks, M., & Graves, N. (2012). How many "friends" do you need? Teaching students how to network using social media. *Business and Professional Communication Quarterly, 75*(1), 80–88. doi:10.1177/1080569911433326

Savin-Baden, M., & Howell Major, C. (2004). *Foundations of problem-based learning*. Birkshire, England: The Society for Research into Higher Education & Open University Press.

Schaefer, M. (2014). *The tao of Twitter: Changing your life and business 140 characters at a time*. New York: McGraw-Hill.

Schwom, B., & Snyder, L. (2012). *Business communication: Polishing your professional presence*. Boston: Prentice Hall.

Silver, D. (2009, February 25). the different between thick and thin tweets. [Blog post]. Retrieved from: http://silverinsf.blogspot.com/2009/02/difference-between-thin-and-thick.html

Stauts, M. (2015, August 7). Your online presence can help or hurt when applying to college. *The Atlanta Journal-Constitution*. Retrieved from www.ajc.com

Tannen, D. (2013). The medium is the metamessage: Conversational style in new media interaction. In D. Tannen. A. Trester. (Eds.), Discourse 2.0: Language and new media (pp. 99-118). Washington, D.C: Georgetown University Press.

Turner, J. (2012, Nov. 2). #InPraiseOfTheHashtag. *The New York Times*. Retrieved from: http://www.nytimes.com/2012/11/04/magazine/in-praise-of-the-hashtag.html?_r=1

Turner, K. (2009). Flipping the switch: Code-switching from text speak to standard English. *English Journal*, *98*(5), 60–65.

Twitter. (n. d.a). Using hashtags on Twitter. Retrieved from: https://support.twitter.com/articles/49309

Twitter. (n. d.b). About your Twitter timeline. Retrieved from: https://support.twitter.com/articles/164083

Vicknair, J., Elkersh, D., Yancey, K., & Budden, M. (2010). The use of social networking websites as a recruiting tool for employers. *American Journal of Business Education*, *3*(11), 7–12.

Wheeler, R. (2008). Becoming adept at code-switching. *Educational Leadership*, *65*(7), 54–58.

Wood, C., Kemp, N., & Waldron, S. (2014a). Exploring the longitudinal relationships between the use of grammar in text messaging and performance on grammatical tasks. *The British Journal of Developmental Psychology*, *32*(4), 415–429. doi:10.1111/bjdp.12049 PMID:24923868

Wood, C., Kemp, N., Waldron, S., & Hart, L. (2014b). Grammatical understanding, literary, and text messaging in school children and undergraduate students: A concurrent analysis. *Computers & Education*, *70*, 281–290. doi:10.1016/j.compedu.2013.09.003

Zappavigna, M. (2012). *Discourse of Twitter and social media: How we use language to create affiliation on the web*. London: Bloomsbury Academic.

ENDNOTES

[1]   For expediency, the terms "casual" and "everyday" writing in this chapter will refer to those that are digital- and computer-mediated.

[2]   This abridged, non-standard discourse is called textese because people tend to use it in SMS or mobile phone text messages; nevertheless, textese is "similar, if not identical, to other popular forms of computer-mediated discourse…and language observed on social networking sites…such as Twitter" (Wood, Kemp, & Waldron, 2014b, p. 282). My use of the term "textese," therefore, encompasses all forms of abbreviated, non-standard writing in digital environments, including SMS text messages, chat messages, and social media posts.

[3]   What this means in the context of the chapter, then, is that students can learn about code sliding and switching at once, and their progress in one area should not cancel out their efforts in the other.

[4]   Importantly, Zappavigna (2014) notes that Twitter-speak can be understood by people who do not use Twitter. Job seekers on Twitter, then, can use discourse specific to the site without automatically compromising their ability to convey a positive, legible image to employers.

[5]   Eventually, I also incorporated the Twitter project into a 400-level Rhetoric of New Media course at FMU.

[6]   Many of my students chose to keep their professional, classroom Twitter accounts public.

[7]   I suggested but did not require that students attach their legal names to their professional Twitter accounts. Because user and profile names were required to "sound" professional, students who opted not to use their full names often used their initials combined with a series of numbers.

[8]   Practically speaking, staggering tweets exposes one to different Twitter users across the globe, which in turns facilitates the formation of a larger, more diverse online network (Schaefer, 2014). Pedagogically speaking, when students tweet throughout the assignment period, they can adjust their approach well before the final grading period.

[9]   Students' prior completion of a cover letter and resume assignment also helped them gain traction on the project, as they already contemplated their career goals and the ways in which their experiences fit within those plans.

Chapter 13
Curating the Public Self:
Helping Students Present an Authentic, Professional Persona via LinkedIn

Erin Trauth
University of South Florida, USA

ABSTRACT

Many 21st century student writers have long since mastered the art of crafting a public image through their social media profiles. However, when it is time to make the transition from personal to professional in their public persona, many students have trouble differentiating between the shades of their lives, and subsequently, create less-than-professional public profiles. In this chapter, I explore ways writing teachers can help students transition from a social media experience limited to friends and family to a public persona for job searches, graduate school applications, and the like. More specifically, I discuss how I used LinkedIn to help student writers create authentic, yet professional, public selves.

INTRODUCTION

I met Reggie[1] two years ago; he was a senior and a student in my course, Technical Writing for Health Science Majors at the University of South Florida. Reggie had a strong personality and voice, a remarkable face-to-face presence, a long list of jobs and internships related to his area of study, and great references. Yet, when we began our employment unit in the course, Reggie told me he was having trouble getting any calls for job interviews. After coming to the conclusion that he looked quite marketable on paper, I asked him to perform a Google search on himself. He reported back to me the next class period with astonishment. His public persona was anything but professional, and he had racked up quite the collection of personal photographs. Some of these photos were not so appropriate for a job search. In addition, he had found a long list of personal rants, links to games and apps, and the like. In other words, he had made no moves to craft his online public persona.

Like Reggie, a majority of Millennials have grown up with all the trappings of a digital society. Reggie and his peers have grown up in an age of self-promotion of accomplishments on Facebook and rants on Twitter. Reggie and his peers often post daily Instagram "selfies," and find entire relationships formed

DOI: 10.4018/978-1-5225-0562-4.ch013

via text messaging. Many Millennials have grown up in a world where much of their lives have been cast to the public, and, as such, many of these 21st century student writers have long since mastered the art of crafting a public image through their social media profiles. However, when students approaching graduation set out to make the transition from personal to professional in their public persona, many students have trouble differentiating between the shades of their lives. Subsequently, they create less-than-professional public profiles, their profile pictures are "selfies," (see Figure 1) and their profile content is written in "text talk."

This, of course, can lead to problems for Millennials when they begin to search and put themselves on the job market. Cassandra Branham and Danielle Farrar (2014) write in "Negotiating Virtual Spaces: Public Writing," "Despite the fact that public writing in the virtual world has become increasingly popular, some people think less and less about what they write online. One particular consequence of this trend is the rise, in the past few years, of employers 'vetting' the online personas of potential employees and scholarship applicants" (p. 1).

Whether we like it or not, employers have long since begun using the capabilities of Internet searching to lay the groundwork for hiring decisions. A survey conducted via Career Builder claims that about one in four U.S. employers research prospective employees via Internet searching. And, further, of those using the Internet to research candidates, 51 percent found information which led to a decision not to hire a given candidate (p. 1). For those employers doing research specifically on social media sites, 63 percent of employers opted to not hire a given candidate based on information revealed in such searches (p. 1). The search information discovered varies from embellished qualifications to lying about an absence; further, 25 percent of the aforementioned employers found "poor communication skills" online, 19 percent found information about candidates drinking alcohol or using drugs, 11 percent found provocative or "inappropriate" photographs, and 8 percent found candidates with unprofessional screen names (p. 1).

In terms of creating positive information about themselves online, one of the best strategies for students is the creation of a LinkedIn profile. Recent Career Builder estimates note that 98 percent of recruiters

Figure 1. A selfie style photograph
Reprinted from Flickr, by P. Tomic 2014. Retrieved from https://www.flickr.com/photos/tomicpasko/14139726176. Copyright 2014 by P. Tomic. Reprinted with permission of Creative Commons Images.

and 85 percent of hiring managers are checking LinkedIn for candidates (1), and so, students would do well to craft a professional persona in this space.

With all of this mind, as teachers of Millenials, we might consider the act of curating one's self on-line. Curating, in the typical sense, means to organize, sift through, and select for presentation. The act of curating public acts of expression and writing involves editing and fine-tuning marketable skills and qualities one possesses. By strategically selecting and bolstering skills and qualifications one wants to showcase, combined with their extensive understanding of digital communication methods, Millenials can curate their best public self for the purposes of their public profiles.

In Reggie's case, I advised him to delete anything inappropriate or overly-personal – in other words, anything he wouldn't want his parents/guardians and his boss to see – and then we moved on to the second most important step: creating a professional LinkedIn profile.

In this chapter, I explore ways writing teachers can help students transition from a social media experience limited to friends and family to a public persona for job searches, graduate school applications, and the like. More specifically, I discuss how I used LinkedIn in undergraduate writing courses, to help student writers create authentic, yet professional, public selves.

THEORETICAL FRAMEWORK

Step One: Clean Up Your Online Act

Because employers are making efforts to search for what is on the Internet regarding their potential future employees, students entering the workforce will usually want to do a pruning of the information that does exist to make sure that the digital foot they're putting forward best represents the professional light in which many of them want to be seen. This involves an initial search on major search engines, i.e. Google, Bing, and Yahoo to see what profiles, posts, and images are tied to their names. Then, depending on what students would not want a potential employer to see, they might work on changing various privacy settings on their past profiles, posts, and images or deleting inappropriate entries, if they exist, altogether. The first round of curating involves a fine-tuning of the information that does already exist.

One helpful initial class activity is to ask students to search for themselves online – and to make sure to click through all tabs on a given search site, i.e. looking for search result images, links, and other areas sometimes not noticed in a general text-based search.

An enlightening class activity is to pair students and have them role play as employer-potential employee. I often ask these "student employers" to search various sites, such as Google, Bing, and Yahoo to see what arises. Then, they should target specific spaces, such as looking up the "potential employee" on Facebook, Twitter, Instagram, LinkedIn, and even sites Millenials might initially consider to be entirely personal, such as Snapchat and Tumblr, Vine, and Youtube, WhatsApp, and Pinterest. Millennial students should realize that nothing in the public realm is out of bounds, and anything they post could potentially boost their profile – or be held against them.

Advise students that if they wouldn't want to share the post, image, or profile in a job interview (see Figure 2 for an example of job-search-inappropriate Twitter postings), they should modify, remove, or ensure privacy for the given entry when they're on the job market. It is important to make special note that default privacy settings for many sites often change – so a vigilant check of these settings is also important as one's job search continues.

Figure 2. Twitter job-related rants
Reprinted from FireMe! App, Retrieved from fireme.l3s.uni-hannover.de. Copyright FireMe! App.

Another area to focus on while curating includes examining associations online, which include user comments Students should consider their online friendships. Online friends posting controversial or risqué material may make a job seeker look "guilty by association" in the eyes of employers searching the names of prospective employees. While writing instructors need not tell students to lose certain friends on their social media pages, asking them to examine such connections and the marks these connections leave on their own online profiles is worthwhile.

Curating, in this sense, is an act of revision – cutting what is not helpful or needed in one's creation of a public and professional persona.

Step Two: Curating the Public Self via LinkedIn Profiles

LinkedIn, a professional profile and networking platform launched in 2003, is used by millions of people globally to search for jobs and discuss professional topics. In October 2015, LinkedIn stated that it boasts more than 400 million users in more than 200 countries (p. 1). With such a wide scope of use, LinkedIn can be a rather useful starting place for Millenials seeking to curate a professional online presence. LinkedIn may be one of the first professional opportunities for students to think about the types of information that would be beneficial to share and promote in online spaces. As such, special attention should be paid to the information LinkedIn encourages its users to share as a virtual resume marketplace and opportunity to create an online professional network in a few clicks of a button.

Despite LinkedIn's increasing usage, Millenials aren't using it as much as other groups; according to PEW research, users aged 50-64 use LinkedIn more often than users aged 18-29. This could mean that those with more professional practice (and thus probably in a position to hire) are on the site (p.1). Although Millennials reportedly under-use LinkedIn, its importance cannot be underestimated. LinkedIn can be a primary vehicle that students use to create (or curate) their online professional selves. Laura Shin (2014) of *Forbes* cautions Millennials that we may be at a point in society that, in most industries, it may actually be frowned upon for future employees to be missing from LinkedIn.

With all of this in mind, I encourage writing instructors to make the creation of a LinkedIn profile part of any professional, technical or business writing syllabus. In many cases, even my junior and senior level students either had never even heard of LinkedIn or had not been actively working on a LinkedIn profile. I now require it as part of the professional, technical or business writing classes I develop, and students often use it to gain internships, jobs, and admissions into graduate schools.

Instructors asking students to create profiles should be careful, however, to not impose any sort of requirements on connections, as making connections on LinkedIn also requires some curating in the sense that it should not be done haphazardly.

Attempting direct LinkedIn connections without first being introduced in person or without being "introduced" by a common contact can often prove detrimental, as many seasoned professionals, or those on LinkedIn for longer periods of time, have perhaps grown wary of incessant requests from people they don't know. If students don't know any connections related to the connections they want to get to know, they might try a more informal space, such as Twitter, to reach out – or by emailing the person directly.

Because many students are unsure about how to design their LinkedIn profiles, I also ask students to research the profile a mid-level employee at a company they find interesting. While the CEO's profile might appear daunting – with its wealth of experience and connections – a mid-level employee might bear insight as to what they should mimic in their own curation of the site. Creating a worksheet or in-class activity in which students research several employees this way – researching everything from profile headlines, to format of resume-related information, to the types of groups the people are active in – and do this perhaps at a few different companies of interest with the end goal of generating a synthesis of the results – can prove to be a fruitful exercise. Students might even find issues of professionalism in these profiles that will help them to shape their own with some things to avoid in mind. In the next section, I will go share my LinkedIn methodology and pedagogy for professional, technical, and business writing courses.

METHODOLOGY AND PEDAGOGY

For the last four years, I have built a LinkedIn profile assignment into my employment project unit in all of my professional and technical writing courses. This includes Technical Writing for Health Science Majors, a 2000-level (sophomore) class, and Professional Writing, a 3000-level (junior) class at the University of South Florida. I have also used a variation of this assignment at the University of Colorado-Colorado Springs in Business Writing, a 2000-level (sophomore) class, and Technical Writing and Presentation (a class primarily for future engineers, a 2000-level (sophomore) class. My assignment is as follows:

Resume Creation

First, it is important to note that I ask students to complete or revise a full resume before creating a LinkedIn profile. Once the first draft of the resume is in the peer review stage, I ask students to begin working on the creation of a LinkedIn profile.

Preliminary LinkedIn Research

Before officially beginning or revising a current LinkedIn profile (a handful of students have a profile in existence already), I ask students to conduct research on people in the field they want to be in on LinkedIn.com. I should note early on that I also allow students to choose another means of building an online presence if they wish to stay away from LinkedIn.com for privacy reasons, and so some of this language will have an "and/or" for using other sites such as Twitter or Facebook, but I have only had this happen once in the past four years. Students are asked to complete worksheet in which they research relevant persons, businesses, and graduate school programs. A sample question from this worksheet is as follows: "Identify at least 2 people currently working in your target career area (i.e. a company CEO or a manager of a company you're interested in). List them here. Then, locate their Linkedin.com pages, groups, and/or professional Facebook/Twitter pages. What topics/articles/research areas are being discussed and shared by these people on their pages relevant to the field you're interested in working in? Provide a summary for at least two people." By researching other people on LinkedIn, students can get a glimpse of how other professionals are curating their own online image on the site.

Then, I ask students to reflect on their experiences researching others in their field on LinkedIn. Com, and I pose them with following question for reflection and planning purposes: "Now, utilizing the research you just conducted, explain how you plan to shape your own professional online presence on your own LinkedIn page and beyond. How can you use the current research and topics being discussed by professionals, journals, organizations, businesses, etc. to shape your own online professional presence in order to help you become a future leader in your field?"

LinkedIn Images

Before fully delving into the creation of the profile, I also ask students to strongly consider their choice of a profile image. In my experience, if left to their own devices, some students will quite often choose images that might be more appropriate for personal Instagram posts – highly-filtered images, less-than-professional dress, and sometimes pictures with friends of a significant other. Though curious, this is a marking of the millennial generation: when one grows up online, the lines between personal and professional often blur when it comes to one's image. One great way to encourage students to opt for more professional – yet still authentic photos – is to have them study LinkedIn photos of well-known-, public profiles of the leaders they wish to emulate. While it might not be necessary for students to go get professional headshots done, they might see that even young leaders and visionaries often use public photos which focus in on their person and show some personality – think natural lighting and more casual dress than the traditional suit-and-tie – but still emulate an air of professionalism. The notes here on LinkedIn images, of course, apply to images in all online spaces. A worthwhile class exercise involves an image quiz, in which instructions project images of randomized profile images, and students can vote and discuss whether or not the projected images would be appropriate for use on public spaces.

LinkedIn Profile Creation

Then, I ask students to complete a LinkedIn profile with the following assignment parameters:

Create a professional profile on LinkedIn. Read the LinkedIn's User Agreement, Privacy Policy and Cookie Policy before you start creating your profile. The profile should be professional and demonstrate involvement with the career community. After completing the project, you can opt to close your account. With your research in mind, now complete and finish your LinkedIn.com profile. After creating an account, you will need to:

- Make your profile public. Include, at minimum:
  - A profile picture (headshot, professional look encouraged)
  - A 1 to 3 paragraph summary of your qualifications and experiences in the "Summary" section (consider using some of what you have on your cover letter to populate this section; this, however, should only be about you and not a specific company)

- A completed, current experience section (including all positions listed on your resume, with job dates, title, company, as well as duties/skills you list on resume)
- A completed, current education section (including all educational experiences listed on your resume, with job dates, title, company, as well as duties/skills you list on resume)
- Any other sections applicable (i.e. groups, skills listings, awards, work samples, etc.) -- (all other sections optional but encouraged) Encouraging students to keep or follow LinkedIn blogs, join relevant professional groups, and connect with human resources representatives and recruiters at companies students would like to work have all proven to be useful exercises, too.

- When you are finished, proofread your profile very carefully. Remember, this is a public profile! Put your best professional foot forward here. Customize your public profile URL.

LinkedIn Peer Reviews

After creating a basic profile, I ask students to peer review one another's profiles in groups of two – four, depending on the class size and time available for this activity. The peer review activity is quite comprehensive. Students use a worksheet and answer the following questions about one another's work:

- Does the LinkedIn profile meet the minimum assignment requirements? If not, what is missing?
- Does the profile appear professional? Why or why not? What can be done to make it even more professional? Is the profile picture professional?
- What 2 to 3 things did this student do particularly well with regard to the LinkedIn profile?
- What 3 to 4 things should the student consider revising and/or expanding?
- What should this person consider adding to their profile to make it stronger?
- What, if anything, should the person remove from their profile?
- If this student were actually applying for the job specified on the job ad you reviewed, how do you think the hiring manager would perceive this person, based on the LinkedIn profile alone? Based on what you see, are they prepared for the job? If not, does it appear as though they are on the right track? (Note: this is much less about actual experience than it is the profile's ability to highlight what this person has done in their own experiences to make them a great candidate for any professional position). What areas could be expanded or made more prominent to help this person appear ready for the job? What you are looking at here is the person's ability to use what they do have to make a good professional impression.

Further Drafting

After the peer review, students revise their profiles and submit an intermediate draft. I provide feedback on this draft; students revise and submit a final draft for a grade.

Final Reflection

After completion of the LinkedIn profile, I ask students to reflect on their process. The assignment details are as follows: *Write a reflective memo that describes and analyzes how you approached, managed, and completed the project. Consider the following list of questions as you compose your reflective memo.*

- What was the purpose of the LinkedIn profile?
- What strategies did you use to understand the needs of your audiences?
- What decisions did you make about content, style, and format? How did you establish your ethos and credibility?
- What research methods did you use for this project? Why?
- What obstacles did you encounter when writing for your LinkedIn profile, and how did you solve those problems?
- What strategies did you apply to evaluate your LinkedIn profile?
- Which part of the LinkedIn profile are you most proud of? Why?

RESULTS

This effort has been a great success, as many of my students have opted to keep and further build their profiles beyond the class parameters, going on to make connections and utilize the site to aid in internship and job searches

At the end of the term, students often thank me for requiring them to get started on this very important part of the online public persona. Many students cite the creation of a LinkedIn profile as a method which helped them to earn the internship or post-graduate job they wanted, as it allowed them to make connections and put their best foot forward online. While the creation of yet another online profile might seem tedious to some, the experience and potential rewards are worth it. A recent student comment from an end-of-course evaluation sums up the experience well: "Liked that I had to make a LinkedIn page. It was a pain but well worth it."

CONCLUSION

Much of the aforementioned information directed to Millenials includes information about how to "clean up" one's digital presence – but does all of this professionalization mean that Millenials cannot still express themselves online? While it's important to make the shift to professional in one's public self, one should not lose all sense of identity and wipe the Internet clean of all information relating to the personal aspects of one's life. All job seekers – and all Millenials, for that matter – should still feel free to have a voice in the public space. In fact, having an opinion on matters is what can set a job seeker apart from another. What matters is the delivery of this information.

Branham and Farrar (2014) write: "[Public writing] does not mean that you cannot express your opinions within your own writing or in response to others, but you should express your opinions in a caring way that shows respect for those opinions that differ from your own. When publishing online, be sure that you are respecting yourself, the members of your online community, others who may read your posts, and the writing space."

Another idea to encourage students to foster a public online identity that fuses professional dealings with personal areas would be facilitating a project in which students created an online personal expression of their professional values, qualifications, or goals using a medium with personal meaning. For example, a student with a love for making movies who aims to become a physical therapist could create a series of web videos interviewing physical therapists about up-and-coming technologies related to the field and post this to a Youtube channel which links to their resume on LinkedIn. A student with a passion for music who wants to become an engineer could relate the two areas and write a blog post describing how the two areas intertwine and can build on one another. The idea is to encourage students to take their passions and find fusions between the professional and the personal – allowing them to express their personal interests in new and interesting ways which may ultimately benefit the entire profession – or, at the very least, make for an interesting video, blog post, or web site tab which may, in the end, make them stand out in a positive way amongst other job candidates.

Sharing this information with students can help encourage them to not only self-monitor and edit (when need be) existing online information and profiles, but can also show that curating a public persona, as described through this chapter, can help create a positive and professional online persona. Putting effort into curating one's public self, then, is not time wasted, and Millenials and their writing instructors can feel confident that work spent constructing public profiles and acts of writing can have an extremely positive impact on their future job prospects.

It may also be worth sharing with students that one's efforts to construct an online self should be considered part of an on-going process. With more of the workforce moving to online spaces, use of online professional spaces such as LinkedIn will increase, and, with continually changing privacy settings, new online friends, continual monitoring will be key even after the Millenials settle into their chosen careers.

REFERENCES

Branham, C., & Farrar, D. (2014). Negotiating Virtual Spaces: Public Writing. *Writing Commons*. Retrieved from http://writingcommons.org/index.php/open-text/new-media/negotiating-virtual-spaces-public-writing/650-negotiating-virtual-spaces-public-writing

FireMe! App. (2016). Twitter Rants [Image]. Retrieved from http://fireme.l3s.uni-hannover.de/fireme.php

Grasz, J. (2006). One-in-Four Hiring Managers Have Used Internet Search Engines to Screen Job Candidates; One-in-Ten Have Used Social Networking Sites, CareerBuilder.com Survey Finds. *Career Builder*. Retrieved from http://www.careerbuilder.com/share/aboutus/pressreleasesdetail.aspx?id=pr331&ed=12/31/2006&sd=10/26/2006

Lienesch, R. (2015). Not All Millennials are Social Media Mavens. *Public Religion Research Institute*. Retrieved from http://publicreligion.org/2015/07/not-all-millennials-are-social-media-mavens/#.Vf7jt-99Vikp

Pinkerton, J. (2013). How to Manage Your Online Image to Advance Your Career. *CompTIA*. Retrieved from http://certification.comptia.org/news/2013/03/27/How_to_Manage_Your_Online_Image_to_Advance_Your_Career.aspx

Ruefman, D. (n. d.). Taking Control: Managing Your Online Identity for the Job Search. Writing Commons. Retrieved from http://writingcommons.org/index.php/open-text/new-media/negotiating-virtual-spaces-public-writing/1210-taking-control-managing-your-online-identity-for-the-job-search

Shin, L. (2014). How to Use LinkedIn: 5 Smart Steps to Career Success. *Forbes*. Retrieved from http://www.forbes.com/sites/laurashin/2014/06/26/how-to-use-linkedin-5-smart-steps-to-career-success/

Single Platform Team. (2014). How to Build a Positive Public Persona. *Single Platform Blog*. Retrieved from: http://www.singleplatform.com/2014/06/09/build-positive-public-persona/

Tomic, P. (2014). Selfie [Photograph]. Retrieved from https://www.flickr.com/photos/tomicpasko/14139726176

ENDNOTE

[1]   Name changed.

Chapter 14
#WordUp! :
Student Responses to Social Media in the Technical Writing Classroom

Kendra N. Bryant
Florida A&M University, USA

ABSTRACT

In this chapter, the author argues that although integrating online social media networks into a traditional writing classroom seems timely, cutting edge, and apropos to students' current past-time activities, teachers have the opportunity to create more meaningful classroom activities with social media if they first: consider students' trepidation regarding such non-traditional classroom activities; and second: realize socially-networked students don't necessarily translate into career-ready students. By way of two in-class Q&A sessions, the author discovers that her Technical Writing students need less instruction on how to use social media academically, and more instruction on how to use social media to brand and market themselves professionally. In a chapter grounded in student response, readers receive her student feedback about the effects of integrating social media networks into their writing classroom in an effort to assist teachers more purposely integrate social media into their traditional classroom spaces.

Teachers need to integrate technology seamlessly into the curriculum instead of viewing it as an add-on, an afterthought, or an event. – Heidi-Hayes Jacobs, Founder of Curriculum Designers and Curriculum21

INTRODUCTION

For the past four years, I have practiced integrating social media into the *Technical Writing, Improving Writing*, and *Freshman Communicative Skills* courses that I teach at Florida A&M University (FAMU). I have incorporated the social media platforms WordPress—and most recently, Twitter and LinkedIn—to my traditional writing courses (whose departmental curriculums make no such requirements), because I wanted my predominantly Black student population to know more about writing with technology than I did when I was a graduate student at University of South Florida (USF) four years ago.

DOI: 10.4018/978-1-5225-0562-4.ch014

As expressed in the Preface at the beginning of this book, unlike my White peers, I was unfamiliar with the trends regarding social media networks' effects on composition, identity, language, and the like. As a result, I found myself quite disengaged from classroom discussions and required online writing assignments. While the *Rhetoric & Technology* course I was taking at the time was designed to enlighten me (and my White peers) about the current trends in Rhetoric & Composition, because I was the only student who seemed to know nothing about social media platforms (aside from MySpace) and their potential for academic/professional use, I felt stupid and unprepared. I felt like I did not belong in a Ph.D. program, and being the only Black student in the English doctoral program only encouraged my feelings of inferiority.

Although I was struggling with the technological demands of my *Rhetoric & Technology* course, I had not realized that my challenges with technology were also familiar to other Black undergraduate students attending USF. While teaching a First Year Composition course that required students to use Blackboard—an online content management system for academic purposes—one of my Black male transfer students claimed that he was dropping out of USF because he couldn't keep up with the university's technological requirements. Although the composition course he was taking with me didn't require online tasks aside from Blackboard, this student, who transferred from a historically black university, felt overwhelmed by the technologies that he said were not required at his former institution. And so, despite my attempts at retaining him, he dropped out.

As a teacher in training, I vowed to integrate writing technologies (beyond Word processing) into my writing classrooms so that no other student would be so discouraged and threatened by technological demands that he would forfeit his (traditional) education. And so, in order to garner my own appreciation for and understanding of online communications technologies, I began including WordPress, a content management system that offers a blogging platform, into the *Professional Writing* courses I was required to teach at USF. I continued my practice at FAMU where the majority of my Black students were like me and my former Black male USF student: they, too, were far removed from the academic and professional possibilities that online writing communities offered its users.

I have integrated WordPress into my traditional writing courses for four years now and have felt a bit like a Mother Theresa of teaching with online writing technologies. I believed, without a shadow of doubt, that my familiarizing my writing students with online writing communities—that both improved their online marketability and forged classroom community—provided them more meaningful learning experiences (Bryant 2013a; Bryant 2013b). And it did. However, this year when I required students to link their Twitter to their WordPress accounts, I realized a trepidation from students I had not realized before.

In an unexpected class discussion, students complained about their Twitter requirement. According to many of them, they either don't use Twitter because it's "messy," or their own Twitter account is "too messy" to share in an academic setting. In other words, student Twitter feeds were inappropriate for the traditional classroom setting. Their Twitter feeds were complete with vulgar images, profane language, and violent video clips, they said. And as a result, students didn't want to connect their Twitter feeds to their WordPress accounts. Instead, they preferred to create new Twitter accounts or to create pseudo Twitter accounts specifically for the course assignment.

During that unexpected classroom discussion, I realized that reviewing a course syllabus that notes technological requirements, polling students' familiarity with WordPress, and assuming that each of my students would benefit from and appreciate my notions regarding social media use in the writing classroom based on my own experiences as a college student, are not enough to determine social media's usefulness in the traditional classroom setting. As a result, I held two Q&A sessions with my students to better understand their fears as well as to gain insights on the effects of my social media assignments per students' explicated experiences.

This chapter, therefore, outlines those two Q&A sessions. Although this chapter is divided into five parts (methodology and pedagogy; teacher-student Q&As; implications; and conclusion), it does not theoretically examine my classroom methodology or pedagogical practices nor does it argue for a particular writing practice or social network platform. Instead, this chapter relies on student feedback in an effort to encourage educators who integrate or plan to include social media networks into their classrooms to be more mindful of their students' hesitancies and trepidations as well as students' needs regarding alternative social media use.

We teachers often assume that our 21ˢᵗ century students are socially networked students, and therefore, require little to no instruction regarding social media use beyond their regular status posting, tagging, and updating. However, as we get to know our students, we will discover our assumptions lead to careless classroom practices—and sometimes even back paddling. Although universities often require its professors to create a semester long syllabus prior to meeting their students, in order to meet students where they are, we have to build relationships with our students first, and from there, we can create classroom assignments that promise to be more meaningful for each of them. With that said, this chapter serves as a reminder that as teachers engage new pedagogical practices, our practices do not become meaningful because they are cutting edge; they are meaningful because they are grounded in purpose.

METHODOLOGY AND PEDAGOGY

Purpose of *Technical Writing:* Course Objectives

FAMU's *Technical Writing* course is not supported by any departmental curriculum. There is no required departmental textbook, no departmental syllabus, and no departmental course objectives. According to the departmental website, however, *Technical Writing* "emphasizes clear expository writing of memoranda, reports, and articles in student's particular field" (famu.edu). With that said, I have free reign regarding my pedagogical approaches to teaching *Technical Writing*. Therefore, I approached the course as if it were a professional writing course with objectives that included: writing resumes, cover letters, personal statements; mastering team skills and interpersonal communication; crafting messages for electronic media; and developing oral and online presentations and portfolios. In an effort to ensure that students were writing in their particular field—which the university's website description details— I required writing assignments that asked students to write expository essays that discuss the current trends in their chosen majors.

Although the last two course objectives were aimed directly at online writing, the entire course required students to engage in online writing. Considering my own experiences and the research (Blair, 1998; Banks, 2006; Snipes, Ellis, & Thomas, 2006; and Blackmon, 2007) that support my notions that most Black students do not have the same access to and/or academic practice with writing with online social media networks as their White counterparts, I integrated WordPress—a content management system and blogging platform—into my *Technical Writing* class. More specifically, students were required to use WordPress for two reasons: 1. to create an online employment portfolio; and 2. to explore their academic and professional interests by way of blogging. Students were also required to create LinkedIn profiles and Twitter accounts, both of which they had to link to their WordPress accounts in order to strengthen their professional online persona and communication skills. Erin Trauth writes about this very idea in her chapter, "Curating the Public Self."

And so, the purpose of *Technical Writing* is to help students compose professional identities by way of traditional writing practices and assignments, coupled with the 21ˢᵗ century demands and expectations of online writing.

Required Resources

Students were required to have only one textbook: *Handbook of Technical Writing*, 11ᵗʰ edition, by Alfred Gerald, Charles Brusaw, and Oliu Walter. They used this textbook to support their in-class writing activities, specifically resumes, cover letters, personal statements, recommendation letters, and memos. They also used their handbooks to aid their practices in grammar, mechanics, and sentence structure as well as paragraph development. The handbook includes chapter readings on blogs, emails, and online presentations, which provided students basic insights regarding their larger online writing assignments. I provided students with additional instruction regarding their social media requirements usually by way of in class lecture, handouts, and supplementary reading materials, as noted in the Implications and Conclusion section later in this chapter.

In addition to their required texts, students were required to have outside of class access to computers and the Internet, maintain a concrete three ring-binder that serves as a traditional writing portfolio, and have already taken and passed (with a C or higher) *Freshman Communicative Skills I & II*. They were also required to use Blackboard, the online academic content management system that FAMU has adopted, where students received class announcements, assignments and instructions, and grades.

Integrating WordPress, LinkedIn, and Twitter

WordPress

Students enrolled in *Technical Writing* were required to use WordPress to create online employment portfolios and to blog about their academic/professional interests. As a content management system, WordPress allows its users to create a website complete with themes, headers, links, static pages, and widgets (applications that take the form of onscreen devices such as clocks, calendars, searching tools, archives, and Twitter feeds). Therefore, each student used WordPress to host his or her required biographical sketch, resume and personal statement—all of which were assigned, peer reviewed, and revised in a traditional classroom setting and later posted on student WordPress accounts.

At about the third week of the semester after student schedules were secured, students—98% of whom claimed to have never heard of WordPress—were given instruction by way of classroom lecture on how to create their WordPress accounts and to utilize the system. In order to limit frustration and to maximize our time, I carefully assisted students in navigating WordPress and offered them detailed instruction. We basically built WordPress together, step-by-step, so that no student was left behind.

Before students posted any of their class assignments online, students were asked to familiarize themselves with WordPress by reading Wikipedia entries about it and to peruse my own website. Then they were required to simply create their accounts, which I orally explained while giving students a virtual tour, if you will, of WordPress. Via the classroom overhead projector, I projected the WordPress site to students, while reciting their online tasks step-by-step. Through orated instruction, students were told to:

1. Go to wordpress.com and create an account using their first and last name as their web address. If students' first and last names are already taken by another user, I require students to use some variation of their name.
2. Create four static pages: About Me, Resume, Personal Statement, and Blog.
3. Assign their WordPress account a title (preferably their first and last name).
4. Include an inspirational quote as their WordPress tagline.
5. Choose a theme that speaks to their professional/academic self.

I allotted about a week for students to complete these online tasks, after which time, I checked each student's progress by way of informal in class presentations where students were required to use the teacher's computer desk to project their WordPress accounts. At that time, students shared their challenges and fixed any hiccups while at the computer station. Additionally, students received ideas from their classmates regarding account themes and design.

After these primary online tasks and in class showcases, as the semester progressed, students were instructed on how to post their two paragraph biographies(About Me), resumes, and personal statements to their respective pages. Before any content was posted online, however, students submitted typed drafts of their writing assignments to class for peer review, and again for my teacher comments, in order to minimize mistakes in grammar, mechanics, sentence structure, and the like. In essence, students still engaged traditional classroom practices: They participated in the writing process, discussed rhetorical elements, and studied business communications in the workplace; however, their online writing component required them to rethink (read: revise) their rhetorical decisions, carefully proofread and edit their work, and shift from a teacher-focused audience to a public audience. Additionally, the course's online writing requirement offered students a space that managed their content, or archived their writing assignments, while providing them an audience that extended the classroom.

Once students posted their biographies (complete with a professional headshot), revised resumes and personal statements to their WordPress accounts—all of which were completed by mid-semester—students spent the remaining semester blogging about the current trends in their academic/professional subject areas. To encourage their blogging practice and in-field research, I offered students their first writing (blogging) prompt: *Who is the person in your academic field that you admire, and why?* Students were not given any other instruction about their blog, except to ensure that their response was one page (at least five paragraphs long) with a clear beginning, middle, and end and was posted to their Blog page. After students completed their first blog, I required each of them to email me their WordPress account link so that I could review student accounts, which by then looked like functional websites and blogging spaces. From that point forward, students received feedback about their WordPress accounts and were required to submit weekly blog posts every Monday. Their instructions for their remaining blog entries were as follows:

Type a one-page blog post on WordPress about a current trend in your academic/professional field. Note: Your post should not simply be a summary of that trend, but your contribution to the current discussion. For instance, a current debate in higher education is whether universities should still grant faculty tenure. My blog post would be my informed opinion/argument re: tenure and promotion at universities.

Add your post to WordPress, and print a copy (in Word) for in class submission.

I incorporated LinkedIn and Twitter into their class requirements about mid-semester, after students had successfully met all of their WordPress requirements and were actively blogging.

LinkedIn

I gave very little instruction to students regarding how to create LinkedIn profiles. First, LinkedIn, which is a website directed for professional networking, is a lot more user-friendlier than WordPress. LinkedIn is neither a website, per se, nor is it a blogging platform. Additionally, while not all of my students had a LinkedIn account prior to theircourse requirement, many of them were familiar with LinkedIn; those of them who were not, were encouraged to peruse Wikipedia's explication and gather information about it. Moreover, since LinkedIn is predominantly made up of user resumes and curriculum vitaes, creating a LinkedIn account simply required students to upload their resumes—which, by mid-semester when students are required to create their LinkedIn profiles, had already been written, revised, and uploaded to their WordPress accounts. With all of that said, the only instruction students were given regarding their LinkedIn accounts is to complete their online profile, including uploading a professional headshot, and linking their LinkedIn accounts to their WordPress accounts in order to maximize their marketability.

Twitter

Students received no instruction for their Twitter use, since the majority of students enrolled in the class already had a Twitter account. Even the students who did not have Twitter accounts didn't need instruction on how to use it, and if they did, their classmates assisted them. (What I have learned as a teacher who integrates computer technologies into the classroom is that the challenges students encounter as a result often lend itself to classroom community.) Nevertheless, like LinkedIn, students were required to link their Twitter accounts to their WordPress accounts, while also including a widget that allowed their Twitter feed to appear directly on their WordPress pages. In an effort to assist students—especially those who were not regularly Tweeting—to post daily tweets, I offered them tweet topics such as: *During Black History month, tweet an "A Moment in Black History" statement, such as a biographical sketch of a Black inventor.* Students were also instructed to use the hashtag #FAMUtechwrite in order to archive their Tweets in one communal space for their classmates and me to read and/or retweet, love, and respond.

Participants and Setting

There were 22 students enrolled in the *Technical Writing* course I taught. The class was predominantly African American with one Vietnamese student and two biracial students—one Black and White, the other Black, White, and Mexican. Students ranged in age; the 20 students who participated in the Q&A included: one 18-year-old, three 19-year-olds, seven 20-year-olds, seven 21-year-olds, one 22-year-old, and one 32-year-old. The majority of the students are first generation college students from low-income households. Many of them were criminal justice majors, while others majored in STEM (science, technology, engineering, and mathematics), psychology, and business administration. While there were no English majors in the course, there were two English minors.

According to an in class questionnaire I distributed in class, each of the student participants—except for one—actively belonged to an online social media network as outlined in Table 1.

Table 1. Student social media use

Social Media Platform	Student Users
Facebook	19
Twitter	19
Instagram	18
SnapChat	13
MySpace	6
LinkedIn	5
Tumblr	3
Other (Reddit, Google+, Vine, MocoSpace, Foursquare, Path, YouTube, GroupMe)	9

Although only one student noted belonging to GroupMe, the majority of the students participated in GroupMe in order to keep up with class assignments and activities. So interestingly, students didn't identify GroupMe as a social media network. Additionally, each student surveyed, with the exception of the 32-year-old student, noted that she began her online social networking activities with MySpace. None of the students had WordPress accounts prior to taking the *Technical Writing* course.

Each student has out-of-class access to computers, and they each access their online social media networks with their smart phones; one student claimed to also use his tablet, while three others still rely on their desktops/laptops. Finally, while the majority of the students surveyed said they had not been required to engage online social media in their other courses, nine students claimed having been required to use online social media in classes such as *Engineering Professionalism, Professional Development*, and *Journalism*.

The Q&A sessions took place during two class periods at Florida A&M University, a historically black university which was founded in 1887 to service "underrepresented" and "underprivileged" students. FAMU is one of the top ranked universities for studies in pharmacy, allied health, and agriculture and is home to one of the most affluent journalism programs in the southern region (*famu.edu*). With circa 8,000 enrolled students, and about 35 English faculty members, the university caps its writing courses at 22 students for *Freshman Communicative Skills I & II* and 25 for the remaining courses including *Technical Writing, Improving Writing*, and *Advanced Composition*.

TEACHER-STUDENT Q&A: PART ONE

The initial questionnaire, which was distributed at the start of the semester, included 13 questions grounded in demographic information. Additionally, questions were grounded in students' social media use, all of which were explicated in the *Participants and Setting* section above. However, there are three questions posed in that initial questionnaire worth sharing here:

1. Do you experience some trepidation/hesitancies when professors require social media in the classroom? Explain.
2. Why do you engage in online social media?

3. How do you think social media could best be used in a writing classroom? In other words, how would you implement social media in the writing classroom if you could?

Student Responses to Question #1

Of the 20 students questioned about their online social media activity, seven of them expressed trepidation about being required to integrate their social media into the traditional classroom space. Their responses are provided in Figure 1.

Figure 1. Student trepidation: students claim uneasiness about using social media in the classroom

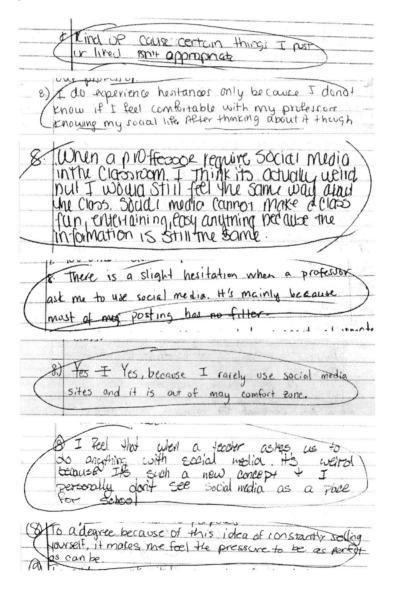

Student Responses to Question #2

All of the students who were asked, "Why do you engage in online social media?" noted that they either use social media for entertainment and information or to stay connected with family and friends. One student even claimed:

I engage in social media because I am an introvert and socializing in person drains me. With social media, I can 'stay on the charger' and be ready to socialize whenever.

None of the students surveyed, however, noted using their online social media networks to create an academic/professional brand and/or to market themselves beyond daily expressions of fanfare.

Student Responses to Question #3

Of the 20 students asked about how they would integrate social media in the writing classroom, half of them claimed that they would use online social media communities as spaces for teacher criticism and writing practice. Surprisingly, students believe that online public writing spaces are ideal for practicing grammar. The other half of students noted that they would integrate online social media communities in the following ways:

- As bulletin boards, if you will, where students post their final compositions to their sites;
- As practice in clear writing and critical thinking where students use Twitter to tweet about complex topics;
- As spaces for self-expression where students "write a post about their day everyday" or "view an event on TV or in person and tweet their thoughts on it";
- As a word board where students "post definitions of new words learned"; and
- As discussion threads.

With the exception of Twitter, students did not identify a particular social media platform for hypothetical assignments. However, one student did claim that "besides LinkedIn and blogs, I can't think of an effective way to implement social media in a writing class."

TEACHER-STUDENT Q&A: PART TWO

After receiving students' initial responses regarding their (surface) interactions with social media, I distributed another more thought-provoking questionnaire intended to probe students' thoughts and behaviors since using social media networks to help them brand their professional/academic selves. I asked students four questions, all of which are boldfaced below with italicized student responses following each of them. While I have not included each student response here, student responses more or less mirror one another.

Question 1: How has using social media in *Technical Writing* made you aware (or not) of how you conduct or create your online profile, and what changes (if any) have you made to your online activity?

Answers:

It is actually helpful that we use social media in class. I had to make a lot of changes to my Twitter that really wasn't professional at all. It made me aware that companies do look at your social media. I believed only athletes had to go through that process. I feel more professional that my Twitter is connected to my Wordpress so I have to watch what I say or do. It has prepared me to face the business world, and my social media won't affect me.

I used social media to connect with family and friends. We would share jokes, and at times, distasteful material. Upon entering this class, I've learned how to use social media to better market myself. I've replaced the jokes with more educational material. I feel more professional and confident. I worry less about who's viewing my sites.

I feel like since I made my website, I'm ready for Corporate America because most people applying for jobs don't have a website. By having a website, I have a slight edge over applicants.

Using social media during this class has made me change what I put out there. It has made me realize that some personal things about how I feel should be kept private. It has also made me feel more professional because I watch my word choice and how I say things.

Prior to enrolling in the Technical Writing class, it was not brought to my attention that people in the professional world would look my profile up on Twitter. Although I would never post anything that I would not want the world to see, I am more professional in the things I write online.

My social media use in Technical Writing class made me look at all of my social media differently. Prior to this course, my online profiles had images and post I would not want any business to look at. Creating these new profiles helped me feel more professional but made me realize that I am not prepared to meet Corporate America.

The use of social media in class came off a bit odd. My awareness definitely piqued in what I post and who I follow. When told we had to use Twitter, I immediately thought about the fact that I had to make a new one because the last was not in the least bit professional.

Question 2: Before *Technical Writing*, how have you used social media to brand your professional/ academic self?

Answers:

I never did, which is crazy, right? I created a LinkedIn account a while ago, but I never actually decided to really do anything with it. I think the concern of not having enough 'stuff behind my name' deterred me from wanting to post really anything academically.

Before this class, I haven't used social media to brand my professional/academic self. I always thought social media should be separate from professional/academic setting.

I never thought of social media to brand myself. I didn't think that I will have a class that would integrate social media as homework.

Before Tech Writing, I did not use online social media to brand my professional/academic self, esides putting where I work and which school I attend on Facebook.

Before Technical Writing, I did not use online social media to brand myself on a professional level because I didn't know that was possible.

The most professional brand I used was making my Gmail account my name and posing a professional picture of myself.

Before Technical Writing I utilized Instagram to brand myself. If I was speaking on a panel or attending a meeting for a particular club, I made sure I constantly posted the flyer with the time and information.

I have utilized LinkedIn to put together a professional profile. I have linked with different recruiters hoping to increase my chances of getting noticed.

I created a LinkedIn page over the summer to stay in contact with any professional connections I made.

Question 3: How do you feel about having social media integrated into your *Technical Writing* class? In other words, would you prefer not to interact with social media at all while taking traditional classes, and if so, why?

Answers:

I like the social media aspect and feel that it is a good addition to the course. It opens the students up to new platforms.

I feel that it is necessary. Although I prefer not to use social media, the work being done in this class is viable. Not saying social media makes it viable, but that social media integrated into the curriculum is a crucial part of being viable.

Some social media sites like Facebook I prefer not to integrate because there is a lot of my personal information that I only share with a selected audience.

Yes, I would prefer not to interact with social media at all while taking traditional classes because social media may be places where you like to vent and hear people's opinions about situations that's not always professional. If you always have to be professional, then what's the point of having social media?

I love it.

I think we should interact on social media in classes because it is teaching us how to conduct ourselves in a professional manner. It shows us how to act in the real world because people are always watching you do.

I like the fact that it opens doors I never really thought about entering before. I do prefer to use it in the class because it forces me to do something I should have been doing.

I feel that it's a new way of teaching that I haven't seen before. It seems appropriate since social media is a big part of life our generation.

It helps a lot that the class uses social media. I never knew about WordPress or LinkedIn at all. It helped better prepare myself to get a job and stand out from other job seekers.

I like the added use of social media. It is very interesting on how modern this approach is.

Questions 4: Before *Technical Writing*, how did you use Twitter, LinkedIn, and/or WordPress?

Answers:

I did not use these social networks before Technical Writing.

Before this class, I had a Twitter, but was not a constant user. I have never heard of WordPress before this class. I have heard of LinkedIn but didn't have an account until this class because I didn't think I had any majorly important professional/academic information that would help me at that time.

Before Technical Writing, I only had a Twitter account. I used it as a site to express my feelings.

Before this class, I used Twitter recklessly. I didn't use the right grammar. I was lazy on what I wrote, but I didn't put everything out there. I knew about LinkedIn but didn't use it. I didn't know anything about WordPress.

Before this class, I never used Twitter at all that much. I didn't know anything about WordPress. I didn't have a LinkedIn. Now I plan to use it as part of my professional future.

I used Twitter to talk to friends, girls, and if I missed any important event, Twitter informs me. I never had neither a LinkedIn nor WordPress. It was my first time hearing about these two sites.

IMPLICATIONS

I had not required students to connect their Twitter accounts to their WordPress threads before this course, and as a result, I realized that my integrating social media into the classroom had been successful thus far because I was integrating WordPress, an online social media network with which students were unfamiliar. None of my *Technical Writing* students were privy to WordPress before taking the course, and less than half of them were familiar with LinkedIn. Those students who were aware of LinkedIn claimed disengagement as a result of their own disinterest and/or feelings of inadequacy.

What I have learned from these students—each of whom is familiar with or do engage Twitter (and other more popular online social media spaces like Instagram, Facebook, and Snapchat)—is twofold:

1. Students do not experience uneasiness about in-class social media use that they either:
    a. Do not regularly use; or
    b. With which they are unfamiliar.
2. Students are not aware of the effects that their online social media use has on their professional branding and job marketability.

Each of the students questioned about his social media interactions began engaging in online social media (specifically, MySpace) while he was an elementary school student. Based on these results, not one of them realized the effects that her online social media networking has on her branding and marketability. In short, most of my college students had been carelessly using social media for the past 7-10 years and maintaining online profiles that discredited their professional selves. While my *Technical Writing* students were adamant about not integrating their Twitter accounts to their in-class WordPress assignments because of the inappropriate content expressed on their Twitter feeds, students had not considered before then the possible effects that their Twitter communications would have on their job marketing. Therefore, students enrolled in a university that promises to graduate career ready students, require writing practice that transcends those often associated with traditional composition courses. After all, today's University is a liaison, if you will, between students and prospective employers.

In addition to realizing that my 21st century *Technical Writing* students needed some insight regarding the effects of online social media use on their job marketing and professional development, students' initial trepidation regarding their required Twitter use made me aware of a privacy issue I had not considered. While I believe that not inviting students' at-home experiences (like their social media network interactions) into the classroom is a disservice to 21st century learners inundated with online social media platforms, I had not considered students' own feelings regarding privacy. My lack of consideration, therefore, made me more aware of other possible issues (like religion, safety, attachment, and vulnerability) I had never considered while integrating social media platforms into the academic setting.

In other words:

How do I integrate a social media requirement in a class where an orthodox Muslim student believes having a social media account infringes upon her religious beliefs? How does a female student who is hiding from an abusive boyfriend maintain her safety in a classroom that requires a social media project? Should a student who has consciously decided to stay off of social media in an effort to focus her attention on her studies, be required to engage online social media platforms? Would requiring a student who has encountered cyber bullying to create an online social media profile be detrimental to his emotional self?

Surely, these issues (and more) can be resolved by allowing students to simply opt out of social media assignments; however, these issues reminded me that no assignment is one-size-fits all—no matter how cutting edge and time appropriate that assignment might be.

CONCLUSION

Writing teachers who aim to assist 21st century students in improving their writing practices must consider writing situations beyond the traditional modes of essay writing; and, they must consider writing environments that extend the classroom location. Therefore, integrating online social media networks into students' writing tasks feels quite necessary. However, as is the case with all new pedagogies, teachers need to feel prepared and able to introduce new teaching practices into the classroom, especially one as dynamic as the 21st century classroom.

I could not have begun to discuss social media with my students if I didn't have and actively use the platforms I ask my students to engage in our classroom writing practices. I have learned to use social media via trial and error; however, I have relied on Wikipedia to provide me with historical underpinnings of each platform as well as explications of the platform's function and feature. I have also googled troubleshooting questions and have often been directed to the platform's troubleshooting guide that I obviously wasn't able to locate prior to my Google search. Because I have and actively use WordPress, LinkedIn, and Twitter accounts, my students trust that I have sufficient skills to teach them about social media beyond their personal, uninhibited uses.

In addition to my own trial and error tutorials, I have perused various books and articles that offer both instruction and theories regarding social media. I have often provided my students with these readings in order to guide our classroom discussions. A few of my classroom staples include: Nicholas Carr's 2008 "Is Google Making Us Stupid?"; Douglas Rushkoff's 2011 *Program or Be Programmed*; Courtland Bovee and John Thill's 2014 "Crafting Messages for Electronic Media," from *Business Communications Essentials: A Skills-Based Approach*, 6th edition; and research from the Pew Research Center at http://www.pewinternet.org/.

Finally, my students are my greatest assets. I seek their help with using recently released social media platforms like Snapchat and Instagram. From my experiences, students are more than happy to teach me how to use these programs, to gain followers, and to access features that have recently been updated and/or added to particular platforms. Students have also assisted me in WordPress use. I have found that once I introduce students to WordPress, and then require weekly tasks with it, students become more adapted to the program than I am. To date, students have assisted me with customizing WordPress headers, adding visible LinkedIn buttons, and creating picture collages. By allowing my students to teach me, I displace the teacher-student hierarchy that often contributes to distance and distrust. As my students and I engage social media use on what feels like equal footing, the classroom becomes a "real life" communal space of shared knowledge, quite reflective of the "virtual" social media spaces to which our students currently belong.

Undoubtedly, online social media platforms that students already engage are worthwhile pedagogical resources, especially for a writing classroom, since each of these platforms require some type of composition. Additionally, because many students are so attached to their social media networks and the technologies that they use to access them, integrating social media into a traditional classroom setting assumingly makes the course more relative, timely, and engaging. However, because of students' regular online social media use—which rarely considers an audience outside of students' family, friends, and followers—students do require some in-classroom instruction regarding how to create (or curate) their professional online personas. They also need to feel safe in a classroom that requires they bring their personal selves, via their online social connections, into the traditional learning environment. In order to achieve these two important tasks, instructors need to know their students, as well as the social media platforms that they are asking students to engage. If teachers are to promise students a meaningful classroom experience, then teachers must attend to students' whole selves—mind, body, and soul—through both an academic and professional lens.

REFERENCES

Banks, A. (2006). *Race, rhetoric, & technology: Searching for higher ground*. Mahwah: Laurence Erlbaum Associates, Inc.

Blackmon, S. (2007). (Cyber)conspiracy theories? African-American students in the computerized writing environment. In P. Takayoshi & P. Sullivan's (Eds.), Labor, writing technologies, and the shaping of composition in the academy: New Directions in computers and composition (pp. 153-166). New York: Hampton Press.

Blair, K. (1998). Literacy, dialogue, & difference in the "electronic contact zone.". *Computers and Composition, 15*(3), 317–319. doi:10.1016/S8755-4615(98)90004-4

Bryant, K. (2013a). Composing online: Integrating blogging into a contemplative classroom. In K. Pytash and R. Ferdig's (Eds.), Exploring technology for writing and writing instruction (pp. 77-99). Hershey: IGI Global.

Bryant, K. (2013b). Me/we: Building an 'embodied' classroom for socially networked, socially distracted basic writers. *Journal of Basic Writing, 31*(2), 51–79.

Gerald, A., Brusaw, C., & Walter, O. (2015). *Handbook of Technical Writing. Boston*. Bedford: St. Martin's.

Snipes, V., Ellis, W., & Thomas, J. (2006). Are HBCUs up to speed technologically? One case study. *Journal of Black Studies, 36*(3), 382–395. doi:10.1177/0021934705278782

Section 5
Re-Envisioning Wikis in the Writing Classroom

Although rarely referred to as a social media platform, the authors in this section invite readers to explore Wiki's capacity for teaching students how to interact with and write for "real" audiences, while improving student writing skills, including their revising and editing practice.

Chapter 15
Using Wikipedia to Teach Written Health Communication

Melissa Vosen Callens
North Dakota State University, USA

ABSTRACT

Unlike first-year writing courses, upper-division writing courses often require students to engage in discipline specific writing. In the author's upper-division course, Writing in the Health Professions, students examine health literacy as it pertains to both oral and written patient-provider communication. Students edit and expand a Wikipedia article for the final course assignment. The advantages of this assignment are threefold. First, students write for an authentic audience, decreasing student apathy. Second, students engage civically, improving health information accessed by millions of people across the world. Finally, students improve content of existing articles and broaden the scope of new articles written, leading to more diverse content and perspectives. In this chapter, the author discusses the above assignment, providing descriptions of scaffolding activities. Potential drawbacks of using Wikipedia to teach students how to write using plain language is discussed, in addition to strategies that might limit these difficulties.

INTRODUCTION

At North Dakota State University (NDSU), a land-grant research institution, I teach several upper-division writing courses: *Writing in the Health Professions*, *Business and Professional Writing*, and *Visual Culture and Language*. Unlike first-year composition courses, upper-division writing courses at NDSU require students to engage in discipline-specific research and writing. These 300-level courses are meant to prepare students for the workplace and / or graduate school. The primary focus of my *Writing in the Health Professions* course is health literacy as it pertains to both oral and written patient-provider communication. According to Osborne (2004), nurse and health literacy advocate, health literacy is "a shared responsibility in which patients and providers each must communicate in ways the other can understand" (p. 2). I believe health literacy is an important and appropriate focus for the course, as it best simulates the writing my students will engage in as healthcare professionals. While I could ask students to review

DOI: 10.4018/978-1-5225-0562-4.ch015

and / or write journal articles, both common upper-division writing assignments, realistically, most of these students will not formally review or write a journal article after graduation.

For the foreseeable future, most of my students will not be attending graduate school or working in a lab in academia. Upon graduation, a majority of the students will enter the workforce as pharmacists or registered nurses. Some students will get promotions from their current employers as they already work as pharmacy technicians, licensed practical nurses, or certified nursing assistants. When in the workplace, most will be asked to write to inform, to educate both colleagues and patients on a variety of work and health-related issues. With either of the above audiences, these students will be expected to write in a clear and concise manner. They will be expected to communicate using plain language. In my course, students quickly learn that plain language does not mean changing the meaning of their message; rather, plain language is using words and concepts people already know and understand. If that is not possible, words and concepts should be clearly defined in a manner that the reader can understand (Osborne, 2004, p. 157). Last summer, I asked students to expand a Wikipedia article of their choosing to hone their ability to communicate in a clear and concise manner. In addition to learning more about how to use plain language, students sharpened their research skills and understanding of how social media can facilitate collaboration. This chapter explores that endeavor, explaining both the benefits and pitfalls of using Wikipedia in a writing course.

THEORETICAL FRAMEWORK

Wikipedia: An Educational Social Media Platform

Some may argue that Wikipedia is not a social media site; rather, as its name suggests, it is an online reference book, an encyclopedia. While it is an online encyclopedia, Wikipedia is also a social media platform because anyone can contribute and exchange information on the site; Wikipedia is a collaborative endeavor. Wikipedia has a community of users that has a common goal: a desire to educate and make knowledge available to every single person on Earth—or at least every single person with access to a computer and the Internet. All Wikipedians (what contributors to Wikipedia are called) have their own user talk pages where they are encouraged to share information about themselves and their personal editing philosophy. They are also encouraged to share their reasoning behind each of their edits and contributions.

In addition to user talk pages, each article on Wikipedia has a talk page in which users can discuss the article's content as well as any edits prior to publishing those changes. Wikipedia encourages discussion on talk pages before changes are made. For talk pages that generate a large amount of conversation, Wikipedia archives these discussions to help keep the talk page easy-to-read and up-to-date (Help: Using talk pages, n.d.). Archiving these discussions documents the collaborative process of contributing users and is a great way to see how an article evolved. Talk areas provide Wikipedians, including student Wikipedians, a chance to communicate, socialize, and learn from one another. In addition to learning about Wikipedia and the collaborative writing process, students working on Wikipedia can improve their editing and grammar knowledge, hone their research skills, and learn how to communicate using plain language.

Collaborative Writing and ELL Learners

If an instructor wants students to learn more about collaborative writing and the Internet, he/she might require students to become active on several articles' talk pages and work with other Wikipedians to develop and tweak content. Developing a relationship with other editors is particularly fruitful for English language learners (ELL) as they learn more about the English language from native speakers across the world. Furthermore, if an instructor wants ELL students to practice their newly acquired skills, he / she might ask the students to translate an article in English to their native language, adding it to their native languages' Wikipedia site. This gives students much needed practice, but also expands Wikipedia, likely introducing more diverse content to different language versions of the site. Similarly, Wikipedia is also a great site to study if one wants to discuss differences between languages and dialects of languages, such as British English and American English. An introductory linguistics course may find this exercise useful.

Editing and Grammar

If an instructor wants students to learn more about grammar, he / she might ask students to edit articles and explain their choices and their editing philosophy to the class. In addition to engaging in a dialogue with their classmates, students may also have to explain their editing choices to other Wikipedians. While this may initially be overwhelming for some students, it is a great exercise in community and collaboration. If the dialogue goes in a negative direction, and it sometimes does, this is a teachable moment. Students can learn more about trolling and how to respond to people who engage in this type of activity on the Internet.

Research

If an instructor wants students to learn more about researching and presenting material from a neutral point-of-view, he / she might ask students to write a new article on a topic of their choosing or develop a "stub" article. A stub article on Wikipedia is an article that has been started, but has been flagged because it lacks content and needs to be developed. Any registered user can start a stub article. Expanding a stub article is a great alternative to traditional reports often assigned in writing courses. Students are still expected to find credible information and summarize and synthesize it. The primary difference between a Wikipedia entry and a traditional report is that students are writing for an audience beyond the four classroom walls. Since students often lack motivation in required general education courses, including first-year and upper-division composition courses, one way to avoid student apathy is to involve students in a writing activity that has an authentic audience (Graham & Harris, 2007, p.124). Writing for people other than their instructor and classmates can be highly motivating for some students, which is what can happen when students contribute to Wikipedia.

Plain Language in the Health Professions

Finally, when I was first assigned to teach *Writing in the Health Professions,* I found it difficult to teach pharmacy and nursing students, who have been immersed in medical jargon and academese for at least three years, to communicate using plain language. Studying Wikipedia, however, was a helpful way for these students to understand what type of information their patients do comprehend and *are* accessing and reading prior to their visits with healthcare providers. For example, Tunick and Brand (2015) note that "an August 2013 Google search yielded over 2 billion hits for 'health information,' 774 million hits for 'cancer information,' and 7.5 million hits for 'pediatric cancer information'" (p. 346). This translates to an incredible number of people seeking written healthcare information on the Internet. Is that information, however, easy to read and medically accurate? In my course, the students explored this question from a variety of angles.

In their study on Web 2.0 use by junior physicians, Hughes, Joshi, Lemonde, and Wareham (2009) noted that all 35 participants mentioned Internet use by patients, "such as receiving and discussing Wikipedia printouts during a patient consultation" (p. 651). This study was a perfect starting point for class discussion, as it helped explain why we were studying social media and plain language in an upper-division writing course. The students' patients and future patients already use Wikipedia. As medical providers, it is in my students' best interest to learn more about the site.

Because of its wide use, I believe it is important for my students to know what information is available on social media. It is also important that they understand how sites like Wikipedia work, as this knowledge will better prepare them for conversations with patients. In addition, because of the wide use of social media, it is important to encourage students to improve information on these sites, as they are near experts in their field.

METHODOLOGY AND PEDAGOGY

Participants

Students enrolled in my asynchronous online *Writing in the Health Professions* were juniors and seniors at NDSU; while most lived in the immediate area, some of the students were three hours away at a satellite campus. All of the students who completed the Wikipedia assignment (14) had been accepted into the nursing professional program, which means they had a minimum GPA of 2.75. For most of the students, they were introduced to genre theory in their first-year writing course(s). After being immersed in their nursing classes for three years, however, most of my students had forgotten about genre theory and how it relates to writing. In addition, there were a small number (three) of non-traditional students, who had returned to school after years in the workforce. These students took first-year English years ago, and some even took the course when it focused more on literature. Because of this, at the beginning of the course, we spent time reviewing genre theory. What are the genre conventions of lab reports? What are the conventions of patient charts? At the start of each unit, we reviewed genre theory and discussed what genre they would be exploring next, including, at the end of the semester, Wikipedia articles.

Purpose

The culminating project required students to improve, by editing and expanding, a Wikipedia article related to healthcare. This was an appropriate culminating project for a variety of reasons. First, by contributing to Wikipedia, students contributed to their field in a large and meaningful way—potentially educating hundreds of thousands of people—as many people use Wikipedia to obtain information. When writing for Wikipedia, students wrote for the general public, which helped them better understand audience and voice. Anyone with a computer and an Internet connection—family, friends, potential employers, and strangers—could see their work. Whether we, as instructors, like it or not, many people use Wikipedia as one of their primary go-to places for information on just about any topic. There were 8,524,715 views per hour during May 2015 on Wikipedia (Wikimedia, 2015). From a medical standpoint, these views were not simply from patients, but also providers. In their study on Web 2.0 use in the medical field, Hughes, Joshi, Lemonde, and Wareham (2009) found that tools like Google or Wikipedia are being "regularly employed in clinical practice by junior physicians" (p. 654). Not only would my students encounter patients using Wikipedia and other Web 2.0 technologies, but they also would likely end up using these resources as medical professionals.

Second, and most importantly for upper-division writing instructors, my students learned how to research a topic, find appropriate and credible sources, and present that information from a concise and neutral point-of-view. Third, students learned how to communicate using plain language. They were required to identify and consider the literacy levels of the general public. Finally, students learned (or relearned) how to properly cite sources and produce grammatically correct documents. As a secondary benefit, but one worth noting, this assignment also brought different and varied voices to the Wikipedia community. Student writers in a variety of disciplines can help make Wikipedia more diverse in regard to content *and* perspective. Based on a survey of 58,000 self-selected Wikipedians, "23% of contributors have completed degree-level education, 26% are undergraduates and 45% have secondary education or less. 87% are men and 13% women" (Wikipedia: Wikipedians, n.d.). In my course, 13 of the 14 students were female; by asking these students to complete this assignment, new female voices were introduced to the site.

Building up to Wikipedia

My students completed several scaffolding activities to ensure they not only understood the nuts-and-bolts of editing and contributing to Wikipedia, but also the community aspect of Wikipedia and how knowledge could be generated collaboratively. It was important to explain clearly why they were being asked to undertake this assignment, as many of my students had been told that Wikipedia is not a resource they should use in the classroom or otherwise. More of this will be discussed in a later section of this chapter, "Pitfalls."

Prior to the Wikipedia assignment, students completed several assignments that helped them think about how their patients find health-related information as well as if they comprehend it. For one of their first assignments, students identified a healthcare-related topic currently covered in the media and compared the popular media stories to peer-reviewed medical research on the same topic. The primary purpose of this assignment was so students learned how to evaluate health information from a variety of sources and see firsthand how accurate the media was at presenting health information. They also learned how to critical analyze a medical report, which is an important skill to have if they are going to take complex medical information and summarize it using plain language for their patients.

By understanding how to analyze medical research as well as how the media informs or misinforms the public, my students are better prepared to have conversations with their patients about evaluating medical information obtained on the Web. Health News Review (http://www.healthnewsreview.org/) provided my students with a set of ten criteria to use when analyzing popular media stories. The criterion helped students perform a systematic review and analysis of the media stories. Their review and analysis ultimately led to an evaluation, an evaluation similar to the ones they would likely have to provide in the workforce and an evaluation they would have to make before adding content to Wikipedia.

In addition, before moving to the Wikipedia assignment, students completed one other systematic review of health information. Students analyzed a healthcare document from a facility of their choosing using Helen Osborne's plain language checklist. These documents were typically patient-education brochures, handouts, or posters hung in pharmacies or clinics. Both of the above assignments helped students understand where patients currently get their information and how accessible and accurate that information might be. It helped them get a better understanding of plain language and how it is or is not used effectively in a healthcare setting. At this point the course, students evaluated Wikipedia articles on the same topic or related topics and chose an article to expand. Since they had already explored the topic in medical journals, popular media stories, and clinic literature, they had a good understanding of the information that was available to patients and what information was correct and what information was being misrepresented.

Resources

The WikiEd Foundation (https://wikiedu.org/) has great resources available to instructors, most of which I used. First, it offered an assignment generator that produced a course schedule for me to use, complete with scaffolding activities. It also offered several brochures related to planning a course, in addition to brochures that could be given to students. In an attempt to create an assignment that met my needs, when completing the assignment generator, I was asked to identify what type of project I was interested in assigning as well as how much time I wished to devote to the assignment. In addition to those questions, I also answered a series of questions that helped generate scaffolding activities that might be appropriate for the class. After I completed the generator, a schedule and rubric for the assignment was produced as well as a course page on Wikipedia. The WikiEd Foundation recommended a course page as it provided a space for my students to converse on Wikipedia, and it also made tracking student work much simpler. Without this function, it would have been difficult to determine what changes students made to articles, particularly if other Wikipedians removed those changes. In addition to the course page, the WikiEd Foundation also had a dashboard for me to use, which made tracking student activity and contributions even easier.

Scaffolding Activities

In my course, students completed several activities prior to editing and expanding an article. These scaffolding activities were required and graded on a complete / incomplete basis. After a brief introduction of the assignment, I led a discussion on Wikipedia use and asked how many students were familiar with it and use it. While most of the students used Wikipedia regularly in their personal lives, not one had edited or added to a Wikipedia entry. None of them had accounts, prior to the course. Because they were used to being consumers, I felt it was important to give them time to explore Wikipedia from the role of critical consumer and producer. Most of the students were surprised they were being asked to use Wikipedia in the classroom, as most had been told not to use it for course assignments. These comments prompted a discussion on our discussion board when is it okay to use Wikipedia as well as why I asked them to contribute to it for a class. First, students completed an online training offered by the WikiEd Foundation. I believe this is imperative step, as it introduced students to Wikipedia as a community, explained the editing process, and described the five pillars for contributing to Wikipedia. In addition to the online training, as mentioned, the WikiEd Foundation also provided handouts for students to use. I required students to read and discuss these handouts on the discussion board. Some of the handouts I used: Editing Wikipedia, Citing Sources on Wikipedia, Evaluating Wikipedia, and Illustrating Wikipedia. These handouts were of high quality and were great resources. It was one less document that I had to create. After completing the training, I asked my students to search for articles related to healthcare. They then evaluated those articles using criteria outlined in the Evaluating Wikipedia brochure provided by the WikiEd Foundation. Students posted their first evaluation to a safe space—on our course management site, Blackboard. This allowed them to obtain feedback from me as well as their peers in the class, honing their analysis skills. It also helped them hone their understanding of the five pillars of Wikipedia before engaging with other Wikipedians. This step was helpful because it also allowed me to answer any questions or concerns students had about the assignment *before* they moved to working on Wikipedia.

This particular activity was also useful because it helped students understand what makes a "good" article to edit. Some articles are already well-developed, particularly in the medical field. They do not need to be expanded. On the other hand, other articles, especially on obscure or relatively new topics, are difficult to edit and expand. I found that it takes a good amount of practice to find articles that need to be edited and can be edited without tremendous difficulty. Next, students were required to learn about the rules for editing medical content. Wikipedia has guidelines established to ensure that appropriate and accurate information is being published. One guideline, for example, reminds Wikipedians editing medical content to avoid medical jargon and to use plain language. This was particularly helpful for my students as they needed practice writing (and speaking) in a manner that all patients can understand. Not all guidelines, however, were as easy for my students to understand and follow. While the strict guidelines are there for good reason, they took some time for students to learn. For example, my students struggled to understand why they could not cite primary sources, likely because they were used to citing these sources in academic papers. They have been taught that peer-review journal articles, and rightfully so, are credible. Unfortunately, they are not appropriate for Wikipedia, an encyclopedia, and it took some time for my students to understand why that was. At this point, we again discussed genre, and students generated genre conventions of a Wikipedia entry.

After they practiced evaluating several different articles, students moved to working on Wikipedia. First, students communicated with one another on their personal user talk pages. This was also a safe space where they could converse with others and learn how to sign their comments, an important part of Wikipedia talk pages. Next, they worked in their own space, their sandbox, to draft article contributions before engaging others. Unlike Blackboard, both of those spaces gave them practice using the Wikipedia editor. Even the students who completed the online training several times (as an instructor, I could see who did) needed time to work in their sandbox to feel comfortable with the Wikipedia editor. After working in their sandbox, I asked students to suggest an edit for an article on the article's talk page. On the talk pages, some students received feedback from other Wikipedians; some did not. I wish I could have waited longer, to see if more students got feedback, but because this was a summer course, I had to keep the unit moving.

At this point, students were ready to make an actual edit. In my eight-week summer class, students only had time to add a few sentences to an article and suggest surface-level edits. In a longer 16-week course, I believe it would be possible for students to expand an article, two or three fold. Whatever the assignment objective, I also believe it is important to provide students with enough time to learn about the Wikipedia community and the guidelines for contributing. Because Wikipedia is a community of volunteers, volunteers who are proud of their work and proud of the value of Wikipedia, it is important—and respectful— for students to learn more about Wikipedia and the Wikipedia community before making any "live" changes to the site.

RESULTS AND DISCUSSION

By editing and expanding an article, my students were able to write for an authentic audience as well as participate actively in the larger community, to help create a better world.

Benefit: Authentic Writing

When writing for Wikipedia, my students wrote for an authentic audience, an audience beyond me, the classroom instructor. According to the Council of Writing Program Administrators (2011):

Effective instruction approaches writing as a whole and varied activity, by its nature including feedback from peers and experts that aims to create authentically communicative results. Most isolated drills and decontextualized instruction have shown no value in improving student writing in large part because authentic writing is always embedded in complex rhetorical situations. (Effective teaching practices in general studies writing classes section, para. 4)

In the assignment, students received feedback from other Wikipedians as well as their classmates and myself. I believe all these relationships were valuable to my students. The Wikipedians helped the students understand the importance of genre, purpose, voice, and audience.

For those unfamiliar with Wikipedia, it may seem as though they are no guidelines, no genre conventions, and no complex rhetorical situations. When I introduced this assignment to my students last summer, nearly all of them said just that. Most of them thought that anything goes on Wikipedia. In reality, all Wikipedia articles must adhere to a set of content guidelines, making a Wikipedia assignment a great way to teach or reinforce genre theory. All Wikipedia articles must be written from a neutral point-of-view, include only information that is verifiable, and contain no original research (Wikipedia: Policies and guidelines, n.d.). When discussing these guidelines with students, I reminded students of how each piece of writing can be categorized by genre. In addition, other Wikipedians also reminded students if they did not adhere to one of the guidelines.

Before the unit, all of my students were unaware of how Wikipedia worked and that professionals, in a variety of fields, were using Wikipedia and contributing to it. One student remarked about her contribution:

Seeing it on the Wikipedia page was really cool, and I felt like the information I contributed was useful. Before this course, I had no idea that anyone could edit Wikipedia articles let alone contribute to them. This is something that even if I had known I would not have done on my own.

In addition, many other students commented that they appreciated learning more about how the site worked, even if they were still unsure if they would use it or call it a credible source. One student commented:

Although it was a good experience to use Wikipedia and post on the site so I gained an understanding of how exactly the information is obtained by Wikipedia, I still will not count it as a reliable and will not be using it.

In addition to providing my students with an authentic audience and the opportunity to learn more about the site itself, one of the other benefits of incorporating the Wikipedia assignment was that my students were able to meaningfully contribute to their discipline.

Benefit: Civic Engagement

By assigning a Wikipedia project, my students had a chance to impact hundreds of thousands of lives. Civic engagement is when students participate actively in the community to "improve conditions for others or to help shape the community's future" (Adler & Goggin, 2005, p. 236). While editing and writing for Wikipedia may not be considered civic engagement in the traditional sense, when my students contributed to Wikipedia, they were improving content area knowledge for everyone in the world. According to Dr. Amin Azzam, a health sciences associate clinical professor at the U.C.S.F. School of Medicine, "If we want to get high-quality information to all the world's population, Wikipedia is not just a viable option, but the only viable option" (Cohen, 2013, para. 8). Dr. Azzam teaches a course for medical students on writing for Wikipedia at his institution.

In my course, one student reflected on contributing to Wikipedia as a form of civic engagement:

This assignment allowed me to write information that I felt was important on a topic and post it to a well-known and highly used website. Posting information for anyone in the world to read about a topic in my field that I wrote is pretty cool.

This is a sentiment I heard from a handful of students in my course evaluations.

Pitfalls

This assignment, however, was not without its challenges. When adopting a similar assignment, prepare for some resistance. My students had been told by previous instructors, and even their parents, that Wikipedia is not a legitimate source of information. Many students told me they were taught in middle school and high school that Wikipedia had no place in the classroom. It was clear that these students believed that writing for Wikipedia was not something they should learn how to do in an upper-division writing course. Some students also struggled to see how this particular assignment related to their chosen profession, immediately dismissing the assignment.

When I shared articles and statistics outlining how Wikipedia was currently being used in the medical profession, many remained skeptical. I remained positive and continued to share resources with them that showed how Wikipedia was being used in a variety of different settings. If assigning a similar assignment, I would encourage instructors to find articles to share with their class that show how Wikipedia is being used in their disciplines, using these articles as a starting point for discussion. These articles can be a great way to "sell" the assignment to students.

In addition to some resistance, some of my students were confused with the editing process and the Wikipedia editing interface. While the Wikipedia editor is much easier to use then it used to be, some of my students found the interface complicated, which is why I believe mandatory training is important. In addition to the mandatory online training, I found it helpful to complete the training myself, so I understood how the Wikipedia editing interface works. In addition to being a resource, I also provided my students with contact information for our university Technology Learning and Media Center.

Because my course was online, I found it extremely difficult to explain the project in general as well as the editing process. I ended up recording video lectures to explain the project and screencasts that walked students through the editing process. When creating screencasts, I would recommend free apps like Jing or Screen-cast-o-matic; both are easy to use. Adopting the scaffolding activities outlined above helped encourage my students to start the project early. Particularly with assignments that require an extensive contribution, I believe it is important that students are not only working on learning the Wikipedia editor, but also developing their content. As an instructor, it is important to provide time for drafting, peer review, and practice, like any other writing assignment. Small, but required, weekly contributions helped my students master the Wikipedia editor interface.

Finally, it is possible for a student's work to be taken down by Wikipedia editors. Sometimes, taking down the material is justified (the student failed to follow the content guidelines), and other times, the reason for taking the material down is not quite as clear. This can lead to difficult conversations with students. While having work taken down would undoubtedly be frustrating, it can also be a great learning moment. It is important to encourage students to engage in a dialogue with the editors that removed their contribution. Learning how the community works is a great secondary lesson of this assignment. Unfortunately, there are a few rogue, rude editors, but this, too, can be a learning experience. Even if work is taken down, it will appear on the edit page of the article the student was working on, so if an instructor was trying to grade a contribution, the instructor would be able to see the work and grade it accordingly. In my course, I did not experience this, but was warned about the possibility by the people at the WikiEd Foundation.

In addition, the people at the WikiEd Foundation told me they are more than willing to step in and indeterminate between students and other Wikipedians. They ensured me that problems do not happen regularly, but I found it reassuring, knowing they are a resource for instructors. The WikiEd Foundation was highly supportive of my students working on Wikipedia. They understood what a powerful learning experience this was for students and that these students can contribute greatly to Wikipedia.

IMPLICATIONS

Despite the difficulties in assigning a Wikipedia project, there are still many reasons to assign a Wikipedia project. More and more schools across the country are asking their students to edit Wikipedia to ensure that high-quality content in a variety of disciplines is available to the English-speaking population of the world. With the supervision of a professor, an expert in a given discipline, the impact one class can have is quite large. According to Heilman et al. (2011), those in the healthcare-related fields should contribute to Wikipedia for a variety of reasons:

- *It may be personally satisfying to provide an important educational service for individuals looking for health information, and to see articles grow that one created or improved.*
- *While not having a high scientific impact, Wikipedia's articles have a high social impact due to its broad readership. In the experience of the authors, a newly created article can often be found*

among the top Google results within a day, often outperforming review articles in highly regarded medical journals.

- *Editing or adding information helps contributing students or professionals master the subject matter and learn more about the evidence underpinning it.*
- *Translating complex ideas into accessible concepts and language is an interesting intellectual challenge, which can help in everyday nontechnical communication with patients.*
- *Writing for Wikipedia teaches modern online communication.*
- *WikiProject Medicine offers participation and recognition in a Web-based international community.*
- *Writing for Wikipedia teaches modern online communication (A call to action section, para. 2)*

If students learn how to contribute to Wikipedia in an educational setting, they may be more likely to continue to contribute after their class or schooling is over.

As mentioned earlier, Wikipedia noted that nearly 90% of Wikipedia editors are white males, which can lead to systematic bias in articles (File: Editor survey report, 2011). By requiring students to complete an assignment such as this one, more female voices will be introduced to Wikipedia and possibly other minority voices as well. This is tremendously important, as different voices improve the content of existing articles and broaden the scope of new articles written. A good experience in the classroom, may lead to students editing Wikipedia on their own time, providing more diverse perspectives and content on the site. At the end of my course, one student expressed her interest to continue editing. She wrote, "I have a new outlook on Wikipedia. I may even spend some time looking at ways of improving article information. I did not know this was an option prior to this class."

CONCLUSION

Wikipedia is a great way to provide students with an authentic writing opportunity as well as engage them civically. For my *Writing in the Health Professions* students, it gave them a chance to improve health information that is accessed by millions of English speaking people around the world. It also gave them practice writing using plain language, a skill they will need in their careers from both a written and oral communication perspective. This is a skill that is needed by not only healthcare professionals, but also professionals in a variety of fields, making Wikipedia an appropriate assignment for students across all majors. While the assignment is not without its problems, I believe the benefits outweigh them tremendously. My students were able to see how a community can work collaboratively to generate knowledge. They also better understood how important it is to making Wikipedia a place with accurate information from diverse perspectives.

REFERENCES

Cohen, N. (2013, September 29). Editing Wikipedia for med school credit. *The New York Times*. Retrieved from: http://www.nytimes.com

Council of Writing Program Administrators. (2011). WPA network for media action. *Effective teaching practices in general studies writing classes.* Retrieved from: http://wpacouncil.org/nma

File: Editor survey report. (2011). *Wikimedia foundation.* Retrieved from https://wikimediafoundation.org/

Graham, S., & Harris, K. R. (2007). Best practices in teaching planning. In S. Graham, C. A. McArthur, & J. Fitzgerald (Eds.), *Best practices in writing instruction* (pp. 119–140). New York: The Guilford Press.

Heilman, J. M., Kemmann, E., Bonert, M., Chatterjee, A., Ragar, B., Beards, G. M., & Laurent, M. R. et al. (2011). Wikipedia: A key tool for global public health promotion. *Journal of Medical Internet Research, 13*(1), e14. doi:10.2196/jmir.1589 PMID:21282098

Help: Using talk pages (n. d.). In *Wikipedia.* Retrieved from https://en.wikipedia.org/wiki/Help:Using_talk_pages

Hughes, B., Joshi, I., Lemonde, H., & Wareham, J. (2009). Junior physician's use of Web 2.0 for information seeking and medical education: A qualitative study. *International Journal of Medical Informatics, 78*(10), 645–655. doi:10.1016/j.ijmedinf.2009.04.008 PMID:19501017

Tunick, R. A., & Brand, S. R. (2015). Social media and health care. In L.S. Wiener, M. Pao, A.E. Kazak, M.J. Kupst, & A.F. Patenaude (Eds.), Pediatric psycho-oncology: A quick reference on the psychosocial dimensions of cancer symptom Management (pp. 345-357).

Wikimedia Foundation. (2015). *May 31, 2015 Wikipedia Statistics.* Available from the Wikimedia Foundation website: http://stats.wikimedia.org/EN/Sitemap.htm

Wikipedia. Policies and guidelines. (2015, July 18). *Wikipedia.* Retrieved from https://en.wikipedia.org/wiki/Wikipedia:Policies_and_guidelines

Wikipedia. Wikipedians. (2015, December 18). In *Wikipedia.* Retrieved from https://en.wikipedia.org/wiki/Wikipedia:Wikipedians

Chapter 16
Designing a Wiki–Based Course for Enhancing the Practice of Writing Skills in the 21st Century:
Moving from Theoretical Grounding into Practical Knowledge

Ahmed Abdulateef Al Khateeb
King Faisal University, Saudi Arabia

ABSTRACT

This chapter describes an intervention of a wiki-based course to enhance the practice of academic writing through the process approach. This course was experimented on a freshmen year class of medical students learning English for specific purposes at a university in Saudi Arabia. This chapter draws on the relevant theories and their relationship to the practice of wikis in learning academic writing. Wikis have been introduced into the teaching of writing to afford collaborative assistance and social support. Accordingly, the chapter demonstrates the structure of the course and details the systematic organization between the in-class teaching and on-wiki practice. The intervention of a wiki-based writing course gives emphasis on the background of the tasks assigned. It points out the essential characteristics of the structure of wiki interface that would enable learners to accomplish the process-oriented wiki-mediated collaborative writing (PWMCW) tasks. This new practice reveals the evaluation of this course with its writing tasks, based on the learners' perspectives.

INTRODUCTION

The practice of academic writing production embodies a challenge for several learners of English academic writing in preparatory year at university in Saudi Arabia. One facet of this challenge is because English is located in Saudi Arabia within the expanding circle which requires its learners, either for speaking or writing, to follow British or American English (Kachru, 1992). Determining the causes related to the

DOI: 10.4018/978-1-5225-0562-4.ch016

deficit of learning academic writing is demanding; yet without a doubt, using old-fashioned methods in teaching academic writing, without taking the advantages of technology, would retain learners' motivation in developing this skill. In some instructional contexts, there is an emphasis on the product approach which neglects the strategies and process writing of making a sound piece of writing (Al-Seghayer, 2011). In this chapter, process writing has been suggested as a solution for the current problem as Al-Hazmi (2006) emphasizes that process writing helps to construct various meanings and realities; enables writers' needs to be raised, discussed and resolved and formulates a channel for expressing individuals' own opinions.

Furthermore, social networking tools, online-based applications and multimedia (e.g., wikis) have positively contributed to the advancement of academic writing practice which has become socially interactive-based. It enforces learning through acts of collaboration. It also looks for members' partnership in groups rather than teammates' competition. According to this view, social relationships and communication skills are encouraged; sense of belonging to a group and being a member of a group is highly provided (Johnson and Johnson, 1999). As this era is called digital age, it is undoubtedly that investigating interaction in online learning has become the tip of the iceberg in the educational research (Roblyer and Ekhaml, 2000; Anderson, 2003). Our concentration in this chapter is that all users should be stimulated socially through engaging into a variety of tasks. Thereby, the more social presence is the more collaboration and interaction is expected to happen.

THEORETICAL FRAMEWORK

The course drew on theories concerning wiki-mediated collaborative writing, and the process approach (i.e. the PWMCW), in order to apply them to classroom and online learning. Such theories support the development of the practices adopted and the incorporation of peer collaboration into the learning process. In other words, the design of this course has been consolidated with theoretical knowledge and these principles:

- Firstly, drawing on social constructivism, the PWMCW (Process-oriented Wiki-Mediated Collaborative Writing) was seen as a joint enterprise between the teacher, learners and their peers in creating new meaning (e.g. Swain, Brooks & Tocalli-Beller, 2002).
- Secondly, the concept of Zone of Proximal Development (ZPD) by Vygotsky, which is the area between the actual development of learners and their level of potential development, was at the heart of this course design as the learners were encouraged to get engaged and expand their thinking, understanding and performance with the help of "experts" (e.g. Lund, 2008).
- Thirdly, in terms of collaborative learning (CL), learners were encouraged to participate in explicit collaborative tasks, mutual communication and knowledge sharing (e.g. Davoli, Monari & Eklundh, 2009).
- Fourthly, the practice of computer-supported collaborative learning (CSCL) was initiated so that the learners could share knowledge asynchronously (e.g. Lehtinen, 2003; Bradley, et al., 2010).
- Finally, motivation in language learning was seen as key so that the opportunity for language learning success was increased (Dörnyei, 1998).

The course was thus designed according to how collaboration, collaborative writing and wiki-based writing can be introduced, nurtured and maintained. It focused on meeting learners' social needs and the strategies that can be used in the future. It gave more attention on pursuing their knowledge, particularly in learning general academic writing. This course depended on creating an engaging experience combined with meaningful tasks using an integrated approach: face-to-face teaching and wiki.

METHODOLOGY

Defining Wikis

The term 'wiki' comes from the word 'wikiwiki' which means 'quick' in the Hawaiian language. A wiki is web-based software that allows users to collaborate in forming the content and to share knowledge. Wikis allow users to create or amend content. Users can have also the features of accepting or rejecting changes provided by participants. It is a form of social networking media and web 2.0 tools that promotes webpages to be more dynamic and user-generated rather than static. Wikis pursue collaborative writing and allow more social support for virtual and real-time communication. Wikis can be embedded along with collaborative writing tasks and the process writing approach as a pedagogical intervention for promoting learning academic writing, as it was conducted in this study. Therefore, the integration of wikis for the development of writing skills fosters collaboration and learner-centred learning and peer feedback.

Defining the Course Goals

Designing the course was initiated to satisfy the research aims, namely exploring the impact of wikis in helping the learners to improve their general academic writing (PWMCW).

As far as the goal of the intervention of a wiki-based course is concerned, it contributed to improving the writing practices of the learners in a way that was meant to be interesting. Research literature shows the impact of using wikis in literacy; such relevant findings enriched the understanding regarding the outcome of this course (Minocha and Thomas, 2007; Choy and Ng, 2007; Hadjerrouit, 2011; Oh, 2014). Accordingly, the educational goals of the course were to help the students to:

- Apply the writing process and its stages and phases, with reference to collaborative writing (CW).
- Practice drafting, thus receiving useful feedback and negotiations from the learners and their peers and the teacher by using wikis; and
- Develop students' awareness concerning their practice of writing in terms of accuracy, content and cohesion in a more interactive way.

In addition, the course is in line with Blooms' Taxonomy, which has been used by West and West (2009) for designing wiki-based projects. West and West highlight the role of knowledge construction and contextual application. Knowledge construction comprises tasks and topics seeking to teach learners to share information and build knowledge based on each other's contributions (ibid). They require students to understand and elaborate on information. The contextual application requires the learners to implement their knowledge in order create new solutions or products. It is very similar to 'Knowledge Construction' because the topics and tasks focus on collaboration and the collaborative processes.

The potential outcomes of using the integrated course (or wiki-based tasks in this course) were:

- On an individual writing level, the learners will be encouraged to create a higher standard of texts with meaningful content gained from reliable resources.
- On a collaborative writing level, the learners will be motivated to practise informative interaction on wikis to make this new concept less awkward.

Describing the Course Components

The course is divided into two components which were designed to complement each other: the face-to-face class (the prescriptive component) and wikis (the integrated component). Much of the content of the whole course was based on delivering a course that was required by the university where the study took place, in the Kingdom of Saudi Arabia. In addition to the course book, task-based learning was also applied. As shown in Table 1, the contribution of the syllabus in this chapter provided new ways of syllabus development to organize learning and make it experiential with lasting impact to extend beyond the classroom. The current syllabus also ensured planning teaching of academic writing by deciding as to which topics are needed to be included.

Table 1. A plan for elements of classroom teaching

Teaching Week	Topics (Elements of Classroom Teaching)	Reference
Week 1	• Course orientation • Program demonstration • Pre-evaluation of the course	Handouts- about wiki
Week 2	• Compound sentences • Coordinating conjunctions	
Week 3	• Listing-order & time-order signals • Listing & outlining	Textbook, Ch. 3
Week 4	• Complex sentences • Sentence errors and fragments	Ch:3
Week 5	• Review types of sentences • Four rules for capitalisation & commas	Ch:3
Week 6	• Describe pictures • Space order/using adding specific details	Ch:4
Week 7	Using adjectives (e.g. adjectives with nouns, adjectives with linking verbs, compound adjectives, adjectives with -*ing* and -*ed*)	Ch:4
Week 8	• Cumulative adjectives & coordinate adjectives (order of adjectives) • Writing sentences with adjectives	Ch:4
Week 9	Holiday	
Week 10	Prepositions and prepositional phrases	Ch:4
Week 11	Mid-term exam	
Week 12	Discussion of the texts produced by the students (on wikis)	
Week 13	• Activities: identifying reasons & examples for outlining • Making outlines with details with specific examples	Ch:5
Week 14	Transition signals with reasons conclusion signals with reasons	Ch:5
Week 15	• Complex sentences with reasons & condition • Subordinators • Additional rules for capitalisation & commas	Ch:5
Week 16	Post- evaluation of the course	

The Prescriptive (Face-to-Face) Teaching

As far as this course is concerned, face-to-face teaching is a requirement for passing the orientation year and one of the university's general subjects for completing the core modules of the academic year. The students are assessed during the face-to-face teaching with a midterm exam (week 11) and a final exam (week 16). This portion of the course is allocated two hours on a weekly basis for a total of 28 hours of actual instruction time. The writing class has a two credit hour in the students' overall credit hours degree plan. In such classes, there was a focus on direct instruction about writing to explain the contents of the textbook, which had been agreed upon by the curricula committee at the university. The class involved explaining various elements of developing learners' competency in writing.

Table 1 demonstrates the wide range of topics covered in the writing lectures during the semester. These oral-oriented classes also included working on a number of activities in the textbook and practice writing a few examples. This traditional form of teaching was to ensure the learners' abilities regarding these elements especially when the learners started applying them on wikis. There were also handouts designed for each topic that included additional exercises to help the students use the new structure on wikis. This was in order to teach the different topics and create a chance for the learners to develop a detailed understanding regarding different elements of writing.

The content of the class involved in this course was identical to that of the three other - classes who received teaching based on the same curricula, but without wikis. This then allowed me to make comparisons between the classes with and without wikis. The textbook used was *Writing Academic English (fourth edition) by Alice Oshima and Ann Hogue*. A number of different variables that draw on the process-oriented approach and engaging the learners with additional un-assessed tasks on wikis were voluntary, unlike the other classes. The rationale behind this integration of the content of the class and wiki was to unite them in order to create a more connected classroom and to make learning to write more effective.

This form of teaching briefly introduced new practices such as facilitating the collaborative writing (CW) practice to empower the students so they could apply this technique exhaustively on wikis. The students were taught how to give constructive feedback and negotiate meanings effectively, as both skills are important in terms of professional leadership as well as in their personal lives (Yang et al., 2006).

I instructed the students that feedback on the wikis must be objective and involve comments on error correction and content accuracy. It was essential to give specific and clear thoughts on how to improve their texts and create multiple ways for learners to communicate amongst themselves and with the teacher. In class then, the participants did role-plays to practice how to give and receive beneficial feedback. This was done by explaining the purpose of feedback, which focuses on the positive aspects, as well as the aspects that need improvement. These classes showed the potential outcomes of practising writing collaboratively, not just individually.

The Integrated (Face-to-Face and Wiki-Based) Teaching

Face-to-face teaching is important because it can meet the needs and interests of many students, and it reinforces the fact there is physical support. On the other hand, teaching through wikis provides more opportunities for live interaction and many-to-many collaboration (Wagner, 2004). In both mediums, peers and teachers can provide continuous feedback, which can be increased using wikis because of the unrestricted time limit. The integrated teaching (class and wiki) can occur by distributing those components which require more emphasis from face-to-face classes and those that can be best conveyed through wikis (e.g. in regard to using common subordinators such as although, even though, so that, … etc.). Therefore, the class can afford explicit instruction for various writing components (e.g., on how to write a compound and complex sentence) and include how to work effectively on collaborative wiki-based tasks in order to attain the maximum benefit of integrating both ways of learning.

The integration of face-to-face writing classes and wikis helps learners to undertake writing in a collaborative form, as Bernard, Rubalcava, and St-Pierre (2000) indicate. In view of that, the learners can develop their basic competences through teachers' instruction and guidance in face-to-face learning environments. The students can also develop their understanding concerning academic writing through peer interaction and successful online (wiki)-based learning communities. Using wikis is helpful for sound negotiation because it increases agreement and diminishes conflicts and helps in finding mutual understanding, which is a vital element for good writing. The intention behind this integration is to create extra time for the learners outside of class to engage in more practice of academic writing in shared environments.

West and West (2009) suggest that several issues should be considered when wikis are to be integrated in a class. Such issues are to provide adequate training on how to use wikis at the beginning the course in order to be familiar with its use. Accordingly, the participants undertook training on how to use the wiki. Some of the basic steps of this training were based on principles proposed by the Australian Flexible Learning Framework (2008). They included how to:

1. Create chunks of text;
2. Edit chunks of text;
3. Make those chunks of text accessible to others;
4. Create comments on those chunks of text with editing and making them accessible to others;
5. Add pictures, sound recordings, and other media files;
6. Receive notifications about the new modifications to old items through Rich Site Summary (RSS); and
7. Recognize types of access to the chunks of text.

The integration between the class and wikis was also designed to be achieved through a number of pedagogical principles. There was emphasis on ensuring that the new elements of face-to-face teaching were understood by the students in order to use them in the texts they published on wikis. The students were encouraged to give oral as well as e-based feedback and be part of small collaborative learning groups. Furthermore, they were taught how to determine the questions and comments that are best discussed in face-to-face classes or on wikis, thus enabling the students to reflect on what they wrote or said. This course shows how the wiki element was planned and delivered during the weekly writing lectures along with the use of process writing, as shown in Table 2. A similar design was identified by Oh (2014), that is, to produce collaboratively and individually-based texts.

Distribution of the Research Methods during the Teaching Course

As part of designing the course, I had to identify a new course based on a combination of collaborative writing on wikis using the process approach (PWMCW) with face-to-face learning. This form of blended learning involved writing classes. There were three main tasks, which were designed in parallel with the contents of the students' textbook. Each task was planned to last for one month. During each month, the

Table 2. A plan of the integration of wiki into writing classes

Teaching Week	Stages of Wiki-Based Activities + Tasks' and Roles' Deadline	Practice of the Process + Mode of Achieving Tasks	Elements of the Course in Face-to-Face Setting	Nature of the Practice of CW + Task Number
1	Ice-breaking, analysing the learners' grades in the writing test (1ˢᵗ semester), Conducting pre-questionnaires and the initial focus groups, training on wiki			
2	Planning (exploration & exhibition) Starts after lecture 2 & ends at the end of week 2	Wiki-based/Group collaboration [Planning- all group members]	Reviewing compound sentences	A writing task (# 1) (brainstorming and researching)
3	Drafting (explanation) Starts after lecture 3 & ends at the end of week 3	Wiki-based/Individual duty (drafting) [Writing -writers]	Listing-order & time-order signals, Listing & outlining	A writing task (#1) (writing and drafting)
4	Expanding and evaluating the writers' texts (elaboration & evaluation). Starts after lecture 4 & ends at the end of week 4	Wiki-based/Group collaboration [Revision -editors and revisers plus writers]	Complex sentences, Sentence errors Fragments	A writing task (# 1) (editing and revising)
5	--------------------	Paper-based (practice for individual writing)	Reviewing types of sentences. Rules for using capitalisation & commas	-----------------------
6	Planning (exploration & exhibition). Starts after lecture 6 & ends at the end of week 6	Wiki-based/Group collaboration [Planning -all group members]	Describing pictures Using space order Adding specific details	A writing task (# 2) (brainstorming and researching)
7	Drafting (explanation). Starts after lecture 7 & ends at the end of week 7	Wiki-based/Individual duty (drafting) [Writing -writers]	Using adjectives (e.g. with nouns, with linking verbs, compound adjectives) Adjectives with -*ing* and -*ed*)	A writing task (# 2) (writing and drafting)
8	Expanding and evaluating the writers' texts (elaboration & evaluation). Starts after lecture 8 & ends at the end of week 8	Wiki-based/Group collaboration [Revision -editors and revisers plus writers]	Cumulative adjectives and coordinate adjectives-Writing sentences with adjectives	A writing task (# 2) (editing and revising)
9	Holiday (one week)			
10	Expanding and evaluating the writers' texts (elaboration & evaluation). Starts after lecture 10 & ends at the end of week 10	Wiki-based/Group collaboration [Revision -editors and revisers plus writers]	Prepositions and prepositional phrases	A writing task (# 2) (editing and revising)
11	Mid-term exam			
12	--------------------	Paper-based (practice for individual writing)	Individual tasks related to the students' writings (for errors which were identified by peers). Discussing some of the students' produced texts	-----------------------
13	Planning (exploration & exhibition). Starts after lecture 13 & ends at the end of week 13	Wiki-based/Group collaboration [Planning - all group members]	Identifying reasons & examples for outlining. Making outlines with giving details	A writing task (# 3) (brainstorming and researching)
14	Drafting (explanation). Starts after lecture 14 & ends at the end of week 14	Wiki-based/Individual duty (drafting) [Writing -writers]	Transition signals with reasons Conclusion signals with reasons	A writing task (# 3) (writing and drafting)
15	Expanding and evaluating the writers' texts (elaboration & evaluation). Starts after lecture 15 & ends at the end of week 15	Wiki-based Group collaboration [Revision -editors and revisers plus writers]	Complex sentences with reason and condition subordinator. Additional rules for using capitalisation & commas	A writing task (# 3) (editing and revising)
16ᵗʰ	Conducting the post questionnaires, the follow-up focus groups, and the delayed Interviews (after six months from running this course)			

participants would take part in collaborative planning (group brainstorming), individual drafting and collaborative revision (editing and revising) on Wikispaces (the type of wiki chosen for this course). In particular, Wikispaces was chosen as it integrates many of Web 2.0 features and services.

Wikispaces offers three types of group space. These are 1) Basic: which is open for everyone but cannot be edited by everyone except by those who have been invited. 2) Plus: which cannot be either seen or edited by others unless invited. 3) Super: which cannot be either seen or edited by others unless invited with additional privileges. For this course, all the wikis were paid for to ensure participants' protection where nobody from other groups or outsiders could see what had been written. The participants would also undertake two individual writing tasks on paper before and after their contributions to the wikis.

Before starting the course, I:

- Prepared learning materials and handouts to simplify the course and to show how to navigate Wikispaces.
- Finalized the layout of the wiki and the content for each group and the necessary modifications such as the type of font and the colors of the scripts.
- Examined the IT facilities (e.g. availability of a network) and the wireless network, along with ensuring the availability of good projectors in order to present some of the participants' works in-class.

Furthermore, during the course I completed the following:

- In the first week, I distributed a pre-evaluation form. The participants were unaware of the new course and the instructor. Yet, it was appropriate to express their expectations based on their former knowledge.
- After completing this form, the participants performed short CW tasks (offline), where they formed their own small groups and started writing texts with their classmates.
- In week 1, I decided it was a good idea to complete the initial form before telling the learners that I would be teaching this course. This promoted their willingness to speak freely and to discuss their past experiences.
- In weeks 2-15, the participants had the opportunity to focus on WMCW in using the writing process.
- In weeks 2-15, I discerned that several collaboratively written texts started to be carefully edited and revised in an attempt to make texts more accurate and have sound content and structure.
- In week 16, after announcing the final grades, I distributed a post-evaluation form. The participants had become more aware of what they were doing in regards to writing supported by wikis and face-to-face interaction. So they were able to give their post-perceptions of the class and express their experiences.

Developing the Course (Wiki-Based) Tasks and the Interface

Structure of the Wiki Interface and Nature of Wiki-Based Tasks

Wikispaces is one of the commonly used social networking platforms that provides building online-based communities. It originated in 2005 by a company called 'Tangient LLC' based in San Francisco. Tangient

Figure 1. Basic wiki-based writing

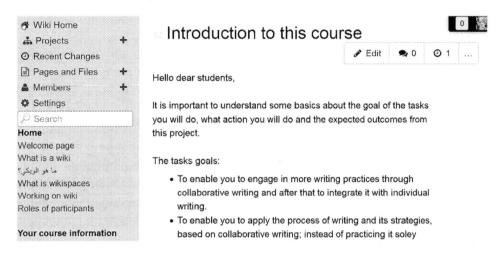

LLC hosts millions of subscribers with over five million wikis for individuals, schools and educational corporations worldwide (Wikispaces website, 2011). As shown below in Figure 1, these constituents provide the basic understanding regarding wiki-based writing and serve to indicate what the participants should do and how they can do it. The interface consisted of four main areas based on Li (2014):

- The first area, *Home*, it detailed the relevant responsibilities to be completed in-class and on wikis as well as the expected outcomes. It concisely demonstrates the roles of the participants to be followed in each task based on the phases of the process approach.
- The second area, *Your Course Information*, comprised a brief introduction to the process writing approach with relevant questions. It included questions on how to practice peer feedback, revising and editing.
- The area entitled *Your Writing Tasks* was designed to demonstrate the core item about the writing tasks. It contained a pre-task activity and a description for each writing task.
- Finally, the fourth area, *Language Resources*, encompassed links to useful learning writing websites plus a free online dictionary for vocabulary searches.

The interface had also detailed information regarding:

- **The Course:** This included the course schedule and a demonstration of the new strategies to be used to achieve each task. It also included how wikis work and how to use it.
- **The Tasks:** These included participants' biographies (self-introduction) and a description of each task. The tasks were introduced one by one rather than all at once.
- **The Language Resources:** These included non-compulsory worksheets, links to some websites on academic writing and on learning English.
- **Additional Material:** This included supplementary materials and useful links

In the present course, three wikis were created. The interface of the first wiki was cloned for the rest of the wikis. There were twenty-one participants who were distributed into three groups (seven members in each group). In keeping with Willis (1996), the components of task-based learning were reinforced in the following tasks: *Pre-task* where topics are introduced by the teachers, *Task cycle* where the students prepare how they do the task and how they report it, and finally *Language focus* where the students examine and analyze the specific features they discover in the task. Consequently, TBL suggests a task as being:

A piece of classroom work that involves learners comprehending, manipulating, producing or interacting in the target language ... in order to express meaning, and in which the intention is to convey meaning rather than to manipulate form. (Nunan, 2006, p: 17)

Three tasks were designed and given to the participants that matched their syllabus content, field of study and contextual background. All three tasks were chosen to represent different learning objectives and unique experiences: solving a problem; analysing a situation; and summarising an academic article. Furthermore, the question types were designed to address different prompts. Prompts are defined as 'sentence openers or question stems' (Weinberger et al., 2005, p: 9) encompassing elaborative details.

Each of these three different tasks lasted for approximately four to six weeks in order to complete the stages of wiki activities, the phases of the process writing and the roles assigned as indicated in Table 2. The students were encouraged to visit the local library in the college in order to use external resources. Library use was considered important to encourage the students to practise reading for writing purposes. This idea endorses the reciprocity between reading and writing, in that writers need to use their talents as readers; where both skills share in conferring pragmatic benefits for the learning process.

Noting the differences between an activity and a task, Goodyear (2005) indicates that *a task* is a prescribed work originated by the instructor whereas *an activity* is what learners get engaged with and what they actually do. Such tasks transfigured the learners' learning potential to write, creating a positive impact on their curiosity, interest, engagement and motivation. A brief introduction of each task is given below:

Task 1: Addressed 'diabetes', one of the common health problems in Saudi society. Since participants were medical students, they were encouraged to write about this syndrome, give information about it and suggest some possible ways to stop it spreading in society. The students were engaged to produce collaborative written texts through gradually moving from the first creation (draft) to the best creation possible. Those texts were expected to be in academic format (relevant to their proficiency level), using process writing strategies among peers.

Task 2: Addressed a different kind of major problem, 'car accidents'. It was intended to let students write about the consequences of car and motor vehicle accidents in Saudi Arabia and the resulting injuries and other health problems. This was to enable the students to reflect on this topic and to elicit the reasons behind this problem. Ideally, in the future when the students have become physicians, they can play a positive role in raising awareness of car accidents to their patients. Similar to task 1, the novice writers were asked to play the same roles of the PWMCW, but changing the roles among themselves.

Task 3: Addressed one of the most enjoyable foods, chocolate. The academic article given to the learners showed how chocolate is produced. Since it is relevant and important to the students' field of study, the article addressed the positive as well as the negative effects and other health-related matters linked with the excessive consumption of chocolate (e.g., relaxing effects, as well as heart disease and high blood pressure). The students were asked to reflect on this debate by creating outlines and then extracting reasons and examples.

Use of the Key Stages of Wiki-Based Activities

Part of determining the content of the course involved referring to the key stages of wiki-based activities as identified by Wheeler (2010). These stages (exploration, exhibition, explanation, expansion and evaluation) are employed as guiding principles for establishing successful wiki-based writing tasks. There has been growing interest in using this model, established by Wheeler, in basic and higher education across several institutions. This model helps the students to make progress with their collaborative writing abilities, although such stages were originally identified as stages of general wiki-based collaborative learning activities. The stages mentioned proceed in line with the process writing approach and its phases of development (planning, drafting and revision).

The stages of exploration and exhibition include preparing learners themselves on how to use wikis and presenting their initial experience of using them. These two stages are the counterpart of the *planning* stage, which involves the organization and prioritization of different ideas based on their relevance to the topics assigned. Explanation comes next, providing the ideas or texts to peers or other people. It is equal to drafting, as the appropriate ideas can be maintained and formulated into texts. Elaboration and evaluation draw learners' attention to editing and revising and giving a value regarding others' texts. It indicates ambiguities and suggested alternatives.

The five phases ascend towards deeper cognitive and meta-cognitive thinking and broader engagement of a concept or skill, in this case, writing. They aim to develop a pedagogical environment ideal for fostering collaborative writing through using wikis, along with social and professional development, since a large community of learners are more interested in presenting their ideas and discoveries on wikis. The phases are deliberately created to stimulate the students' shared discussion of knowledge, which is borrowed from the theoretical framework of the current study.

Use of the Process Writing Approach (in a Collaborative Form)

The process approach is one of many teaching approaches to learning writing. The primary goal of this approach is to deal with writing in a more sensible and meaningful way. In other words, the students have a key role in developing their ideas, their repertoire of vocabulary, and structures around the topics assigned. Based on the findings of Storch (2005), the students are directed to focus on process writing by drawing their attention to the importance of spending adequate time and effort on planning (pre-writing), drafting (focus on preparing) and evaluation (post-writing that includes editing and revising).

There is a deeper focus on the process approach for this particular class, as they need to understand the practice of writing in detail, what each phase involves, and how writing a text occurs. It also helps the learners to generate ideas organically, to develop and communicate ideas and to decide on the appropriate content. The course applies the process writing approach in a collaborative form in order to combine the efforts of learners in groups and as individuals. The first and last phases of the process approach (planning, editing and revising) in collaborative writing requires the learners (or group members) to have explicit roles (e.g. reporting main ideas) to be achieved in a collaborative process. As there are two areas in each wiki, planning is intended to be accomplished on the discussion thread whereas drafting and revising is on the main wiki pages.

Initially, in this approach, the learners were asked to prepare the preliminary versions of the texts in isolation, by the individual, despite the fact that writing in general is considered as a social product (Ede and Lunsford, 1990). Students were required to recognise the features of the process approach and how each stage is different in order to promote reflective learning. This can also be reinforced through collaborative work. When the students begin to consider reflection as part of the process in terms of learning writing skills during the process approach, it causes an increase in their positive feelings related to the experience, a better ability to identify related issues and find solutions to problems. They can observe the gradual movement to the more demanding phases that require shared and critical thinking. The purpose of relying on this approach is to encourage the students to use it initially with the assistance of the teacher and the help of their peers so they can use it individually or collaboratively with their peers in the future.

Use of Specific Assigned Roles

Allocating specific roles for continued learning, particularly when writing in a collaborative format, could facilitate the solution of problems which are caused by writing: psychological, cognitive and linguistic. There were roles allocated to the students in order to practice the phases of wiki-based activities and the process writing approach. The allocated roles (planners, drafters, editors and revisers) were assigned with key questions to facilitate writing practice and to give students the opportunity to choose the roles they liked in each task, as group members distributed those roles among themselves.

The role of the teacher is seen to be complex in integrated teaching, as it involves being a moderator or facilitator and is therefore just as important as the participants' roles. The roles undertaken by the participants are essential, especially as each role is played by a different individual. This is achieved in order to provide ample time for learners to practice free writing and brainstorming. They might also produce multiple drafts until they are satisfied with their work. Learners can edit and revise someone's drafts that are easier, and this is a helpful way to get various opinions and feedback.

The practice of the roles allocated in the writing process can be more achievable when using collaborative writing platforms such as wikis (Storch, 2013). Storch emphasizes that on wikis, each role can be carried out more effectively, as they allow students to outline and organize their ideas in an interactive way. For that reason, it is crucial for the learners to understand the roles that are assigned according to the desires of the group members and their competence and abilities. There is also the possibility of exchanging these roles across different tasks, so they can experience the three major roles of writing.

- Planners need to think about the topics assigned, prepare the relevant ideas and develop their ideas into full texts. They are responsible for determining the audience targeted and what is hoped to be accomplished.
- Drafters are responsible for collecting and turning the segmented ideas into texts. Based on the ideas already given, they develop an introduction, discussion and conclusion in a coherent and cohesive way.
- Editors/revisers are responsible for improving the quality of the first written drafts. Students are required to be familiar with this role because it encourages peer response and better understanding of readership.

As shown in Table 2, a plan for the integrated course was constructed in accordance with Littlejohn and Pegler (2007) who proposed a plan for a number of synchronous and asynchronous tools to be used in face-to-face teaching. In this plan, the basic components are mode, instructor's and students' role(s), tasks/activities and resources. Another plan is suggested by Murphy and Southgate (2011) considering the following: mode, teacher's and students' activities, and resources. Taking these plans into account plus inserting some adaptation, this researcher's proposed plan summarized the procedures of integrating wikis using the writing process into normal writing classes. As the semester was composed of sixteen teaching weeks, it was sensible to divide the elements of the course according to those weeks. It was planned that each phase, stage or role would start when the lecture finished and last until the next lecture began in the following week.

In each lecture, there was a brief discussion about what needed to be accomplished on the wikis in the following week. This created an opportunity for the students who required further face-to-face support and to inquire about any difficulties they might still be experiencing and that they had not been able to solve online. The PWMCW was gradually introduced into the class through two steps adapted from the Australian Flexible Learning Framework (2008). As a first step, the participants would receive a number of emails from their instructor about the significance of using wikis in their writing course and why it was so important to actively participate on the wiki. The second step was the actual performance which included the following:

1.   Orienting to wikis via provision of training on wikis;
2.   Defining how wikis are used throughout the course;
3.   Determining the learning outcomes and the purpose of using wikis in the writing course and
4.   Defining the acceptable and unacceptable usage and guidelines for posting.

Moreover, a group of strategies were adopted from West and West (2009) in order to ensure that the students could develop connection between face-to-face and online tasks. The strategies included motivating learners and promoting their perceptions towards collaboration. The participants were also encouraged to collaborate on wiki outside classes by:

1.   Developing teams and roles;
2.   Developing a sense of community;
3.   Giving sufficient time for collaboration;
4.   Giving feedback and
5.   Comparing different visions and inferring their similarities and differences.

The design of this course was to enable the learners to understand the rules and structures of academic writing that are taught in-class as well as to practice other skills such as the ability to engage in shared discussions to complete the wiki-based tasks.

RESULTS

The course participants had a chance to evaluate the wiki-based course for the practice of learning academic writing and its related tasks. This evaluation is useful as it illuminated further insights about this course and its related tasks from the participants' points of view. Furthermore, the participants had been given time to make decisions regarding their own learning throughout the term, therefore their input was valuable. Chapelle (2007) asserts that learners' evaluation of their learning materials and tasks assigned that are facilitated through technology-assisted language learning could boost their understanding for a better innovative learning environment. On this basis, the participants pinpointed three major issues that are seen as crucial for delivering an effective PWMCW course as reported in the post-evaluative questionnaire.

Analysis of the Post-Evaluative Questionnaire

In this questionnaire, most of the participants gave positive responses that disclosed higher percentages of agreement and satisfaction with various aspects of the course, focused on the PWMCW, as shown in Tables 3 and 4.

Quality Assurance for the Designed Layout

The first procedural issue raised by the participants concerned quality in the design of (and active work) on wikis and with their tasks. The views of the participants, who expressed the importance of designing clear content in an attractive way while providing continuous training and instructional guidance, are shown in the following excerpts:

Student 1: *I think the subdivisions in the website are well-organised. I see it really well-organised and very, very systematic. These areas can be easily recognised as there is a main page to draft. There is also history to identify any addition. The task is on a side.*
Student 2: *In fact I didn't note any complexity or the possibility of losing my way. It might be at the beginning, but we become used to it, it became very comfortable since all of its categories were clear.*
Student 3: *I thought how difficult that would be, but then I realized later when I logged in how easy it would be to deal with because of the layout was helpful.*

Table 3. Participants' responses for the evaluative questionnaire (1)

Item Description		Yes	No
Was the introduction to Wikispaces enough?	Response %	8 **90**	2 10
Do you wish to integrate wiki-mediated collaborative writing in your regular writing instruction in classes?	Response %	12 **69**	8 40
Were you pleased with your group?	Response %	17 **85**	3 15
Were the tasks new, informative, interesting and related to your future career?	Response %	17 **85**	3 15
Were there any difficulties related to the technical side of the course?	Response %	6 30	14 **70**
Were there any difficulties in dealing with the tool bar on the wiki?	Response %	4 20	16 **80**
Were the questions given for each role (i.e. collaborative planning, drafting and collaborative revision) sufficient?	Response %	19 **95**	1 5
Was it confusing to work on more than one area: 'discussion' and 'main wiki page' areas?	Response %	19 **95**	1 5

Table 4. Participants' responses for the evaluative questionnaire (2)

Item Description				
Was the timing for each task: long, satisfactory or short?		**Long**	**Satisfactory**	**Short**
	Response %	1 5	18 **90**	1 5
Was the number of members in each group: big, sufficient or small?		**Big**	**Sufficient**	**Small**
	Response %	2 10	18 **90**	- -
Was the nature of achieving the tasks: clear (easy) or confusing (difficult)?		**Easy**		**Difficult**
	Response %	18 **90**		2 10

Thus, in order to ensure a high quality PWMCW course with effectively designed layouts, there are a number of studies that identify models to ensure this feature. Minocha and Thomas (2007) consider the following aspects to be important: access and motivation, online socialization, information giving and receiving, knowledge construction and development. Liu (2010) highlights that wiki-based layouts should reduce learners' anxiety related to online posting; encourage their online participation and acceptance of using social tools and promote the feeling of usefulness of incorporating such tools. Hadjerrouit (2011) also shows the importance of:

- Starting with gathering information about the chosen topics;
- Creating the necessary links and hyperlinks;
- Assessing the content of these pages; and
- Providing opportunities for peer review.

Fair Distribution of Groups and Individuals

The participants expressed the importance of fairness in the distribution of groups and individuals through applying procedures that determine the proficiency levels of the participants. Fair distribution is a determiner for establishing interdependence, or mutuality, and allowing synthesis of new information among individuals. Both are key elements in online collaborative learning as was discovered by Ingram and Hathorn (2004).

Also, a group of instructors, from the same research context, were consulted in order to seek their advice about the achievement level for each participant. These instructors had already taught such participants and had experience about them. A further procedure was applied by consulting the scores and levels of achievement which participants had achieved in the previous term in their writing course.

Despite the effort carried out by myself in organizing the participants in a fair way, a handful of the participants, as emphasized in the examples below, asked why they had been allocated to a certain group, and with certain peers, rather than others which they thought would be more appropriate.

Student 4: *I think group members should be distributed similarly. I mean, you need good, average and slow learners (.) all within one group. I think the distribution of members in the groups wasn't fair.*

Student 5: *I mean students shouldn't only be evaluated by scores. There are other things which are necessary to know about students before giving any test or distributing a role.*

Student 6: *It [the distribution of individuals] depends on students' willingness and acceptance of this idea.*

The indicated contributions have resonance with Einon (2010) who emphasizes the importance of the users' agreement on the distribution of groups and individuals, the duties assigned and the timeline for when the project should be completed. Yet, it was realized that it is hard to be absolutely fair in the distribution of the individuals in their groups. The most important thing is the adoption of as many procedures and strategies as possible to ensure consistency in the distribution of individuals in a systematic way. Each learning group should have a similar number of individuals with mixed abilities.

Notwithstanding, discussion with participants prior to starting the distribution process of individuals in certain groups and is perhaps a potential procedure for ensuring fairness. The participants can also distribute themselves according to what they think is comfortable but in keeping with some general principles agreed from the beginning. It is most likely that self-distribution of groups and individuals of themselves can reinforce learners' distributed cognition. Distributed cognition is 'a process in which cognitive resources are shared socially in order to extend individual cognitive resources or to accomplish something that an individual agent could not achieve alone' (Lehtinen, 2003, p: 12).

Consideration of Satisfactory Grading 'or Assessment'

The participants drew attention to the status of assessment for the new course and its related tasks. It must be noted that the participants mentioned this issue because they thought that the un-assessed subjects were less important than the assessed (e.g. biology, autonomy and physics). They also felt that allocating fair marks, is essential since they study several subjects and usually concentrate more on subjects with higher mark allocations. The indicated subjects carried higher marks compared to the minimal marks assigned to the individually-produced texts.

Besides this, the collaboratively-produced texts on wikis were not assessed at all, and this led several participants to consider it as an elective course. Such tasks were not assessed because the purpose was not to force the participants to achieve the tasks and not everyone was required to take part. Yet, a number of the participants pointed out the consequence of assessment on their motivation as shown in the excerpts given below, regardless of their interest in the new classes and tasks.

Student 7: *Yah, so we tell ourselves that instead of wasting an hour everyday working on un-assessed work, it's better to do more on the biology course.*

Student 8: *... but if there are no marks we won't become highly interested in it. I mean other things might have more priority.*

Student 9: *[Student] we may say we have subjects that have more priority in which I must succeed or need to concentrate on to increase my accumulative GPA (Grade Point Average).*

Student 10: *Marks give motivation and force you to work.*

It is true to say that there was satisfactory collaboration and participation. However, the minimal assessment of the individually-produced texts did not increase the motivation of the participants to be socially interactive. If there had been more allocated marks, there would have been more collaboration than they in fact accomplished. The participants stated their preference for PWMCW more than traditional writing but that assessment should be integrated to give them more enthusiasm. Such extended tasks should be assessed in order to make participants more able to pursue social interaction. It was evident that the participants thought that creating well-constructed writing in wikis was determined by assessment and the allocation of sufficient marks, reflecting what was recognised by Coniam and Ki (2008).

There were a few marks allocated to the products of the individually-based texts produced before and after collaboration. However, the students wanted further details about how the process and product of the collaboratively-oriented texts would be assessed. Although the participants stated the importance of assessing what they do in groups, they were also concerned about how assessment would be accomplished for their collaborative product. This feeling highlighted the need to make accurate grading criteria 'to avoid one-sentence pages, to reward good effort, and to provide feedback' (Cronin, 2009). Correspondingly, Hazari, North and Moreland (2009) agree with this view. These researchers confirm that sound assessment 'should set clear performance expectations, and include consideration for both the process and product used by team members to develop the final deliverable for the assignment' (p: 189).

Practical Considerations for the Course Implementation

The new course emphasizes not only the product, but also the process, which could contribute to the construction of a good piece of writing (Al-Seghayer, 2011). Following this practice creates more chances for learners, particularly beginners, to construct meaning during their learning of writing. It also constitutes a channel through which individuals can express their own opinions by demonstrating and discussing their writing needs and how they can be met. For this reason sound wiki-based courses need to consider the steps shown below. The same steps are agreed by Stanley (2013). An instructor, is encouraged to:

1. Plan a writing lesson for a writing topic that is interesting and can be discussed in a collaborative way;
2. Set up a wiki platform (one or many based on the number of participants);
3. Ask the participants to join and contribute to the wiki(s);
4. Conduct specific training (by showing learners how wiki works, its advantages, and things they need to be aware of);
5. Set up a plan for fulfilling the tasks and the distribution of roles; and
6. Set up a plan to revise all the amendments contributed by each individual.

Undeniably, the new course is not always necessarily beneficial, as participants may sometimes show biased opinions influenced by their learning groups rather than what they as individuals think. It is crucial to apply the PWMCW within a complete pedagogical model for teaching writing appropriately and creatively. This model must entail how tasks and roles can be fulfilled. Wikis are tools which alone do not result in effective learning; rather, such learning mostly depends on learners' understanding of collaboration and their response to the assigned tasks.

Following well-planned models, such as those ones already explained by Minocha and Thomas, 2007; Liu, 2010 and Hadjerrouit, 2011, should decrease the difficulty of composing texts, explaining how to start and how to revise. Yet, such pedagogical models might involve a few difficulties regarding: setting appropriate time limits, maintaining awareness of and providing adequate training and technical support. The technical support involves dealing with the website, of Wikispaces when it fails, teaching learners how to update the content and how to use the proper browser.

There were challenges which were hard for the instructor to deal with and provide full support for all the students. They exhibited needs for emotional and psychological support during their social interaction at a distance, because of lacking verbal interaction. This support is necessary to ensure learners' capacities for generating new written texts in line with the given description for each task; and they need to do this within a specific time by responding to the roles as agreed among peers (Ducate, Anderson and Moreno, 2011). In this study, I adapted collaborative and individual tasks without grading. Only the individual tasks were graded as the course guide outlines.

This result showed that the students were less likely to be involved in activities unless they were assigned marks. Hazari, North and Moreland (2009) advocate the necessity of identifying a robust marking scale in order to let writers assess their contributions. It was not easy to persuade the students to work actively without assessing them on their collaborative effort. It is striking to observe the influence of rewarding by grades on students' achievement. In harmony with Kummer (2013), who claims that rewarding students by marks is the foundation for intrinsic and extrinsic motivation even in higher education.

The new course, relying on the PWMCW, also needs great patience, effort and skill from instructors. I was responsible for giving comprehensive feedback and general guidelines. Such given feedback is highly dependent on 'the effectiveness of the instructor in promoting group collaboration, the instructor's role in creating the course conditions and climate for establishing an online community...' (Choy & Ng, 2007, p: 209-226).

The participants described a difficulty concerning applying the new course in regular classes. This is because the classes are built on an individual basis rather than by the inclusion of groups, especially in exams. Conforming with Lund (2008):

This approach has been at odds with more traditional and dominating forms of testing and assessment... Focus on coursework, process, collaboration...This is a shift that, at least to some extent, is more aligned with a sociocultural view of learning and teaching. (p: 35)

Based on the given steps and challenges reported in this chapter which are related to the pedagogical implications, this chapter concludes that the PWMCW and its related tasks, along with a number of the principles suggested here, should be officially adopted for writing classes and perhaps for other classes, but with the utmost degree of planning and organization. This practice should be part of the course design for different subjects that seek to enhance learners' abilities in writing skills and collaboration.

DISCUSSION AND CONCLUSION

Reconsidering the course designed for this study is important as the inclusion of recommendations and guidance is invaluable for future users, including myself and other teachers. There were a number of lessons learned from this course. As the main goal of the course was to improve the writing skills of English learners as a second/foreign language (L2/FL), the main three core foci of the course (wiki, collaborative writing and the process approach) contributed to the target of learning writing skills in a novel way. Moreover, choosing authentic tasks, using Wikispaces, designing an area for planning and another for drafting and revising, creating collaborative learning environments and reinforcing collaborative and individual writing simultaneously were all helpful in meeting the course goal Those elements supported the course, so it is essential that they remain.

Other features were found to be less effective so they should be dropped. The prescription of the entire course details in advance was important, however, this should not be to the extent that there is no flexibility whatsoever. Flexibility and planning for additional time are vital in course design, particularly if technology is integrated in the project or it seeks to establish integrated learning. This can provide more room for adjustment of less desired practices and replace it with those that are more interesting. Learners should be included in the design process with teachers, e.g. in relation to the size of the groups and the adequacy of training.

Other features were found to be beneficial but need further adaptation. The learners expressed a desire to conduct more face-to-face meetings to discuss their wiki-based interactions and what they hoped to achieve. The learners had to be repeatedly reminded about their roles as active learners who take responsibility for their own learning. Furthermore, it was essential to explain more about the different way of assessment using wikis, which is formative-based in order to provide more interactive, useful feedback and the expected outcomes.

As this course mainly focused on assessing the individual tasks, the assessment of collaboratively-produced work was also seen as indispensable. It would be more useful if participants were given more intensive training on how to deliver peer feedback and if there were several tasks so that each group of learners could select the tasks they like. If I have the opportunity to repeat this course, I will run a second phase in which the same participants will be introduced to the tasks and requested to write texts according to their own process so they can decide on the type of collaborative writing and the approach that they wish the writing process to take.

REFERENCES

Al-Hazmi, S. (2006). Writing and reflection: Perceptions of Arab EFL learners. *South Asian Language Review*, *16*(2), 36–52.

Al-Seghayer, K. (2011). *English teaching in Saudi Arabia: Status, issues, and challenges*. Riyadh: Hala Printed Co.

Anderson, T. (2003). Getting the mix right again: An updated and theoretical rationale for interaction. *The International Review of Research in Open and Distributed Learning*, *4*(2).

Bernard, R. M., Rubalcava, B. R., & St-Pierre, D. (2000). Collaborative online distance learning: Issues for future practice and research. *Distance Education*, *21*(2), 260–277. doi:10.1080/0158791000210205

Bradley, L., Lindstrom, B., & Rystedt, H. (2010). Rationalities of Collaboration for Language Learning in a Wiki. *ReCALL*, *22*(2), 247–265. doi:10.1017/S0958344010000108

Chapelle, C. A. (2007). Challenges in evaluation of innovation: Observations from technology research. *International Journal of Innovation in Language Learning and Teaching*, *1*(1), 30–45. doi:10.2167/illt041.0

Choy, S. O., & Ng, K. C. (2007). Implementing Wiki Software for Supplementing Online Learning. [AJET]. *Australasian Journal of Educational Technology*, *23*(2), 1–14. doi:10.14742/ajet.1265

Cronin, J. J. (2009). Upgrading to Web 2.0: An Experiential Project to Build a Marketing Wiki. *Journal of Marketing Education*, *31*(1), 66–75. doi:10.1177/0273475308329250

Davoli, P., Monari, M., & Eklundh, K. S. (2009). Peer activities on Web-learning platforms—Impact on collaborative writing and usability issues. *Education and Information Technologies*, *14*(3), 229–254. doi:10.1007/s10639-008-9080-x

Dörnyei, Z. (1998). Motivation in second and foreign language learning. *Language Teaching*, *31*(03), 117–135. doi:10.1017/S026144480001315X

Ede, L., & Lunsford, A. A. (1990). *Singular texts, plural authors: Perspectives on collaborative writing*. Illinois: SIU Press.

Einon, G. (2010). Managing computer-supported collaboration. In H. Donelan, K. Kear, & M. Ramage (Eds.), *Online communication and collaboration: a reader*. Oxon: Routledge.

Goodyear, P. (2005). Educational design and networked learning: Patterns, pattern languages and design practice. *Australasian Journal of Educational Technology*, *21*(1), 82–101. doi:10.14742/ajet.1344

Hadjerrouit, S. (2011). A collaborative writing approach to wikis: Design, implementation, and evaluation. *Issues in Informing Science and Information Technology*, *8*, 431–449.

Hazari, S., North, A. & Moreland, D. (2009). Investigating pedagogical value of wiki technology. *Journal of information Systems*, 20(2), 187-198.

Ingram, A., & Hathorn, L. (2004). Methods for Analysing Collaboration in Online Communications. In T. S. Roberts (Ed.), *Online Collaborative Learning: Theory and Practice*. Hershey, PA: Information Science Publishing. doi:10.4018/978-1-59140-174-2.ch010

Johnson, D. W., & Johnson, R. T. (1999). Making cooperative learning work. *Theory into Practice*, *38*(2), 67–73. doi:10.1080/00405849909543834

Kachru, B. B. (1992). *The other tongue: English across cultures*. University of Illinois Press.

Kummer, C. (2013). Students' Intentions to Use Wikis in Higher Education. *Wirtschaftsinformatik*. Retrieved from http://files.figshare.com/1035208/ Structural_Equation_Modeling.pdf

Lehtinen, E. (2003). Computer-supported collaborative learning: An approach to powerful learning environments: *Unravelling basic components and dimensions*.

Li, M. (2014). *Small Group Interactions in Wiki-Based Collaborative Writing in the EAP Context* [Unpublished PhD thesis]. University of South Florida.

Littlejohn, A., & Pegler, C. (2007). *Preparing for Blended E-learning*. Abingdon, New York: Routledge.

Liu, X. (2010). Empirical testing of a theoretical extension of the technology acceptance model: An exploratory study of educational wikis. *Communication Education*, *59*(1), 52–69. doi:10.1080/03634520903431745

Lundin, R. W. (2008). Teaching with Wikis: Toward a Networked Pedagogy. *Computers and Composition*, *25*(4), 432–448. doi:10.1016/j.compcom.2008.06.001

Minocha, S., & Thomas, P. G. (2007). Collaborative Learning in a Wiki Environment Experiences from a software engineering course. *New Review of Hypermedia and Multimedia*, *13*(2), 187–209. doi:10.1080/13614560701712667

Murphy, L., & Southgate, M. (2011). The Nature of the 'blend': Interaction of Teaching Modes, Tools and Resources. In M. Nicolson, L. Murphy, & M. Southgate (Eds.), *Language Teaching in Blended Contexts. Scotland* (pp. 13–28). Dunedin.

Nunan, D. (2006). *Task-based language learning*. Cambridge: Cambridge University Press.

Oh, H. (2014). Learners' Writing Performance, Revision Behavior, Writing Strategy, and Perception in Wiki-mediated Collaborative Writing. *Multimedia-Assisted Language Learning, 17*(2), 176–199.

Oshima, A., & Hogue, A. (2005). *Writing Academic English* (4th ed.). Longman.

Roblyer, M. D., & Ekhaml, L. (2000). How interactive are your distance courses? A rubric for assessing interaction in distance learning. *Online Journal of Distance Learning Administration, 3*(2).

Stanley, G. (2013). *Language Learning with Technology: Ideas for Integrating Technology in the Classroom*. Cambridge: Cambridge University Press.

Storch, N. (2005). Collaborative writing: Product, process, and students' reflections. *Journal of Second Language Writing, 14*(3), 143–173. doi:10.1016/j.jslw.2005.05.002

Storch, N. (2013). *Collaborative writing in L2 classrooms*. Multilingual matters.

Swain, M., Brooks, L., & Tocalli-Beller, A. (2002). 9. Peer-Peer Dialogue as a Means of Second Language Learning. *Annual Review of Applied Linguistics, 22*(1), 171–185.

Wagner, C. (2004). Wiki: A technology for conversational knowledge management and group collaboration. *Communications of the Association for Information Systems, 13*(13), 265–289.

Weinberger, A., Ertl, B., Fischer, F., & Mandl, H. (2005). Epistemic and social scripts in computer–supported collaborative learning. *Instructional Science, 33*(1), 1–30. doi:10.1007/s11251-004-2322-4

West, J. A., & West, M. L. (2009). *Using Wikis for On-line collaboration: The power of the Read-Write Web*. San Francisco, CA: Jossey-Bass.

Wheeler, S. (2010). Open content, open learning 2.0: Using Wikis and Blogs in Higher Education. In U.-D. Ehlers & D. Schneckenberg (Eds.), *Changing Cultures in Higher Education: Moving Ahead to Future Learning* (pp. 103–114). Springer. doi:10.1007/978-3-642-03582-1_9

Willis, J. (1996). *A Framework for Task-Based Learning*. Harlow: Longman.

Yang, M., Badger, R., & Yu, Z. (2006). A comparative study of peer and teacher feedback in a Chinese EFL writing class. *Journal of Second Language Writing, 15*(3), 179–200. doi:10.1016/j.jslw.2006.09.004

Compilation of References

Adsanatham, C. (2012). Integrating assessment and instruction: Using student-generated grading criteria to evaluate multimodal digital projects. *Computers and Composition, 29*(21), 152–174. doi:10.1016/j.compcom.2012.04.002

Ahmed, L. (2014). Confessions of a teenage activist. Retrieved from https://lemeesahmed.wordpress.com/

Alexander, J. (2006). *Digital youth: Emerging literacies on the World Wide Web*. Cresskill, NJ: Hampton Press.

Alexander, J., & Rhodes, J. (2014). *On multimodality: New media in composition studies*. Urbana: National Council of Teachers of English.

Al-Hazmi, S. (2006). Writing and reflection: Perceptions of Arab EFL learners. *South Asian Language Review, 16*(2), 36–52.

Ali, I., & Byard, K. (2013). Student perceptions on using blogs for reflective learning in higher educational contexts. *AUT University Department of Economics Working Paper Series, 2013*(6).

Allen, G. (2008). *Language, Power, and Consciousness: A Writing Experiment at the University of Toronto. Teaching Composition: Background Readings* (T. R. Johnson, Ed.). New York: Bedford St. Martin's.

Al-Seghayer, K. (2011). *English teaching in Saudi Arabia: Status, issues, and challenges*. Riyadh: Hala Printed Co.

Anderson, T. (2003). Getting the mix right again: An updated and theoretical rationale for interaction. *The International Review of Research in Open and Distributed Learning, 4*(2).

Anson, C. M. (1999). Distant voices: Teaching and writing in a culture of technology. *College English, 61*(3), 261–280. doi:10.2307/379069

Arola, K. L. (2010). The design of web 2.0: The rise of the template, the fall of design. *Computers and Composition, 27*(1), 4–14. doi:10.1016/j.compcom.2009.11.004

Arola, K., Sheppard, J., & Ball, C. E. (2014). *Writer/designer: A guide to making multimodal projects*. MacMillan Education.

Association for Education in Journalism and Mass Communication. (2010). AEJMC: Social Media in the Classroom.

Association, A. L. S. (2014). The ALS Association extends 'thank you' in new message [Press release]. Retrieved from www.alsa.org/news/archive/als-association-thankyou-video.html

Bakhtin, M. (2001). Marxism and the Philosophy of Language. In Bizzell & Herzberg (Eds.), The Rhetorical Tradition: Readings from Classical Times to the Present (pp. 1206-1245). Bedford St. Martin's.

Banks, A. (2006). *Race, rhetoric, & technology: Searching for higher ground*. Mahwah: Laurence Erlbaum Associates, Inc.

Banks, A. J. (2006). *Race, rhetoric, and technology: Searching for higher ground*. New Jersey: Lawrence Erlbaum Associates, Inc.

Baron, D. (2009). *A better pencil: Readers, writers, and the digital revolution*. New York, NY: Oxford University Press.

Bartholomae, D. (1985). Inventing the university. In V. Villanueva (Ed.), *Cross talk in comp theory: A reader* (2nd ed., pp. 623–653). Urbana, IL: National Council of Teachers of English.

Barton, D., & Hamilton, M. (1998). *Local literacies: Reading and writing in one community*. New York: Routledge. doi:10.4324/9780203448885

Bauerlein, M. (2011). *The digital divide: arguments for and Against Facebook, Google, texting, and the Age of Social Networking*. USA: Archer Perigee, Penguin Books.

Baughman, D., & Siegel, M. (Producers), & Baughman, D. & O'Hara, J. (Directors). (2010). *Bhutto* [Motion Picture]. USA: First Run Features.

Berkelaar, B., & Buzzanell, P. (2015). Online employment screening and digital career capital: Exploring employers' use of online information for personnel selection. *Management Communication Quarterly*, *29*(1), 84–113. doi:10.1177/0893318914554657

Berlin, J. (1996). *Rhetorics, poetics, and cultures: Refiguring college English studies*. Urbana, IL: NCTE.

Berlin, J. (2003). *Rhetorics, poetics, and cultures*. West Lafayette, IN: Parlor Press.

Bernard, R. M., Rubalcava, B. R., & St-Pierre, D. (2000). Collaborative online distance learning: Issues for future practice and research. *Distance Education*, *21*(2), 260–277. doi:10.1080/0158791000210205

Bitzer, L. F. (1968). The rhetorical situation. *Philosophy & Rhetoric*, *1*, 1–14.

Bizzell & Herzberg (Ed.), (2001). *The Rhetorical Tradition: Readings from Classical Times to the Present. New York*. Bedford: St. Martin's.

Blackmon, S. (2007). (Cyber)conspiracy theories? African-American students in the computerized writing environment. In P. Takayoshi & P. Sullivan's (Eds.), Labor, writing technologies, and the shaping of composition in the academy: New Directions in computers and composition (pp. 153-166). New York: Hampton Press.

Blair, A. (2013). Democratising the learning process: The use of Twitter in the teaching of politics and international relations. *Political Studies Association*, *33*, 135–145.

Blair, K. (1998). Literacy, dialogue, & difference in the "electronic contact zone.". *Computers and Composition*, *15*(3), 317–319. doi:10.1016/S8755-4615(98)90004-4

Blood, R. (2002). *The weblog handbook: Practical advice on creating and maintaining your blog*. Cambridge, Massachusetts: Perseus Books.

Boggs, G. L., & Kurashige, S. (2012). *The next American revolution*. Berkeley: University of California Press.

Bolter, D., & Grusin, R. (1999). *Remediation: Understanding new media*. Boston, MA: MIT Press.

Bombardieri, M. (2006, July 9). Life away from home 101: Orientations warn students of drugs, Facebook, Texas Hold'em. *The Boston Globe*. Retrieved from http://www.boston.com/news/education/higher/articles/2006/07/09/life_away_from_home_101/?page=full

Boon, S., & Sinclair, C. (2009). A world I don't inhabit: Disquiet and identity in Second Life and Facebook. *Educational Media International*, *46*(2), 99–110. doi:10.1080/09523980902933565

Bosker, B. (2013, October 22). Beheadings belong on Facebook. *The Huffington Post.* Retrieved from http://www. huffingtonpost.com/2013/10/22/facebook-beheading-videos_n_4144886.html

Bouton, K. (2015, July 17). Recruiting for cultural fit. *Harvard Business Review.* Retrieved from www.hbr.org

Bovee, C., & Thill, J. (2014). Business communication today (12th ed.). Boston: Pearson.

boyd, d. (2008a). Why youth [heart] social network sites: The role of networked publics in teenage social life. In D. Buckingham (Ed.), *Youth, identity, and social media* (pp. 119-142). Cambridge, MA: The MIT Press.

boyd, d. (2008b). Can social network sites enable political action? *International Journal of Media and Cultural Politics, 4*(2), 241-44.

Boyd, D. M., & Ellison, N. B. (2008). Social network sites: Definition, history, and scholarship. *Journal of Computer-Mediated Communication, 13*(1), 210–230. doi:10.1111/j.1083-6101.2007.00393.x

Bradley, L., Lindstrom, B., & Rystedt, H. (2010). Rationalities of Collaboration for Language Learning in a Wiki. *ReCALL, 22*(2), 247–265. doi:10.1017/S0958344010000108

Brandt, D. (1990). *Literacy as involvement: The acts of writers, readers, and texts.* Carbondale: Southern Illinois Univ. Press.

Brandt, D. (2014). *The Rise of Writing: Redefining Mass Literacy.* Cambridge: Cambridge UP.

Branham, C., & Farrar, D. (2014). Negotiating Virtual Spaces: Public Writing. *Writing Commons.* Retrieved from http://writingcommons.org/index.php/open-text/new-media/negotiating-virtual-spaces-public-writing/650-negotiating-virtual-spaces-public-writing

Brooke, C. G. (2009). *Lingua fracta.* Creskill, NJ: Hampton Press.

Brosh, A. (2011, May 6). FAQ (Blog). Retrieved from http://hyperboleandahalf.blogspot.com/p/faq_10.html

Brosh, A. (2013). *Hyperbole and a half: Unfortunate situations, flawed coping mechanisms, mayhem, and other things that happened.* New York, NY: Simon & Schuster.

Brown, V., & Vaughn, E. D. (2011). The writing on the (Facebook) wall: The use of social networking sites in hiring decisions. *Journal of Business and Psychology, 26*(2), 219–225. doi:10.1007/s10869-011-9221-x

Brubaker, A. T. (2006). Faculty perceptions of the impact of student laptop use in a wireless Internet environment on the classroom learning environment and teaching.

Bruffee, K. (1984). Collaborative learning and the "conversation of mankind". *College English, 46*(7), 635–652. doi:10.2307/376924

Bryant, K. (2013). Composing online: Integrating blogging into a comtemplative classroom. In K. Pytash & R. Ferdig (Ed.), Exploring technology for writing and writing instruction. (pp. 77-99). Hershey, PA, USA: IGI Global.

Bryant, K. (2013a). Composing online: Integrating blogging into a contemplative classroom. In K. Pytash and R. Ferdig's (Eds.), Exploring technology for writing and writing instruction (pp. 77-99). Hershey: IGI Global.

Bryant, K. (2013b). Me/we: Building an 'embodied' classroom for socially networked, socially distracted basic writers. *Journal of Basic Writing, 31*(2), 51–79.

Buck, E. (2015). Assessing the efficacy of the rhetorical composing situation with FYC students as advanced social media practitioners. *Kairos: A Journal of Rhetoric, Technology, and Pedagogy, 19*(3). Retrieved from http://kairos.technorhetoric.net/

Buck, S. (2012, September 4). 12 things students should never do on social media. *Mashable*. Retrieved from http://mashable.com/2012/09/04/students-social-media-warnings/

Buck, A. (2012). Examining digital literacy practices on social network sites. *Research in the Teaching of English*, *41*, 9–38.

Bunn, M. (2011). How to read like a writer. *Writing Spaces: Readings on Writing*, 2, 71-86. Retrieved from http://writingspaces.org/sites/default/files/bunn--how-to-read.pdf

Burke, K. (1941). *The philosophy of literary form: Studies in symbolic action*. Baton Rouge: Louisiana State University Press.

Burwell, C. (2013). The Pedagogical Potential of Video Remix. *Journal of Adolescent & Adult Literacy*, *57*(3), 205–213.

CareerBuilder Survey. (2015). Thirty-five percent of employers less likely to interview [Press release]. Retrieved from http://www.careerbuilder.com/share/aboutus/pressreleasesdetail.aspx?sd=5%2f14%2f2015&siteid=cbpr&sc_cmp1=cb_pr893_&id=pr893&ed=12%2f31%2f2015

Carlson, S. (2010). The Net Generation Goes to College. *The Chronicle of Higher Education*: Information Technology, A34.

Carr, D. (2015, January 4). Selfies on a stick, and the social-content challenge for the media. *The New York Times*. Retrieved from http://www.nytimes.com/2015/01/05/business/media/selfies-on-a-stick-and-the-social-content-challenge-for-the-media.html?_r=0

Carr, N. (2008). Is Google making us stupid? What the Internet is doing to our brains. *The Atlantic*. Retrieved from http://theatlantic.com

Castek, J., Coiro, J., Guzniczak, L., & Bradshaw, C. (2012). Examining peer collaboration in online inquiry. *The Educational Forum*, *76*(4), 479–496. doi:10.1080/00131725.2012.707756

Castells, M. (2009). *The Rise of The Network Society: The Information Age: Economy, Society and Culture*. Oxford, UK: Wiley-Blackwell.

Caulfield, S., & Ulmer, A. (2014). Capacity limits of working memory: The impact of media multitasking on cognitive control in the adolescent mind. *American Academy of Pediatrics National Conference & Exhibition*.

Chandler, D., & Munday, R. (2011). Horizon of expectations. Oxford Dictionary of Media and Communication. Oxford: Oxford University Press. Retrieved from http://www.oxfordreference.com.proxy.bsu.edu/view/10.1093/acref/9780199568758.001.0001/acref-9780199568758-e-1217 doi:10.1093/acref/9780199568758.001.0001

Chapelle, C. A. (2007). Challenges in evaluation of innovation: Observations from technology research. *International Journal of Innovation in Language Learning and Teaching*, *1*(1), 30–45. doi:10.2167/illt041.0

Chen, H. L. (2009). *Electronic portfolios 2.0*. Sterling, VA: Stylus Publishing.

Choy, S. O., & Ng, K. C. (2007). Implementing Wiki Software for Supplementing Online Learning.[AJET]. *Australasian Journal of Educational Technology*, *23*(2), 1–14. doi:10.14742/ajet.1265

Clark, J. (2009). The digital imperative: Making the case for a 21st-century pedagogy. *Computers and Composition*, (27): 27–35.

Cohen, N. (2013, September 29). Editing Wikipedia for med school credit. *The New York Times*. Retrieved from: http://www.nytimes.com

Coiro, J. (2009). Rethinking online reading assessment: How is reading comprehension different and where do we turn now. *Educational Leadership*, *66*, 59–63.

Coiro, J. (2012). The new literacies of online reading comprehension: Future directions. *The Educational Forum, 76*(4), 412–417. doi:10.1080/00131725.2012.708620

Consigny, S. (1974). Rhetoric and its situations. *Philosophy & Rhetoric, 7*, 175–186.

Coogan, D. (1998). Email 'tutoring' as collaborative writing. In *Wiring the Writing Center*. Logan, UT: Utah State University Press.

Cooper, M. M., & Selfe, C. L. (1990). Computer conferences and learning: Authority, resistance, and internally persuasive discourse. *College English*, 1990, 849–869.

Cordell, R. (2010, May 28). Disposable Twitter accounts for classroom use [Blog post]. http://chronicle.com/blogs/profhacker/disposable-twitter-accounts-for-classroom-use/40145

Council of Writing Program Administrators (CWPA). (2014, July 17). *WPA Outcomes Statement.* Retrieved from http://wpacouncil.org/positions/outcomes.html

Council of Writing Program Administrators. (2011). WPA network for media action. *Effective teaching practices in general studies writing classes.* Retrieved from: http://wpacouncil.org/nma

Cronin, J. J. (2009). Upgrading to Web 2.0: An Experiential Project to Build a Marketing Wiki. *Journal of Marketing Education, 31*(1), 66–75. doi:10.1177/0273475308329250

Crystal, D. (2008). *Txtng: The Gr8 Db8.* Oxford: Oxford University Press.

Cummins, H. J. (2006, March 30). Students' Facebook faces adult invasion; Facebook, a web world for college students, now gets visits from prospective employers. *Star Tribune.* Retrieved from http://www.highbeam.com/doc/1G1-143881218.html

Curtis, S. (2013, August 19). Five biggest social media blunders of 2013. *The Telegraph.* Retrieved from http://www.telegraph.co.uk/technology/social-media/10252609/Five-biggest-social-media-blunders-of-2013.html

Cushman, E. (1998). *The struggle and the tools: Oral and literate strategies in an inner city community.* Albany: State University of New York Press.

Darling, J. (2015). Community and citizenship in the computer classroom. *Hybrid Pedagogy.* Retrieved from http://www.digitalpedagogylab.com/hybridped/community-and-citizenship-in-the-computer-classroom/

Davoli, P., Monari, M., & Eklundh, K. S. (2009). Peer activities on Web-learning platforms—Impact on collaborative writing and usability issues. *Education and Information Technologies, 14*(3), 229–254. doi:10.1007/s10639-008-9080-x

De Jonge, S., & Kemp, N. (2012). Text message abbreviations and language skills in high school and university students. *Journal of Research in Reading, 35*, 49–68. doi:10.1111/j.1467-9817.2010.01466.x

DeAndrea, D. C., Shaw, A., & Levine, T. R. (2010). Online language: The role of culture in self-expression and self-construal on Facebook. *Journal of Language and Social Psychology, 29*(4), 425–442. doi:10.1177/0261927X10377989

Dean, T. (1989). Multicultural classrooms, monocultural teachers. *College Composition and Writing, 40*(1), 23–37.

Decarie, C. (2010). Facebook: Challenges and opportunities for business communication students. *Business Communication Quarterly, 73*(4), 449–452. doi:10.1177/1080569910385383

DeVoss, D. N., Johanson, J., et al. (2003). Under the radar of composition programs: Glimpsing the future through case studies of literacy in electronic texts. In Bloom, Daiker and White (Eds.), Composition studies in the new millennium: Rereading the past, rewriting the future (pp. 157-173). Carbondale: Southern Illinois University Press.

DeVoss, D. &Ridolfo, Jim. (2009). Composing for Recomposition: Rhetorical Velocity and Delivery. *Kairos: A Journal of Rhetoric. Technology, and Pedagogy, 13*(2), n2.

DeVoss, D. N. (2013). *Understanding and composing multimodal projects. New York, NY*. Bedford: St. Martin's.

Donaldson, J. (2014). The maker movement and the rebirth of constructionism. *Hybrid Pedagogy*. Retrieved from http://www.hybridpedagogy.com/journal/constructionism-reborn/

Donham, J. (2014). College ready–What can we learn from first-year college assignments? An examination of assignments in Iowa colleges and universities. *School Library Research, 17*, 1–22.

Donnelly, K. (2013, September 20). Graduates could be 'Googled' out of jobs over online posts. *Irish Independent*. Retrieved from www.independent.ie

Dörnyei, Z. (1998). Motivation in second and foreign language learning. *Language Teaching, 31*(03), 117–135. doi:10.1017/S026144480001315X

Dorwick, K. (1996). Rethinking the Academy: Problems and Possibilities of Teaching, Scholarship, Authority, and Power in Electronic Environments. *Kairos*.

Douglass, F. (1898). From narrative of the life of Frederick Douglass, an American slave. In L. Jacobis Editor (Ed.), A world of ideas (pp. 327-340). Boston: Bedford/St. Martin's.

Drouin, M., & Driver, B. (2014). Texting, textese and literacy abilities: A naturalistic study. *Journal of Research in Reading, 37*(3), 250–267. doi:10.1111/j.1467-9817.2012.01532.x

Duggan, M., Ellison, N. B., Lampe, C., Lenhart, A., & Madden, M. (2015). Demographics of key social networking platforms pew research center. Retrieved from www.pewinternet.org

Duggan, M., Ellison, N., Lampe, C., Lenhart, A., & Madden, M. (2015, January 9). Social Media Update 2014. *Pew Research Center*. Retrieved from http://www.pewinternet.org/2015/01/09/social-media-update-2014/

Ebner, M., Lienhardt, C., Rohs, M., & Meyer, I. (2010). Microblogs in higher education: A chance to facilitate informal and process-oriented learning? *Computers & Education, 55*(1), 92–100. doi:10.1016/j.compedu.2009.12.006

Ede, L., & Lunsford, A. A. (1990). *Singular texts, plural authors: Perspectives on collaborative writing*. Illinois: SIU Press.

EDUCAUSE Center for Applied Research. (2008). ECAR Study of Undergraduate Students and Information Technology.

Einon, G. (2010). Managing computer-supported collaboration. In H. Donelan, K. Kear, & M. Ramage (Eds.), *Online communication and collaboration: a reader*. Oxon: Routledge.

Elavsky, M. C. (2010). Social Media in the Classroom.

Elbow, P. (1973). *Writing without teachers*. New York, NY: Oxford University Press.

Elbow, P. (1981). *Writing with power, writing without teachers*. Oxford: Oxford UP.

Ellis, K. (2014). Civic engagement. Retrieved from http://kristinaellisfinalproject.blogspot.com/

Emarketer Inc. (2013). Digital set to surpass TV in time spent with US media: Mobile helps propel digital time spent [Press release]. Retrieved from http://www.emarketer.com/Article/Digital-Set-Surpass-TV-Time-Spent-with-US-Media/1010096

Emig, J. (1971). *The composing process of twelfth graders*. NCTE Press.

Emig, J. (1983). *The web of meaning*. UK: Heinemann Educational Books.

Facebook. (n. d.). *Facebook community standards.* Retrieved from https://www.facebook.com/communitystandards

Facebook. (n. d.). *What happens after you click 'report.'* Retrieved from https://www.facebook.com/notes/facebook-safety/what-happens-after-you-click-report/432670926753695

Faigley, L. (2003). The challenge of the multimedia essay. In Bloom, Daiker and White (Eds.), Composition studies in the new millennium: Rereading the past, rewriting the future (pp. 174-187). Carbondale: Southern Illinois University Press.

Farmer, B., Yue, A., & Brooks, C. (2008). Using blogging for higher order learning in large cohort university teaching: A case study. *Australasian Journal of Educational Technology, 24*(2), 123–136. doi:10.14742/ajet.1215

Ferdig, R. E., & Trammell, K. D. (2004). Content delivery in the "blogosphere." *T.H.E. Journal Online.* Retrieved from http://thejournal.com/articles/2004/02/01

Ferdig, R., & Trammell, K. (2004). Content delivery in the 'blogosphere.'[Technological Horizons in Education]. *T.H.E. Journal, 31*(7).

Ferguson, K. (2012). Everything is a remix. Retrieved from vimeo.com/kirbyferguson

Ferguson, K. (2012, August). Embrace the remix [Video file]. Retrieved from www.ted.com/talks/kirby_ferguson_embrace_ the_remix.html

Fernandes, J., Giurcanu, M., Bowers, K. W., & Neely, J. C. (2010). The writing on the wall: A content analysis of college students' Facebook groups for the 2008 presidential election. *Mass Communication & Society, 13*(5), 653–675. doi:10.1080/15205436.2010.516865

Ferriter, W. M. (2010). Why teachers should try Twitter. *Educational Leadership, 67*(5), 73–74.

Fife, J. M. (2010). Using Facebook to teach rhetorical analysis. *Pedagogy, 10*(3), 555–562. doi:10.1215/15314200-2010-007

File: Editor survey report. (2011). *Wikimedia foundation.* Retrieved from https://wikimediafoundation.org/

FireMe! App. (2016). Twitter Rants [Image]. Retrieved from http://fireme.l3s.uni-hannover.de/fireme.php

Flower, L. (2008). *Community literacy and the rhetoric of public engagement.* Carbondale: Southern Illinois UP.

Ford, S., Green, J., & Jenkins, H. (2013). *Spreadable media: Creating value and meaning in a networked culture (post-millennial pop).* New York, NY: New York University Press.

Freire, P. (1972). *Pedagogy of the oppressed.* New York: Herder and Herder.

Fulwiler, T. (1982). The personal connection: Journal writing across the curriculum. In T. Fulwiler & A. Young (Eds.), *Writing and reading across the curriculum.* Urbana, Illinois: National Council of Teachers of English.

Gee, J. (1989). Literacy, discourse and linguistics: Introduction. *Journal of Education, 171,* 5–17.

Gerald, A., Brusaw, C., & Walter, O. (2015). *Handbook of Technical Writing. Boston.* Bedford: St. Martin's.

Gerben, C. (2014). Free and easy: a Rubric for evaluating everyday technology. *The Writing Instructor.* Retrieved from http://parlormultimedia.com/twitest/gerben-2014-03

Gergitis, J. M., & Schramer, J. J. (1994). The collaborative classroom as the site of difference. *JAC, 14*(1), 187–202.

Gerodimos, R., & Ward, J. (2007). Rethinking online youth civic engagement: Reflections on web content analysis. In B. D. Loader (Ed.), *Young citizens in the digital age: Political engagement and new media* (pp. 114–126). New York, NY: Routledge.

Godwin-Jones, R. (2003). Emerging technologies: Blog and wikis: Environments for on-line collaboration. *Virginia Commonwealth University. Grading Student Papers: Some guidelines for commenting on and grading students' written work in any discipline.* Retrieved from https://www.cte.umd.edu/teaching/resources/GradingHandbook.pdf

Gooblar, D. (2014, July 2). The obvious benefits of in-class writing assignments. *The Chronicle Vitae.* Retrieved https://chroniclevitae.com/news/588-the-obvious-benefits-of-in-class-writing-assignments

Goodwin-Jones, B. (2003). Blogs and wikis: Environments for on-line collaboration. *Language Learning & Technology, 7*(2), 12–16.

Goodyear, P. (2005). Educational design and networked learning: Patterns, pattern languages and design practice. *Australasian Journal of Educational Technology, 21*(1), 82–101. doi:10.14742/ajet.1344

Grabill, J., Hart-Davidson, W., Pigg, S., Curran, P., McLeod, M., Moore, J., . . . Peeples, T. … Brunk-Chavez, B. (2010, September 7). *The Writing Lives of College Students.* Retrieved from http://www2.matrix.msu.edu/wp-content/uploads/2013/08/WIDE_writinglives_whitepaper.pdf

Graff, G. (2003). *Clueless in academe: How schooling obscures the life of the mind.* New Haven, CT: Yale University Press.

Graham, S., & Harris, K. R. (2007). Best practices in teaching planning. In S. Graham, C. A. McArthur, & J. Fitzgerald (Eds.), *Best practices in writing instruction* (pp. 119–140). New York: The Guilford Press.

Grasz, J. (2006). One-in-Four Hiring Managers Have Used Internet Search Engines to Screen Job Candidates; One-in-Ten Have Used Social Networking Sites, CareerBuilder.com Survey Finds. *Career Builder.* Retrieved from http://www.careerbuilder.com/share/aboutus/pressreleasesdetail.aspx?id=pr331&ed=12/31/2006&sd=10/26/2006

Gunraj, D., Drumm-Hewitt, A., Dashow, E., Upadhyay, S., & Klin, C. (2016). Texting insincerely: The role of the period in text messaging. *Computers in Human Behavior, 55,* 1067–1075. doi:10.1016/j.chb.2015.11.003

Guynn, J. (2014, March 03). Ellen DeGeneres selfie on Twitter is Oscar gold for Samsung. *Los Angeles Times.* Retrieved from http://articles.latimes.com/2014/mar/03/business/la-fi-tn-ellen-degeneres-selfie-twitter-oscars-samsung-20140303

Hacktivist [Def. 1]). (n. d.). *Oxford Dictionaries.* Retrieved from http://www.oxforddictionaries.com/us/definition/american_english/hacktivist

Hadjerrouit, S. (2011). A collaborative writing approach to wikis: Design, implementation, and evaluation. *Issues in Informing Science and Information Technology, 8,* 431–449.

Haefeli, S. (2013). Using blogs for better student writing outcomes. *Journal of Music History Pedagogy, 4*(1), 39–70.

Hallin, A. (2004). A Rhetoric for Audiences: Louise Rosenblatt on Reading and Action. Lunsford, A. (Ed.), Reclaiming Rhetorica: Women in the Rhetorical Tradition (pp. 285-303). Pittsburg: University of Pittsburg Press.

Hall, S. (1997). *Representation: cultural representations and signifying practices.* Los Angeles: SAGE Publications.

Hassett, J., Spuches, C., & Webster, S. (1995). Using electronic mail for teaching and learning. *To Improve the Academy.*

Hawisher, G., & Selfe, C. (Eds.). (1991). *Evolving perspectives on computers and composition studies: questions for the 1990s.* Urbana, IL: National Council of Teachers of English.

Hawk, B. (2007). *A Counter-history of composition: Toward methodologies of complexity.* Pittsburgh, PA: University of Pittsburgh Press.

Hazari, S., North, A. & Moreland, D. (2009). Investigating pedagogical value of wiki technology. *Journal of information Systems, 20*(2), 187-198.

Heiberger, G., & Harper, R. (2008). Have You Facebooked Astin Lately? Using Technology to Increase Student Involvement. *New Directions for Student Services*, 2008, 3–25.

Heilman, J. M., Kemmann, E., Bonert, M., Chatterjee, A., Ragar, B., Beards, G. M., & Laurent, M. R. et al. (2011). Wikipedia: A key tool for global public health promotion. *Journal of Medical Internet Research*, *13*(1), e14. doi:10.2196/jmir.1589 PMID:21282098

Help: Using talk pages (n. d.). In *Wikipedia*. Retrieved fromhttps://en.wikipedia.org/wiki/Help:Using_talk_pages

Helsper, E., & Enyon, R. (2010). Digital natives: Where is the evidence? *British Educational Research Journal*, *36*(3), 503–520. doi:10.1080/01411920902989227

Hess, M. (2006). Was Foucault a plagiarist? Hip-hop sampling and academic citation. *Computers and Composition*, *23*, 280–295.

Hobbs, R. (2015). Twitter as a pedagogical tool in higher education. In R. Lind (Ed.), *Producing theory in a digital world 2.0*. New York: Peter Lang.

Hocks, M. E. (2008). Understanding visual rhetorics in digital writing environments. In T. R. Johnson (Ed.), *Teaching composition: background readings* (pp. 337–362). New York, NY: Bedford St Martin's.

Holub, R. C. (1984). *Reception theory: A critical introduction*. London: Methuen.

Honan, E. (2003). *Teachers as researchers: Using the four resources model as a map of practices. Teachers as leaders: Teacher education for a global profession. International yearbook on teacher education. 48th world assembly*. Melbourne, Australia: ICET.

Huckin, T. (1992). Context-sensitive text analysis. In Methods and methodology in composition research (pp. 84-104).

Hughes, B., Joshi, I., Lemonde, H., & Wareham, J. (2009). Junior physician's use of Web 2.0 for information seeking and medical education: A qualitative study. *International Journal of Medical Informatics*, *78*(10), 645–655. doi:10.1016/j.ijmedinf.2009.04.008 PMID:19501017

Ingram, A., & Hathorn, L. (2004). Methods for Analysing Collaboration in Online Communications. In T. S. Roberts (Ed.), *Online Collaborative Learning: Theory and Practice*. Hershey, PA: Information Science Publishing. doi:10.4018/978-1-59140-174-2.ch010

Ipsos (2014). Ipsos Millenial Social Influence Study. Retrieved from http://corp.crowdtap.com/socialinfluence

Isaac, M. (2015, August 3). For mobile messaging, GIFs prove to be worth at least a thousand words. *The New York Times*. Retrieved from http://www.nytimes.com/2015/08/04/technology/gifs-go-beyond-emoji-to-express-thoughts-without-words.html

Jacobis, L. (Ed.). (2013). *A world of ideas. Boston*. Bedford: St. Martin's.

Jacquemin, S. J., Smelser, L. K., & Bernot, M. J. (2014). Twitter in the higher education classroom: A student and faculty assessment of use and perception. *Journal of College Science Teaching*, *43*(6), 22–27.

Jaschik, S. (2014, January 28). Snow hate. *Inside Higher Ed*. Retrieved from https://www.insidehighered.com/news/2014/01/28/u-illinois-decision-keep-classes-going-leads-racist-and-sexist-twitter-attacks

Jenkins, H., Purushotma, R., Clinton, K., Weigel, M., & Robinson, A. (2006). *Confronting the challenges of participatory culture: Media education for the 21st century*. Chicago: The MacArthur Foundation.

Jobvite Survey. (2014). Social recruiting survey (Press release). Retrieved from https://www.jobvite.com/wp-content/uploads/2014/10/Jobvite_SocialRecruiting_Survey2014.pdf

Johnson, D. (2014). Reading, writing, and literacy 2.0: Teaching with online texts, tools, and resources, K-8. Teachers College Press: Columbia University.

Johnson, D. W., & Johnson, R. T. (1999). Making cooperative learning work. *Theory into Practice*, *38*(2), 67–73. doi:10.1080/00405849909543834

Johnson-Eilola, J., & Selber, S. (2007). Plagiarism, Originality, Assemblage. *Computers and Composition*, *24*, 375–403.

Johnson, W. (1943). You can't write writing. *Etc.; a Review of General Semantics*, *1*(1), 25–32.

Jones, J. (2010, March 9). The creepy treehouse problem (Blog post). Retrieved from: http://chronicle.com/blogs/profhacker/the-creepy-treehouse-problem/23027

Junco, R., Heiberger, G., & Loken, E. (2011). The effect of Twitter on college student engagement and grades. *Journal of Computer Assisted Learning*, *27*(2), 119–132. doi:10.1111/j.1365-2729.2010.00387.x

Kachru, B. B. (1992). *The other tongue: English across cultures*. University of Illinois Press.

Keengwe, J., & Onchwari, G. (2011). Fostering meaningful student learning through constructivist pedagogy and technology integration. *International Journal of Information and Communication Technology Education*, *7*(4).

Keengwe, J., Onchwari, G., & Agamba, J. (2014, December). Promoting effective e-learning practices through the constructivist pedagogy. *Education and Information Technologies*, *19*(4), 887–898. doi:10.1007/s10639-013-9260-1

Kemp, F. (2010). *Introduction to Rhetorical Theory Course*. Texas Tech University.

Kemp, N., Wood, C., & Waldron, S. (2014). do i know its wrong: Children's and adults' use of unconventional grammar in text messaging. *Reading and Writing: An Interdisciplinary Journal*, *27*(9), 1585–1602. doi:10.1007/s11145-014-9508-1

Kim, D. (2014). The rules of Twitter. *Hybrid Pedagogy*. Retrieved from http://www.hybridpedagogy.com/journal/rules-twitter/

King, M., Jr. (1963). Letter from Birmingham jail. In L. Jacobis (Ed.), A world of ideas (pp. 375-392). Boston: Bedford/St. Martin's.

Knobel, M., & Lankshear, C. (2008). Remix: The art and craft of endless hybridization. *Journal of Adolescent & Adult Literacy*, *52*(1), 22–34.

Koh, A. (2015). Teaching with the Internet; or How I learned to stop worrying and love the Google in my classroom. *Hybrid Pedagogy*. Retrieved from http://www.hybridpedagogy.com/journal/teaching-with-the-internet-or-how-i-learned-to stop-worrying-and-love-the-google-in-my-classroom/

Krause, S. D. (2008). When blogging goes bad: a Cautionary tale about blogs, email lists, discussion, and interaction. In T. R. Johnson (Ed.), *Teaching composition: background readings* (pp. 325–336). New York, NY: Bedford St Martin's.

Kress, G. (2010). *Multimodality: A social semiotic approach to contemporary communication*. London, England: Routledge.

Kristof-Brown, A. (2000). Perceived applicant fit: Distinguishing between recruiters' perceptions of person-job and person-organization fit. *Personnel Psychology*, *53*(3), 643–671. doi:10.1111/j.1744-6570.2000.tb00217.x

Kummer, C. (2013). Students' Intentions to Use Wikis in Higher Education. *Wirtschaftsinformatik*. Retrieved from http://files.figshare.com/1035208/ Structural_Equation_Modeling.pdf

Kuznekoff, J., Munz, S., & Titsworth, S. (2015). Mobile phones in the classroom: Examining the effects of texting, twitter, and message content on student learning. *Communication Education, 63*(3), 344–365. doi:10.1080/03634523. 2015.1038727

LaFrance, A. (2014, March 25). When did group pictures become 'selfies'? *The Atlantic.* Retrieved from http://www. theatlantic.com/technology/archive/2014/03/when-did-group-pictures-become-selfies/359556/

Lambert, J., & Cuper, P. (2008). Multimedia technologies and familiar spaces: 21st-century teaching for 21st-century learners. *Contemporary Issues in Technology & Teacher Education, 8*(3), 264–276.

Lehr, F. (1995). Revision in the writing process. *ERIC Digest, ED379664*(1995-00-00). Retrieved from eric.ed.gov

Lehtinen, E. (2003). Computer-supported collaborative learning: An approach to powerful learning environments: *Unravelling basic components and dimensions.*

Lenhart, A. (2015). *Teens, social media & technology overview 2015.* Retrieved from http://www.pewinternet. org/2015/04/09/teens-social-media-technology-2015/

Lenhart, A., Arafeh, S., Smith, A., & Macgill, A. (2008). *Writing, Technology and Teens.* Retrieved from http://www. pewinternet.org/2008/04/24/writing-technology-and-teens/

Lenhart, A., Sousan, A., Amith, A., & Macgill, A. R. (2008). Writing, technology, and teens. *Pew Internet and American Life Project.* Retrieved from http://www.pewinternet.org

Leslie, P., & Farmer, E. (2008). Post-secondary students' purposes for blogging. *International Review of Research in Open and Distance Learning, 9*(3).

Lessig, L. (2008). *Remix: Making art and commerce thrive in the hybrid economy.* New York, NY: Penguin.

Lethem, J. (2007). The ecstasy of Influence. *Harpers Magazine.* Retrieved from http://harpers.org/archive/2007/02/ the-ecstasy-of-influence/

Leu, D. J. Jr, Kinzer, C. K., Coiro, J., & Castek, J. (2013b). New literacies: A dual-level theory of the changing nature of literacy, instruction, and assessment. In R. B. Ruddell & D. Alvermann (Eds.), *Theoretical models and processes of reading* (pp. 1150–1181). Newark, DE: International Reading Association. doi:10.1598/0710.42

Li, M. (2014). *Small Group Interactions in Wiki-Based Collaborative Writing in the EAP Context* [Unpublished PhD thesis]. University of South Florida.

Lienesch, R. (2015). Not All Millennials are Social Media Mavens. *Public Religion Research Institute.* Retrieved from http://publicreligion.org/2015/07/not-all-millennials-are-social-media-mavens/#.Vf7jt99Vikp

LinkedIn. (n. d.). About Us. Retrieved from: https://www.linkedin.com/about-us

Lin, M.-F., Hoffman, E., & Borengasser, C. (2013). Is social media too social for class? A case study of Twitter use. *TechTrends, 57*(2), 39–45. doi:10.1007/s11528-013-0644-2

Littlejohn, A., & Pegler, C. (2007). *Preparing for Blended E-learning.* Abingdon, New York: Routledge.

Liu, X. (2010). Empirical testing of a theoretical extension of the technology acceptance model: An exploratory study of educational wikis. *Communication Education, 59*(1), 52–69. doi:10.1080/03634520903431745

Livinstone, S., Couldry, N., & Markham, T. (2007). Youthful steps towards civic participation: Does the Internet help? In B. D. Loader (Ed.), *Young citizens in the digital age: Political engagement and new media* (pp. 21–34). New York, NY: Routledge.

Locker, K., & Kienzler, D. (2015). *Business and administrative communication* (11th ed.). Boston: McGraw-Hill.

Loeb, P. (2010). Soul of a citizen (new and revised edition). New York: St. Martin's Press.

Loeb, P. (Ed.). (2004). *The impossible will take a little while*. New York: Basic Books.

Luke, A., & Freebody, P. (1999). Further notes on the four resources model, reading online. Retrieved from http:www. readingonline.org/research/lukefrebody.html

Lundin, R. W. (2008). Teaching with Wikis: Toward a Networked Pedagogy. *Computers and Composition, 25*(4), 432–448. doi:10.1016/j.compcom.2008.06.001

Lunsford, A. A. (2015). Writing addresses, invokes, and/or creates audiences. In L. Adler-Kassner & E. Wardle (Eds.), Naming what we know: Threshold concepts of writing studies (pp. 20-21). Boulder: Utah State University Press.

Lunsford, A. (2007). *Writing Matters: Rhetoric in public and private lives*. Athens, GA: University of Georgia Press.

Lunsford, A., Ede, L., Moss, B., Papper, C., Walters, K., & Brody, M. (2012). *Everyone's an author with readings*. New York: W.W. Norton & Company.

Lutkewitte, C. (Ed.). (2014). *Multimodal composition: a critical sourcebook. Boston*. Bedford: St. Martin's.

Maitre, M. (2006, August 22). Myspace 101: Colleges urge caution. *Inside Bay Area*. Retrieved from http://www.inside-bayarea.com/dailyreview/localnews/ci_4218247

Manovich, L. (2005, November 15). Remix and remixability. Rhizome. Retrieved from rhizome.org/discuss/view/19303/

Maranto, G., & Barton, M. (2010). Paradox and promise: MySpace, Facebook, and the sociopolitics of social networking in the writing classroom. *Computers and Composition, 27*(1), 36–47. doi:10.1016/j.compcom.2009.11.003

Margetson, D. (1991). Why is problem-based learning a challenge? In D. Boud & G. Feletti (Eds.), The Challenge of Problem Based Learning (pp. 36-44). London: Kogan.

Markel, M. (2014). *Technical communication* (11th ed.). Boston: Bedford/St. Martin's.

MarketingProfs. (2013). Social takes up 27% of time spent online. Retrieved from http://www.marketingprofs.com/charts/2013/10582/social-takes-up-27-of-time-spent-online

Marshall, K. (2015, June 1). Rethinking Twitter in the classroom. *Chronicle Vitae*. Retrieved from https://chroniclevitae.com/news/1021-rethinking-twitter-in-the-classroom

Marwick, A. E., & boyd, . (2010). I tweet honestly, I tweet passionately: Twitter users, content collapse and imagined audience. *New Media & Society, 13*(1), 114–133. doi:10.1177/1461444810365313

Mayer-Schonenberger, V., & Cukier, K. (2013). *Big data: A revolution that will transform how we live, work, and think*. New York, NY: Houghton Mifflin.

McCloud, S. (1993). *Understanding comics: the invisible art*. New York, NY: HarperCollins.

McCominsky, B. (2000). *Teaching composition as a social process*. Logan, UT: Utah State University Press.

McKay, B., & McKay, K. (2010). *The pocket notebooks of 20 famous men*. Retrieved from http://www.artofmanliness.com/

McNeill, R., Jr. (2011). Adapting teaching to the millennial generation: A case study of a blended/hybrid course. *International CHRIE Conference-Refereed Track. Paper 3.*

McWhorter, J. (2013, February). John McWhorter: Texting is killing language [Video File]. Retrieved from http://www.ted.com/talks/john_mcwhorter_txtng_is_killing_language_jk

Mesch, G. S., & Coleman, S. (2007). New media and new voters: young people, the Internet and the 2005 UK election campaign. In B. D. Loader (Ed.), *Young citizens in the digital age: Political engagement and new media* (pp. 35–47). New York, NY: Routledge.

Miller, C., & Shepherd, D. (2004). Blogging as social action: A genre analysis of the weblog. University of Minnesota. Retrieved from http://www.webcitation.org/5j9YtAGiO

Miller, C., & Shepherd, D. (2009). Blogging as social action: A genre analysis of the weblog. In S. Miller's (Ed.), The Norton book of composition studies. (pp. 1450-1473). New York: W.W. Norton & Company, Inc.

Miller, C. (1884). Genre as social action. *The Quarterly Journal of Speech, 70*(2), 151–167. doi:10.1080/00335638409383686

Miller, C., & Shepherd, D. (2009). Questions for genre theory from the blogosphere. In J. Giltrow & D. Stein (Eds.), *Genres in the Internet: Issues in the theory of genre.* Amsterdam: John Benjamin's Publishing. doi:10.1075/pbns.188.11mil

Miller, P. (2008). *Sound Unbound.* Boston, MA: MIT Press.

Minocha, S., & Thomas, P. G. (2007). Collaborative Learning in a Wiki Environment Experiences from a software engineering course. *New Review of Hypermedia and Multimedia, 13*(2), 187–209. doi:10.1080/13614560701712667

Moffett, J., & Wager, B. (1991). *Student-centered language arts, K-12.* Portsmouth: Heinemann.

Monster.com. (n. d.). Search results. Retrieved from: http://career-advice.monster.com/searchresult/employment.aspx

Moody, M. (2010). Teaching Twitter and beyond: Tips for incorporating social media in traditional courses. *Journal of Magazine & New Media Research, 11*(2), 1–9.

Morey, S. (2014). *The new media writer.* Southlake, TX: Fountainhead Press.

Murphy, D. (2013, November 6). Woman behind Boston marathon bombing costume blasts critics. *NY Daily News.* Retrieved from http://www.nydailynews.com/news/national/woman-behind-boston-marathon-bombing-costume-blasts-critics-article-1.1508156

Murphy, L., & Southgate, M. (2011). The Nature of the 'blend': Interaction of Teaching Modes, Tools and Resources. In M. Nicolson, L. Murphy, & M. Southgate (Eds.), *Language Teaching in Blended Contexts. Scotland* (pp. 13–28). Dunedin.

Myers-Scotton, C., & Ury, W. (1977). Bilingual Strategies: The Social Functions of Codeswitching. *Journal of the Sociology of Language, 13*, 5–20.

National Writing Project. DeVoss, D., Eidman-Aadahl, E., & Hicks, T. (2010). Because digital writing matters: Improving student writing in online and multimedia environments. San Francisco, California: Jossey-Bass.

Navas, E. (2012). *Remix theory: The aesthetics of sampling.* New York, NY: Springer.

New London Group. (2014). From a pedagogy of multiliteracies: designing social futures. In C. Lutkewitte, (Ed.), Multimodal composition: a critical sourcebook (pp. 193-210). Boston: Bedford St. Martin's.

Nordloff, J. (2014). Vygotsky, scaffolding, and the role of theory in writing center work. *Writing Center Journal, 34*(1), 45–64.

Nunan, D. (2006). *Task-based language learning.* Cambridge: Cambridge University Press.

Oh, H. (2014). Learners' Writing Performance, Revision Behavior, Writing Strategy, and Perception in Wiki-mediated Collaborative Writing. *Multimedia-Assisted Language Learning, 17*(2), 176–199.

Oleson, Frances B. (1999). Is it a diary? A journal? - No, it's a writer's notebook. *Language Arts Journal of Michigan, 15*(2), 17-22.

Ophir, E., Nass, C., & Wagner, A. D. (2009). From the Cover: Cognitive control in media multitaskers.*Proceedings of the National Academy of Science.*

Optimizing Facebook engagement – the effect of post length. (2012, June 27). *Smart Data Collective*. Retrieved http://www.smartdatacollective.com/morgan-j-arnold/52456/optimizing-facebook-engagement-effect-post-length

Oravec, J. A. (2002). Bookmarking the world: Weblog applications in education. *Journal of Adolescent & Adult Literacy, 45*(7), 616–621.

Oshima, A., & Hogue, A. (2005). *Writing Academic English* (4th ed.). Longman.

Palmeri, J. (2012). *Remixing composition: A history of multimodal writing pedagogy*. Carbondale: Southern Illinois University Press.

Palmer, P. (1983). *To know as we are known: Education as a spiritual journey*. New York, NY: Harper One.

Palmer, P., & Zajonc, A. (2010). *The heart of higher education: A call to renewal*. San Francisco, CA: Jossey-Bass.

Pariser, E. (2011). *The filter bubble: How the new personalized web is changing the way we read and how we think*. New York, NY: Penguin.

Pegrum, M. (2011). Modified, multipled, and (re-)mixed: Social media and digital literacies. In M. Thomas (Ed.), *Digital education: Opportunities for social collaboration* (pp. 9–36). New York: Palgrave Macmillan.

Peluso, D. C. C. (2012). The fast-paced iPad revolution: Can educators stay up to date and relevant about these ubiquitous devices? *British Journal of Educational Technology, 43*(4), E125–E127. doi:10.1111/j.1467-8535.2012.01310.x

Penney, J., & Dadas, C. (2014). (Re)Tweeting in the service of protest: Digital composition and circulation in the occupy Wall Street movement. *New Media & Society, 16*(1), 74–90. doi:10.1177/1461444813479593

Perkins, D., & Salomon, G. (1992). *Transfer of learning. International Encyclopedia of Education* (2nd ed.). Boston, MA: Pergamon Press.

Perrin, A. (2015). Social media usage: 2005-2015. *Pew Research Center*. Retrieved from http://www.pewinternet.org/2015/10/08/social-networking-usage-2005-2015/

Pew Internet and American Life Project. (2010). Social Media & Mobile Internet Use among Teens and Young Adults.

Pew Research Center. (2014). Social networking fact sheet. Retrieved from http://www.pewinternet.org/fact-sheets/social-networking-fact-sheet/

Pingdom, A. B. (2012). Report: Social network demographics in 2012. Retrieved from http://royal.pingdom.com/2012/08/21/report-social-network-demographics-in-2012/

Pinkerton, J. (2013). How to Manage Your Online Image to Advance Your Career. *CompTIA*. Retrieved from http://certification.comptia.org/news/2013/03/27/How_to_Manage_Your_Online_Image_to_Advance_Your_Career.aspx

Pitts, M., & Bennett, J. (2011). *Just do it: Tips for avoiding procrastination*. Retrieved from http://www.law.georgetown.edu/academics/academic-programs/legal-writing-scholarship/writing-center/usefuldocuments.cfm

Planning, C. (n. d.). Radford University. Retrieved from http://www.radford.edu/content/career-services/home/students.html

Poling, C. (2005). Blog on: Building communication and collaboration among staff and students. *Learning and Leading with Technology*, *32*(6), 12–15.

Pope, J. (2006, Aug 2). Students warned about networking sites. *USA Today*. Retrieved from http://usatoday30.usatoday.com/tech/news/internetprivacy/2006-08-02-facebook-orientations_x.htm

Preliminary report on English composition teaching by a committee of the English Section of the Central Division of the Modern Language Association. (1910). Bulletin Iowa State College of Agriculture and Mechanic Arts, IX(3).

Prensky, M. (2001). Digital natives, digital immigrants. Retrieved from http://www.marcprensky.com/writing/Prensky%20-%20Digital%20Natives,%20Digital%20Immigrants%20-%20Part1.pdf

Prensky, M. (2001). Digital natives, digital Immigrants. Retrieved from http://www.marcprensky.com/writing/Prensky%20-%20Digital%20Natives,%20Digital%20Immigrants%20-%20Part1.pdf

Prensky, M. (2001). Digital natives, digital immigrants. *On the Horizon*, *9*(5), 1–6. doi:10.1108/10748120110424816

Prensky, M. (2001). Digital natives, digital immigrants. *On the horizon.*, (9): 1–6.

Purcell, K., Buchanan, J., & Friedrich, L. (2013). *The impact of digital tools on student writing and how writing is taught in schools.* Retrieved from http://www.pewinternet.org/2013/07/16/the-impact-of-digital-tools-on-student-writing-and-how-writing-is-taught-in-schools/

Purdy, J. (2010). The changing space of research: Web 2.0 and the integration of research and writing environments. *Computers and Composition*, *27*(1), 48–58. doi:10.1016/j.compcom.2009.12.001

RAND Reading Study Group. (2002). *Reading for understanding: Toward an R&D program in reading comprehension.* Santa Monica, CA: RAND.

Rice, J. (2012). *Digital Detroit: Rhetoric and space in the age of the network.* Carbondale: Southern Illinois University Press.

Rideout, V. (2012). *Children, teens, and entertainment media: The view from the classroom a national survey of teachers about the role of entertainment media in students' academic and social development, a Common Sense Media research study.* Retrieved from https://www.commonsensemedia.org/research/

Rivera, L. (2015, May 30). Guess who doesn't fit in at work. *The New York Times*. Retrieved from: http://nyti.ms/1d61kMt

Roblyer, M. D., & Ekhaml, L. (2000). How interactive are your distance courses? A rubric for assessing interaction in distance learning. *Online Journal of Distance Learning Administration*, *3*(2).

Rosenblatt, L. (1983). Literature As Exploration (4th ed.). New York: MLA.

Rosenblatt, L. (1977). What We Have Learned: Reminiscences of the NCTE. *English Journal*, *66*(8), 88–90.

Rounasville, A., Goldberg, R., & Bawarshi, A. (2008). From incomes to outcomes: FYC students' prior genre knowledge, meta-cognition, and the question of transfer. *WPA*, *32*(1), 97–112.

Ruefman, D. (n. d.). Taking Control: Managing Your Online Identity for the Job Search. Writing Commons. Retrieved from http://writingcommons.org/index.php/open-text/new-media/negotiating-virtual-spaces-public-writing/1210-taking-control-managing-your-online-identity-for-the-job-search

Rushkoff. (2010). *Program or be programmed: Ten commands for a digital age.* Berkeley: Soft Scull Press.

Sabatino, L. (2014). Improving writing literacies through digital gaming literacies: Facebook gaming in the composition classroom. *Computers and Composition, 32*, 41–53. doi:10.1016/j.compcom.2014.04.005

Sacks, M., & Graves, N. (2012). How many "friends" do you need? Teaching students how to network using social media. *Business and Professional Communication Quarterly, 75*(1), 80–88. doi:10.1177/1080569911433326

Safronova, V. (2014, December 20). Millennials and the age of Tumblr activism. *The New York Times.* Retrieved from http://www.nytimes.com/2014/12/21/style/millennials-and-the-age-of-tumblr-activism.html

Santos, M. C., & Leahy, M. H. (2014). Postpedagogy and web writing. *Computers and Composition, 32*, 84–95. doi:10.1016/j.compcom.2014.04.006

Savin-Baden, M., & Howell Major, C. (2004). *Foundations of problem-based learning.* Birkshire, England: The Society for Research into Higher Education & Open University Press.

Schaefer, M. (2014). *The tao of Twitter: Changing your life and business 140 characters at a time.* New York: McGraw-Hill.

Schroeder, J., & Boe, J. (2004). An Interview with Ken Macrorie: 'Arrangements for Truthtelling'. *Writing on the Edge, 15*(1), 4–17.

Schwom, B., & Snyder, L. (2012). *Business communication: Polishing your professional presence.* Boston: Prentice Hall.

Scott, G. G., Sinclair, J., Short, E., & Bruce, G. (2014). It's not what you say, it's how you say it: Language use on Facebook impacts employability but not attractiveness. *Cyberpsychology, Behavior, and Social Networking, 17*(8), 562–566. doi:10.1089/cyber.2013.0584 PMID:24949532

Selber, S. (2004). *Multiliteracies for a digital age.* Carbondale: Southern Illinois University Press.

Selfe, C. (2010, April). If you don't believe that you're doing some good with the work that you do, then you shouldn't be doing it: An interview with Cindy Selfe. *Composition Forum, 21.* Retrieved fromhttp://compositionforum.com/issue/21/cindy-selfe-interview.php

Selfe, C. (1999). *Technology and literacy in the twenty-first century: The importance of paying attention. Carbondale and Edwardsville.* IL: Southern Illinois University Press.

Selfie [Def 1]. (n. d.). *Oxford Dictionaries.* Retrieved from http://www.oxforddictionaries.com/us/definition/american_english/selfie

Shaughnessy, M. P. (1976). Diving in: An introduction to basic writing. In V. Villanueva (Ed.), *Cross talk in comp theory: A reader* (2nd ed., pp. 311–317). Urbana, IL: National Council of Teachers of English. doi:10.2307/357036

Shifman, L. (2013). *Memes in digital culture.* Cambridge, MA: MIT Press.

Shin, L. (2014). How to Use LinkedIn: 5 Smart Steps to Career Success. *Forbes.* Retrieved from http://www.forbes.com/sites/laurashin/2014/06/26/how-to-use-linkedin-5-smart-steps-to-career-success/

Shipka, J. (2011). *Toward a composition made whole.* Pittsburgh, PA: University of Pittsburgh Press.

Shirky, C. (2014). Why I asked my students to put away their laptops. *Medium.* Retrieved from https://medium.com/@cshirky/why-i-just-asked-my-students-to-put-their-laptops-away7f5f7c50f368

Shor, I. (1996). *When students have power: Negotiating authority in a critical pedagogy.* Chicago: University of Chicago Press.

Silver, D. (2009, February 25). the different between thick and thin tweets. [Blog post]. Retrieved from: http://silverinsf.blogspot.com/2009/02/difference-between-thin-and-thick.html

Single Platform Team. (2014). How to Build a Positive Public Persona. *Single Platform Blog*. Retrieved from: http://www.singleplatform.com/2014/06/09/build-positive-public-persona/

Sirc, G. Serial composition. In S. A. Selber (Ed.), *Rhetoric and Technologies* (pp. 56–73). Columbia, SC: University of South Carolina Press.

Snipes, V., Ellis, W., & Thomas, J. (2006). Are HBCUs up to speed technologically? One case study. *Journal of Black Studies*, *36*(3), 382–395. doi:10.1177/0021934705278782

Social Networking Fact Sheet. (2014). *Pew Research Center*. Retrieved from http://www.pewinternet.org/fact-sheets/social-networking-fact-sheet/

Social networking fact sheet. (n. d.). *Pew Internet*. Retrieved from http://www.pewinternet.org/fact-sheets/social-networking-fact-sheet/

Stanley, G. (2013). *Language Learning with Technology: Ideas for Integrating Technology in the Classroom*. Cambridge: Cambridge University Press.

Starkey, L. (2012). *Teaching and learning in the digital age*. New York, NY: Routledge.

Starnes, T. (n. d.). Facebook explains why they blocked Kirk Cameron. *Fox News*. Retrieved from http://radio.foxnews.com/toddstarnes/top-stories/facebook-explains-why-they-blocked-kirk-cameron.html

Stauts, M. (2015, August 7). Your online presence can help or hurt when applying to college. *The Atlanta Journal-Constitution*. Retrieved from www.ajc.com

Stommel, J. (2012). The Twitter essay. *Hybrid Pedagogy*. Retrieved fromhttp://www.hybridpedagogy.com/journal/the-twitter-essay/

Storch, N. (2005). Collaborative writing: Product, process, and students' reflections. *Journal of Second Language Writing*, *14*(3), 143–173. doi:10.1016/j.jslw.2005.05.002

Storch, N. (2013). *Collaborative writing in L2 classrooms*. Multilingual matters.

Summary health statistics for U.S. children: National health interview survey, 2007. (2009). *CDC Vital and Health Statistics*, 10(239).

Swain, M., Brooks, L., & Tocalli-Beller, A. (2002). 9. Peer-Peer Dialogue as a Means of Second Language Learning. *Annual Review of Applied Linguistics*, *22*(1), 171–185.

Swartz, J. (2010). MySpace, Facebook, and multimodal literacy in the writing classroom. *PraxisWiki: Kairos: A Journal of Rhetoric, Technology, and Pedagogy*. Retrieved from http://kairos.technorhetoric.net/praxis/tiki-index.php?page=Multimodal_Literacy

Taggart, D., & Pall, A. (2014). #Selfie. [Recorded by The Chainsmokers]. On The Chainsmokers [digital download]. Los Angeles: Dim Mak Records.

Takayoshi, P., & Selfe, C. (2007). Thinking about modality. In C. Selfe (Ed.), *Multimodal composition: Resources for teachers* (pp. 1–12). Cresskill, NJ: Hampton Press.

Takayoshi, P., & Sullivan, P. (2007). *Labor, writing technologies, and the shaping of composition in the academy*. New Jersey: Hamilton Press, Inc.

Tannen, D. (2013). The medium is the metamessage: Conversational style in new media interaction. In D. Tannen. A. Trester. (Eds.), Discourse 2.0: Language and new media (pp. 99-118). Washington, D.C: Georgetown University Press.

Teens, social media & technology overview 2015. (2015, April 9). *Pew Internet.* Retrieved from http://www.pewinternet. org/2015/04/09/teens-social-media-technology 2015/

The New London Group. (1996). A pedagogy of multiliteracies: Designing social futures. *Harvard Educational Review*, (66): 60–93.

The skills/qualities employers want in new college graduate hires. (2014, November 18). *National Association of College and Employers.* Retrieved http://www.naceweb.org/about-us/press/class-2015-skills-qualities-employers-want.aspx

The University of Pittsburgh Study of Writing: A Report on Writing in the School of Arts and Sciences Undergraduate Curriculum (2009). Retrieved from http://www.academic.pitt.edu/assessment/resources.html

Thomas, M. (2011). *Deconstructing digital natives: Young people, technology, and the new literacies.* New York, NY: Routledge.

Tomaszewski, J. (2011). Writing lesson: Better blogs. *Education World.* Retrieved from http://www.educationworld. com/a_lesson/better-blog-writing.shtml

Tomic, P. (2014). Selfie [Photograph]. Retrieved from https://www.flickr.com/photos/tomicpasko/14139726176

Tumblr. (n. d.). Retrieved from tumblr.com

Tunick, R. A., & Brand, S. R. (2015). Social media and health care. In L.S. Wiener, M. Pao, A.E. Kazak, M.J. Kupst, & A.F. Patenaude (Eds.), Pediatric psycho-oncology: A quick reference on the psychosocial dimensions of cancer symptom Management (pp. 345-357).

Turkle, S. (2011). The tethered self: Technology reinvents intimacy and solitude. In *Continuing Higher Education Review* (pp. 7528-7531).

Turkle, S. (2012, February). Sherry Turkle: Connected, but alone? [Video File]. Retrieved from http://www.ted.com/ talks/sherry_turkle_alone_together

Turkle, S. (2012). *Alone together.* New York: Basic Books.

Turner, J. (2012, Nov. 2). #InPraiseOfTheHashtag. *The New York Times.* Retrieved from: http://www.nytimes. com/2012/11/04/magazine/in-praise-of-the-hashtag.html?_r=1

Turner, K. (2009). Flipping the switch: Code-switching from text speak to standard English. *English Journal, 98*(5), 60–65.

Turner, K. H. (2009). Flipping the switch: Code-switching from text speak to formal language. *English Journal, 98*(5), 60–65.

Twitter. (n. d.a). Using hashtags on Twitter. Retrieved from: https://support.twitter.com/articles/49309

Twitter. (n. d.b). About your Twitter timeline. Retrieved from: https://support.twitter.com/articles/164083

Urbanaski, H. (2008). *"I hate to write. I can't do it.": First-Year Composition and the Resistant Student Writer* [Dissertation]. Lehigh University.

VanEpps, C. (2012). Blogging as a strategy to support reading comprehension skills. *Education Masters.*

Vatz, R. E. (1973). The myth of the rhetorical situation. *Philosophy & Rhetoric, 6*(3), 154–161.

Vicknair, J., Elkersh, D., Yancey, K., & Budden, M. (2010). The use of social networking websites as a recruiting tool for employers. *American Journal of Business Education, 3*(11), 7–12.

Vie, S. (2014). In defense of 'slacktivism': The Human Rights Campaign Facebook logo as digital activism. *First Monday*, 19(4-7). Retrieved from http://firstmonday.org/article/view/4961/3868

Vie, S. (2008). Digital divide 2.0: "Generation m" and the online social networking sites in the composition classroom. *Computers and Composition*, *25*(1), 9–23. doi:10.1016/j.compcom.2007.09.004

Vygotsky, L. S. (1978). Interaction between learning and development. In M. Cole, V. John-Steiner, S. Scribner, & E. Souberman (Eds.), *Mind in society: The development of higher psychological processes* (pp. 79–91). Cambridge, MA: Harvard University Press.

Vygotsky, L. S. (1981). The genesis of higher mental functions. In J. V. Wertsch (Ed.), *The concept of activity in soviet psychology* (pp. 144–188). Armonk, NY: Sharpe.

Wagner, C. (2004). Wiki: A technology for conversational knowledge management and group collaboration. *Communications of the Association for Information Systems*, *13*(13), 265–289.

Wandel, T., & Beavers, A. (2010). Playing around with identity. In S. C. Wittkower (Ed.), *Facebook and philosophy* (pp. 89–96). Chicago, IL: Open Court.

Wardle, E. (2007). Understanding 'transfer' from FYC: Preliminary results of a longitudinal study. *WPA*, *31*(1/2), 65–85.

Watkins, S. C. (2009). *The young and the digital: What the migration to social-network sites, games, and anytime, anywhere media means for our future.* Boston, MA: Beacon.

Weinberger, A., Ertl, B., Fischer, F., & Mandl, H. (2005). Epistemic and social scripts in computer–supported collaborative learning. *Instructional Science*, *33*(1), 1–30. doi:10.1007/s11251-004-2322-4

West, J. A., & West, M. L. (2009). *Using Wikis for On-line collaboration: The power of the Read-Write Web.* San Francisco, CA: Jossey-Bass.

Wheeler, R. (2008). Becoming adept at code-switching. *Educational Leadership*, *65*(7), 54–58.

Wheeler, S. (2010). Open content, open learning 2.0: Using Wikis and Blogs in Higher Education. In U.-D. Ehlers & D. Schneckenberg (Eds.), *Changing Cultures in Higher Education: Moving Ahead to Future Learning* (pp. 103–114). Springer. doi:10.1007/978-3-642-03582-1_9

Wikimedia Foundation. (2015). *May 31, 2015 Wikipedia Statistics.* Available from the Wikimedia Foundation website: http://stats.wikimedia.org/EN/Sitemap.htm

Wikipedia. Policies and guidelines. (2015, July 18). *Wikipedia.* Retrieved fromhttps://en.wikipedia.org/wiki/Wikipedia:Policies_and_guidelines

Wikipedia. Wikipedians. (2015, December 18). In *Wikipedia.* Retrieved fromhttps://en.wikipedia.org/wiki/Wikipedia:Wikipedians

Williams, E. (2009, February). Evan Williams: The voices of Twitter users [Video File]. Retrieved from http://www.ted.com/talks/evan_williams_on_listening_to_twitter_users

Willis, J. (1996). *A Framework for Task-Based Learning.* Harlow: Longman.

Wilson, M., & Gerber, L. (2008). How generational theory can improve teaching: Strategies for working with the "Millennials." *Currents in Teaching and Learning*, *1*(1), 29–44.

Wolf, M. (2007). Learning to think in a digital world. In M. Bauerlein (Ed.), The digital divide: Arguments for and against Facebook, Google, texting, and the age of social networking (pp. 34-37). New York, NY: Penguin.

Wolff, W. (2013). Interactivity and the invisible: What counts as writing in the age of web 2.0. *Computers and Composition*, *30*(3), 211–225. doi:10.1016/j.compcom.2013.06.001

Wood, C., Kemp, N., & Waldron, S. (2014a). Exploring the longitudinal relationships between the use of grammar in text messaging and performance on grammatical tasks. *The British Journal of Developmental Psychology*, *32*(4), 415–429. doi:10.1111/bjdp.12049 PMID:24923868

Wood, C., Kemp, N., Waldron, S., & Hart, L. (2014b). Grammatical understanding, literary, and text messaging in school children and undergraduate students: A concurrent analysis. *Computers & Education*, *70*, 281–290. doi:10.1016/j.compedu.2013.09.003

Wood, D., Bruner, J. S., & Ross, G. (1976). The role of tutoring in problem solving. *Journal of Child Psychology and Psychiatry, and Allied Disciplines*, *17*(2), 89–100. doi:10.1111/j.1469-7610.1976.tb00381.x PMID:932126

Writing 2011: National assessment of educational progress at grades 8 and 12. (2011). *National Center for Education Statistics*. Retrieved from http://www.nationsreportcard.gov/

Wysocki, A. F. (2004). *Writing new media*. Utah State UP.

Yakin, I., & Tinmaz, H. (2013). Using Twitter as an instructional tool: A case study in higher education. *TOJET: The Turkish Online Journal of Educational Technology*, *12*(4), 209–218.

Yancey, K. (1998). *Reflection in the writing classroom*. Logan, Utah: Utah State University Press.

Yancey, K. B. (2004). Made not only in words: Composition in a new key. *College Composition and Communication*, *56*(2), 297–328. doi:10.2307/4140651

Yancey, K., Robertson, L., & Taczak, K. (2014). *Writing across contexts: Transfer, composition, and sites of writing*. Boulder, CO: Utah State University Press.

Yang, M., Badger, R., & Yu, Z. (2006). A comparative study of peer and teacher feedback in a Chinese EFL writing class. *Journal of Second Language Writing*, *15*(3), 179–200. doi:10.1016/j.jslw.2006.09.004

Zappavigna, M. (2012). *Discourse of Twitter and social media: How we use language to create affiliation on the web*. London: Bloomsbury Academic.

Zappen, J. P., Gurak, L. J., & Doheny-Farina, S. (1997). Rhetoric, Community, and Cyberspace. *Rhetoric Review*, *15*(2), 400–419. doi:10.1080/07350199709359226

About the Contributors

Kendra N. Bryant holds a Ph.D. in English with an emphasis in Rhetoric & Composition from The University of South Florida, Tampa. Her interests rest in writing with technology as well as African American rhetoric, novel, and poetics. She has published chapter essays on literary figures such as Zora Neale Hurston, Alice Walker, and Maya Angelou. Kendra's other works appear in Exploring Technology for Writing and Writing Instruction and The Journal of Basic Writing. Additionally, she is published in Studies in Popular Culture, the quint, and Trayvon Martin, Race and American Justice: Writing Wrong. At the time of this publication, Kendra was an assistant professor of English at Florida A&M University, Tallahassee, where she edited and compiled its Freshman Communicative Skills II required reader, *Writing from the Hill: An Introduction to Writing about Literature*. She is now teaching at The University of North Georgia, Oconee.

* * *

Elisabeth H. Buck is an Assistant Professor of English at the University of Massachusetts Dartmouth. She researches and teaches digital literacies, writing program/writing center administration, and rhetorical approaches to popular culture.

Shannon Butts is a doctoral student at the University of Florida working in writing and media studies. Her research interests include visual rhetoric, remix writing, digital DIY, rhetorics of resistance, and the circulation of parody and popular media. Shannon's work examines the hybrid ecology of material and digital making – investigating the feedback loop between physical space and digital platforms through the circulation of visual rhetoric. As a co-founder of UF's TRACE Innovation Initiative, Shannon also works with data mining and augmented reality technologies to critically analyze the impact of media. In addition, Shannon teaches courses focused on remix and remediation, visual rhetoric, and writing through media.

Melissa Vosen Callens is currently an assistant professor of practice in instructional design and communication at North Dakota State University, Fargo. Her research and teaching interests include online pedagogy, emerging media and classroom technology, and representations of race and gender in popular culture. Her writing can be found in *Rhetoric Matters: Language and Argument in Context*, *English Journal, 100 Entertainers Who Changed America: An Encyclopedia of Pop Culture*, and *A Sense of Community: Essays on the Television Series and Its Fandom*, among other publications.

Jill Darling completed an MFA in creative writing and a Ph.D. in Twentieth Century American Literature and Culture. Her research and writing interests include poetics, writing pedagogy. cultural studies, and creative nonfiction.

Christine Fiore was born and raised in Queens, New York, and moved to the San Francisco area in 1996. She is an early education teacher and blogger, and the mother of a 21-year-old college student daughter.

Katherine Fredlund is currently an assistant professor at Indiana State University. She designed and taught ISU's first New Media Writing course, and the course is now offered regularly as a junior-level composition course within the general education program. In Fall 2016, she will begin a new position as the Director of Writing at the University of Memphis. Her research has appeared or is forthcoming in College English, the Rhetoric Review, Peitho, Feminist Teacher, and elsewhere.

Brian C. Harrell is currently teaching First-Year English Composition at The University of Akron. His interests include synchronous distance learning, elearning, Web 2.0, social media, visual rhetoric, and the death narrative. He currently sits on the Board of Trustees of the Bioethics Network of Ohio and is active in the Two-Year College Association Midwest, National Council of Teachers of English, and The Conference on College Composition and Communication.

Ken Hayes is an assistant professor of composition in the department Language and Literature at Southwestern Oklahoma State University, in Weatherford, OK. He received his Ph.D in Rhetoric and Writing from Bowling Green State University in Bowling Green, OH, in 2015. His research interests include Digital Literacies, Social Networking Site Composition, Composition Pedagogy, and issues in First Year Composition.

Ahmed Abdulateef Al Khateeb is a PhD holder from the University of Southampton, UK and works as an assistant professor in the Department of English Language, King Faisal University, Saudi Arabia. His main research interests include technology-enhanced language learning, online testing and language assessment, English for academic/specific purposes, digital literacy and cognitive linguistics.

Meghan McGuire is an Assistant Professor of English at the University of Delaware. There she teaches courses in technical and professional communication, including business and technical writing, environmental communication, and online representation. Her research interests include the significance of public discourse in social media and how it impacts the commemoration and curation of information in large-scale events, as well as how technology and new media affects technical and professional communication.

Stephanie N. Phillips is currently a doctoral student in rhetoric and composition at the University of South Florida where she serves as the assistant to the graduate rhetoric and composition program. Her research interests include climate change, social media, and feminist studies.

Amy E. Rubens is Assistant Professor of English and co-coordinator of the Graduate Certificate Program in Professional Writing at Radford University in Radford, Virginia. Within business and professional writing, Dr. Rubens has research interests in writing for the job search and hiring process; writing for social media; and learning in problem-based and experiential settings. Currently, she is conducting a study of college students' perceptions of the hiring process and the ways a rhetorically grounded approach to teaching resumes and cover letters influence those beliefs. In her spare time, Dr. Rubens enjoys crocheting, cooking vegetarian meals, and spending time with her family.

Erin Trauth is the Associate Director of Composition and instructor of professional and technical writing at the University of South Florida. She earned her doctorate in Technical Communication and Rhetoric at Texas Tech University. She conducts research on front-of-package food labels and regulatory policies surrounding this communication, public health communication, risk communication, professional and technical writing, composition pedagogy, and computer-mediated communications.

Clarissa J. Walker is a writing instructor and a doctoral student in Rhetoric and Composition at the University of Rhode Island. Focused on web-based activism rhetoric of African-derived communities, her research examines cyber-identity narratives, rhetorical (mis)representation and web content to track the development of the online activist ethos. She received her MA in International Relations from Boston University in 2003; this followed a career as a professional print journalist, during which her work was published in the *Augusta Chronicle* (Morris Communications), *The Pacific Daily News* (Gannett) in Micronesia, *The Miami Herald* (now, McClatchy Communications), *Upscale Magazine* and *the Palm Beach Post*.

Index

H

health communication 247
health literacy 247
health science 221, 225
high road transfer 98
Hook 190-191, 194, 198

I

integrated teaching 263, 270
internet research 127, 129, 191

J

job search 200, 202, 206, 221, 223
journaling 175, 185, 194, 198

L

life writing 37, 92, 116, 125
LinkedIn 206, 221-229, 231, 233-234, 236, 239, 241-244

M

marketability 232, 236, 243
media 1-7, 10-11, 14-18, 21, 26, 29, 32-38, 40-41, 48-49, 51-60, 63-64, 68-70, 74-80, 83-89, 91-92, 96-104, 106-114, 116-122, 125, 127, 129, 138, 151-160, 163-171, 173-177, 179-182, 187, 191, 195-196, 198, 200-204, 206, 208-211, 213-216, 221-224, 231-234, 236-245, 248, 250-252, 256, 261
memes 96, 104-107, 111-114, 118-119, 121-122, 125, 129, 146, 167
meta-cognition 98-99
metamessages 201, 205, 215
Mickey Hess 74, 77
millennial student 154, 158-161, 185
multimodal 2-3, 11, 14, 16, 51-52, 55-56, 58, 75, 78, 83, 116, 119, 130, 134, 144, 158, 176, 206
multitasking 159, 191, 198

N

networking 4, 11, 34, 40, 54, 133, 135, 138-141, 152, 173, 176, 202-203, 207, 224, 236-237, 243, 260-261, 266

O

online employment portfolio 233
online presence 201-202, 204-207, 213, 224-226
online spaces 4-5, 116, 134, 224, 226, 229

P

page-based formats 75, 91
pedagogy 3, 5, 15-17, 20, 37-38, 51-52, 54-56, 58, 66, 69, 74-75, 77, 99, 118, 120, 133, 146, 151, 153, 156-160, 163, 175, 205, 225, 233, 250
plain language 247-253, 257
problem-based learning 200, 205-206, 211, 215-216
process approach 259-260, 264, 269-270, 276
professional discourse 119, 123-125
professional presence 200-201, 216, 226
professional writing 91-92, 116, 121-122, 147, 205-206, 225, 232-233, 247
public persona 221-223, 228-229

R

reading comprehension 14-15, 19-20, 24-25
reception theory 163-166, 170, 175-177
reflection 9-11, 18, 41, 51, 53-56, 58-60, 63-64, 66, 68, 80, 104, 109-110, 128-129, 141, 226-227, 270
remediation 78, 83-85, 88-89
remix writing 74-78, 80, 83-84, 89, 91
rhetoric 1, 4, 17, 32, 38, 53, 63-64, 78, 85, 99, 102, 107-108, 113, 134, 151, 154, 163, 232
rhetorical analysis 38-39, 41-48, 78-83, 89, 91, 114, 141, 143, 145-146, 165
rhetorical knowledge 97-99, 103, 114
rhetorical methods 75, 91
rhetorical practices 54, 83, 92, 96, 102
rhetorical sensibilities 201, 214
rhetorical situation 15, 19-20, 44, 64, 96, 98, 100, 102, 111, 113, 120-121, 137
rhetorical/audience awareness 133, 135-136
rhetorically savvy 214
rubric 2, 25-26, 28, 182, 194, 198, 252

S

social media 1-7, 10-11, 14-18, 21, 26, 29, 32-38, 40-41, 48-49, 51-54, 56-57, 59-60, 63-64, 69, 75-79, 83, 88, 91-92, 96-104, 106-114, 116-122, 125,

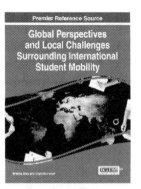
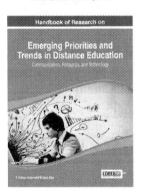

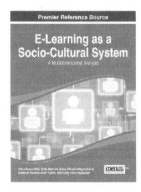

Printed in the United States
By Bookmasters